Kiana Busch

An Architecture-based Approach for Change Impact Analysis of Software-intensive Systems

The Karlsruhe Series on Software Design and Quality
Volume 30

Chair Software Design and Quality
Faculty of Computer Science
Karlsruhe Institute of Technology

and

Software Engineering Division
Research Center for Information Technology (FZI), Karlsruhe

Editor: Prof. Dr. Ralf Reussner

An Architecture-based Approach for Change Impact Analysis of Software-intensive Systems

by
Kiana Busch

KIT Scientific Publishing

Karlsruher Institut für Technologie
Institut für Programmstrukturen und Datenorganisation

An Architecture-based Approach for Change Impact Analysis of Software-intensive Systems

Zur Erlangung des akademischen Grades einer Doktorin der Ingenieurwissenschaften von der KIT-Fakultät für Informatik des Karlsruher Instituts für Technologie (KIT) genehmigte Dissertation

von Kiana Busch, geb. Rostami

Tag der mündlichen Prüfung: 16. Juli 2019
Referent: Prof. Dr. Ralf H. Reussner
Korreferentin: Prof. Dr. Barbara Paech

Impressum

KIT Scientific Publishing

Karlsruher Institut für Technologie (KIT)
KIT Scientific Publishing
Straße am Forum 2
D-76131 Karlsruhe

KIT Scientific Publishing is a registered trademark of Karlsruhe Institute of Technology.
Reprint using the book cover is not allowed.

www.ksp.kit.edu

Print on Demand 2020 – Gedruckt auf FSC-zertifiziertem Papier

ISSN 1867-0067
ISBN 978-3-7315-0974-5
DOI: 10.5445/KSP/1000098183

Abstract

This thesis presents an architecture-based and model-based approach to change propagation analysis of software-intensive technical systems, which considers heterogeneous elements from different domains.

One main property of software-intensive technical systems is sustainability. Sustainable systems have to continuously change due to internal change triggers, such as error corrections, or external change triggers, such as changing environments[1]. The quality attribute, which is concerned with the propagation of a change in a system, is referred to as maintainability[2]. Thus, maintainability can be considered as a relevant quality attribute of sustainable systems.

A change to an element of a system can result in further changes to other system elements. If system elements belong to different domains (e.g., information systems, business processes, or automated production systems), changes can propagate across several domains. For example, an automated production system can involve mechanical and electrical/electronic components, as well as control software. If mechanical and/or electrical/electronic components such as sensors change, they can also affect the corresponding control software. Additionally, there are different ways to implement a change request. This can lead to different implementation costs and can affect the quality attributes of the changed system. Estimating the affected elements in advance can support the process of decision making by analyzing the effects of a change in advance. However, manual estimation of changes can be costly and time-consuming. Hence, there is a need for an approach, which can automatically analyze the change propagation across different domains.

[1] Meir Lehman. "On understanding laws, evolution, and conservation in the large-program life cycle". In: *Journal of Systems and Software* 1 (1979), pp. 213–221.

[2] ISO/IEC 25010:2011. *Systems and software engineering – Systems and software Quality Requirements and Evaluation (SQuaRE) – System and software quality models.* 2011.

One possible category of approaches addressing this issue is based on models to analyze the change effort in different scenarios. However, most approaches in this category mainly focus on the change propagation in only one domain. They neglect the effort of changing affected elements in other domains. Neglecting affected elements results in inadequate change effort estimation.

To address the aforementioned issues, this thesis presents a generic methodology to support automated change propagation across several domains. The generic methodology can be instantiated in a specific domain to obtain a change propagation analysis approach in this domain. Thus, the generic methodology aims at improving the development process of a model-based change propagation analysis approach by reusing the existing concepts and best practices. The generic methodology is based on the Karlsruhe Architectural Maintainability Prediction (KAMP) approach, which is concerned with the change propagation analysis in information systems[3]. Further main contributions of this thesis are as follows: i) Software systems are a main part of business processes of organizations. Thus, they affect each other during the evolution in a mutual way. For this purpose, the methodology was instantiated in business processes as an extension of the KAMP approach to consider these mutual effects during the change impact analysis. ii) A further approach was developed as an instance of the methodology to support the change propagation in automated production systems based on the metamodels of mechanical and electrical/electronic components, as well as control software according to the IEC 61131-3 standard. Thus, this approach enables the analysis of the change propagation in system elements from different sub-domains of automated production systems. iii) The previous approaches to change propagation analysis in information systems, business processes, and automated production systems consider the change propagation caused by a change request at system level. However, the change requests can in general be specified at requirements level. Thus, this contribution complements the previous contributions by extending the existing instances of the methodology to include the requirements changes. These extensions are based on models representing requirements and design decisions. iv) Instances of the methodology use change propagation

[3] Kiana Rostami et al. "Architecture-based Assessment and Planning of Change Requests". In: *Proceedings of the 11th International ACM SIGSOFT Conference on Quality of Software Architectures*. ACM, 2015, pp. 21–30.

rules to estimate the effects of a change. To avoid the recurring technical code and to improve the readability of the change propagation rules, a domain-specific rule language was developed. v) A new comprehensive and multidimensional categorization of change triggers in business processes was developed based on the results of a literature review.

The contributions of this thesis regarding the change propagation analysis were evaluated using case studies in each domain. The precision and the recall of the automatically generated results for different case studies were calculated by comparing the tasks of the generated results to implement the change scenarios with the corresponding manually created task lists. Additionally, to evaluate the effort reduction by an automated approach to change propagation analysis, the following two metrics were compared: i) the ratio of the number of model elements, which have to be considered manually, to the number of all model elements, and ii) the ratio of the number of model elements generated by the automated approach in each domain to the number of all model elements. In information systems and business processes, the community case studies "Common Component Modeling Example (CoCoME)" and "modular Rice University Bidding System (mRUBiS)" were used. A set of change scenarios for each case study was created based on the aforementioned category of change triggers in business processes to evaluate the corresponding approach. To analyze the external validity of the generic methodology, the automated production systems were considered. For this purpose, the instance of the generic methodology in this domain was applied to the community case study "extended Pick and Place Unit (xPPU)", which represents a lab-size plant. This plant consists of mechanical and electrical/electronic components, as well as control software according to the IEC 61131-3 standard.

Zusammenfassung

Die vorliegende Dissertation präsentiert eine automatische domänenübergreifende Wartbarkeitsanalyse basierend auf der Architektur der Systeme, in deren Entwicklung und Evolution verschiedene Domänen zusammenarbeiten müssen.

Eine der integralen Eigenschaften software-intensiver technischer Systeme ist ihre Langlebigkeit. Langlebige Systeme unterliegen kontinuierlichen Anpassungen aufgrund externer Änderungen, wie Änderungen ihrer Umgebung, oder auch interner Änderungen, wie zum Beispiel Fehlerbeseitigungen[4]. Die Eigenschaft des Systems, die angibt, welcher Aufwand erforderlich ist, um ein System gemäß eines gegebenen Änderungsszenarios zu ändern, wird als Wartbarkeit bezeichnet[5]. Somit ist Wartbarkeit ein wichtiges Qualitätsattribut langlebiger Systeme.

Eine initiale Änderung an einem Element im System kann weitere Änderungen an anderen Systemelementen zur Folge haben. Stammen die betroffenen Systemelemente aus mehreren Domänen, wie zum Beispiel aus den Domänen der Informationssysteme, Geschäftsprozesse oder automatisierten Produktionssysteme, können sich die Änderungen auch über mehrere Domänen hinweg mit Abhängigkeiten in alle Richtungen ausbreiten. Ein automatisiertes Produktionssystem kann zum Beispiel aus mechanischen und elektrischen Bauteilen, sowie Steuerungssoftware bestehen. Eine Änderung an mechanischen und/oder elektrischen Bauteilen, wie zum Beispiel Sensoren, kann zu Folgeänderungen in der entsprechenden Steuerungssoftware führen. Zudem gibt es viele unterschiedliche Möglichkeiten, wie eine Änderungsanfrage in einem System umgesetzt werden kann. Verschiedene Möglichkeiten zur Umsetzung einer Änderungsanfrage

---

4 Meir Lehman. "On understanding laws, evolution, and conservation in the large-program life cycle". In: *Journal of Systems and Software* 1 (1979), S. 213–221.

5 ISO/IEC 25010:2011. *Systems and software engineering – Systems and software Quality Requirements and Evaluation (SQuaRE) – System and software quality models.* 2011.

können zu verschiedenen Änderungsaufwänden, sowie unterschiedlichen Systemen bezüglich ihrer Qualitätsattribute führen. Das Abschätzen der Änderungsfolgen hat deshalb besondere Relevanz im Entscheidungsprozess. Jedoch können manuelle Änderungsabschätzungen mit hohem Zeit- und Kostenaufwand verbunden sein. Somit kann eine automatische und domänenübergreifende Änderungsausbreitungsanalyse vor der Umsetzung einer Änderungsanfrage die Vorhersage der Änderungsaufwände und den Entscheidungsfindungsprozess zu deren Umsetzung unterstützen.

Eine Möglichkeit zur automatischen Änderungsausbreitungsanalyse ist ein modell-, sowie szenariobasierter Ansatz zur Wartbarkeitsabschätzung, der Systeme aus mehreren Domänen berücksichtigt. Jedoch konzentrieren sich bestehende modellbasierte und szenariobasierte Ansätze meist auf die Änderungsausbreitung in einer Domäne und vernachlässigen Änderungsaufwände der Elemente aus Domänen, die in einer gegenseitigen Abhängigkeitsbeziehung zur betrachteten Domäne stehen. Dies führt zu einer unzureichenden Abschätzung der Änderungsauswirkungen.

Die vorliegende Dissertation stellt eine generische Methode für eine automatische und domänenübergreifende Änderungsausbreitungsanalyse vor. Durch die Instanziierung der generischen Methode in verschiedenen Domänen kann ein vollständiger Ansatz zur automatischen Änderungsausbreitungsanalyse in der jeweiligen Domäne erstellt werden. Somit hat die generische Methode zum Ziel, den Entwicklungsprozess einer modellbasierten Änderungsausbreitungsanalyse durch die Wiederverwendung von bestehenden Konzepten zu verbessern. Die generische Methode basiert auf dem Karlsruhe Architectural Maintainability Prediction (KAMP) Ansatz zur Änderungsausbreitungsanalyse in Informationssystemen[6]. Weitere Beiträge dieser Dissertation können wie folgt zusammengefasst werden: i) Software-Systeme sind integrale Bestandteile der Geschäftsprozesse moderner Unternehmen. Daher beeinflussen sich Software-Systeme und Geschäftsprozesse gegenseitig während der Evolution. Angesichts komplexer gegenseitiger Beeinflussung bietet der Ansatz als eine Instanz der generischen Methode und eine Erweiterung des KAMP-Ansatzes eine automatische Änderungsausbreitungsanalyse in den sich gegenseitig beeinflussenden Domänen der

[6] Kiana Rostami u. a. "Architecture-based Assessment and Planning of Change Requests". In: *Proceedings of the 11th International ACM SIGSOFT Conference on Quality of Software Architectures*. ACM, 2015, S. 21–30.

Informationssysteme und der Geschäftsprozesse. ii) Basierend auf Metamodellen zur Darstellung von mechanischen und elektrischen Teilen, als auch der Steuerungssoftware im Standard IEC 61131-3 für speicherprogrammierbare Steuerungen wurde ein weiterer Ansatz (ebenfalls als eine Instanziierung der generischen Methode) für die Domänen der automatisierten Produktionssysteme entwickelt. Mit dem Ansatz ist es möglich Änderungen über Systemelemente aus mehreren Sub-Domänen von automatisierten Produktionssystemen zu verfolgen, um eine umfassende Liste von Wartbarkeitsaufwänden zu erstellen. iii) Die Änderungsauslöser können sich entweder auf Architekturmodellebene oder auf Anforderungsebene befinden. Basierend auf Modellen zur Erfassung von Anforderungen und Entwurfsentscheidungen in der Domäne der Informationssysteme, Geschäftsprozesse, sowie automatisierten Produktionssysteme wurden die bestehenden Instanzen der generischen Methode zur Berücksichtigung von Anforderungsänderungen erweitert. Somit ergänzt dieser Beitrag die bisherigen Beiträge bezüglich der domänen-spezifischen Änderungsausbreitungsanalysen. iv) Die Änderungsausbreitung in den Instanzen der Methode wird durch Änderungsausbreitungsregeln betrachtet. Hierzu wurde eine domänenspezifische Sprache zum Beschreiben der häufig benutzten Änderungsausbreitungsregeln zur besseren Lesbarkeit der Regeln sowie zur Vermeidung von technischem Code vorgestellt. v) Weiter wurde ein mehrdimensionales Kategorisierungsschema für die Änderungsauslöser in Geschäftsprozessen basierend auf den Ergebnissen einer umfassenden Literaturrecherche vorgestellt.

Die Beiträge dieser Dissertation zur automatischen Änderungsausbreitungsanalyse wurden anhand von Fallstudien in der jeweiligen Domäne evaluiert. Für jede Fallstudie wurde die Genauigkeit der Ergebnisse des jeweiligen Ansatzes im Vergleich zu manuell erstellten Ergebnissen angegeben. Zudem wurde die Aufwandsersparnis durch eine automatische Änderungsausbreitungsanalyse anhand des Vergleichs zweier Metriken gezeigt: i) Die erste Metrik repräsentiert die Rate der Anzahl der tatsächlich zu ändernden Modellelemente zur Anzahl der gesamten Modellelemente. ii) Die zweite Metrik repräsentiert die Rate der Anzahl der vom Ansatz vorgeschlagenen Modellelemente zur Anzahl der gesamten Modellelemente. Für die Validierung des Ansatzes zur automatischen Änderungsausbreitungsanalyse in den Domänen der Informationssysteme und der Geschäftsprozesse wurde basierend auf den Ergebnissen der systematischen Literaturrecherche zur

Ermittlung der Änderungsauslöser in Geschäftsprozessen repräsentative Änderungsauslöserklassen identifiziert. Diese repräsentativen Änderungsauslöserklassen wurden jeweils auf die Community-Fallstudien “Common Component Modeling Example (CoCoME)” und “modular Rice University Bidding System (mRUBiS)” angewendet. Für die externe Validität der Methode wurde die Domäne der automatisierten Produktionssysteme betrachtet. Hierzu wurde die Instanz der Methode zur automatischen Änderungsausbreitungsanalyse in der Domäne der automatisierten Produktionssysteme auf die Community-Fallstudie “extended Pick and Place Unit (xPPU)” angewendet. Die betrachtete Anlage beinhaltet die elektrischen und mechanischen Bauteile sowie die Steuerungssoftware im Standard IEC 61131-3 für speicherprogrammierbare Steuerungen.

Danksagung

Zunächst möchte ich mich bei meinem betreuenden Professor Ralf Reussner bedanken. Er hat mich schon zu Studienzeiten für die Wissenschaft begeistern können. Während meiner Zeit als Doktorandin hat er mir immer wieder neue Möglichkeiten eröffnet und aufgezeigt und mich dabei unterstützt mein Forschungsthema voranzubringen. Auch sehr herzlich möchte ich mich bei Doktor Robert Heinrich für unzählige Feedback-Runden und Publikationsprojekte bedanken. Viele Gespräche mit ihnen waren für mich stets eine Quelle der Inspiration.

Zudem möchte ich mich bei Professorin Anne Koziolek und Professorin Birgit Vogel-Heuser für wertvolle Diskussionen und erfolgreiche Publikationsprojekte bedanken. Ebenfalls sehr bedanken möchte ich mich bei Professorin Barbara Paech, sowie den Professoren Bernhard Beckert, Andreas Oberweis, Gregor Snelting, Rainer Stiefelhagen und Walter Tichy für ihr wertvolles Feedback in Promotionsgesprächen.

Mein besonderer Dank gilt meinem besten Freund Axel für seine Unterstützung in meinem Leben. Mit ihm konnte ich zahlreiche Diskussionen über das Thema meiner Forschungsarbeit führen. Ebenfalls bedanken möchte ich mich bei meiner Familie, insbesondere bei Nasrin dafür, dass sie immer für mich da ist.

Auch bei allen Mitarbeitern der SDQ und ARE Forschungsgruppen möchte ich mich sehr herzlich für die schöne Atmosphäre und tolle Zusammenarbeit bedanken. Insbesondere bei Sandro Koch, Angelika Kaplan, Johannes Stammel, und Dominik Werle möchte ich mich für die intensive Zusammenarbeit bei der Betreuung von Studierenden und gemeinsamen Publikationen bedanken.

Ebenfalls bedanken möchte ich mich herzlich bei den von mir betreuten Studierenden insbesondere Jakob Bach, Angelika Kaplan, Sandro Koch,

Martin Löper, Timo Maier, Maximilian Peters, und Jannis Rätz für die sehr gute Zusammenarbeit und inspirierende Gespräche.

Contents

1. Introduction

This thesis presents a generic methodology to develop change propagation analysis approaches. Instances of the methodology in different domains can be used to analyze the change propagation in the corresponding domain. This chapter discusses the research goal and questions derived from research problems, which resulted in the development of the methodology and its instances.

1.1. Motivation

As software-intensive technical systems are in operation for many years, they can be considered as sustainable systems [Vog+17]. Sustainable systems have to change continuously to provide their functionality. This can be considered as a generalization of the Lehman's law [Leh79] regarding the *continuing change* of systems, which do not consist only of software. The "degree of effectiveness and efficiency with which a product or system can be modified by the intended maintainers" is defined as maintainability [ISO11]. Thus, maintainability can be considered as one of the main quality attributes of sustainable systems [HBK18]. According to the above definition, the maintainability of a system correlates with the effects of changes in this system. The changes can have their source within a system, also referred to as *internal change triggers*, or outside a system, also referred to as *external change triggers* [AJ00]. An example of the internal change triggers is the category of the *corrective maintenance*, as introduced by Swanson [Swa76]. This type of the maintenance is concerned with the changes caused by failures and errors in the system [Swa76]. By contrast, the *adaptive maintenance* can be considered as an external change trigger, as it is caused by changes in the environment [Swa76]. Additionally, a change in a system can cause further changes in the system, also known as *change propagation*. Hence, the maintainability of a system depends not only on the system under study, but also on the specific change request. In other words, a system can be easier to maintain for certain change requests, while it is harder to maintain for other requests at the same time. In order to determine the maintainability of a system for a change request in advance, the effects of this request on the system have to be estimated.

The process of estimating the effects of a change starts with a change request, which initially affects a set of system elements. Bohner refers to this set as the Starting Impact Set (SIS) [Boh02]. The change propagates from the SIS to other system elements. The set of system elements, which have to actually change due to the SIS, is called Actual Impact Set (AIS) [Boh02]. However, the *change propagation analysis* can only estimate the set of affected system elements. In other words, this set is not necessarily equal to the AIS. The result set of the analysis is also referred to as Candidate Impact Set (CIS) [Boh02]. As the change propagation analysis can overestimate the AIS, the CIS can include system elements, which are not actually affected [Boh02]. It is also possible to underestimate the AIS. In this case, affected system elements are missing in the result of the change propagation analysis [Boh02]. According to Bohner [Boh02], the main goal of the change propagation analysis is that both sets CIS and AIS are as close as possible. This goal is one of the main challenges during the development of an approach to change propagation analysis.

The estimation of the effects of a change request correlates with how a change request is implemented. There are often more than one possibility to implement a change [Sta15]. This depends on the SIS, which results from the change request. In other words, different SIS can lead to different implementations of a change request. This results in different efforts and costs depending on how to implement a change request. Thus, estimating the efforts of different implementations in advance can help in the decision-making process [Sta15]. Summarized, one challenging task during the change propagation analysis is to identify the appropriate implementation of a change request in advance.

Software-intensive technical systems can be composed of elements, which originate from different domains. In this context, the term *domain* refers to a discipline, which comprises systems providing different functionality, but addressing similar business and technical needs, and are subject to common requirements and terminology. Thus, the term *domain* refers to two dimensions: While the first dimension regards application domains, the second dimension is concerned with abstraction levels. Examples of domains are Information Systems (IS), Business Processes (BP), and automated Production Systems (aPS).

System elements from different domains can influence each other. Examples of domains affecting each other are IS and BP, as IS can be considered as a main part of the BP in organizations. Mooney et al. categorize the effects of IS on BP in *automational, informational*, or *transformational* effects [MGK96]. This example shows that system elements from different domains seldom evolve in isolation, but rather co-evolve. Thus, it is not sufficient to consider only one domain during the change propagation analysis [Ros+17a]. Summarized, a further challenging task during the estimation of the change effort is considering the affected domains and their effects on each other.

Software-intensive technical systems do not comprise only software, but also other elements such as hardware (e.g., sensors or actuators). In other words, a domain can consist of further sub-domains. For example, the systems in aPS can comprise mechanical and electrical/electronic components, as well as control software [Vog+17]. Changing a mechanical and/or electrical/electronic component in these systems can lead to further changes in the control software [Hei+18]. For example, a change to a sensor in a plant can lead to a change in the corresponding functionality in the control software [Vog+14a]. If the change propagation analysis considers only the mechanical and/or electrical/electronic components, the effects of the change on the control software are missing in the result. Additionally, the approach has to consider the change propagation between hardware and software of a system, and from a system to its behavior. Summarized, a change propagation analysis approach has to be able to deal with the heterogeneity of system elements.

The development process of a system involves not only the structure of the system, but also different organizational and/or technical artifacts [Sta15; Con68; Boh02]. For example, after the change requests have been implemented in a system, the system has to be tested [Boh02]. This task causes further efforts in the implementation of the change requests. Motivated by

Conway's law, there is a dependency between the communication structures in an organization and the resulting system [Con68]. Thus, it is important to consider the system not in isolation but rather regarding other influencing factors such as the organization, as also introduced by other researchers such as Stammel [Sta15]. There are also further project-planning tasks, which also have to be considered during the implementation of a change request [Sta15]. An example of these tasks is assigning a task to the responsible staff in an organization during the implementation of a change request [Sta15]. Summarized, a further challenging task is identifying and considering different organizational and technical artifacts, which are relevant for the change propagation analysis of a specific system.

Current approaches mainly focus on the change propagation analysis in systems comprising elements from only one domain [HBK18]. Thus, they neglect the effects of a change to the system elements in one domain on the system elements in other domains [HBK18]. In other words, to analyze the change propagation across different domains, the results of different approaches developed independently of one another have to be combined. However, there are fundamental differences between the approaches developed in different domains, or even between different approaches developed in the same domain [HBK18]. For example, the change propagation analysis can be performed manually, automatically, or semi-automatically. Further, the approaches can be based on different concepts, such as model-based approaches (e.g., [Sta15]) or code-based approaches in IS (e.g., [Wei81]). There are also further categories or several sub-categories of the aforementioned categories. For example, the model-based approaches can use general-purpose modeling languages such as Unified Modeling Language (UML) (e.g., [BLO03]) or can be based on the modeling languages tailored to the domain or even to the system under study (e.g., [Hei+18]). In general, not every category of change propagation analysis approaches can be generalized to other domains (e.g., code-based approaches in IS). Additionally, there are also different ways to calculate the output of an approach based on the input of the approach. For this purpose, different types of algorithms can be used [HBK18]. Even, the outputs of the approaches can vary [HBK18]. While some approaches calculate the effort of a change, for example based on experts' experience or predefined metrics (e.g., [Boe+00]), other approaches aim at identifying the affected system elements without calculating the costs of the changes (e.g., [RT01]). Even though we consider

only one category of the change propagation analysis approaches, their results can be at different levels of abstraction. Summarized, neither different change propagation analysis approaches from different domains nor the results of them can be easily combined to obtain a domain-spanning change propagation analysis approach [HBK18]. Thus, there is a need for an approach, which analyzes the change propagation across domains.
The problems and challenges discussed in this section can be summarized as follows:

Problem 1: Different ways to implement a change request: A change request can be implemented in different ways, which lead to different costs of the development. Identifying the appropriate implementation in advance supports the decision-making process. Thus, a challenging task during the implementation of a change request is to identify the appropriate implementation in advance.

Problem 2: Co-evolution of different domains: System elements affected by a change request can belong to different domains. In other words, different domains affect one another during their evolution. This leads to co-evolution of different domains. Thus, considering the affected domains and their effects on each other is one of the main challenges during the change effort estimation.

Problem 3: Heterogeneity of elements: System elements that belong to different domains are often heterogeneous. For example, a system can consist of hardware (e.g., actuators and sensors) and software. Hence, the change propagation analysis approach has to be able to consider heterogeneous system elements.

Problem 4: Mismatch of approaches in different domains: One solution idea to address the previous problems regarding heterogeneous elements from different domains is to combine the change propagation analysis approaches from these domains or their results. However, change propagation analysis approaches from different domains cannot be easily combined to obtain a change propagation analysis approach covering different domains. It is also difficult to combine their results. The main reasons for the problems regarding the compatibility of approaches with each other is that both approaches and their results are at different abstraction levels, are designed due to different goals, or can deal only with specific types of systems or elements (e.g., code-based or model-based approach).

Problem 5: Additional organizational and technical efforts: A change request does not affect only the system elements, but can also cause organizational and technical efforts. These efforts are usually caused by adapting artifacts such as test cases or documentations. Thus, a further challenging task is to identify and consider these efforts for a specific system and a given change request.

1.2. Research Problems

The previous section discussed the problems and challenges during the development of an approach to change propagation analysis, which has to consider the co-evolution of systems from different domains. This section summarizes the discussed problems to derive the main research problems, which this thesis addresses.

Research problem 1: No common language for heterogeneous elements: Software-intensive technical systems are sustainable systems, which, in general, are composed of heterogeneous elements. As discussed by *problem 3*, if the approach cannot consider the heterogeneous elements of a system, the results of the approach cannot fully consider the efforts of a change on this system. The main problem is caused due to the fact that there is not any common language to describe the heterogeneous elements. Additionally, different approaches for specific types of elements are not compatible to each other, as described by *problem 4*. Nevertheless, it is desirable to estimate the effects of a change to the heterogeneous elements of a continuously evolving system in advance. This is mainly important due to *problem 1*, as different ways to implement a change can have different effects on a system. In particular, different implementation ways can also influence different quality attributes of a system such as maintainability of the system for future changes. Summarized, it is difficult to estimate the effects of a change to one system element on other system elements due to their heterogeneity and lack of a common language.

Research problem 2: Undocumented mutual dependencies:
Heterogeneous elements of software-intensive technical systems can originate from different domains, as described by *problem 2*. However, these elements depend on one another and, thus, affect one another in a mutual way during the evolution. These mutual dependencies between heterogeneous elements from different domains are often undocumented. This applies to the context of a system, as a change can also cause organizational and technical efforts (cf. *problem 5*). Summarized, these factors make the prediction of the change propagation more challenging.

1.3. Research Idea

This section describes the research ideas to address the research problems discussed in the previous section.

One possible solution to abstract from the heterogeneity of systems' elements is to use architectural models, as they represent the "structure, function, or behavior" of a system in an abstract way [SV06, p. 18]. To use models as a main part of systems, as well as their development and evolution, they have to be defined in a formal way [SV06]. For this purpose, a formal modeling language can be used [SV06]. Metamodels define the main constructs of a modeling language and their relations [SV06]. Thus, model-based approaches can be used to analyze the change propagation in software-intensive technical systems involving heterogeneous elements from several domains.

Using a model-based approach correlates with the question regarding the relevant system properties for a change propagation analysis approach, which the system model has to represent (cf. [Sta73]). One possible solution is the use of models representing the *system's structure*, also known as *system's architecture*, as the main artifact during the change propagation analysis. The structure of a system consists of system elements and their relationships. Using the system's structure as the main artifact is motivated by the reason that "a system's architecture is the set of principal design decisions made during its development and any subsequent evolution" [MT10, p. 1]. Additionally, the system's structure affects the quality attributes of a system [Ros+15b; Sta15; TMD09]. To consider the impact of affected organizational and technical artifacts, the system's structure can be annotated by these artifacts [Ros+15b; Sta15]. Thus, considering these artifacts in addition to the system's structure can help to estimate the effects of a change request more completely [Ros+15b; Sta15].

To enable the change propagation between heterogeneous elements and across different domains, a dependency analysis can be used. The concept of dependency analysis has been used by many researchers in different ways especially in the context of change propagation analysis (e.g., program slicing [Wei81]). In this context, the idea of a dependency analysis, in a broader sense, is to utilize the different types of dependencies between different types of systems' elements for the change propagation analysis (e.g., [Sta15]). For this purpose, the relevant types of dependencies for the change propagation between the potentially affected types of systems' elements have to be identified. The types of systems' elements in a single or different domains and the types of their dependencies can be derived from the metamodel describing the systems' structure, as it represents different element types and the relations between them [Con68; SV06].

To combine different change propagation analysis approaches developed in different domains and/or their results, there is a need for a generic guideline for developing such approaches. On the one hand, the guideline has to homogenize the results of different approaches to make them compatible with one another by providing a generic framework. On the other hand, it has to abstract from individual implementations to allow the development of approaches at different granularity levels. Especially, the guideline must not assume a specific programming language or a metamodeling framework. Additionally, the guideline has to be applicable to different domains and the system within them. Thus, the guideline shall be mainly considered conceptually.

1.4. Research Goal and Questions

To address the research problems discussed previously the following research goal was defined.

Overall Research Goal: Generalize the existing architecture-based approaches to change propagation analysis in information systems to a domain-spanning approach based on the system's architecture and process design, which can also consider the effects of changing different technical and organizational artifacts over the development and the evolution process of a system.

To achieve this goal, the main research question was defined as follows:

Main Research Question: Is an architectural model a suitable abstraction to identify change effort across domains?

To analyze the main research question constructively, the following research questions were derived from the main research question and were designed to address both research problems:

Research Question 1: How can model-based and architecture-based approaches to change propagation analysis in information systems be generalized to a generic approach, which can be applied to the systems comprising heterogeneous elements from different domains?

Research Question 2: How can the effects of a change be identified based on the architecture and using different technical and organizational artifacts over the development and the evolution process of a system in order to reflect the mutual dependencies between heterogeneous elements?

1.5. Context of Thesis

In the previous sections, the main research ideas, goals, and questions were presented. This section describes the scope of the thesis and the main assumptions on the context.

System development process: This thesis proposes approaches to analyze the maintainability of systems in terms of estimation of change efforts. The development process of a system in several development models involves different phases such as design, implementation, and maintenance. Thus, the main usage contexts of the proposed approaches are the later phases of the development process (e.g., during the operation and maintenance [Som06]). Nevertheless, they can also be used in the earlier development phases (e.g., during the design phase [Som06]). In these phases, the approaches help to analyze the effects of frequent or potential future changes on the design to develop a system with regard to these changes. Even though the changes to the system in the later phases of the development process may differ from the estimated changes in the earlier phases of the development process, the system can be designed in accordance to maintainability characteristics by considering frequent or potential changes. In this way, the efforts for this type of changes can be reduced.

Systems' architecture: As described in Section 1.3, the approaches are based on the idea of dependency analysis. Thus, they can be applied to the class of systems, which can be described as interconnected elements. The granularity of elements differs depending on different influencing factors such as phases of the development process. While the elements in the earlier development process are rather coarse-grained, they can be decomposed into fine-grained elements in the later development process. The more fine-grained the elements of a system, the more precise the efforts of a change to them can be estimated. However, regardless of the granularity of elements, the approaches can be applied to this class of systems.

Modeling concepts: The approaches described in this thesis can be applied to a wide range of systems involving heterogeneous elements from different domains. Thus, the approaches have to abstract from the heterogeneity of systems and their elements. For this purpose, modeling concepts were used to describe the system at an abstract level, as discussed in Section 1.3. Thus, one of the main assumptions to use the proposed approaches is that the elements of a system and their relationships can be modeled.

Static change propagation analysis: One of the classification of dependency analysis approaches in IS is static and dynamic change propagation analysis approaches, or a combination of them, depending on whether the change propagation analysis approach uses only the structure of a system or run-time analysis (cf. [Kil08; Tip95] especially in context of program slicing). Although this classification was developed for IS, it can be generalized to systems in other domains. The approaches presented in this thesis are mainly concerned with the change effort estimation on the basis of systems' structure. Thus, the approaches can be considered as static change propagation analysis approaches in a broader sense, as they can be applied not only to IS, but also to other domains. In other words, the approaches are not applicable to the behavior of systems at run-time (i.e., dynamic change propagation analysis). However, the behavior of a system can be seen as linked activities by considering the connection to its environment. In this case, the behavior of a system and the relationship between the system's elements and its behavior can also be modeled. In this way, the effects of a change to the system on its behavior or vice versa can be analyzed.

Domain experts: Different roles are involved during the development of a system. The proposed approaches aim at providing support to domain experts by the maintainability analysis. A *domain expert* refers to an expert in a specific domain. In the context of this thesis, the role of the domain expert can be narrowed to the experts who are concerned with the maintainability of the system under study in a specific domain. Note that domain experts are not necessary the same persons, who are concerned with the development of a change propagation analysis approach. Examples of domain experts can be software architects in IS, process designers in BP, and plant manufacturers in aPS [HBK18]. This role is differently called by different researchers. For example, Sommerville referred to this role as *maintenance engineer* in [Som06].

Change requests: Change requests are often formulated in natural language. Identifying the initial change in a system based on a change request is not a trivial task and has to be undertaken by domain experts [Sta15]. Thus, the proposed approaches assume that initial changes to systems based on a given change request are known in advance.

1.6. Contributions

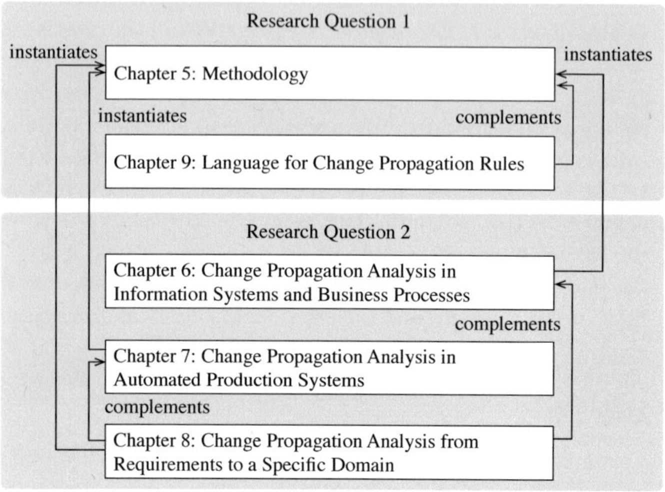

Figure 1.1.: Correspondence between the research questions and the contributions of this thesis

This section gives an overview of the contributions of this thesis and how they answer the identified research questions to address the overall research goal. Figure 1.1 gives an overview of the correspondence between the contributions and the chapters of this thesis on the one hand and the research questions on the other hand. In the following, the contributions and their correspondence to the research questions are discussed in more detail.

A Methodology to change propagation analysis: The methodology provides a generic guideline to develop a change propagation analysis approach in a specific domain. It is based on an approach to change propagation analysis in IS. The methodology abstracts from the heterogeneity of individual system elements by using modeling concepts. The change propagation analysis is mainly based on the system's structure, which can be annotated with different technical and organizational artifacts. The idea of the change effort estimation is based on the dependency analysis between the heterogeneous elements. Thus, the methodology answers the *first research question*.

Two interconnected change propagation analysis approaches in IS and BP: The approaches provide the functionality to estimate the change propagation during the co-evolution of IS and BP. The approach to change propagation analysis in BP was developed by instantiating the methodology to this domain. It can be considered as an extension of the originally developed approach in IS. These approaches estimate the effects of a change request not only in one of both domains, but also between both domains with regard to mutual dependencies between a BP and the corresponding IS. Thus, this contribution answers the *second research question*, as it considers the mutual dependencies between heterogeneous elements from two domains, which influence each other during their co-evolution.

A change propagation analysis approach in aPS: The approach considers the heterogeneous elements of aPS sub-domains, namely mechanical and electrical/electronic components, as well as control software. Thus, the approach combines further modular approaches to analyze these sub-domains by instantiating the methodology to them. In this way, the approaches enable domain experts to analyze the change propagation in each sub-domain and between them. Additionally, the approaches provide the functionality to analyze the effects of a change request on the behavior of aPS. Thus, this contribution answers the *second research question*, as it considers the mutual dependencies between heterogeneous elements from different sub-domains of aPS.

Requirements as change triggers: Considering requirements in the change propagation analysis improves the traceability of changes from requirements to the corresponding system elements. This is based on, how a change request has to be specified: If a change is initially specified at system level, the initial change is a model element in the model of the system's structure or behavior. If a change is initially specified at requirements level, the change propagation has to be analyzed first from the affected requirements to the model elements of the system's structure or behavior. The change can then propagate to the other system elements as in the first case. The analysis was also developed as a further instantiation of the methodology. Thus, considering the requirements as a further source of change triggers for different domains complements the previously described contributions regarding the change propagation analysis in IS, BP, and aPS. Hence, this contribution answers the *second research question.*

A Language for change propagation rules: The language enables domain experts to describe common change propagation rules. For this purpose, the language provides a reduced set of language elements to improve the development of common rules. In this way, it abstracts from the technical code needed by a General-purpose Programming Language (GPL) such as Java. The language aims at improving the maintainability and the readability of the rules. It can be applied to heterogeneous elements regardless of the domain and the system under study. Thus, the language complements the contribution of the maintainability analysis methodology and was developed to partially answer the *first research question.*

A category of change triggers in BP: The category was developed regardless of a specific sub-domain in BP and, thus, can be used in different organizations. It can be used not only to estimate the potential risks and sources of changes, but also during the requirements engineering with regard to potential future changes and risks. This categorization mainly contributes to the *evaluation* of the approaches to change propagation analysis in IS and BP. For this purpose, comprehensive sets of change requests for two case studies were developed based on this categorization.

These sets cover groups of change triggers along different dimension of this category.

As described previously, the methodology was instantiated in different domains to obtain change propagation analysis approaches. The methodology was developed to answer the first research question regarding the generalization of a change propagation analysis originally developed in IS to a generic guideline, which can be applied to the systems comprising heterogeneous elements from different domains. Thus, it was evaluated regarding the relevancy and the comprehensiveness by analyzing individual instances at a high abstraction level. In other words, the evaluation mainly targets at the degree of reuse for each part of the methodology by considering its instances.

Different instances of the methodology were designed to answer the second research question regarding the change propagation analysis using the system's architecture based on the mutual dependencies between heterogeneous system elements from several domains, while considering different technical and organizational artifacts. Thus, they provide the functionality to analyze the change propagation across heterogeneous elements from different domains. Hence, the instances of the methodology were also evaluated using case studies regarding the quality of their results. The quality mainly refers to the coverage of the results and the actually affected system elements in the results in comparison to the system elements in the results, which are not actually affected, and the system elements, which are missing in the results.

1.7. Outline

This chapter discussed the problems and challenges domain experts face, while developing a change propagation analysis approach with regard to mutual dependencies between heterogeneous elements originating from different domains. Based on these problems, the overall research goal was defined. The research questions, which address the overall goal, were derived from the research problems. Additionally, this chapter gave an overview of the contributions of this thesis, which answer the research questions. The reminder of this thesis is organized as follows:

Chapter 2 presents the foundations and concepts for the contributions of this thesis. This mainly includes the concepts of model-driven software development, the metamodels used to develop the approaches of the thesis, and the change propagation analysis approach in IS, which is generalized to be applicable to other domains.

Chapter 3 mainly discusses the state of the art and the related work to the change propagation analysis in different domains and the language to specify the change propagation rules.

Chapter 4 illustrates two running examples. The first example was designed to illustrate the problems of the change propagation analysis and the corresponding approaches in the dependent domains of IS and BP. The second example represents a minimal plant in aPS, to which the approaches to change propagation analysis for the mechanical and electrical/electronic components, as well as the control software in aPS were exemplary applied.

Chapter 5 presents the generic methodology, which is based, in a broader sense, on an approach to change propagation analysis in IS. To obtain a complete change propagation analysis approach in a specific domain, the generic methodology has to be instantiated in this domain.

Chapter 6 describes, how the methodology can be instantiated in the domains of IS and BP, which influence each other in a mutual way during their co-evolution. The proposed instance is one of the possible instantiations of the methodology in these domains.

Chapter 7 describes further instantiations of the methodology to aPS. As aPS comprises mechanical and electrical/electronic components, as well as software, several interrelated instances are created, which are concerned with the change propagation in each sub-domain and the behavior of aPS.

Chapter 8 complements the contributions of the previous two approaches by extending the domain-specific approaches to include the change propagation analysis in requirements and design decisions.

Chapter 9 presents a language to support common patterns of change propagation rules used in approaches to change propagation analysis.

Chapter 10 describes a new comprehensive categorization of change triggers in BP. It is designed to identify categories of change triggers in BP based on the results of a literature review.

Chapter 11 presents the evaluation of the discussed contributions. It starts with the evaluation of the methodology, followed by the evaluation of the developed instances. The categorization of change triggers in BP contributes to the evaluation of the instance of the methodology in BP. This chapter includes, further, the evaluation of the language to change propagation rules.

Chapter 12 presents a summary of the contributions as well as the evaluation results. Additionally, it outlines possible future work.

2. Foundations

This chapter presents the foundations of this thesis. The first section describes the main concepts of the Model-Driven Software Development (MDSD) and the tool support. Section 2.2 gives an overview of change impact analysis in general. An overview of the Palladio Component Model (PCM) is given in Section 2.3. While the PCM is mainly used to model the structure of IS, the metamodel for BP is proposed in Section 2.4. The requirement metamodel is proposed in Section 2.5. Section 2.6 presents the standard used in this thesis for the control software in aPS. The metamodel for the hardware of aPS is introduced in Section 2.7. The last section of this chapter presents the change impact analysis approach, on which the methodology and the approaches presented in this thesis are based.

2.1. Model-Driven Software Development

MDSD is a software development paradigm, which is based on models. For this reason, the term *model* and its characteristics has first to be introduced. There are various definitions of a model. In Rational Unified Process, a model is defined as "a semantically closed abstraction of a system" [Kru04, p. 286]. Another definition introduced by Stahl and Völter is as follows: "A model is an abstract representation of a system's structure, function or behavior" [SV06, p. 18]. Depending on the research area there are also other definitions of a model. However, models have common characteristics according to several definitions. The model concept this thesis refers to is based on the model theory of Stachowiak [Sta73]. According to this theory [Sta73], the models have the following characteristics: i) A model represents the original. The original can be a model. ii) A model is an abstraction of the original and involves only relevant properties to creators or users of the model. iii) A model can replace the original for specific subjects and for specific functions within a specific time period. Section 2.1.1 describes the main concepts of MDSD and their relations. The tool support for viewing and editing models, as well as code generation is given in Section 2.1.2.

2.1.1. Modeling Languages

The main idea of MDSD is modeling a software system and generating code from these models. Thus, one of the goals is to automate the software development. In this context, models cannot be considered as only a documentation of software systems, but also an integral part of them. Thus, models in MDSD have to be described in an abstract and a formal way. The abstraction means the reduction to important aspects of the software system. The formalization is based on a *Domain Specific Language (DSL)*. For this purpose, a formal *modeling language*, which is independent of a specific platform, but is tailored to a specific domain is used. The *domain* narrows the area of interest or knowledge. Then, several transformations allow generating code from models. However, it is also possible to generate models from models [SV06].

The constructs of a modeling language (i.e., the concepts in a domain) and the relations between them are defined by the *metamodel*. In other words, a metamodel, which comprises a set of metaclasses, involves the specification of the abstract syntax and semantics of a modeling language. The *abstract syntax* of a language defines its structure. A specific graphical or textual notation of the abstract syntax is represented by the *concrete syntax*. However, not all constraints and criteria for a well-formed language can be defined by its abstract or concrete syntax. They are defined by the *static semantics* of the language. The dynamic semantics of a language specify the meaning of its constructs and elements. Figure 2.1 illustrates the relations between the terms described previously. In this context, the instances of metamodels are considered as *models*. A metamodel is an instance of a *meta-metamodel* [SV06].

Two main categories of DSL are internal DSL and external DSL: An external DSL has a dedicated syntax and a corresponding parser. In other words, an external DSL in general has its own grammar. By contrast, an internal DSL

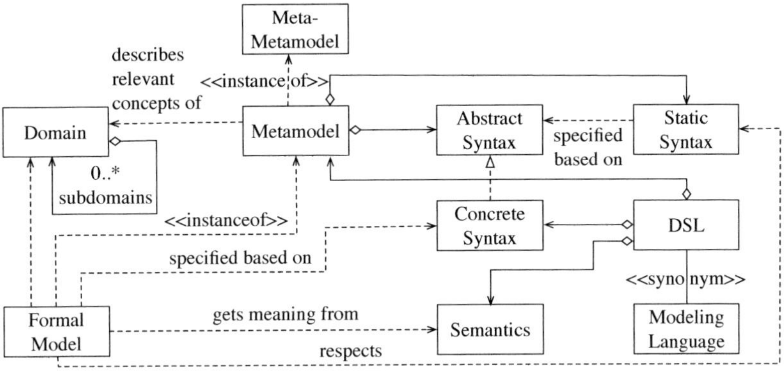

Figure 2.1.: Relations between modeling concepts [SV06, p. 56]

can be seen as a specific type of Application Programming Interface (API). Thus, it depends on the syntax of the host language [Fow10].

A further differentiating aspect is imperative vs. declarative languages. A declarative programming language is concerned with "what is to be computed, but not necessarily how it is to be computed" [Llo94, p. 1]. The latter is called an imperative programming language.

DSL can be executable, non-executable, or only executable to some degree [MHS05]. In other words, a distinction is made between DSL, from which executable code can be generated and DSL, from which no executable code can be generated [Fow10]. For example, a DSL can compile to another programming language, which can compile to byte code [Fow10].

2.1.2. Eclipse Modeling Framework

The Eclipse Modeling Framework (EMF) [1] is a modeling framework to create and edit structured data models. It is developed for Eclipse Integrated

[1] `https://www.eclipse.org/modeling/emf`

Development Environment (IDE) [2]. For this purpose, it provides the self-describing metamodel language ecore [3]. Models can be specified based on ecore. Other features such as runtime support for the models are also provided by EMF. Further, it allows code generation for the models [Ste+09].

As a part of EMF, Xtext [4] is developed. Using Xtext textual DSL can be developed. Xtext provides a grammar language with a syntax, which is similar to Extended Backus-Naur Form (EBNF). Further, it provides support for the generation of a parser, as well as a metamodel and the corresponding code. Further, Xtext provides additional features such as editors [EV06].

One of the languages, which is implemented in Xtext is the expression language Xbase [5]. Xbase has a similar syntax as Java. The code written in Xbase can compile to Java code. Xbase can be embedded in a DSL. The Java dialect Xtend [6] has also a similar syntax as Java and compiles to Java.

The syntax of the language for change propagation rules presented in this thesis is specified in EBNF. To present the terminal symbols' quotation marks (i.e., " . . . ") are used. The optional parts of the rules are presented in brackets (i.e., [. . .]). Different alternative parts of a rule are separated by pipes (i.e., |). Commas (i.e., ,) are used for the concatenation. Non-terminals can also include white spaces [Pat].

2.2. Change Impact Analysis

Maintainability is defined by ISO/IEC as the "degree of effectiveness and efficiency with which a product or system can be modified by the intended maintainers" [ISO11]. Thus, the maintainability of a system correlates with the propagation of a change in the system. A change can be considered as a transition of one state to another (from *AS-IS* to *TO-BE*) [Nwo+18]. It is desirable to estimate the TO-BE state by a change in advance. "The ability to determine what parts are related to what other parts according to

[2] https://www.eclipse.org

[3] https://download.eclipse.org/modeling/emf/emf/javadoc/2.9.0/org/eclipse/emf/ecore/package-summary.html

[4] https://www.eclipse.org/Xtext

[5] https://www.eclipse.org/Xtext/documentation/305_xbase.html

[6] https://www.eclipse.org/xtend

specific relationships" is proposed by Arnold and Bohner in [AB93, p. 2] as *traceability*. In this context, the *change impact analysis* can be defined as "the activity of identifying what to modify to accomplish a change, or of identifying the potential consequences of a change" [AB93, p. 1]. Although this definition is originally proposed in the domain of IS, the change propagation analysis approaches for other domains presented in this thesis are also based on this definition. This definition distinguishes between a change, also referred to as the trigger of a change, and the potential consequences of this change. A *change trigger* presents an event causing the change, while potential consequences of a change are known as the *change impact* [Nwo+18]. Thus, the less the impact of a change trigger in a system, the easier the system can be maintained regarding this change trigger. If the change impact analysis is conducted at the model level, the result is a set of affected or impacted model elements. A model element is affected by a change, "if a modification to that element or its implementation may be needed to accomplish a change" [BLO03, p. 6]. One method to identify the affected model elements is based on the change propagation rules. Change propagation rules can be executed repeatedly to determine a transitive closure of directly and indirectly affected elements. *Rule* is defined by Briand et al. as "a specification ... of how to derive several collections ... of elements, corresponding to elements of different types ..., that are potentially impacted by a particular change ... " [BLO03, p. 6]. Although this definition is originally introduced to specify the change propagation rules for the UML models based on Object Constraint Language (OCL) constraints, it can also be used as a general definition of change propagation rules.

2.3. Palladio Component Model

The PCM [Reu16] enables software architects to model a component-based software architecture. The PCM as a Architecture Description Language (ADL) considers different viewpoints of a software architecture, namely structural, behavioral, and deployment. It can be used to predict different quality aspects of a software system such as performance [Reu16], maintainability [Sta15; Ros+15b], or reliability [Bro+12]. In general, the PCM is composed of the following metamodels with respect to different developer roles: i) The *Component Repository Model* supports component developers by modeling components and interfaces. ii) The *System Model* allows software architects to model the software architecture by assembling the components. iii) The *Execution Environment Model* enables component deployers to define the underlying hardware nodes. iv) The *Component Allocation Model* supports component deployers to specify the deployment of components on hardware nodes. v) The *Usage Model* allows domain experts to model the interaction of users with the software system [BKR09; Reu16].

In the following, PCM or its extensions are used to model the software architecture or its behavior.

2.4. Metamodel of Business Processes

A *BP* is defined by the Terminology & Glossary of the Workflow Management Coalition Specification as "a set of one or more linked procedures or activities which collectively realise a business objective or policy goal, normally within the context of an organizational structure defining functional roles and relationships" [Wor99, p. 10]. The change propagation analysis approach between IS and BP in this thesis is based on the metamodel of BP, proposed by Heinrich [Hei14]. According to [Hei14, p. 105], "the BP design represents the usage profile of the IS on an abstract level". The proposed metamodel can be considered as a set of connected activities, as shown in Figure 2.2 [Hei+17]. `Activities` are used to model hierarchically nested BP [Hei+17]. A BP model consists of a set of BP. Each BP can be modeled as a `ScenarioBehaviour`. A `ScenarioBehaviour` is composed of a set of `AbstractUserActions`, which contain all control flow model elements from the UsageModel of PCM [BKR09; Hei14; Hei+17]. An `EntryLevelSystemCall` is a "call of services at system provided roles" [BKR09, p. 11]. Thus, `EntryLevelSystemCalls` represent the system steps in a BP, which are performed automatically by IS [Hei+17]. Further, the PCM was extended by `ActorStep`, `AcquireDeviceResource`, and `ReleaseDeviceResource`, as illustrated in Figure 2.2 [Hei+17]. All activities between two related `AcquireDeviceResource` and `ReleaseDeviceResource` need the usage of a specific device to be performed [Hei+17]. `ActorSteps` are activities, which are manually performed by the actors (i.e., human) [Hei+17]. This metamodel is based on the Business Process Model and Notation (BPMN) [Obj11] with focus on the mutual dependencies between IS and BP.

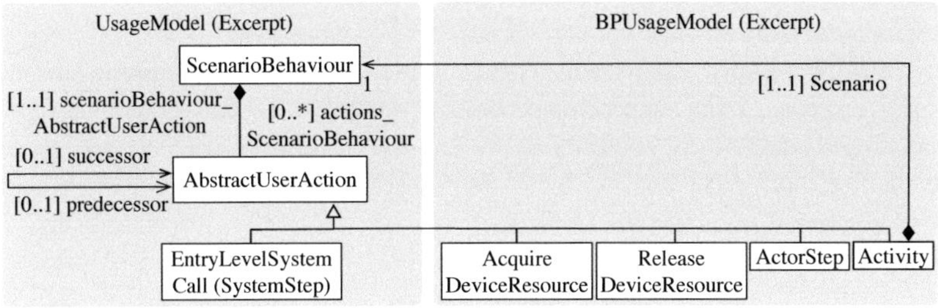

Figure 2.2.: Metamodel of the BP design [Hei14; Hei+17]

2.5. Requirements Engineering

This section clarifies the terminology used in this thesis regarding different concepts of the requirements engineering and gives an overview of the formalizations of the discussed concepts. *Requirements engineering* is defined by the IEEE standard 29148 as an “interdisciplinary function that mediates between the domains of the acquirer and supplier to establish and maintain the requirements to be met by the system, software or service of interest” [IEE11, p. 8]. The standard states the relationship between the roles of an acquirer (i.e., other synonyms such as “buyer, customer, owner, and purchaser” [IEE11, p. 3] are also possible.) and a supplier as, the acquirer “acquires or procures a product or service from a supplier” [IEE11, p. 3]. *Requirement* represents a “statement which translates or expresses a need and its associated constraints and conditions” [IEE11, p. 5]. Glinz distinguishes in [Gli07] three categories of requirements: i) *system requirements*, ii) *project requirements*, and iii) *process requirements*. System requirements involve i) *functional requirements*, ii) *performance requirements and specific quality requirements*, as well as iii) *constraints* [Gli07]. Examples of specific quality requirements are reliability, usability, security, availability, portability, and maintainability [Gli07]. This categorization is based on the IEEE standards [IEE90; IEE98], which explicitly mention the performance requirements and on the fact that there is no standardized definition of non-functional requirements (see the terminology discussion by Glinz [Gli07]). However, he defined the term *non-functional requirement* as "an attribute of or a constraint on a system" [Gli07, p. 5]. *Constraint* is an "externally imposed limitation on system requirements, design, or implementation or on the process used to develop or modify a system" [IEE11, p. 4]. *Attribute* is defined by the IEEE standard as an "inherent property or characteristic of an entity that can be distinguished quantitatively or qualitatively by human or automated means" [IEE11, p. 3].

The architecture of a software system embraces the main design decisions [TMD09]. However, many researchers use the term *design decision* without clarifying its definition. One of the few discussions on this topic is proposed by Taylor et al. in [TMD09]. According to their discussions, "design decisions encompass every aspect of the system under development" [TMD09, p. 58]. In particular, examples of these aspects can be "system structure", "functional behaviour", "interaction", "non functional properties", and "system's implementation" [TMD09, p. 58]. However, a design decision can be implemented in different ways. For this purpose, Hahn and Schuller introduced in [HS15] the term *option* in IS, which connects the design decisions with a certain software architecture. Thus, an option can be considered as a possible implementation, which has its rationals. Although several of the introduced terms were originally defined in IS, they can also be used in a broader sense. Thus, this thesis uses these concepts not only in IS, but also in BP and aPS.

After requirements elicitation, they can be expressed in a natural-language text or as a formal model [IEE11]. A formal model allows structured and systematic capture of relevant requirements, design decisions, and options, as well as a better traceability in the change propagation analysis [Dur14]. This provides further supports for automation using tools. One possible way to formalize the requirements is the use of metamodels, as proposed by Durdik [DR13; Dur14] and Küster [Küs13]. This thesis is based on the aforementioned metamodels of [DR13; Dur14; Küs13; HS15] to establish traceability links between the requirements and the system under study over the design decisions and options. In the following, the relevant metaclasses of these metamodels are described in more detail.

Figure 2.3 illustrates the relationship between requirements, decisions, and options. The `Relations` metamodel is proposed by Hahn and Schuller [HS15] as an extension of the aforementioned metamodels by Durdik [DR13; Dur14] and Küster [Küs13] to allow the traceability between different requirements, decisions, and options. Thus, it defines several possible relation types (e.g., to document that there is a conflict between two design decisions). Figure 2.3 shows various relation types. Various relation types enable traceability, as the change propagation can be analyzed based on these relations. Inheriting from the metaclass `TraceableObject` allows access to the pre-defined relation types. The following sections give an overview of metamodels of requirements, design decisions, and options, as proposed by [DR13; Dur14; Küs13; HS15].

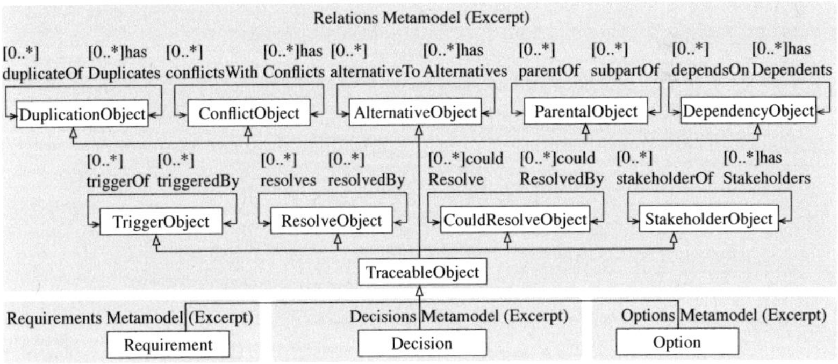

Figure 2.3.: Relationship between requirements, design decisions, and options [HS15], adapted from [Küs13; Dur14; DR13]

2.5.1. Metamodel of Requirements

The `Requirements` metamodel is shown in Figure 2.4. It is mainly based on the aforementioned categorization, proposed by Glinz [Gli07]. According to this categorization, a requirement can regard a system, a process, or a project. A system requirement can be a constraint on the system, a functional requirement, or a quality requirement [Gli07; HS15; Dur14].

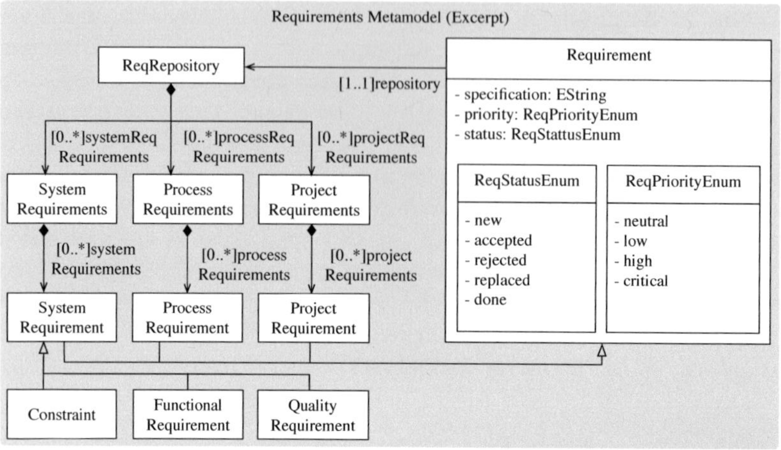

Figure 2.4.: Metamodel of requirements [HS15], adapted from [Küs13; Dur14; DR13]

2.5.2. Metamodel of Options

Figure 2.5 illustrates the `Options` metamodel, proposed by Hahn and Schuller [HS15]. As described previously, options present possible solutions [HS15]. Software architects can annotate the rationale of each option [HS15]. The decision-making process involves selecting the appropriate options and describing their rationales [HS15; Dur14]. The rational of an option can be considered as the reason, why the option is needed (adapted from the IEEE standard [IEE11]). An option can also be a text option or a constraint. Further, the metamodel allows annotating various decision status for an option such as open or taken [HS15].

The metamodel depicted in Figure 2.5 illustrates the `Options` metamodel at a high level of abstraction. These options can also be further refined to allow a fine-grained traceability. As a software architecture presents a set of design decisions during its development and evolution [TMD09; MT10], options can be further refined to include architectural options. Figure 2.6 illustrates this refinement involving the architectural options and their refinements for the PCM as metamodel files. The architectural options involve

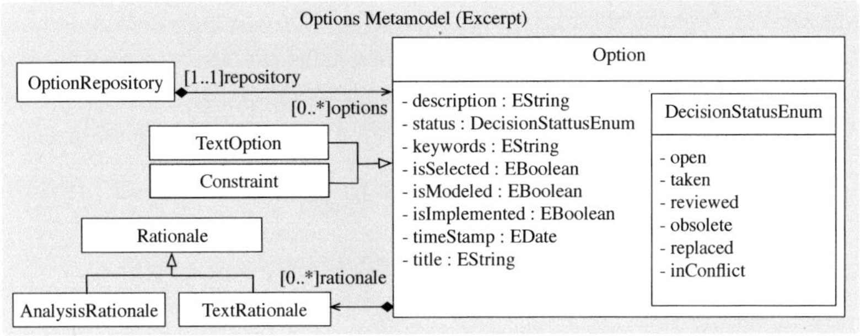

Figure 2.5.: Metamodel of options [HS15], adapted from [Küs13; Dur14; DR13]

further options regarding *interfaces*, *components*, *data types*, and *deployment*. These options can also be further refined. Examples of *deployment*-specific options can be *move component*, *never allocate to specific nodes*, or *allocate together*. PCM was used as a possible metamodel describing the software architecture. Thus, other metamodels are also possible due to the provided modular metamodels. The metaclasses of `PCMArchitectureOption` metamodel references the metaclasses of PCM. For example, the PCM-specific metaclass in `PCMArchitectureOption` metamodel regarding *never allocate to specific nodes* references the affected *allocation context* and the *resource container* from the PCM [HS15; Küs13; Dur14; DR13].

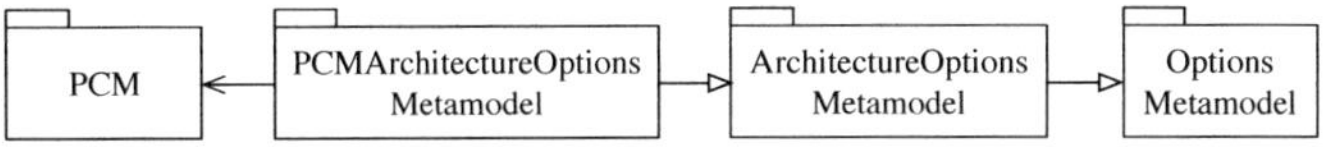

Figure 2.6.: Relationship between the metamodels of options, architectural options, and PCM architectural options and the PCM [HS15], adapted from [Küs13; Dur14; DR13]

2.5.3. Metamodel of Design Decisions

The metamodel presented in Figure 2.7 is concerned with documenting the decisions and the corresponding rationale. The use of the decision concept allows selecting the appropriate options to fulfill the requirements. Similar to the `Options` metamodel, `DecisionStatusEnum` allows documenting the current status of a decision (e.g., open or taken) [HS15; Küs13; Dur14; DR13].

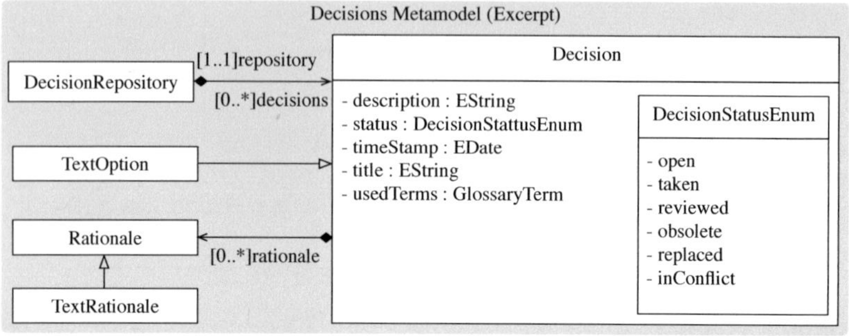

Figure 2.7.: Metamodel of decisions [HS15], adapted from [Küs13; Dur14; DR13]

2.6. The IEC 61131-3 Standard

This section gives an overview of the standard International Electrotechnical Commission (IEC) 61131-3 [IEC13]. This standard is used to program control software, which is deployed on Programmable Logic Controllers (PLC) [Vog+17; Bus+18c]. Although there are several standards for programming PLC, this standard is used in most manufacturing systems and, thus, can be stated as "the state of industrial practice in the next 5 - 10 years" [Vog+15, p. 14]. There are several dialects of this standard. This thesis uses the dialect developed by CodeSys V3.1 [AG], as it is very similar to the original specification and provides a run-time environment for simulating the control software [Bus+18c]. Further, this dialect provides also object-oriented features [Wer09], which result in "a more efficient code reuse and increased safety and stability of software" [Vya13, p. 9]. Additionally, it allows a modular design of programs [Dus+15].

IEC programs are structured using configurations, as illustrated in Figure 2.8. Processing units of a PLC are represented by resources. Following this standard, an IEC software is structured with regard to Program Organization Units (POU). POU can be programs, function blocks, or functions in the IEC standard and can be executed by tasks. Several programs can be assigned to one resource. Functions act as stateless procedures. A function block contains input and output variables, as well as a set of operations accessing these variables. In contrast to functions, function blocks can access global variables. Thus, they can be considered as stateful. The object-oriented extension provides further features such as methods or interfaces [JT01; IEC13].

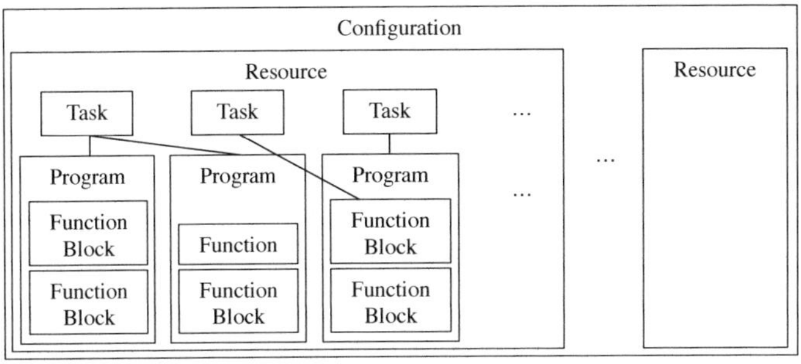

Figure 2.8.: Simplified structure of an IEC program, adapted from the IEC software model [IEC13]

2.7. Metamodel of Mechanical and Electrical/Electronic Parts of Automated Production Systems

This work is based on the metamodel representing the structure of the aPS hardware [Hei+18; Koc17]. This metamodel represents a domain-specific modeling language, which is based on Automation Markup Language (AML) models developed by Technische Universität München (TUM) [Vog+17]. AML is a general-purpose modeling language, which does not represent the specific types of artifacts in an aPS [Hei+18]. Therefore, AML models are not suitable for change propagation algorithms based on rules, as the rules are based on the specific types of artifacts [Hei+18]. The domain-specific metamodel based on the AML models is described in the following in more detail.

As there are many different elements in aPS, two metamodels were developed at two abstraction levels. The first metamodel represents a plant at a high abstraction level and, therefore, enables modeling any plant. This metamodel is referred to in the following as the *abstract metamodel*. However, its metaclasses can be further refined to model a specific plant more precisely. This is the second metamodel, which is designed at a lower abstraction level. It contains mainly the metaclasses needed to model the Extended Pick and Place Unit (xPPU), which is a lab-size community case study in aPS. In other words, the xPPU can be modeled using this metamodel more precisely. However, this metamodel is limited to the xPPU or plants that are similarly structured. The second metamodel is referred to hereinafter as the *specific metamodel* [Hei+18].

2.7.1. Abstract Metamodel of Automated Production Systems

Figure 2.9 gives an overview of the abstract metamodel of the aPS hardware. This metamodel can describe a plant at an abstract level. Following this metamodel, a plant can consist of several structures. A structure can contain components and modules. Thus, it can be considered as a composition of components and modules. Structures present complex elements. In other words, the use of structures allows grouping the artifacts of a plant and modeling a plant at a higher abstraction level. Thus, they can be used to improve the reusability of models [Hei+18].

Modules are artifacts in a plant, which can be assembled by plant manufacturers using components and other modules [LS17]. By contrast, components are provided by third-party vendors [LS17]. For example, a motor module can have components for the communication. Components can represent both mechanical and electrical/electronic elements. An example of a component can be a screw [Hei+18].

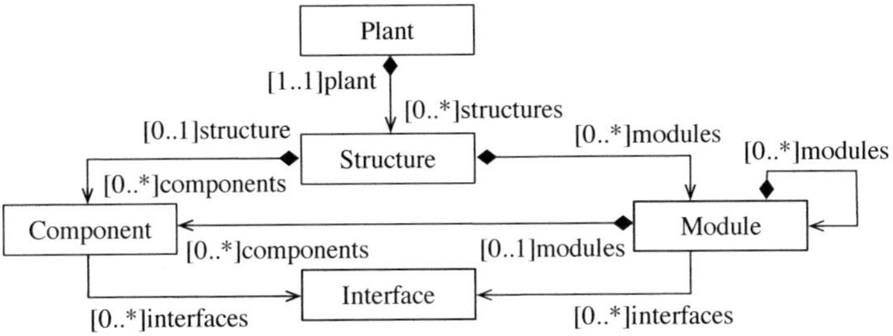

Figure 2.9.: Abstract metamodel of aPS [Koc17; Hei+18]

Both modules and components can have interfaces. Interfaces can be considered as general. In other words, an interface can be a communication interface or a physical interface for fixing an artifact to a plant [Hei+18].

2.7.2. Specific Metamodel of Automated Production Systems

As described previously, the abstract metamodel can be refined to allow modeling a specific plant more precisely. The metamodels presented in this section were designed to model the xPPU. As the xPPU is a community case study for industrial manufacturing plants, it is composed of the typical artifacts of an industry plant [Hei+18; Gol+15; Vog+14a]. Although this metamodel is tailored to the xPPU, the abstract metamodel can also be extended by further elements for any plants containing elements, which do not exist in the xPPU. To extend the abstract metamodel to a specific one, the specific components and modules in the plant under study have to be metamodeled [Hei+18].

2.7.2.1. Components

As described in Section 2.7.1, components are artifacts, which can be purchased from third parties. According to this definition, a component in an aPS model can be considered as a black box. However, they can be grouped together according to their types [Hei+18]. Examples of this grouping are bus components, as shown in Figure 2.10. Bus components (e.g., `BusBox`, `BusSlave`, or `BusCable`) are used for communication of other artifacts within a system [Koc17; Hei+18].

Components can be composed of other components, which can be mechanical and electrical/electronic components. Thus, composite components cannot be considered in general as purely mechanical components or purely electrical/electronic components. However, these components can also be specialized. In contrast to modules, composite components are provided by third-party vendors and are not assembled by plant manufacturers [Hei+18].

Mechanical components and electrical/electronic components can be further refined. Figure 2.10 illustrates the refinement (i.e., specialization) of these components in the specific metamodel. This metamodel can also be extended by further specializations [Hei+18].

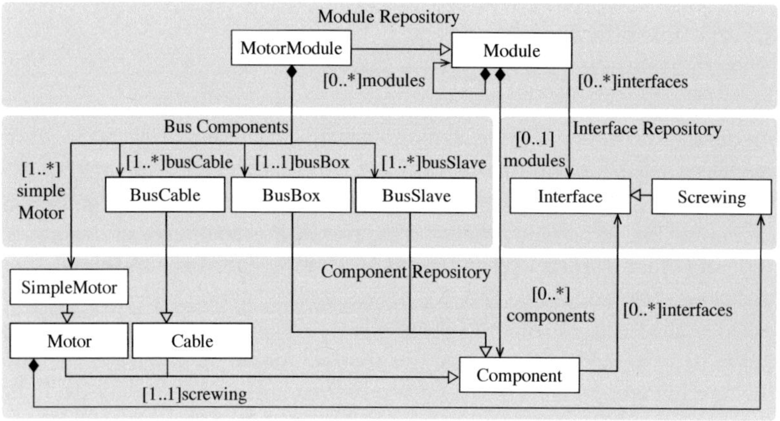

Figure 2.10.: Specific Metamodel of aPS - An excerpt [Koc17; Hei+18]

2.7.2.2. Modules

As described in Section 2.7.1, a module is composed of components or other modules. In the following, the composition of components and modules for the `MotorModule` of the xPPU is exemplary described. Figure 2.10 illustrates the components and modules of the `MotorModule`. The `Motor` has a physical interface for fixing (i.e., `Screwing` in Figure 2.10). This interface enables assembling the motor to the rest of the plant. This physical fixation represents an interface. Further, there is a need for a bus communication to control the motor. Bus boxes, bus slaves, and bus cables are specializations of the bus communication. In addition, the `MotorModule` requires a real motor (see the `SimpleMotor` in Figure 2.10). Thus, the `MotorModule` consists of other modules, components (e.g., the `SimpleMotor`), and interfaces (e.g., the `Screwing`). It is conceivable that a motor could be provided by a third party vendor as a black box. In this case, the motor is a component and not a module [Hei+18].

2.7.2.3. Structures

Modules and components can be grouped into coarse-grained elements to improve the reusability of elements. As described previously, these elements are called structures. An example of a structure in the specific metamodel is the crane structure. The crane is composed of several components such as the mechanical component arm. In addition to components, it contains various modules such as turning table. Each module can be composed of further components and modules.

2.8. Karlsruhe Architectural Maintainability Prediction

The methodology presented in this thesis can be considered as the generalization of the Karlsruhe Architectural Maintainability Prediction (KAMP) approach [SR09; Sta15; Ros+15b]. KAMP is an approach to change propagation analysis in the domain of IS. It considers the architecture of a software system as the main artifact. The analysis of the change propagation is based on rules, which consider the relationship between the model elements of the software architecture. Further, the software architect can annotate the software architecture with organizational and technical information. In this way, KAMP considers the impact resulted by these artifacts [SR09; Sta15; Ros+15b].

The approach is composed of a preparation phase and a change request analysis phase [SR09; Sta15; Ros+15b]. Both phases are described in the following in more detail.

During the preparation phase of KAMP [Sta15; Ros+15b], the software architect models the architecture of the software system. The architecture model is based on a simplified version of the PCM. In this version, a further metamodel represents the internal dependencies between the provided roles and the required roles of a component. In other words, this version omits modeling the Service EFFect specification (SEFF) [BKR09]. Additionally, the software architect can annotate the software architecture with additional information such as source code, build configuration, test cases, deployment, or staff. The software architect can model the software system either manually or using a reverse engineering approach. An example of these approaches is Source Code Model eXtractor (SoMoX), which is proposed by Krogmann in [Kro12]. This approach reconstructs a PCM model of a component-based software. Source Code Model eXtractor for Karlsruhe Architectural Maintainability Prediction (SoMoX4KAMP) is an extension of SoMoX detecting the organizational and technical artifacts, such as build specification based on heuristics (e.g., naming convention for example for `pom.xml` or `Makefile`) [Ros+17c].

The next phase is the change request analysis phase. KAMP analyzes the propagation of a change request in the software architecture automatically. For this purpose, it uses a rule-based algorithm for the change propagation analysis. This algorithm is composed of a set of change propagation rules. The change propagation rules consider the relationship between the metaclasses of the PCM. Each rule represents a change propagation from an affected metaclass to a further metaclass. Thus, a transitive closure of the affected model elements based on the change request can be calculated. The granularity of the change propagation is based on components, interfaces, and data types. After identifying all potentially affected elements of the software architecture, KAMP calculates the affected organizational and technical artifacts. The result is a task list containing all model elements, which can be affected by a change request [SR09; Sta15; Ros+15b].

3. State of the Art

This section gives an overview of the related work to this thesis. The presented approaches are structured according to the main contributions of this work and the domains under study (i.e., IS, BP, or aPS). Section 3.1 discusses the relevant approaches to change propagation analysis in IS. The change propagation analysis approaches in the domain of BP are presented in Section 3.2. The approaches, which consider the co-evolution of IS and BP are proposed in Section 3.3. Section 3.4 presents the model-based approaches to change impact analysis in aPS. As requirements can also cause the change propagation, the approaches to this topic are discussed in Section 3.5. Section 3.6 gives an overview of the domain-specific languages to specify the change propagation rules. An overview of the metamodels for the control system and more especially for the standard IEC 61131-3 is given in Section 3.7. The last section summarizes the discussion of the state of the art regarding the change propagation analysis in various domains.

3.1. Change Propagation in Information Systems

In IS there are several approaches addressing the change propagation analysis and cost estimation [Leh11b; Leh11a]. One of the most relevant approaches is program slicing. This approach is originally introduced by Weiser [Wei81]. A program slice is described by Tip [Tip95, p. 1] as "the parts of a program that (potentially) affect the values computed at some point of interest". The program slicing refers to the method of reducing the program to the program slice [Wei81; Tip95]. Since introducing this approach, several types of program slicing and methods to calculate the program slices are developed [Tip95]. Static and dynamic program slicing are the main categories of these methods [Tip95]. While the static program slicing does not rely on the input of the program, the dynamic program slicing considers the known inputs of the program [Tip95; GGS96]. One of the efficient methods to calculate the program slices is based on the Program Dependence Graph (PDG) [OO84; GGS96]. The edges of a PDG represent the data and control dependencies of a program [GGS96]. The literature review of Tip [Tip95] gives a detailed overview of the approaches to program slicing. The idea of program slicing is also generalized to slicing methods for the UML models, as described by [LR11; KMS05].

Different types of graphs are used by several approaches to analyze the change propagation. One of the most relevant approaches is proposed by Reps [Rep82]. The presented algorithms are based on dependency graphs representing the functional dependencies of attributes. Based on a dependency graph, characteristic graphs are constructed, which represent the transitive dependencies in the dependency graph. The provided algorithms can identify the attributes affected by a change and update their values. The cost of the algorithm is proportional to the values affected by the change. This property is referred to as time optimal [Rep82], as these algorithms are “asymptotically optimal in time” [RT87, p. 9].

In the context of object-oriented programs, there are several approaches to change propagation analysis. One of the important approaches is proposed by Ryder and Tip in [RT01]. This approach is based on call graphs and addresses the problems caused by subtyping and dynamic dispatch. The change propagation is analyzed on the granularity of classes, methods, and fields. This analysis helps to identify the affected regression test drivers. This also allows further analyses regarding regression testing such as identifying the changes that do not affect any tests.

The previous approaches are based on graphs (e.g., PDG or call graphs) to analyze the change propagation. However, there are a wide variety of categories of approaches. The review provided by Lehnert [Leh11a] covers 150 approaches from 1991 to 2011. A taxonomy and a classification of the change propagation approaches are provided based on this review [Leh11b]. The provided taxonomy contains the following dimensions: i) analysis scope, ii) utilized techniques, iii) entity granularity, iv) analysis style, v) tool support, vi) language, vii) scalability, and viii) experimental results [Leh11b]. He divided the scope of the analyzed approaches into three categories: i) code, ii) models, and iii) miscellaneous artifacts (e.g., documentation). Due to this review, 65 % of the analyzed approaches are based on the source code. Further, most approaches neglect the effects of changes on the miscellaneous artifacts. Thus, there is a need for approaches based on a holistic view of the system under study to consider not only the code, but also the miscellaneous artifacts.

The proposed methodology in this thesis generalizes the idea of the architecture-based and model-based approach KAMP [Sta15; Ros+15b] in IS (see Section 2.8). Hence, the resulting instances of the methodology are scenario-based and architecture-based change propagation analysis approaches. Although the change propagation analysis in IS is outside of the scope of this thesis, the remainder of this section presents most relevant related work in this research area. A detailed overview of these approaches is given in [Sta15; Ros+15b].

Software Architecture Analysis Method (SAAM) [Kaz+94] is one of the earliest approach to analyze the software architecture regarding different quality attributes based on scenarios. The approach is composed of several steps. The first step is to identify a reference architecture (i.e., canonical functional partitioning as it is called by the authors) for the domain under study. The results of the first step is, then, mapped the structural decomposition of the software architecture. The next step is concerned with identifying the most relevant quality attributes, which have to be used to analyze the architecture. Although the approach can be applied to different quality attributes, the paper discusses the modifiability in more detail. To assess the software architecture regarding the chosen quality attribute, a set of scenarios (i.e., tasks) has to be identified. In the modifiability example, this set can contain likely changes. Finally, the software architecture is assessed regarding, whether and how well it fulfills the chosen quality attributes. Thus, the approach can also be used to compare and rank different architecture candidates.

A successor to SAAM is the Architecture Tradeoff Analysis Method (ATAM) [Kaz+98], which makes trade-offs between different quality attributes such as modifiability or performance explicit. In this way, it evaluates the architectural design regarding the fulfillment of requirements. The method comprises various steps, which can be conducted iteratively. In the first step, the usage scenarios of the resulting system have to be gathered.

To ensure whether the gathered scenarios are relevant for different quality attributes, the method suggests clarifying requirements of the system, constraints relating to design space, and system's environment with regard to different quality attributes. Hence, different architecture candidates can be obtained and the number of potential possibilities can be limited. These steps lead to a set of requirements, usage scenarios, quality attributes, and initial architecture candidates. Then, different architecture candidates have to be assessed regarding the identified quality attributes in isolation. The next step is concerned with identifying the sensitivity points (i.e., attributes or parameters in the architecture, which changes result in a considerable change in the quality attributes). The elements in the architecture, which can affect several sensitivity points at the same time, are considered to be the trade-off points. After each iteration, the analysis results have to be compared to the requirements of the system. If the system fulfills the requirements, the design or the implementation of the software can be refined.

While the previous both approaches are concerned with different quality attributes, Bengtsson and Bosch present in [BB99] an approach to architecture-level prediction of software maintenance. Their approach uses the software architecture and a set of change scenarios as input to estimate the maintenance effort. In particular, domain experts choose a set of representative change scenarios for a given architecture. The weights of change scenarios can be chosen either based on expertise of domain experts or maintenance data from earlier scenarios. In the next steps, the size of both the whole system and the affected parts of it has to be estimated. Based on this information, the effort for each scenario can be estimated as a weighted average.

Similar to the previous approach, Architecture-level Modifiability Analysis (ALMA) [Ben+04] was designed to analyze the modifiability of a software system at the architecture level. This approach also involves several steps. In the first step, the overall goal has to be defined. ALMA differentiates between three goals during the modifiability analysis at the architecture level: i) change effort estimation, ii) flexibility analysis of the architecture regarding different change types, and iii) comparing different architecture candidates to identify the optimal one. In the next step, a description of the software architecture has to be prepared with regard to the components of the system and their relationships, as well as the relationship between the system and its environment. Then, a set of relevant and representative change scenarios have to be identified. The next step of ALMA is concerned with changing the software architecture with regard to the change scenarios and evaluating the affected parts of the architecture. The results of the evaluation can be documented qualitatively or quantitatively. These results have to be analyzed with regard to the overall goal of the change propagation analysis.

The previously described scenario-based approaches mainly focus on the software system and neglect the activities regarding project management. One of the approaches considering the role of the architecture of a software system in the project management, is proposed by Paulish [Pau01]. He describes the main steps during the process of an architecture-centric project management, as illustrated in Figure 3.1. After identifying the market requirements during the *requirements analysis*, the *global analysis* is concerned with influencing factors on the resulting product. The *risk analysis* is the next step in this process. The output of these steps (i.e., a list of product features) and a modularized *architecture design* are the inputs of the *release planning* step. The *software development plan* deals with project's costs, schedule, and organization, while focusing on the first release in an incremental development. During the software development, the *team members* have to be *manged. Mid-course correction*s refer to changes in the plan (e.g., due to unforeseen circumstances). Finally, the software product is released in the *release delivery* step. Additionally, the author clarifies the roles and responsibilities of software architect and project manager in more detail.

One of the main concepts in the presented process is considering the software architecture in the process of project planning. This concept is also considered by other researchers, such as Stammel [Sta15]. The approaches presented in this thesis also generalize this concept. They consider the effort of project planning activities along with the architecture of a system for the change propagation analysis.

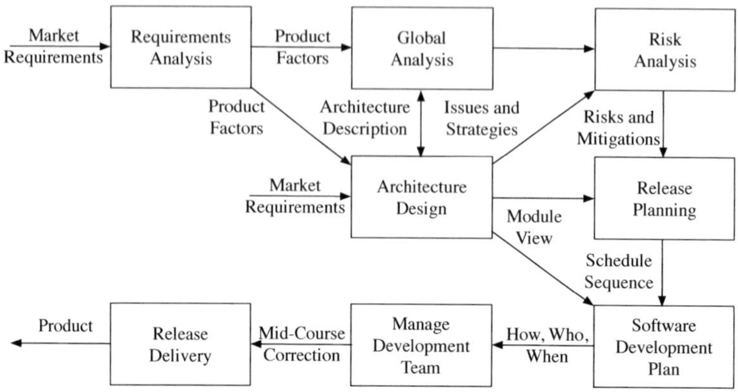

Figure 3.1.: Steps of a project management approach based on software architecture [Pau01, p. 8]

3.2. Change Propagation in Business Processes

One of the contributions of this thesis is the change propagation analysis in BP and between BP and IS. Thus, this section describes the approaches to change propagation analysis in BP, while the next section gives an overview of the approaches considering the co-evolution of BP and IS. Some of these approaches are based on the change patterns in BP provided by Weber et al. [WRR08]. The related approaches to change propagation in BP can be divided into two categories. The first category consists of approaches focusing on the migration of instances of a schema after a schema modification, also referred to as dynamic changes by Rinderle et al. [RWR06b; RWR06a]. The second category of approaches supports the change propagation in collaborative BP. This category contains also approaches, which consider the change propagation in the models of a BP at different abstraction levels. There are also further categories regarding the change propagation and restoring the consistencies. An example of these categories is restoring the consistencies between the business rules and the BP schemata (e.g., the approach of Lezoche [LMT08]). As these approaches are not within the scope of this thesis, they are not further considered in this section. In the following, the approaches of the aforementioned categories are discussed in more detail.

3.2.1. Dynamic Change Propagation in Business Processes

This section describes the approaches to dynamic change propagation analysis in BP. These approaches deal with the migration of instances after changing the BP schema.

Kradolfer and Geppert describe in [KG99] the problems arising when modifying the workflow schema (e.g., creation or modification of workflow types). Based on these changes, a new version of the affected workflow type is created and stored in the schema. The correctness of the schema can be checked using the defined schema invariants. Their approach checks whether the existing instances of the workflow types can be migrated to the new version. Then, the workflow instances are migrated to the new type, if possible. However, their approach focuses only on the change propagation analysis in BP. Further, they neglect the propagation of changes in workflow instances. Additionally, they do not consider additional artifacts that are affected by a change but are not covered by the schema.

Based on the workflow model ADEPT, several approaches are developed to deal with the propagation of changes to the process type [Rei+05; RD98]. After a change to the workflow schema, the compliance of process instance with the affected type is checked. For this purpose, they offer correctness criteria based on the control flow and data flow. Thus, the change propagation from an affected schema to its instances can be considered. However, the proposed approaches consider only the change propagation in BP. The changes to technical and organizational artifacts are also omitted.

Sadiq et al. differentiate in [SMO00] between the changes at the level of workflows (i.e., an automation of BP) and at the level of their instances. They identified five types of workflow changes: *flush*, *abort*, *migrate*, *adapt*, and *build*. These changes can be done by the following operations: *adding tasks*, *removing tasks*, *changing the properties* of a task such as allocated resources, and *modifying the order* of tasks. Then, the compliance criteria are discussed for the existing instances to switch them to the new workflow model. In [SO99] Sadiq and Orlowska present a framework to support the dynamic modification based on a modification methodology. The methodology consists of three phases: defining the modification, conforming to the modification, and effectuating the modification. However, the approach does not support the change propagation between the model of the workflow design and the model of the IS architecture supporting the workflow. Again, the approach neglects the effects of a change to technical and organizational artifacts.

The authors of [Yoo+08] propose an approach to define the schema modification rules in an eXtensible Markup Language (XML) rule language. These rules can be used to modify the schema. Further, the instances of the schema can be migrated to the new schema. However, the proposed approach does not support the change propagation in an instance or between instances of a schema. Further, they neglect the effects caused by changing the corresponding IS. The approach does not consider the effects of changing technical and organizational artifacts, as well.

3.2.2. Change Propagation in Collaborative Processes

This category of approaches is concerned with the change propagation analysis in collaborative processes. This is based on the idea that a change can propagate from a process of one partner to the processes of other partners, as the execution of a process may involve other partners [FRR12; Fdh+15]. These processes are called collaborative processes [FRR12; Fdh+15].

Fdhila et al. analyze in [FRR12; Fdh+15] the change propagation in collaborative scenarios. The interaction between collaborating partners is defined by the choreography model. They provide change propagation algorithms for the change operations *replace*, *update*, *insert*, and *delete*. These algorithms are based on the structure of BP. Using the *delete* change operation as an example, the authors show different scenarios to deal with the change propagation in the semantic of BP. However, they do not offer an automatic approach to change propagation analysis and the calculation of a transitive closure in the instances of a BP. Further, the effects of changes on the IS and technical and organizational artifacts are neglected.

The approach described in [RWR06b] is also concerned with the change propagation analysis in case of process choreographies. The authors consider the change propagation from the private processes of one partner to its public processes. If the changed public processes of this partner and the public process of the other partners are inconsistent, further actions are necessary. In this way, the change can propagate to the public and private processes of other partners. The proposed DYnamic CHOReographies (DYCHOR) framework [RWR06a] uses a formal model based on a finite state automata. Using this automata, the approach deals with *additive* and *subtractive* change operations. However, the approach neglects the change propagation between a BP and the IS supporting the BP. Further, the approach does not consider the effects of changing technical and organizational artifacts.

The approach of Kurniawan et al. [Kur+12] analyzes the change propagation in a collection of interrelated processes, a so-called process ecosystem. A change can cause inconsistencies in this ecosystem. Thus, the change propagation can be considered as restoring the consisting equilibrium. The approach maps the models of BP design to nodes and the relationships between the nodes to constraints. In this way, restoring the consisting equilibrium can be considered as a constraint satisfaction problem. Further, two algorithms were proposed to restore the equilibrium in the process ecosystem. This approach also neglects the effects of a change on the IS supporting the BP and technical and organizational artifacts.

The approach of Weidmann et al. [Wei+11] is concerned with the change propagation between the BP models at different abstraction levels. The authors propose the concept of change queues to implement the change operations. The change queues represent ordered lists of change operations. The changes in the queue have to propagate to the process models at the neighboring levels. Then, the elements have to be corresponded to elements at the current level. The change is considered as accepted after defining the correspondence. In this way, two process models at different abstraction levels can be synchronized. However, this change propagation is limited to BP and neglects IS. Again, they do not consider technical and organizational elements, which are affected by a change.

Weidlich et al. [WWM09] consider the situation, in which there are different process models with overlapping content. The approach uses the activities from process models that correspond to each other. In contrast to the previous approach, this approach can also be used for process models that are not defined at different abstraction levels. The change propagation can then be calculated based on the behavioral profiles of these activities. The behavioral profiles define three relations between two nodes in a process graph: *strict order*, *exclusiveness*, and *observation concurrency* relation. Similar to the previous approaches, this approach does not consider the effects of changes on IS and on technical and organizational artifacts.

The main limitation of the approaches presented in this section is that they do not consider the co-evolution of IS and BP. The effects of changes on technical and organizational artifacts are neglected, as well. Further, most approaches do not analyze the change propagation in the instances of a BP metamodel.

3.3. Change Propagation between Information Systems and Business Processes

There are several research papers indicating the importance of the co-design of BP and IS to reduce the gap between the IS and the BP requirements in organizations [LSB02]. Based on this idea, the Co-Design of Business and IT Systems (Co-BITS) method was developed as a guideline for the co-design [SKL12]. However, this method describes a manual process of the co-design. There are further works identifying the similarities of IS and BP [Van+07], describing the mutual dependencies between BP and IS [Aer+04], providing related metamodels [WGK00], or presenting a methodology to integrate the knowledge of different stakeholder groups [Gas08]. However, none of the previously mentioned approaches considers an automated change propagation analysis regarding the co-evolution of BP and IS. Thus, this section considers only the approach focusing on the change impact analysis.

Jamshidi and Pahl use graph matching to identify the changes in the model of the BP design [JP12]. Based on a specific change and change pattern, the model of the software architecture can be changed. However, they neglect the change propagation in each of these models based on the initial change. Further, they do not consider affected organizational and technical artifacts such as test cases in the process of change propagation analysis.

Sunkle et al. [Sun+13] developed an Enterprise Architecture (EA) ontology based on the modeling language Architecture-Animate (ArchiMate) [17]. Their approach is based on a set of cross-grained change propagation rules. The rules are based on heuristic between the nature of different relations, namely *accesses*, *assignedTo*, *usedBy*, *realises*, *triggers*, and *composedOf* between the concepts (e.g., behavioral concept). However, the change propagation rules are modeled at a very high abstraction level. Thus, insufficient semantics in relations can result in a high number of false positives as specified by Bohner [Boh02]. Further, the approach does not consider the impact of the change requests to the other artifacts that are not modeled by EA.

Boer et al. also present in [Boe+05] a similar approach to change propagation analysis based on ArchiMate. They use the relationships *access*, *assign*, *use*, *realize*, and *trigger* to formulate coarse-grained heuristics describing the change propagation. The heuristics present guidelines during the change impact process. An example of a *use* relationship can be: *Entity B uses the functionality of service A*. A possible heuristic is also: "If A is modified, B may need to be modified as well, because the older functionalities may no longer be declared in A" [Boe+05, p. 3]. This is an example of a coarse-grained change propagation rule. There is also a need for more semantics for the relations to avoid too many false positives. Additionally, the approach does not consider the effects of a change on the other artifacts such as documentation or test cases.

Bodhuin et al. present in [Bod+04] a coarse-grained strategy as a guideline for identifying misalignments between BP and IS caused by a change. This is done by identifying metrics such as technological coverage. Given thresholds for these metrics, their values can be evaluated. The authors propose to consider the nature of different relations, namely *include*, *dependOn*, *use*, *composedOf*, and *dependOn* in the UML notation. Based on these relations, four very coarse-grained change propagation rules are specified as follows: A change to an activity in BP and/or a component in IS can propagate to a further activity in BP and/or to a further component in IS. However, they do not provide an automatic approach to change impact analysis. Further, they did not identify fine-grained change propagation rules based on the relations between BP and IS. Thus, a change propagation at this level of abstraction can lead to "impacts explosion without semantics" as described by Bohner [Boh02, p. 5]. Additionally, the approach does not consider the impact of a change request on technical and/or organizational artifacts such as adapting the documentation.

Avia et al. propose in [AG14] a set of coarse-grained actions based on a set of coarse-grained rules in the case of change. The rules describe the combination of different values, namely change types (i.e., *modification*, *deletion*, and *insertion*), the roles of components (i.e., *enabler* and *requester*), and the types of the relationships (i.e., *necessary* and *useful*). The actions are guidelines to solve the misalignments. An example of an action is: "If there are new requirements, a first option is to modify the enabler in order to satisfy the new requirements" [AG14, p. 8]. "In this case, the relationship type remains as "necessary"" [AG14, p. 8]. The proposed approach does not present an automatic approach to change impact analysis. Without further semantics, the change propagation may lead to a high number of false positives.

As discussed for the aforementioned approaches, there is a need for an automated change propagation analysis approach, which considers more semantics to reduce the number of false positives. Further, considering affected technical and organizational artifacts such as documentation can lead to more precise change propagation results.

3.4. Model-based Change Propagation Analysis in Automated Production Systems

In aPS there are a few attempts in the research area of the change propagation analysis and maintainability estimation [Hei+18]. One of the common methods of cost estimation is based on the number of input or output signals [Vog14]. In recent years, metamodels are used by several approaches to manage the complexity of aPS [Hei+18]. However, there is still a lack of a domain-spanning metamodel in aPS [Vog+17]. Thus, one way to model such systems is the use of UML, as discussed in Section 3.4.1. UML diagrams are based on a single metamodel and are usually class-based models, as described by Lin et al. [LGJ07]. Another way is to use domain-specific modeling languages, which are tailored to specific users of a domain [LGJ07]. The approaches based on domain-specific languages are described in Section 3.4.2.

3.4.1. Change Propagation based on UML Models

This section describes the approaches to change propagation analysis and difference calculation based on UML models.

In [BLO03] the authors present a change impact analysis approach based on UML models. This approach identifies the changes between two versions of a UML model (i.e., before and after the change). It uses a set of change propagation rules in OCL to calculate a transitive closure of the model elements affected by the change. Further, they use a distance measure between the initially affected element and the elements identified as changed to prioritize the results.

Kelte et al. [KWN05] present an approach to calculate the differences between two UML models encoded in XML Metadata Interchange (XMI) files. The approach is based on the algorithm Longest Common Subsequence (LCS) to identify the similarities between strings. Thus, it does not need any identifiers of diagram elements. However, this approach does not analyze the change propagation.

The approach of Dam and Winikoff [DW10] aims at resolving the inconsistencies for UML models using OCL constraints. For this purpose, they check the constrains in the models, after changes were made to these models. For each constraint violated by a change, a repair plan is generated. Then, the costs of the repair plans are calculated. The approach presents the cheapest plan to the user.

Delta-P [Sot07] is an approach to compare models based on the Semantic Web techniques. For this purpose, the model is transformed to the Resource Description Framework (RDF) notation – a triple-based notation. Then, the models are compared based on the unique identifiers. The result is a comparison model. The last step identifies the change patterns in the comparison model. This approach does not calculate the change propagation and the ripple effects caused by a change.

Wolter et al. [WKH07] present an approach to compare UML models based on ontologies. Ontologies are used to define the architecture of the products. In contrast to the other approaches, they do not use any naming similarities. Thus, the results of the approach do not rely on the naming of the single classes. However, their approach does not consider the propagation of changes.

Scharf and Zündorf present an approach in [SZ11] to identify the differences between several model versions and to merge them. However, the approach does not support the change propagation in the models.

The previously described approaches were originally developed in the domain of IS. UML models were not originally defined to describe the aPS systems and, thus, cannot cover the whole semantics of aPS. In [LGJ07] the authors describe the differences and benefits of the domain-specific modeling languages in contrast to UML as a general-purpose modeling language: i) UML models rely on the same metamodels, whereas the syntax and the semantic of the domain-specific models are defined by their own metamodels. In other words, they are tailored to a specific group of usage and users. ii) The domain-specific models can be considered as instance-based models, whereas the UML diagrams are usually class-based models [LGJ07]. Further, none of the previously described approaches considers the impact of other artifacts than code such as technical and organizational artifacts (e.g., documentation and test cases).

3.4.2. Change Propagation based on Domain-specific Models

In aPS there are various undocumented dependencies between the involved disciplines and their objects [Jäg+11]. These dependencies and the complexity of the aPS systems make the estimation of the change impact even more challenging [Vog+15]. Thus, there is a need for systematic models representing the engineering workflow in aPS [Jäg+11]. The importance and the use of models in the recent aPS approaches are discussed in [Vog+15]. This section describes the maintainability approaches in aPS, which are based on domain-specific models.

Biffl et al. [Bif+15] provide an approach to support linking and versioning different engineering artifacts. For this purpose, the plant planner provides a model of the plant structure. Then, domain experts add their engineering results such as AML files to a folder. A parser can detect different file types such as Computer Aided Engineering eXchange (CAEX) or COLLAborative Design Activity (COLLADA). After detecting the files, it generates a model based on the folder contents. A further parser analyzes the file contents based on XML Schema Definition (XSD) to generate Ecore-based metamodels using the libraries provided by EMF. This enables versioning different engineering artifacts. A linking metamodel allows generic links between several artifacts. Further, the quality of the link models can be checked by OCL queries. However, this approach does not support change impact analysis. It cannot derive a task list for a change request in the plant.

The approach presented by Ladiges et al. [LFL16] learns models by observing the input and output signals of the control system of a plant. It is based on the assumption that the state of these systems can be modeled using discrete events [All10]. The approach records the binary signals between the sensors and actuators on the one hand and the PLCs on the other hand. Based on these traces, behavioral models are generated. The system is then monitored to detect the behavioral changes. However, the approach neglects the structural change propagation in the plant and does not consider the effects of a change on the control software.

Lin et al. present in [LGJ07] an algorithm to calculate the differences between domain-specific models. The domain-specific models are mapped to hierarchical graphs. The algorithm starts with the top-level model elements and analyzes the submodels hierarchically. It calculates a mapping set and a difference set. However, the approach does not consider the change propagation in a domain-specific model and does not derive maintenance task lists.

In [LLE17] an approach is presented to extract variability information from product variants. It extracts traces from features and relates the features to the corresponding implementation artifacts. Thus, all implementation artifacts of all variants should exist. The other assumption is that the features of the product variants are known. However, the proposed approach does not consider the change propagation and the generation of maintenance task lists.

The approach of Pietsch et al. [Pie+15] compares models to generate edit scripts used in delta modules. The resulting edit script can be considered as a new delta module. In the next steps different relations between the data modules are analyzed (e.g., conflicts). Several operations such as *intersect* can be used to create new delta modules based on the existing delta modules. Then, a related product can be generated by a feature combination. Again, this approach does not analyze the structure of aPS systems regarding the change propagation and does not derive maintenance task lists.

Prähofer et al. present in [Prä+16] a feature-oriented modeling framework. They use several models based on components, for example for product management or system configuration. The system implementation can be represented as an Abstract Syntax Tree (AST). A system dependence graph is calculated based on the AST, which contains the control and the data flow of the system implementation. The features and components are connected to the code. This allows the application of a change impact analysis method. However, the approach is not based on the structure of an aPS system to analyze the change impact. Further, it cannot generate the corresponding maintenance task lists.

The approaches described in this section are based on domain-specific models. However, they do not consider the propagation of changes in the architectural model of the system. Further, none of the approaches uses a domain-spanning model (i.e., hardware and software) for change impact analysis. Additionally, only a subset of approaches considers the technical and/or organizational artifacts, which can also be affected by a change (e.g., documentation or Electronic Computer-Aided Design (ECAD) designs).

3.5. Change Propagation Analysis based on Requirements Modification

The approaches, which analyze the change propagation from requirements to specific systems can be divided into several subcategories due to the domain under study. As this thesis considers the domains of IS, BP, and aPS, the related approaches to this topic can be divided in further categories, accordingly. The following sections discuss the aforementioned categories in more detail:

3.5.1. Change Propagation Analysis in Information Systems and Business Processes based on Requirements Modification

This section gives an overview of the related work, which is concerned with change propagation analysis in IS and BP triggered by a change to requirements. For this purpose, this section starts with approaches focusing on change propagation analysis from requirements to IS. Then, it presents approaches, which are concerned with analyzing the change propagation from requirements to BP. Finally, the section discusses the approaches to change propagation analysis from requirements to both IS and BP.

In IS, Ramesh and Jarke present in [RJ01] a reference model for requirements traceability based on analyzing traceability tools and structured interviews with 26 organizations in several business areas. The metamodel comprises the metaclasses *object*, *stakeholder*, and *source*. Further, they differentiate between high-end users and low-end users regarding their traceability experience and needs. Thus, they provide further reference models for each group of users. Although the proposed models can be further used for the change propagation analysis, the paper does not provide in-depth information about the algorithms to determine the affected requirements or system elements.

To support the consistency between requirements and software architecture, Vogelsang et al. propose a model-based approach in [Vog+14b]. First, the approach formalizes the requirements from artifacts such as use cases. In the next step, the software architecture has to be modeled. The approach relates the requirements to the architecture by connecting the input and the output of the specifications and the architectures. In this way, it is mainly concerned with early detection of inconsistencies. However, the proposed approach does not analyze the propagation of changes from requirements to IS.

Goknil et al. present several approaches to tracing changes in requirements [Gok+14; Gok+11] and from requirements to the software architecture [GKB16]. The approaches are based on rules, which use formal models representing requirements and their relations to the software architecture. Using these rules, the approaches identify the affected requirements and parts of the architecture. Although these approach use more fine-grained semantics of relations, the model of architecture is still at a high abstraction level without differentiating between different types of architectural elements. This can lead to a high overestimation of the results.

The Goal Business Process Management (GoalBPM) approach aims at connecting the BP models to the stakeholders' goals. The approach uses BPMN [Obj11] for modeling BP and KAOS [Res07] for modeling goals, as stakeholders' goals are closely connected to requirements. For this purpose, the relationships between stakeholders' goals, as well as between stakeholders' goals and activities in the BP model have to be modeled. In this way, changes to the goals or to the BP can be traced to each other in order to identify whether the BP satisfies the goals. However, this approach was conceptually designed and has to be conducted informally and manually. Thus, it remains unclear how the propagation of a change can be analyzed in detail.

[ES05] is one of the few approaches concerning the co-evolution of requirements on the one hand and IS and BP on the hand. It presents a framework involving five dimensions. Each dimension regards a challenge in requirements engineering during the co-evolution (e.g., *understanding the consistency relationships between the co-evolving entities*). Further, they illustrated how the framework can be used based on an application example. Again, the paper does not propose in-depth information about algorithms for analyzing the propagation of change.

3.5.2. Change Propagation Analysis in Automated Production Systems based on Requirements Modification

In aPS, Requirements reflect "the stakeholders' needs and therefore the intention of the plant as well as demanded properties to be competitive and economic" [Vog+15, p. 7]. Thus, requirements changes (e.g., changing *market requirements*) can be considered as a main change trigger in aPS [Vog+15]. Vogel-Heuser et al. describe in [Vog+15, p. 4] the complex dependencies between requirements and the aPS satisfying them during the evolution as "not all changes of requirements can be fulfilled by changes of only the software or only the physical parts alone. Quite often in an aPS, changes of the mechanical and/or the electrical/electronic parts are required, which lead to a subsequent adaptation of the software". Hence, a change propagation analysis approach, which considers the requirements changes, has to provide a holistic view on the system to avoid overlooking parts of the plant under study. To achieve this, a "semi-formal system requirements specifications" can be used [Vog+15, p. 3]. Belgran and Säfsten refer in [BS09] to a study conducted in ten Swedish companies, which shows that a detailed specification of requirements rarely exists in practice [BP95]. However, informal specifications "do not facilitate tests for completeness, unambiguity and consistency" [FL00, p. 2]. Thus, the maintenance of requirements remains an open issue in aPS [Vog+15].

Legat et al. present in [LFV13] an evolution model for industrial plant at a high abstraction level. According to their model, evolution drivers for a specific plant result in changing requirements. These changes result in changing the corresponding properties of a plant. Additionally, the application of the evolution model on a community case study is discussed. However, the proposed model is abstract and mainly illustrates the evolution of a plant conceptually.

The modeling approach of Fay et al. [Fay+15] considers different development artifacts such as requirements, hardware, and software in aPS. The proposed Systems Modeling Language (SysML)-based approach differentiates between functional and non-functional requirements. The functional requirements can be further refined by other requirements. Additionally, they use *validity* relation to represent that a component of a system satisfy a specific functional requirement. However, the proposed approach mainly focuses on modeling a whole system including its requirements and does not analyze the change propagation.

Ladiges et al. [Lad+13] illustrate the effects of changes to a system on the fulfillment of its non-functional requirements using a case study. For this purpose, the authors categorize the evolution scenarios at a high abstraction level. According to this categorization, the change triggers are not necessarily the requirements, but the system can be directly changed without adapting the descriptions of requirements. The latter one leads to a gap between the requirements documentation and the system. The categorization was applied to several evolution scenarios of the case study. However, the influences of changes on the non-functional requirements are mainly illustrated and a solution idea is outlined without providing a modeling language and the corresponding algorithm for change propagation analysis.

Jamro focuses in [Jam15b] on requirements modeling for control software based on the IEC 61311-3 standard. The SysML-based modeling approach considers both functional and non-functional (i.e., mainly performance) requirements. Additionally, an explicit modeling of Human Machine Interface (HMI) requirements is also possible. Each requirement has a unique id and can be described as a text field. The functional requirements refer to POU in an IEC software and can be verified by unit tests. Further, the approach allows modeling the performance requirements resulted from executing POU and device communications. However, this approach also neglects the change propagation analysis with regard to a system and its requirements.

3.5.3. Discussion on Approaches to Change Propagation Analysis based on Requirements Modification

The previously described subsections gave an overview on related work to change propagation analysis in different domains triggered by a change to requirements. The approaches to this topic in different domains are designed at different levels of abstraction and are concerned with different aspects such as documentation of requirements, identification of tracing links, or change impact analysis. While in some domains such as IS, there are several approaches dealing with a wide range of the aforementioned aspects, there are only a few approaches to this topic in other domains such as aPS. The majority of approaches in aPS present formal models for persisting requirements. A subset of these approaches is based on SysML. Thus, these approaches neglect the change propagation from requirements to the system satisfying them. This issue can also be generalized to the evolution of models and to other domains, as discussed by Etien and Salinesi [ES05]. The authors concluded that "several approaches ... do not provide indications concerning evolution of the current models. They help to construct new one" [ES05, p. 3]. Further, there are several approaches in different domains such as IS, BP, or aPS discussing the relevance of considering the requirements changes and, thus, describing the change propagation only conceptually and at a high abstraction level. In other words, these approaches do not provide concrete solutions for this issue. Further, there are only a few approaches analyzing the propagation of change from requirements to the systems in more than one domain. Summarized, there is a need for an approach to change propagation analysis based on requirements modification, which can be extended to other domains.

3.6. Domain-specific Languages for Specifying the Change Propagation Rules

As the approaches proposed in this thesis are based on change propagation rules, this section gives an overview of the languages for describing change propagation rules. There are several approaches, which use UML models to describe the architecture of a system. One of the most used languages to describe the expressions for the UML models is OCL [OMG06; HZ04]. There are two types of expressions: i) They can be defined as constraints or invariants for a model in a formal way. ii) They can also be used to query the elements of a model [OMG06; HZ04].

Several approaches use OCL to define constraints and rules for models. An example of these approaches is the approach of Dam and Winikoff [DW11]. This approach uses OCL constraints to describe consistencies in models. If a model changes, the constraints have to be checked. A repair plan is created in the case of inconsistency. However, this can cause a more specific description of dependency relationships in the models. There is an additional need for further logic to automatize the generation of repair plans. The approach proposed by Briand et al. [BLO03] is based on OCL to define change propagation rules. It compares two versions of UML models to identify the differences between them. However, the rules are specified in an imperative manner. Additionally, they are tailored to the modeling language UML. This increases the overhead of the adaptation of the analysis to other modeling languages or domains. Summarized, although OCL can be used to specify the change propagation rules, it was not originally designed with respect to this topic. This can lead to complex change propagation rules, which cannot be maintained or adapted easily.

Lehnert et al. propose in [LFR13] a rule-based approach to identify the affected elements. They consider UML models, source code, and test cases. 180 change propagation rules identify the potentially affected elements based on the currently affected elements, the change type, and the related elements in a fine-grained manner. The rules are described in [LFR13] in a XML-based notation. Similar to the previous approaches, the rules are specified in an imperative manner. Thus, it is difficult to adapt fine-grained and imperative rules to other modeling languages or disciplines. However, the focus of this section is on the languages, which are tailored to specifying change propagation rules. Thus, the remaining part of this section discusses the domain-specific languages to change propagation rules and a language, which enables traversing the graph elements in an efficient way.

Müller and Rumpe propose in [MR15] an approach to change propagation analysis. Their approach compares UML models to identify the differences between them. These changes invoke rules, which were described in a DSL. However, the proposed DSL by the authors cannot be used to describes rules to identify the affected elements. The rules generate checklists of the predefined development tasks.

VIATRA Query Language (VQL) is a query language for Ecore metamodels. It is based on graph patterns. Further, it provides support for various features, such as aggregation patterns [Ber+11]. Although VQL is an expressive model query language and can also be used to specify the change propagation rules, it was not originally designed with regard to this issue.

3.7. Metamodel of Control Software in Automated Production Systems

This section describes the related work, which specifies the metamodels for the control software. Although this thesis focuses on the IEC 61131-3 standard, the related approaches also cover a broader ranges of standards for the control software. As the IEC 61131-3 standard is currently one of the most used standards in industry, it can be used to cover various applications in the manufacturing systems [Vog+15].

The approach of Thramboulidis [Thr04] is one of the first attempts to metamodel the control software in aPS. The approach is based on the concept of function blocks in IEC 61499 as building blocks in distributed control systems. To support control engineers during the development, the approach combines the UML models and the function block construct.

UML for Process Automation (UML-PA) [KV07] aims at combining the UML with the standard IEC 61311-3 and its object-oriented extension. To provide more support to practitioners in aPS, UML-PA considers only a subset of all UML diagrams. For example, the behavior of the software can be modeled using the state machines. Further, UML-PA provides unambiguous modeling elements for aPS.

Witsch adapted the UML profiles for the control software in the approach plcML [Wit13]. plcML provides class diagrams to model the structure of the control systems. It also allows adapting the UML state-charts to PLC state-charts for the control software. PLC state-charts are deterministic. They allow modeling the behavior of a control software using states and transitions. The control software under study is the 3rd edition of IEC 61311-3 [Wer09]. This edition represents an object-oriented extension of IEC 61311-3.

A markup language is proposed in [EMO07] to model the control software following the standard IEC 61311-3. The model allows generating the automation project of a PLC. The model is based on the Component-based Software Engineering (CBSE) concepts. The software model is composed of two types of components. The first type of components organizes the structure (i.e., the architecture) of a software (e.g., configuration, resource, or task). The second type of components is the computational units (i.e., POU).

However, a metamodel, which specifies the types of different elements of a control software and their relationships, is needed to analyze the change propagation more precisely.

A 3 + 1 language for distributed industrial control systems is presented in [Mar+10; EM12]. The language provides different views for specifying control systems. The first view defines the control strategies at a high abstraction level. The second view deals with the hardware architecture and the physical equipment. The software architecture is the third view. The last view connects the aforementioned views to create a consistent model of the system. The software engineering view provides modeling concepts such as configuration or program. However, the proposed metamodels and their abstractions are not suitable for an appropriate change propagation analysis. For example, there is no difference between the specific POU types [Mar+10], which can be crucial for the propagation of change.

Another 3 + 1 view model for Model Integrated Mechatronics (MIM) is proposed by Thramboulidis in [Thr10]. This view model is based on SysML [OMG12]. The MIM architecture is composed of four layers: mechatronic Layer, application layer, resource layer, and mechanical process layer [Thr05]. The SysML view is used for the mechatronic layer. To model the software the IEC 61499 standard is used. The model decomposes the software based on function blocks, as described in [DT11]. As the metamodel focuses mainly on function blocks, the abstraction of this metamodel is not suitable for an appropriate change propagation analysis.

A dependency model is introduced by Feldmann et al. in [Fel+16]. This model represents the call semantics between different elements of a control program during the compilation process. Thus, it is represented by a directed labelled graph. The nodes in the graph represent the elements of the control software such as POU or global variables. As one of the requirements of the dependency model is its application to a wide range of control software, the edges specify only four dependency types between the nodes (i.e., *read*, *write*, *call*, and *execute*). This dependency model was extended by two further edge types (i.e., *jumps to* and *sequential function chart transition*) to include the control flow between the POUs. Although this dependency graph is one of the fine-grained models, it is still at a high abstraction level. Thus, it can result in a high number of false positives during the change propagation analysis.

Several approaches proposed in this section are based on UML. However, UML without any modifications is not the appropriate way to model the control software [Thr04; KV07]. The main reasons are: i) Most aPS domain experts are not familiar with the language concepts of UML [Thr04], ii) the mapping between the modeling elements of UML and the concepts of a standard for control software (e.g., function blocks in IEC 61499) is not straightforward [Thr04], and iii) many UML modeling elements are superfluous in aPS [KV07]. For these reasons, this thesis introduces a new metamodel for the object-oriented extension of IEC 61311-3 [Rät17; Bus+18c]. This metamodel is tailored to the domain of aPS and to the language concepts of the standard. Thus, it aims at supporting domain experts with concepts, with which they are familiar. Further, it reduces the modeling elements to those, which are necessary to model the structure of the system and to estimate the change propagation.

In a model-based change propagation analysis, the granularity of the metamodel and its instances affects the precision of the change propagation results [Ros15; Bus+18c; Hei+18]. Various metamodels proposed in this section describe the system's structure only in a coarse-grained manner. Thus, the results of the analysis can contain too many false positives. In other words, the high abstraction level can result in the "impacts explosion without semantics" [Boh02, p. 5].

3.8. Discussion

This chapter discussed the state of the art regarding the main contributions of this thesis. Most approaches to change propagation analysis, which were discussed in this chapter, are limited to only a specific domain (e.g., IS, BP, or aPS). Thus, these approaches do not consider the effects of changes to the artifacts of one domain on the artifacts of the other domains. However, this is important to analyze the impact of a change more precisely and to support the co-evolution of different domains (e.g., the co-evolution of IS and BP).

The heterogeneity of approaches in different domains and their results makes them difficult to compare [HBK18]. Further, the idea of various approaches such as several code-based approaches in IS cannot be generalized to the other domains. Thus, the approaches introduced in this thesis are based on the architecture of systems in a specific domain. An architecture-based approach can be generalized to other domains, as it allows analyzing the change propagation based on the structure of the system [HBK18].

Similar to the proposed approaches in this thesis, most approaches presented in this chapter are based on models. The use of models allows to analyze the change propagation even in the early development phases [Leh11b]. Additionally, models abstract from details and, thus, allow overcoming the complexity of the systems in a domain [Hei+18]. Various approaches are based on the general-purpose modeling languages such as UML. However, UML is not always the appropriate modeling language due its "single definition for syntax and static semantics" and "class-based" nature, as described by [LGJ07, p. 3]. Thus, Lin et al. [LGJ07] suggest using a domain-specific modeling language to define the concepts, with which the users of a specific application domain are familiar. Further, as UML is originally developed in the domain of IS, the elements of other domains cannot be mapped to UML concepts [Thr04].

A further limitation of most approaches to change propagation analysis is neglecting the technical and organizational artifacts, which are affected by a change [Ros+15b; Sta15; Ros+17a; Hei+18]. Lehnert describes in [Leh11a] that only 4 % of 150 approaches analyzed during the review consider the effects of a change on software artifacts such as documentation. The result of the review also shows that only 7 % of approaches analyze the effects of changing requirements. Therefore, there is a need to involve such artifacts in the change propagation process.

4. Running Examples

The proposed approaches in this thesis are developed to analyze the change propagation in a specific domain, namely IS, BP, and aPS. A simple example in each domain should be used to illustrate the steps of each approach. The following sections describe the running examples in each domain.

4.1. Media Store Example

The Media Store example [Reu16] is used to discuss the steps of the approaches to change propagation analysis in IS and BP. Media Store was originally introduced in [HKR11] as a simple component-based software system. It was originally designed to reason about the performance of component-based software systems [HKR11]. Further, development artifacts such as requirements or PCM models are available. Media Store was extended continuously to new requirements and technologies [Reu16]. It is implemented as a Java Platform, Enterprise Edition (Java EE)-based case study demonstrating a host system for audio files [Reu16; SK16]. Further, there are several change scenarios for Media Store illustrating the effects of design decisions on different quality attributes such as performance [Reu16].

4.1.1. Model of Software Architecture

As described previously, Media Store serves as a host system for audio files [Reu16]. Figure 4.1 illustrates the initial architecture of the Media Store example. Media Store has a three-tier architecture. In the following, the components of Media Store's software architecture are described:

- The `WebGUI` component is the front-end component and represents the presentation layer. This component enables users to register to and log into the system. Further, it allows uploading and downloading the audio files [Reu16].
- The `MediaManagement` component is the main component in the business logic. It coordinates the communication between components. Further, it answers the download requests of users [Reu16].
- The `UserManagement` component provides services for the registration and login of users [Reu16].
- The `UserDBAdapter` component enables the `UserManagement` component to query the DataBase component and update the data in the `DataBase` [Reu16].
- The `ReEncoder` component re-encodes the audio files requested by users [Reu16].
- The re-encoded audio files are forwarded to the `TagWatermarking` component, which watermarked the audio files using tags [Reu16].

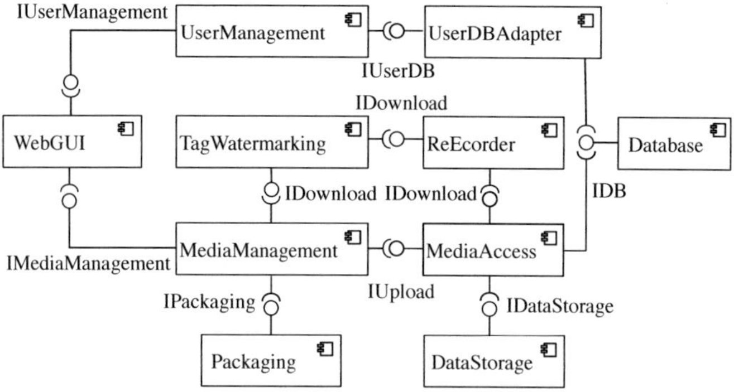

Figure 4.1.: Software architecture of Media Store [Reu16]

- If users want to download more than one audio file, the `Packaging` component compresses the requested audio files to an archive file [Reu16].
- The `DataBase` component is the main component in the persistence tier storing user information and metadata of audio files [Reu16].
- The audio files themselves are stored in a separate database, which is represented as the `DataStorage` component in Figure 4.1 [Reu16].

To illustrate the approaches in the thesis, a slightly modified variant of the Media Store example, introduced in [Reu16], is chosen. The reason for that is, that the original variant of Media Store does not have some relevant model elements to illustrate the approaches. An example of a modification is adding a composed data type `user` that contains the personal information a user provides during the registration.

4.1.2. Model of Business Process

There is a main usage model for Media Store [Reu16]. The usage model consists of the following main system steps: First the user can register to the system. Then they have to log into the system. After a successful log-in, a list of available audio files are displayed to the users. Then they can download or upload audio files [Reu16].

This usage model is extended by the corresponding actor steps to create a simple BP. Figure 4.2 illustrates the BP based on the Media Store usage model. As described in Section 2.4, the usage model is modeled using actor steps (i.e., marked with *AS:* in Figure 4.2) and system steps (i.e., all other activities in Figure 4.2). Similar to the architecture of Media Store, a slightly modified variant of its BP is chosen. For example, the users need to enter personal information and their national identification number to register to Media Store. This is modeled as data object `identity card` for the input of the first actor step. This data object corresponds to the data type `user` containing the personal information of a specific user. The personal information of users is stored in the `DataBase` component. The defined BP is used to illustrate the steps of the change impact analysis approach for BP.

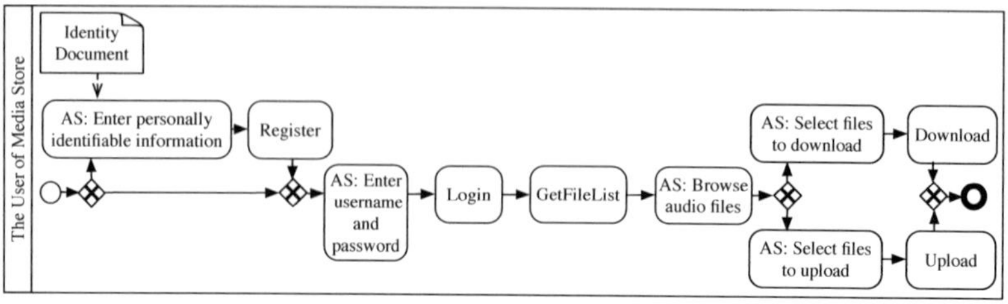

Figure 4.2.: Overview of the Media Store's BP

4.2. Minimal Plant Example

To illustrate the approach to change propagation analysis in aPS a Minimal Plant example is used. The Minimal Plant example is based on the Pick and Place Unit (PPU) and the xPPU [Vog+14a]. It consists of a conveyor and two connected ramps at the conveyor. Further, an optical sensor is installed at the end of the conveyor to detect the work pieces. Two shapes of work pieces can be differentiated, namely a cylinder and a cuboid shape. Additionally, there is a pneumatic cylinder as pusher to push the work pieces to the corresponding ramp. Similar to the xPPU, the Minimal Plant example has an operation panel providing a start button. Pressing the start button allows starting the operation mode [Vog+14a].

4.2.1. Model of Mechanical and Electrical/Electronic Parts

The Minimal Plant example can be modeled using the abstract metamodel of aPS (see Section 2.7.1) and the specific metamodel of aPS (see Section 2.7.2). The conveyor and its connected sensors and ramps can be modeled as a structure. The structure consists of two ramp components and the following main modules: a conveyor belt, a motor, a pusher, and an optical sensor. Each module consists of further components. For example, the conveyor belt consists of a band and a frame, on which several other modules, components, and interfaces are mounted. Figure 4.3 gives a simplified overview of the hardware of the Minimal Plant example, as a reduced variant of the xPPU [Vog+14a]. This figure shows a simplified instance of an abstract metamodel to illustrate the Minimal Plant example. As the instance of the specific metamodel is similar to the instance of the abstract metamodel, it is omitted in the following. The only difference between both instances is that the instance of the specific metamodel contains the specific types of elements such as optical sensor as a type instead of the module as a type.

4.2.2. Model of Software

The Minimal Plant example is a PLC-based plant. The control software is assumed to be programmed using the IEC 61131-3 standard. The behavior of the Minimal Plant example is also based on the xPPU [Vog+14a]. The initialization process of the conveyor initializes the local variables. After the operator pressed the start button, the conveyor is initialized. During the initialization, the conveyor runs for a short time. After a successful initialization, the control software starts the operation mode. The work pieces are conveyed to the ramps. An optical sensor is used to detect the specific types of work pieces at the extension position. After a specific shape of work pieces was detected, the pusher is extended to push the work piece of a specific type to the ramp [Vog+14a].

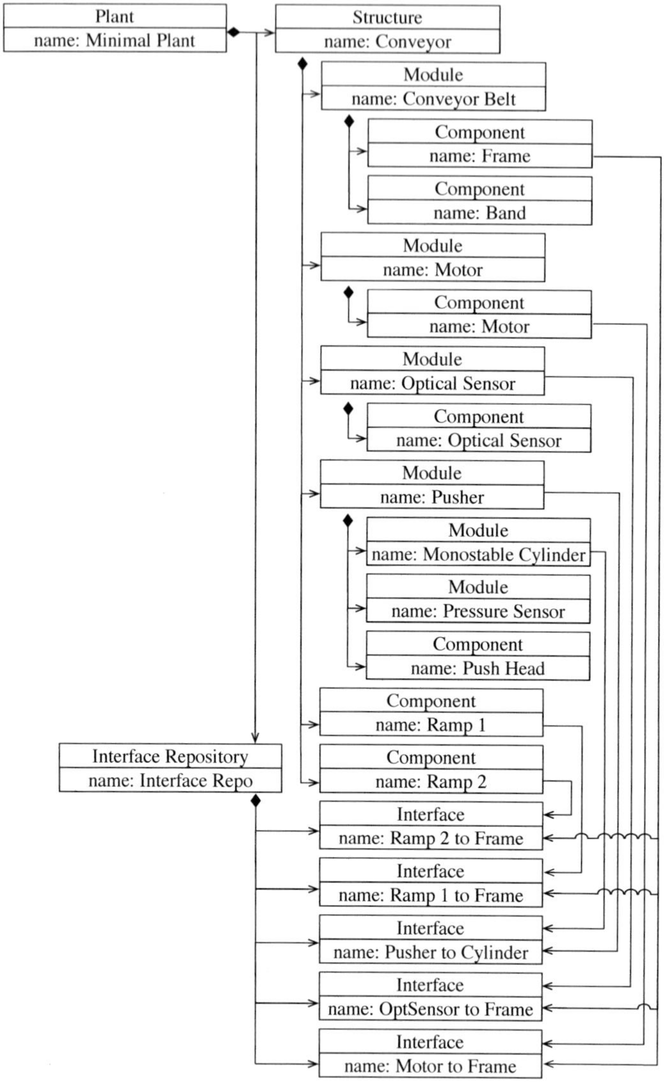

Figure 4.3.: Overview of the hardware of the Minimal Plant example as a reduced variant of the xPPU [Vog+14a]

5. Maintainability Analysis Methodology

Sustainable systems have to be continuously changed in order to be able to provide their functionality correctly over time [Ros15; Leh79]. Thus, sustainable systems have to be maintainable. Maintainability of a system can be considered as the extent, to which a system can efficiently and effectively be modified by given changes [ISO11]. In other words, the maintainability of a system considers the required effort to implement a change request in a system [HBK18]. Thus, the maintainability of a system does not depend only on the system under study, but also on both the system under study and the upcoming change requests.

In general, the sustainable systems contain heterogeneous elements from different domains such as IS, BP, or aPS. In the context of this thesis, a *system element* represents a part of the system. Similar definitions are also proposed by other authors. For example, Conway states in [Con68, p. 2] "any system of consequence is structured from smaller subsystems which are interconnected". He describes the process of identifying the subsystems recursively, as a subsystem can be considered as a system [Con68]. This process can be iteratively repeated "until we are down to a system which is simple enough to be understood without further subdivision" [Con68, p. 2]. Similar to the Conway's definition, the definition used in this thesis does not demand further characteristics of the system elements such as their granularity, as the choice of an element in a system depends on the context and the usage.

According to [Con68, p. 2], "a description of a system ... must delineate each of the subsystems and how they are interconnected". In the context of this thesis, this description corresponds to the system model, which describes the system elements and their relationships.

An example of systems comprising heterogeneous elements is an aPS (e.g., a plant), which in general consists of mechanical, electrical/electronic components and software [Vog+17; Hei+18]. A system element in this example can be a mechanical component such as a physical table or a crane arm.

During the change implementation phase, the system elements from different domains influence each other in a mutual way [Ros+17a; HBK18]. Thus, it is not sufficient, if a change propagation analysis approach focuses on the maintainability of systems in only one domain. In other words, the maintainability analysis approaches have to consider heterogeneous system elements from several domains and their mutual dependencies [Ros15; Ros+17a; HBK18].

Most approaches presented in Chapter 3 are designed to analyze the change propagation in systems in only one domain. Thus, they do not consider the effects of a change request to system elements in one domain on the dependent system elements in other domains. The results of different approaches from different domains can be difficultly combined to obtain a domain-spanning change propagation analysis. The main reasons for the incompatibility of approaches and their results are that the approaches are often tailored to specific types of systems (e.g., code-based approaches) and are designed at different levels of abstraction [HBK18]. The aforementioned factors make the need for an approach essential, which analyzes the change propagation across domains.

This chapter proposes a general methodology to analyze the change propagation in heterogeneous system elements from different domains [HBK18]. Thus, the methodology was designed to answer the *first research question.*

The remainder of this chapter is structured as follows: Section 5.1 gives an overview of the methodology. The methodology consists of two types of metamodels and algorithms: i) The metamodels and algorithms that can be applied in all domains. This is described in Section 5.2. ii) The metamodels and algorithms that have to be extended or defined for the domain under study. Section 5.3 discusses these metamodels and algorithms in more detail. The process of instantiating the methodology in a specific domain is given in Section 5.4. Section 5.5 summarizes the contributions of this chapter.

The results of this chapter have been published in the papers [Ros15; HBK18] and partially (e.g., duplicate elimination, supporting users' decision by reducing task list, or sorting the task list in the instance of the methodology in IS and BP) in the papers [Ros+17a; Bus+18a].

5.1. Generic Methodology for Domain-Spanning Change Propagation Analysis

This section proposes the generic methodology for the domain-spanning change propagation analysis. The methodology was developed as a generic guideline for model-based approaches to change propagation analysis. It aims at improving the development process by providing generic (i.e., domain-independent) metamodels and algorithms for all change propagation analysis approaches, as well as guidelines for the development of a change propagation analysis approach in a specific domain in terms of modular metamodels and algorithms. As the methodology is defined independently of a specific domain and can be instantiated in different domains, it can be considered as generic. Initially, the methodology was mainly developed as a generalization of two change propagation analysis approaches in the domain of IS [Sta15; Ros+15b; Ros+17b] and BP [Ros+17a]. However, it is mainly based on the change propagation analysis approach in IS [Sta15; Ros+15b]. The generic methodology can be instantiated in a new domain to develop a change propagation analysis approach in the domain under study. In this thesis, the resulting change propagation analysis approach is also referred to hereinafter as an *instance of the methodology*. The resulting change propagation analysis approaches are mainly based on the *system's structure*, also known as *system's architecture*, reflecting system' elements and their relationships [Con68]. Using the structure of a system as the main artifact is due to the fact that "a system's architecture is the set of principal design decisions made during its development and any subsequent evolution" [MT10, p. 1]. Additionally, different quality attributes of a system such as maintainability or performance are affected by its structure [Ros+15b; Sta15; TMD09].

The input of the resulting change propagation analysis approach (i.e., the instance of the methodology) is the model of the systems in the domain and a set of change requests referring to the changing elements in a system model. The initial change requests are referred to hereinafter as *seed modifications* [HBK18]. A seed modification in an instance refers to a model element representing an affected system element [Sta15]. Model elements representing the elements of a system structure are called *structural elements* in the following. The instances of the methodology use a *change propagation algorithm* to analyze the change propagation in the system model based on the input and to calculate the output. The output of an instance is a list of potential maintainability tasks to implement the seed modifications. The output is called hereinafter as *task list* [HBK18; Sta15]. Each task in the task list refers to an element of the system model that is potentially affected by the seed modifications. Further, each task has a *task type*, which defines how to change the specific model element [HBK18; Sta15]. An example of a task can be *delete interface I.* While *interface I* represents the affected element, *delete* represents the task type [HBK18; Sta15]. A task in a task list can also have *sub-tasks.* In this example, a sub-task could be *modify the corresponding signatures* [HBK18; Sta15].

As the development process of a system involves not only the structure of the system or the connection to its environment, but also different organizational and technical artifacts (e.g., test cases or documentation), the maintainability analysis has also to consider these artifacts [Ros+15b; Sta15]. Model elements corresponding to the organizational and technical artifacts are referred to hereinafter as *context elements* [Ros+15b; Sta15]. These elements are not part of the system model. Considering context elements in addition to elements regarding the structure and the behavior of a system in the domain under study during the maintainability analysis is also motivated by the Conway's law [Con68]. According to this law, "organizations which design systems (in the broad sense used here) are constrained to produce designs which are copies of the communication structures of these organizations" [Con68, p. 4]. Thus, each task can also have *follow-up tasks,* which reference the context elements. In the previous example, a follow-up task could be *update test cases* [HBK18; Sta15]. In this way, the task lists are mainly derived based on the elements of the system's structure and behavior. Additionally, the corresponding context elements can also be considered for each task. This allows a more comprehensive effort estimation with a holistic view on the system under study, the project and the organization, as well as the involving roles and the responsible staff (see [Ros+15b; Sta15] for IS). While this chapter gives an overview of the methodology, concrete instances of the methodology, as well as the corresponding metamodels and change propagation algorithms to derive the task lists in different domains are described in the following chapters. In general, the methodology can be instantiated to the systems with the following characteristics regarding their structure and behavior, as well as the propagation of changes in these systems:

- **Systems' structure:** As described previously, the systems in a specific domain can be specified as a set of structural elements that can be connected to each other [HBK18]. Examples of these are systems that are composed of components and their interfaces. Components and interfaces in this example represent general components and interfaces. Examples of components can be software components or components in the domain of aPS [HBK18]. In this context, the interfaces can be provided or required by software components [Reu16]. Further, the interfaces can present physical interfaces for the fixation of mechanical components or the communication interfaces of the electrical components [Hei+18]. To instantiate the methodology in a domain, the systems' structure in this domain has to be defined by a metamodel. The methodology does not depend on a certain type of metamodel. Thus, it can be used for any metamodel with the aforementioned properties.
- **Systems' behavior:** Conway demands a further characteristic for a system description: "A description of a system … must describe the system's connections to the outside world" [Con68, p. 2]. This is particularly important to analyze the impact of a change in a system on its outside world. For example, changing a software system may lead to changes in its provided services. This affects the interaction between the software and its users [Cha+01]. This can be considered as changes in the behavior of the software. In general, a change may only affect the behavior of a system. Further, a change to the structure of a system may affect its behavior (i.e., regarding its connection to its environment as proposed by Conway [Con68]). To analyze the change propagation in the behavior of a system, its behavior has to be described as activities that are connected to each other. Similar to the system's structure, the activities are also generally defined. For example, the activities can be performed by a

human actor [Hei+17] or a system such as a software, an electrical/electronic, or a mechanical system [HBK18]. To represent the behavior in a domain, metamodels with the previously described characteristics have to be defined. The methodology can be instantiated to analyze the impact of a change on the behavior regardless of the type of the metamodels.

- **Rule-based change propagation analysis:** The instances of the methodology need to implement a change propagation algorithm to analyze the change propagation. In general, the change propagation algorithm can be composed of a set of *change propagation rules.* A change propagation rule from element A to element B describes, if element A changes, the change propagates to element B [HBK18; Bus+18b]. Element A is referred to hereinafter as the *source element* and element B as the *target element* hereinafter. Change propagation rules are based on the dependencies between the metaclasses of the aforementioned metamodels describing the system's structure or its behavior. In other words, a change propagation rule is described for all systems in a specific domain [Bus+18b]. Thus, change propagation rules highly depend on the metamodels of the systems' structure and behavior [Bus+18b]. Domain knowledge is required to specify change propagation rules.

Figure 5.1 gives an overview of the generic methodology. The rectangles with rounded corners represent the algorithms, while the other rectangles represent the metamodels. The algorithms and metamodels of the methodology are referred to hereinafter as *the elements of the methodology* in the following. Note that the methodology should be considered as a guideline to develop an approach to change propagation analysis. It does not require the use of a specific modeling language or a certain programming language. For example, domain experts can either develop a metamodel or use `Enum` and GPL code instead, if it is possible. Another example is the usage of a GPL or a DSL to describe the algorithms. The methodology consists of two main parts:

- **Domain-independent part of the methodology:** The first part contains the domain-independent elements of the methodology. During the development of the methodology, they were conceptual elements, which can occur in several domains. Factoring out these elements enables using them in different domains. In the following, the reason for choosing different conceptual elements are described in more detail [HBK18].

- **Domain-specific part of the methodology:** The second part contains domain-specific elements, which have to be instantiated in a domain. The second part can be divided into two further parts: an obligatory part and an optional part. The obligatory part contains elements that need to be defined or extended in a new domain in order to instantiate the methodology. The optional part contains methodology elements that can be extended in a new domain if required. This optional elements of the methodology is represented by dashed rectangles in Figure 5.1 [HBK18].

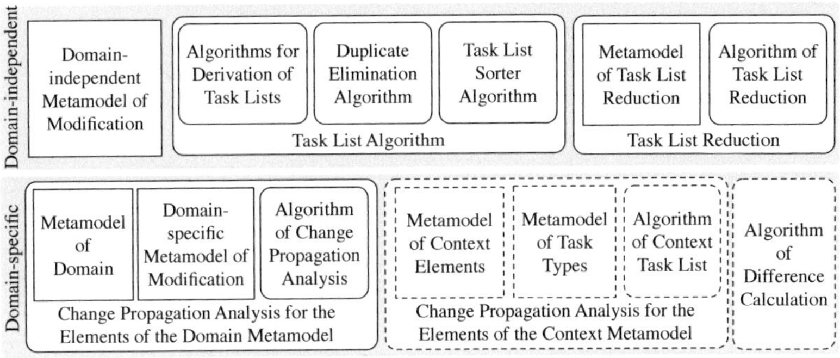

Figure 5.1.: Overview of the methodology for the domain-spanning change propagation analysis [HBK18, p. 2]

Section 5.2 describes the domain-independent metamodels and algorithms of the methodology in more detail, while the domain-specific metamodels and algorithms of the methodology are described in Section 5.3.

5.2. Domain-independent Elements

This section describes the metamodels and algorithms of the methodology that can be used in any instance of the methodology. The domain-independent elements involve a metamodel to represent the modification regardless of the domain, algorithms for creating and managing task lists, as well as a metamodel and the corresponding algorithm for supporting human decisions by reducing task lists. The following subsections describe these metamodels and algorithms in more detail:

5.2.1. Domain-independent Metamodel of Modification

Identifying the potentially affected element types in a specific domain plays an important role during the development of a change propagation analysis approach in this domain. These element types mainly refer to the concrete metaclasses of the system's structure and behavior described previously. In other words, it is important to know whether the instances of a metaclass representing system elements can in principle be affected by a change. Thus, the types of system elements that can be potentially affected by a change need to be metamodeled. Further, the source types and the target types of system elements in a change propagation rule have to be determined. The source types and the target types can be especially important for example to reproduce the cause of the propagation of false positives. *False positives* in a task list are model elements referring to elements in the systems' structure or behavior that are not actually affected by a change [Ros+15b]. Thus, a domain-independent metamodel representing modifications has to reflect the previously described properties of change propagation.

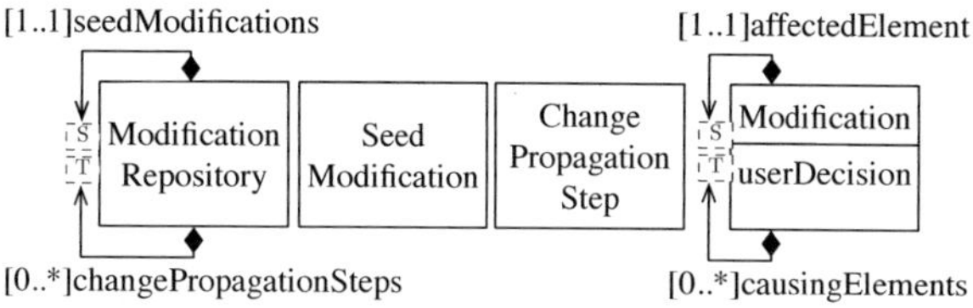

Figure 5.2.: Domain-independent metamodel of modification - Simplified excerpt

Figure 5.2 illustrates the domain-independent metamodel of modification. It shows the common metaclasses of modification in different domains regarding the change propagation analysis at a high abstraction level. The set of model elements and the corresponding metaclass of the domain-independent metamodel of modification are described in the following [HBK18]:

- The first class of model elements refers to the set of all model elements in a domain, which can be potentially affected by a change. `Modification` metaclass in Figure 5.2 represents this set at the metamodel level. If a change propagates between two elements, one element is the cause of the change (i.e., *causing element* in Figure 5.2) and the other element is the affected element by the change (i.e., *affected element* in Figure 5.2). Causing element and affected element in Figure 5.2 represent source element and target element in a change propagation rule.
- The second class of model elements refers to the set of all model elements in a domain, which domain experts can initially select as changed elements. `SeedModification` metaclass in Figure 5.2 represents this set at the metamodel level. The set of metaclasses that can be seed modifications is a subset of the set of metaclasses that can be potentially changed (i.e., the previously described class of model elements).
- A change propagation step refers to affected model elements that have the same change cause. `ChangePropagationStep` metaclass in Figure 5.2 represents this set at the metamodel level.
- The task list is composed of a set of all `SeedModification` and the set of all `ChangePropagationSteps`. `ModificationRepository` in Figure 5.2 represents a task list at the metamodel level.

The aforementioned metaclasses have to be extended to instantiate the methodology in a new domain. *Domain-specific metamodel of modification* in Figure 5.1 describes the extension of the *Domain-specific metamodel of modification* metamodel for a new domain.

5.2.2. Task List Algorithms

In addition to metamodels, algorithms play an important role to create and manage task lists. These algorithms can be used in the instances of the methodology. Which algorithm is necessary in a specific change propagation analysis approach depends on the overall goal of the change propagation analysis and the usage context. For example, some algorithms are necessary to create deterministic task lists for the same input. Using these algorithms, the generated task lists are duplicate-free and sorted. The following sections describe these algorithms in more detail.

5.2.2.1. Algorithm for Derivation of Task Lists

This section proposes a basic algorithm to derive and manage the task lists (see Algorithm 1 in pseudo-code). This algorithm mainly calls further domain-independent and domain-specific algorithms and gather their results.

In the first phase, the algorithm calls the corresponding algorithms to calculate a base task list. To calculate a base task list, the propagation of changes in the model of system's structure and behavior in a specific domain has to be analyzed. Additionally, further activities have to be carried out based on differences between two versions of a system model: i) the *base version* representing the system's structure and behavior before any change and ii) the *target version* representing the system's structure and behavior after changes. Examples of these changes are deleting or adding model elements. The actual change propagation and the activities caused by the difference calculation (e.g., by refining existing generic algorithms for difference calculation) for the elements of different domains have to be implemented in each domain separately, as they require domain knowledge (i.e., domain-specific *Algorithm of Change Propagation Analysis* and *Algorithm of Difference Calculation* in Figure 5.1). These algorithms are described in the follow-up chapters of this thesis for BP, aPS, and requirements in more detail. Thus, this phase of the algorithm gathers this information from different domain-specific algorithms. `BaseTaskList` in Algorithm 1 represents the result of this phase of the algorithm. This task list contains the initial changes and the structural model elements that are potentially affected by the initial changes.

In the next phase, the algorithm for derivation of task lists calls a further algorithm to eliminate the duplicates in the task list. The *algorithm of duplicate elimination* is described in the following section in more detail (see Section 5.2.2.2).

During the implementation of change requests, it is not always sufficient to only analyze the change propagation in the system's structure and behavior, as the change can also cause technical, management, or organizational efforts [Sta15]. In other words, the metamodel of the system's structure and behavior may not be sufficient to estimate the total effort of a change request [Sta15]. The reason for this is that a change may affect elements that are not considered by the metamodel of the system's structure and behavior (i.e., context elements) [Sta15; Ros+15b].

To consider the activities caused by context elements, the next phase of Algorithm 1 is a call to the corresponding algorithms to extend the tasks of the base task list to include the context elements. Similar to the first step of the algorithm, the instances of the methodology in each domain have to determine i) which context elements are affected by a change to structural elements and ii) how they change. The reason for this is that the effort resulted from changing context elements requires domain knowledge and cannot be generalized for all domains. These algorithms are also described in the follow-up chapters for BP and aPS. For example, *component C* may be affected by a change. *Component C* can be tested by *test case T*. In this phase, the task *change component C* is extended by further tasks such as *adapt test T* or *execute test T* [Sta15]. This example shows that annotating a task list regarding specific task types requires domain knowledge and has to be implemented in each domain separately (i.e., *Metamodel of Task Types* and *Algorithm of Context Task List* in Figure 5.1). Thus, this phase of the algorithm gathers the extended task lists of the domains, in which the methodology is instantiated.

In the last phases, Algorithm 1 calls the corresponding algorithm to sort the task list. The *task list sorter algorithm* is described in Section 5.2.2.3 in more detail. The result of this phase of the algorithm is an annotated task list (i.e., `AnnotatedTaskList` in Algorithm 1). The annotated task list contains the base task list and the corresponding context model elements affected by the change.

Algorithm 1 Algorithm for Derivation of Task Lists

Input: BaseVersion ▷ The metamodel instances before changes
Input: TargetVersion ▷ The metamodel instances after changes
$BaseTaskList = \emptyset$ ▷ Task list containing the modified domain elements, as well as the added and removed domain elements
$AnnotatedTaskList = \emptyset$ ▷ Base task list annotated with context elements
if $BaseVersion \neq \emptyset \, and \, TargetVersion \neq \emptyset$ **then**
  $BaseTaskList = Calculate\ base\ task\ list\ based\ on\ TargetVersion\ and\ BaseVersion$
  $Remove\ duplicates\ from\ BaseTaskList$
  $AnnotatedTaskList = Calculate\ annotated\ task\ list\ based\ on\ TargetVersion,\ BaseVersion,\ and\ BaseTaskList$
  $Sort\ AnnotatedTaskList$
end if

5.2.2.2. Duplicate Elimination Algorithm

It is possible that redundant tasks occur in a task list. In general, redundant tasks refer to the same model element and have the same task type. However, other definitions of redundant tasks are also possible depending on usage context. For example, the tasks that refer to the same model element but have different task types can also be considered as redundant. The redundant tasks are referred to hereinafter as *duplicates*. Duplicates can have several causes. In the following some causes for duplicates in a task list are discussed. In general, more than one seed modification can result in duplicates, as different change propagation rules for different seed modifications can cause duplicates in a task list. Further, duplicates can also occur in a task list for only one seed modification, as different concatenation of change propagation rules can result in duplicates. In addition, duplicates can occur in a task list due to several change propagation rules that have the same affected element. However, it is important to have duplicate-free task lists to better estimate the effort of a change request and to have comparable task lists [Ros+17a; HBK18].

The methodology provides an algorithm to eliminate duplicate tasks in a task list. The duplicate elimination is mainly based on merging the tasks, which refer to the same model element of the system's structure and behavior and have the same task type. The idea of this algorithm is described in the following.

Let A be a set of all tasks in the generated task list and let R be the set of the tasks that have been already considered by the algorithm. In other words, R is the result set comprising unique tasks, as these tasks have not been eliminated as duplicate by the algorithm (hereinafter also referred to as the *set of duplicate-free tasks*).

To eliminate the duplicates, each task in the task list $a \in A$ has to be compared to all considered tasks (i.e., R). In the next step, the subset of these tasks, which refer to the same model element of the system's structure and behavior and has the same task type as the task under study (i.e., a), has to be identified. If this subset is empty, the task under study has to be added to the set of duplicate-free tasks (i.e., R). This algorithm can be recursively applied to all sub-tasks and/or follow-up tasks until the base case. In the base case, the algorithm merges two tasks, which refer to the same model element of the system's structure and behavior and has the same task type. In other words, it removes one of two identical tasks. Each of both tasks can have (merged) sub-tasks and (merged) follow-up tasks. However, the sub-tasks and follow-up tasks of both tasks may differ. In this case, the algorithm adds the sub-tasks and follow-up tasks of one of both tasks to the other task and remove the first task. In this way, it recursively merges the tasks, as well as the sub-tasks and the follow-up tasks.

Although the methodology provides an algorithm to merge duplicate tasks in a task list, there are already various algorithms to eliminate duplicates. As the methodology is independent of a specific tool, technology, or programming language, domain experts can also use an existing algorithm to obtain a duplicate-free task list.

5.2.2.3. Task List Sorter Algorithm

In order to generate a deterministic task list for the same seed modifications, the task lists have to be sorted after duplicate elimination. Thus, the methodology provides an algorithm, which can sort tasks together with their sub-tasks and follow-up tasks. Although the methodology provides a sorting algorithm, any sorting algorithm or its extension and modification can be used. The only prerequisite is that the algorithms have to be able to sort tasks on the top level, the sub-tasks, and the follow-up tasks, if this hierarchy of tasks is used in a certain instance of the methodology.

5.2.3. Task List Reduction

The output of an instance of the methodology in a specific domain (i.e., a change propagation analysis approach) is a task list. This task list can contain false positive tasks. An example of a false positive task in IS could be a task that refers to a third-party component, which was bought and, thus, cannot be changed [Ros+15b; Ros+17a]. A false positive can cause other false positives in the task list, as the change propagation rules are applied to the affected elements during the change propagation analysis. Thus, it is important to consider the tacit knowledge of domain experts during the change propagation analysis to avoid the propagation of false positives [HBK18]. The following metamodel and algorithm reduce the task lists by considering the decision of domain experts during the change propagation analysis.

5.2.3.1. Metamodel of Task List Reduction

This metamodel considers the basic decisions of a domain expert on a task [HBK18]. These decisions can be either `Confirm`, `Exclude`, or `Default`. After the generation of the task list, the decisions on all tasks are set to `Default`. `Default` shows that no decision was made manually on this task so far. The domain expert can set the decision on a false positive task to `Exclude` and a true positive task to `Confirm`. In this way, the propagation of false positives can be avoided.

To support domain experts in their decisions, the affected model elements (i.e., tasks) that cause a change to a further task are grouped for this task. In this way, model elements that cause a chain of change propagation can be identified. `CausingElement` and `AffectedElement` in Figure 5.2 show this relationship of the change propagation between model elements. Knowing the causing elements of changing model elements can help domain experts identify the cause of the propagation of false positives and, thus, can support the decision-making process.

5.2.3.2. Algorithm of Task List Reduction

As described previously, domain experts can annotate false positives in a task list with `Exclude`. This triggers Algorithm 2, which considers their decisions. After a task is annotated with `Exclude`, its referenced model element is also annotated with `Exclude`. The model element referenced by an excluded task is referred to hereinafter as *excluded model element*. Then, all tasks that have this model element as the causing element have to be removed from the task list. It is also conceivable that more than one model element are the causing elements of a task. Let set $G = \{g_1, \ldots, g_m\}$, where $m \in \mathbb{N}$, contains all model elements that are referenced by the tasks in the task list. Model elements $g_2, \ldots, g_m \in G$ can all be the `CausingElements` for a change in a task referencing model element g_1. In particular, set G contains all model elements that have to be analyzed. The relation between two model elements in the task list $g_1 \in G$ and $g_2 \in G$, where changes to g_2 cause further changes to $g_1 \in G$, is defined by *HasCausingElement* relation.

Algorithm 2 first removes all tasks, which are initially annotated with `Exclude` from the task list. These model elements can be themselves `CausingElements` for other affected model elements. The model elements that have the excluded model elements as `CausingElement` are defined by set X. However, the members of set X can also have other model elements as `CausingElements`, which are not excluded. The if expression in the algorithm checks, whether all `CausingElements` of a member of X are excluded model elements. In other words, if the if condition for a member of X is true, this model element has no `CausingElements`. This model element is then removed from the set of all model elements that have to be analyzed (i.e., set G). In the last step, the algorithm adds this model element to the set of all excluded model elements that have to be analyzed in the next iterations (i.e., set B). The algorithm terminates when set B is empty.

5.3. Domain-specific Elements

The previous section described metamodels and algorithms, which can be used in all domains. To be able to instantiate the methodology in a

Algorithm 2 Algorithm of Task List Reduction

Input: G ▷ The set of all model elements referenced by the task list
Input: B ▷ The set of model elements initially excluded
$D = \emptyset$ ▷ The set of model elements excluded until the current iteration
$G = G \setminus B$
while $\exists b \in B$ **do**
  $D = D \cup \{b\}$
  $B = B \setminus \{b\}$
  $X = \{a \in G | (a, b) \in HasCausingElement\}$
  $n = |X|$ ▷ The cardinality of set X
  for $k = 1 ; k \leq n ; k++$ **do**
    $Y = \{a \in G | (x_k, a) \in HasCausingElement\}$
    if $Y \subseteq D$ **then**
      $G = G \setminus \{x_k\}$
      $B = B \cup \{x_k\}$
    end if
  end for
end while

specific domain, the domain-specific metamodels and algorithms of the methodology have to be defined or extended. The following methodology elements have to be considered as guidelines to develop an instance of the methodology. The concrete metamodels and algorithms in a specific domain are described in the following chapters. The domain-specific metamodels and algorithms can be either mandatory or optional.

5.3.1. Change Propagation Analysis for Elements of Domain Metamodel

This part of the methodology contains the obligatory metamodels and algorithms. It consists of two metamodels to describe the domain under study and the changes in the domain. The latter is referred to hereinafter as *domain-specific metamodel of modification.* In addition to both metamodels, the algorithm for analyzing the change propagation has to be specified in a specific domain. To instantiate the methodology in a new domain, these metamodels and algorithm have be defined or extended in this domain. The following sections discuss the metamodels and algorithm in more detail.

5.3.1.1. Metamodel of Domain

To analyze the change propagation, the domain under study has to be metamodeled. The metamodel of the domain has to represent the properties that are relevant for the maintainability analysis. It involves aspects regarding the structure of systems in the domain, the data flow, and the behavior of these systems. The following aspects should be considered when metamodeling a new domain:

Structure The instances of the methodology aim at analyzing the change propagation in the structure of the systems in different domains. Thus, the structure of systems in a domain has to be metamodeled. For example, a system can consist of components and their composition in an architectural description language such as UML [RJB04] or PCM [BKR09; Reu16]. The granularity of this metamodel plays an important role in the precision of the change propagation analysis. The more fine-grained the system's structure is metamodeled, the more precise the task lists can be generated. However, the granularity of the metamodel is not the only factor in the precision of the task lists. Other factors are, for example, the granularity of the system model and the change propagation rules. Domain experts usually create the metamodel of the system's structure in a specific domain [HBK18].

Data Flow The change can propagate in a system due to the data flow. For example, a data dependency graph can be utilized to analyze the change propagation [LOA00]. The data flow can also be the cause of change propagation between two domains. The type of the data that has to be metamodeled depends on the domain. For example, the data in IS can be represented by data type [BKR09], while the physical data objects in the real world can represent the data in BP [Ros+17a]. Signals can represent the data in aPS [Hei+18; Koc17]. However, different types of data can usually be converted or transferred to each other. Thus, the data flow can be used to analyze the propagation of changes in different domains [HBK18].

Behavior The behavior of a system can also be affected by a change. A change can directly affect the behavior of a system. At the same time, a change to a system can lead to changes in its behavior. In other words, a change to the system's structure can directly affect its behavior or indirectly due to the data flow. The importance of considering the behavior during the change propagation analysis is discussed by several works. For example, Chapin et al. describe in [Cha+01] that a change in an IS can have a high impact on the experience of its users and the corresponding BP [HBK18].

5.3.1.2. Domain-specific Metamodel of Modification

This metamodel extends the domain-independent metamodel of modification by domain-specific metaclasses. In other words, an instance of the methodology extends the metaclasses in Figure 5.2, as described in the following:

- `Modification`: In a specific domain, this metaclass has to be extended by other metaclasses. Each metaclass references the corresponding metaclass of the metamodel of the domain, which can be potentially affected by a change.
- `ChangePropagationStep`: The concrete change propagation steps in a specific domain group the specific metaclasses extending the `Modification` metaclass with the same cause. For example, a change propagation step could be due to the data dependency [Sta15; Ros+15b].
- `SeedModification`: A subset of all metaclasses that can be potentially changed in a specific domain (i.e., the extensions of the `Modification` metaclass) can be initially affected by a change in this domain. In other words, instances of only these metaclasses can be marked as changed by domain experts. `SeedModification` has to be extended to include these metaclasses in a specific domain.
- `ModificationRepository`: In order to be able to create task lists in a new domain, a `ModificationRepository` metaclass in this domain has to be defined, which extends the `ModificationRepository` metaclass of the methodology.

5.3.1.3. Algorithm of Change Propagation Analysis

As described previously, the change propagation algorithms can be composed of a set of change propagation rules. Such an algorithm can work iteratively. In other words, the change propagation rules are iteratively applied to the newly affected model elements, until there are no newly affected elements. The change propagation rules are based on the elements of the metamodel of the domain under study and the domain-specific metamodel of modification [HBK18]. Thus, the change propagation rules depend highly on the domain under study and have to be specified by domain experts [Bus+18b]. The change propagation rules can be either in a GPL such as Java or in a DSL, which is tailored to this problem [Bus+18b; HBK18]. To support domain experts by specifying change propagation rules, a DSL was developed, which is described in Chapter 9.

5.3.2. Change Propagation Analysis for Elements of Context Metamodel

As described previously, the context elements can also be affected by a change request. These elements are domain-specific and can be associated to the elements of the metamodel of the domain under study. Thus, the modification of a domain element can cause the modification of the corresponding context elements. For example, if a component is changed in IS, the corresponding test cases can also be affected [Sta15; Ros+15b]. A change can also involve different roles (e.g., the software architect role in IS [Ros+15b] or the system engineer role in aPS [Hei+18]), as implementing a change requires the coordination of the tasks of different roles [Sta15]. Therefore, if information regarding context elements is available in the domain under study, it should be considered in the change propagation analysis.

Context elements need not necessarily be used in all usage context of the methodology. An example of this is an early phase of the development, in which no concrete system exists. Consequently, the context elements cannot be modeled. Sometimes, considering the domain elements can be sufficient in the change propagation analysis. This depends on the overall goal of these approaches. For example, if domain experts are interested in a rough estimation of the change propagation, context elements need not necessarily be modeled. Another reason for considering these elements as optional is the development effort of a methodology instance. Omitting these elements during the development lowers the development costs. Thus, this part of the methodology can be considered as optional [HBK18].

The following sections describe the metamodels and algorithms for instantiating the methodology for the context elements.

5.3.2.1. Metamodel of Context Elements

As described at the beginning of this chapter, organizational and technical artifacts, also called context elements, play an important role in the change effort estimation, as they cause additional effort during the change implementation [Sta15]. These model elements are not parts of the metamodel of the domain, as the metamodel of the domain mainly represents the systems in this domain and their connection to their environment. This metamodel contains the context model elements in a certain domain, which are relevant for the maintainability analysis. For example, it may be important to calibrate a plant in aPS, if changes to a component or a module of it are made [Vog+17; Hei+18]. In this example, the calibration information can represent a context element. Further, the context elements can also be the elements that are involved in the change propagation analysis. For example, if activities in BP are changed, knowing the affected organizational units may help plan the implementation of the changes [Ros+17a]. As the metamodel of the domain can be considered as the main artifact in the change propagation analysis, the elements of the context metamodel have to reference the elements of the domain metamodel. This allows identifying the corresponding elements of the context metamodel while analyzing the change propagation in the elements of the domain metamodel.

5.3.2.2. Metamodel of Task Type

As described previously, a task in a task list can have a task type representing how to change the affected elements in a specific domain. Thus, task types depend on a specific domain, such as writing or executing tests. This metamodel consists of the task types in a specific domain [Sta15; HBK18]. As task types show different changes of the elements of the domain or context metamodel, the metamodel of task types has to reference the corresponding elements of the domain or context metamodels. As it is sometimes sufficient to know if an element of the domain or context metamodel is changed regardless of the type of the change, this metamodel can be considered as optional [HBK18].

5.3.2.3. Algorithm of Context Task List

This algorithm identifies the affected context elements and can implement how the context elements are involved during a change to the domain elements. Additionally, this algorithm can also consider the specific task types. For example, if a component is changed, its test cases may need to be adapted and re-executed. By contrast, if the component is removed, its tests cases have to be removed [Ros+15b; HBK18]. Thus, domain knowledge is required to implement the algorithm of context task list. Further, as the metamodel of context elements is optional, the algorithm of context task list has to be considered as optional.

5.3.3. Algorithm of Difference Calculation

It is conceivable that a change can affect the way the elements in a system model are connected to each other. In other words, a change can affect the structure of systems in a domain, for example by adding or removing system elements [HBK18]. The same applies to their behavior such as adding or removing activities. To identify such changes, the difference between the system's structure and behavior before and after the change has to be calculated. For this reason, the algorithm of difference calculation is needed to calculate the differences between the system models before the change (i.e., `BaseVersion` in Algorithm 1) and the system models after the change (i.e., `TargetVersion` in Algorithm 1). For this purpose, existing generic algorithms to calculate the differences between model elements can be used. The results of these algorithms may need to be further refined based on the knowledge of domain experts and the usage context. The result of this algorithm is then gathered by Algorithm 1 [Sta15; Ros+15b; HBK18]. As calculating the differences between the system's structure and behavior may not be always necessary to analyze the change propagation, this algorithm is considered as optional [HBK18].

5.4. Process of Instantiating the Maintainability Analysis Methodology

The previous sections describe different methodology elements and their rationale. This section gives an overview of the process of instantiating the methodology in a specific domain.

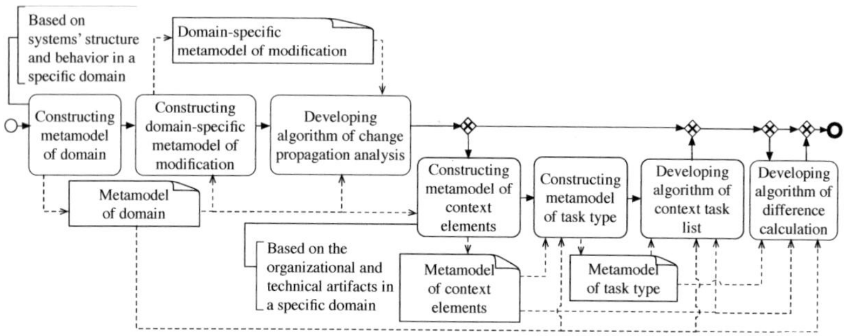

Figure 5.3.: Process for instantiating the methodology

Figure 5.3 illustrates in a BPMN-similar notation [Obj11] how to instantiate the methodology to obtain a change propagation analysis approach. While the first three activities are mandatory, the last four activities can be considered as optional. This figure illustrates all possible inputs (i.e., data objects) of each activity. In other words, the concrete instantiations of different methodology elements can have different input data objects.

The first activity is concerned with analyzing the systems in a specific domain and constructing a metamodel, which describes the systems' structure and behavior, as well as the data flow in this domain. In the next activity, the system elements that are potentially affected by a change have to be identified. Then, domain experts have to construct a domain-specific metamodel of modification based on the identified system elements and the metamodel of the domain. The next activity deals with analyzing the change propagation between different system elements. Based on the results and the previous two metamodels, domain experts develop the algorithm of change propagation analysis. Instantiating these three methodology elements allows creating a change propagation analysis approach, which considers only the domain elements.

If there are organizational and technical artifacts, which have a considerable impact during the change propagation analysis, the next three activities in Figure 5.3 have to be considered. The first activity is concerned with identifying the relevant organizational and technical artifacts and creating the metamodel of context elements. During the next activity, the domain experts have to identify and metamodel the corresponding task types. Developing the algorithm of context task list allows describing, which context elements are affected by a change to a domain element and how they have to be changed.

If domain experts are also interested in a before and after comparison, they can develop the corresponding functionality in the last activity of this process.

5.5. Conclusions

This chapter presented a maintainability analysis methodology, which was designed to provide a guideline for developing change propagation analysis approaches. The methodology abstracts from the heterogeneity of elements by using modeling concepts and is, thus, applicable to different domains, which fulfill the following characteristics: i) The structure of the systems in these domains can be described as a set of structural elements and their connections. ii) The effects of a change to a system on its behavior can be analyzed by considering the relationship between the system and its outside world, as described by Conway [Con68]. iii) The propagation of a change in a system and to its behavior has to be describable by the means of change propagation algorithms. This can be seen as a generalization of the dependency analysis. Thus, the methodology considers the structure of a system as the main artifact during the change propagation analysis.

In general, the methodology comprises two main parts: While the first part does not depend on a specific domain and is, thus, applicable to any domain, the second part has to be instantiated in a domain to develop a change propagation analysis approach. The second part comprises a mandatory part, which is needed in an instance of the methodology and an optional part, which can be used to mainly capture the effects of changing elements that are not part of the system's structure or behavior. The latter one involves the organizational and technical artifacts, which can also be affected by a change. In this way, the methodology can be applied to systems comprising heterogeneous elements from different domains. Summarized, this contribution answers the *first research question.*

6. Change Propagation Analysis in Business Processes

IS are used more and more in organizations to support their BP (e.g., SAP ERP [MW13]) [Ros+17a]. In general, BP can be expressed as a set of ordered activities, which can be actor steps or system steps [Hei+17]. Thus, changing an actor step or a system step can cause further changes in other actor steps and system steps [Ros+17a]. In other words, the evolutions of IS and BP are closely interwoven. Several authors identified different categories of impacts of an IS on the BP. For example, Moony et al. categorized the impact of an IS into *automational*, *informational*, and *transformational* effects [MGK96]. In other words, there are mutual dependencies between BP and IS [Ros+17a]. For example, we assume that users of Media Store [Reu16] need to enter only a username and password during the registration (see Chapter 4). New regulations force users to enter more information such as the date of birth or the national identification number. Thus, the BP of Media Store needs to be changed. Further, the software of Media Store needs also to be changed to handle this information. By contrast, a change to IS can cause further changes to BP and can affect users' behavior [Cha+01]. For example, if the software of the Media Store provides an alternative option for login (e.g., via an existing social profile account), the corresponding activities in its BP have to be adapted. Thus, BP and IS co-evolve during their life cycle [Ros+17a]. Consequently, the mutual dependencies between IS and BP need to be considered while analyzing the maintainability. These mutual dependencies make the change propagation analysis more difficult, as thc maintainability of IS and BP cannot be considered in isolation [Ros+17a].

Using models improves understanding, structuring, and analyzing of BP [Ros+17a]. To consider the mutual dependencies in the change propagation analysis, BP and IS have to be co-designed [LSB02]. In other words, the metamodels of IS and BP have to present their mutual dependencies [WGK00]. However, most approaches presented in Chapter 3 consider the change propagation in only one domain (i.e., either IS or BP). Thus, they do not allow a cross-disciplinary change propagation analysis. They are only a few approaches considering both IS and BP. However, most of these approaches propose only guidelines to calculate the change propagation at a very high level of abstraction. The change propagation analysis at a high level of abstraction can result in "impacts explosion without semantics" [Boh02, p. 5]. Further, they either do not automatically analyze the change propagation or do not estimate the efforts needed to implement a change as an activity list [Ros+17a]. Additionally, the impact of changing the context elements is omitted by most approaches.

To address the aforementioned issues, this chapter presents a model-based approach to automatically analyze the change propagation in BP and between BP and IS. This approach considers mutual dependencies between BP and IS. Thus, it was designed to answer the *second research question*. The proposed approach can be considered as the instantiation of the generic methodology (see Chapter 5) to BP. It extends the approach of Stammel [Sta15; Ros+15b; Ros+17b], which is limited to change propagation analysis in IS [Ros+17a].

Section 6.1 gives an overview of the change propagation analysis approach in IS and BP. Section 6.2 presents the change propagation analysis in the domain metamodel of BP. The change propagation analysis for the context elements in BP is introduced in Section 6.3. Section 6.4 describes the difference calculation during a before and after comparison. The chapter concludes in Section 6.5 with an overview of the contributions.

The results of this chapter have been appeared in the papers [Ros+17a; Bus+18a] and partially (e.g., the instantiation of the methodology in BP) in the paper [HBK18]:

6.1. Change Propagation Analysis for Co-evolution of Information Systems and Business Processes

This section presents the model-based approach Karlsruhe Architectural Maintainability Prediction for Business Processes (KAMP4BP). It analyzes the change propagation in BP during the co-evolution of IS and BP. This approach was developed as two interconnected instances of the methodology in IS and BP. Although the methodology was originally the generalization of both approaches, instantiating the methodology to obtain these approaches served as a first proof of the methodology concept. The change propagation analysis approach in IS is an extension of the original Karlsruhe Architectural Maintainability Prediction for Information Systems (KAMP4IS) (cf. [Sta15; Ros+15b]) to enable the analysis of the change propagation between IS and BP. For this purpose, the approach KAMP4IS had to be extended to analyze the change propagation in IS at a more fine-grained level of abstraction (e.g., at the signature and event level instead of interface level). In addition to the development of KAMP4BP, the combination of both approaches KAMP4IS and KAMP4BP allows analyzing the change propagation between BP and IS. Thus, KAMP4IS and KAMP4BP supports software architects and process designers during the co-evolution. In this chapter, *software architects and process designers*, as well as *domain experts* are used interchangeably.

Figure 6.1 gives an overview of the KAMP4BP approach. The approach consists of three phases: i) the preparation phase, ii) the impact phase, and iii) the post-analysis phase [Ros+17a].

The first phase of KAMP4BP is the preparation of the input. In general, software architects and/or process designers prepare the input of the approach manually. The preparation of input involves modeling the architecture of IS, the design of BP, and the data flow. If context elements, such as messaging in BP, need to be considered in the change propagation analysis, information about these elements has also to be provided. Then, domain experts have to select the initially changed elements as seed modifications [Ros+17a].

In the impact phase, KAMP4BP automatically calculates a temporary task list for the seed modifications. For this purpose, it uses the change propagation algorithms to calculate the change propagation in IS and BP. The approach generates a temporary task list, which contains only domain elements potentially affected by the seed modifications. If domain experts provided context model elements, KAMP4BP extends the temporary task list to include the efforts of changing these elements [Ros+17a].

As described in Chapter 5, the methodology provides the functionality to perform the post-analysis phase. For example, this phase merges the redundant tasks to eliminate the duplicates and sorts the tasks in the task list. If domain experts exclude the tasks, which are not affected by the change, this phase regenerates the task list (i.e., task list reduction in Section 5.2.3) according to these decisions [Ros+17a].

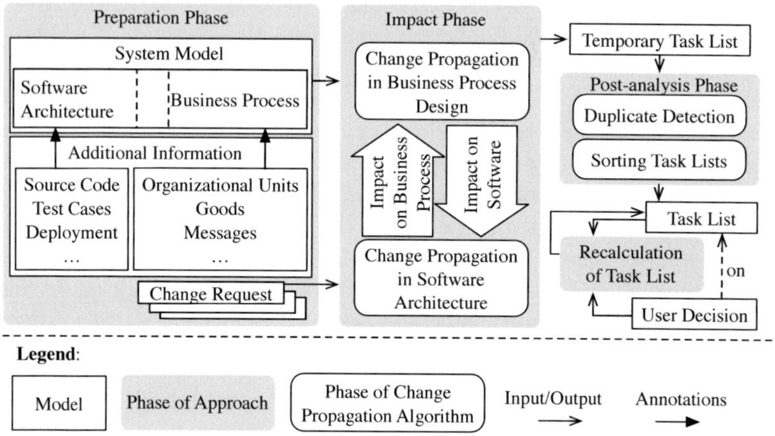

Figure 6.1.: Overview of the KAMP4BP approach [Ros+17a; Bus+18a]

The following sections describe how to instantiate the methodology to BP to implement a change propagation analysis approach for this domain.

6.2. Change Propagation Analysis for Elements of Domain Metamodel

This section presents the metamodels and algorithms that are required to instantiate the methodology to BP.

6.2.1. Metamodel of Domain

To analyze the change propagation in a specific domain, metamodels of systems' structure and behavior, as well as the data flow should be provided, as described in Chapter 5. The following sections discuss the metamodels of IS and BP with respect to these aspects.

In the following, specific metamodels in IS and BP were chosen to model the structure, data flow, and behavior. These metamodels create the foundation for developing further metamodels and algorithms to create instances of the methodology. For example, seed modifications in BP and IS can refer only to the metaclasses of the metamodels, which have been chosen in this step. It is important to note that other metamodels representing the structure, data flow, and behavior are also conceivable.

In general, to obtain a change propagation analysis approach, which fulfills the requirements, domain experts need to know the effects of this choice. Several factors influence this choice such as development costs and the granularity of the analysis results. These influencing factors are discussed in more detail in Section 11.4.2 based on the evaluation results. The decision on the appropriate metamodels for the analysis results from a trade-off between different influencing factors.

6.2.1.1. Structure

As described in Chapter 5, the system's structure plays an important role in the change propagation analysis. In order to be able to analyze the change propagation between BP and IS, the change propagation in the structure of IS needs to be analyzed. For this purpose, KAMP4IS [Sta15; Ros+15b] can be used to analyze the change propagation at the level of components and interfaces. However, a change propagation at this level is too coarse-grained to consider the mutual dependencies between IS and BP. Therefore, KAMP4IS has to be extended by a more fine-grained change propagation analysis. This includes for example a change propagation analysis based on the signatures of an interface instead of the interface (cf. [Sta15]). Similar to the initially developed KAMP4IS, the extended KAMP4IS is based on PCM to represent the systems' structure in IS.

Figure 6.2 illustrates an excerpt from PCM. The presented metaclasses were used to extend KAMP4IS to enable a change propagation between IS and BP. An `Interface` can be an `OperationInterface` comprising `OperationSignatures` [BKR09] or an `EventGroup`, which allows event-based communication [Rat13]. An `EventGroup` contains at least one `EventType`, which represents an event sent and received by components [Rat13]. Both `OperationSignatures` and `EventTypes` are `Signatures`. A `Signature` can have parameters of specific `DataTypes`. An `OperationSignature` can also have a return type of a certain `DataType` [BKR09]. Further, Figure 6.2 shows the relationship between the `EntryLevelSystemCall` metaclass from the UsageModel of PCM to the `OperationSignature` metaclass from the RepositoryModel of PCM [BKR09]. `EntryLevelSystemCalls` present the service calls to the provided roles of a system [BKR09].

6.2.1.2. Data Flow

The data flow between IS and BP can be utilized to analyze the change propagation between these domains, as it can be the cause of the change propagation. To metamodel the data flow in BP, the data object concept based on BPMN [Obj11] was used [Ros+17a]. The data object concept represents the data objects in the real world. Actors in BP can use data objects. Thus, data objects can serve as inputs or outputs of actor steps. They can be either composite or collection data objects. An example of a composite data object is the identity document in the Media Store example that is used by its users. Further, data objects in BP can have corresponding data types in IS. In the previous example, the information of the identity card in a BP can correspond to the user information in the `DataBase` component. Figure 6.3 illustrates the corresponding metamodel – DataModel. It consists of the abstract metaclass `DataObjetcs`

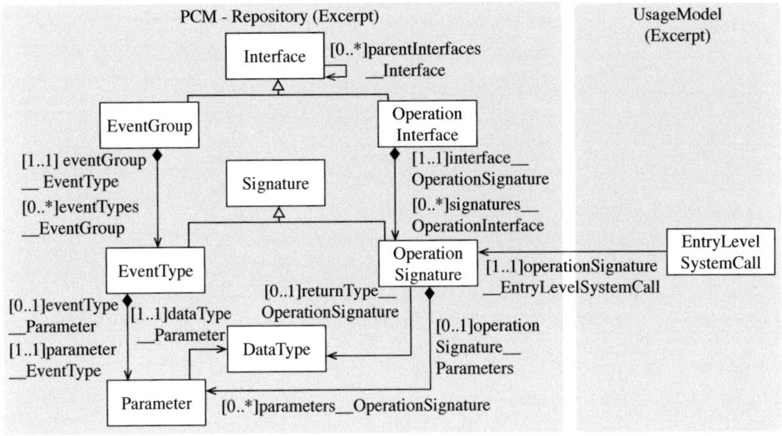

Figure 6.2.: Relationship between the metamodel of PCM RepositoryModel and UsageModel [BKR09]

and the metaclasses `CollectionDataObject` and `CompositeDataObject`. Figure 6.3 shows that `DataObjects` of different types can be composed to a `CompositeDataObject`. By contrast, a set of `DataObjects` of the same type represents a `CollectionDataObject` [Ros+17a]. Further, the figure presents the relationship between `DataObject` from DataModel and `DataType` from UsageModel. This relationship can be used to analyze the change propagation between IS and BP.

6.2.1.3. Behavior

The behavior of a system can also be important to estimate the effort of a change request. A change to IS can propagate to their user interfaces. This change has a high impact on the experience of users and BP [Cha+01]. Thus, the metamodels of BP have to consider the co-design of IS and BP [LSB02]. KAMP4BP is based on the BPUsageModel as an extension of PCM UsageModel representing BP regarding the aforementioned co-design (see the metamodel of BP in Section 2.4). BPUsageModel consists of the following main metaclasses: actor steps, system steps, acquire device resources, and release device resources, as discussed in Section 2.4. Figure 6.4 illustrates

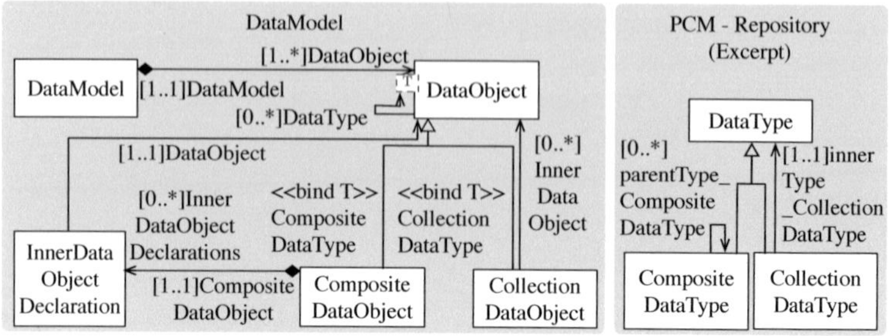

Figure 6.3.: Overview of the metamodel of DataModel and an excerpt of `DataType` in the PCM's RepositoryModel [HBK18]

the relationship of the excerpts from BPUsageModel, PCM UsageModel, and DataModel, which are relevant for the change propagation analysis. The system step metaclass of BPUsageModel represents the `EntryLevelSystemCall` of PCM [Hei+17]. As described previously, Figure 6.4 shows the extension of BPUsageModel to enable `ActorStep` to use `DataObjects` as input or output [Ros+17a]. The aforementioned relationship can be utilized for the change propagation analysis between IS and BP.

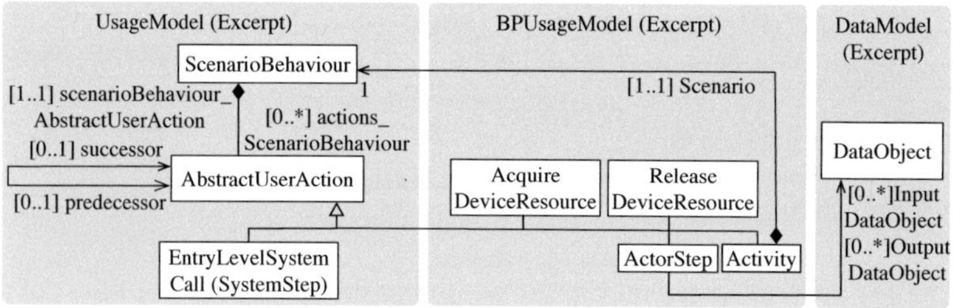

Figure 6.4.: Relationship between PCM UsageModel [BKR09], BPUsage-Model [Hei+17], and DataModel [Ros+17a]

Example

In this section the metamodels described previously are applied to the Media Store example introduced in Section 4.1. In the following, the three aspects regarding the structure, the data flow, and the behavior of Media Store are discussed:

Structure: As Media Store is a component-based software system, its structure is modeled using PCM. The system model is composed of components (e.g., `TagWatermarking` or `ReEncoder`) requiring and providing interfaces (e.g., `IDownload`).

Data flow: Different data types in the software of Media Store are also defined using PCM. An example of a data type could be the composite data type `AudioCollectionRequest` composed of other data types such as the `Size` of the composed audio files. The DataModel enables process designers to model the data flow in BP. An example of a data object could be the `Identity Document`, from which users can enter their personal information such as national identification number during the registration. This information could be stored as data types in the `DataBase` component.

Behavior: The behavior of Media Store can be modeled using BPUsageModel [Hei+17]. Figure 4.2 shows a simplified BP model of Media Store as a sequence of actor steps and system steps.

6.2.2. Domain-specific Metamodel of Modification

To analyze the change propagation in IS and BP, it is necessary to identify the metaclasses of the metamodel of domain that can be potentially affected by a change. The following sections illustrate the metamodels of modification for IS and BP.

6.2.2.1. Information Systems

The basis of the change propagation analysis in IS is generally provided by KAMP4IS [Sta15]. However, there is a need for fine-granular metamodels representing affected elements in IS to analyze the change propagation between BP and IS. As described previously, KAMP4IS analyzes the change propagation at the level of components and interfaces. Thus, the corresponding metamodels have to be extended to allow the change propagation analysis at the level of signatures and events. Furthermore, the metamodels have to be adapted in accordance to the generic methodology of the change propagation analysis (see Section 5.3.1.2).

6.2.2.2. Business Processes

This metamodel represents the changes for the potentially affected metaclasses of PCM UsageModel, BPUsageModel, and DataModel. The metaclasses of this metamodel refer to metaclasses of the aforementioned metamodels that can be potentially changed. To illustrate the relationship between this metamodel and the methodology, the corresponding metaclasses of the methodology are illustrated in the following. Further, the extensions of different metaclasses of the domain-independent metamodel of modification (see Chapter 5) are discussed:

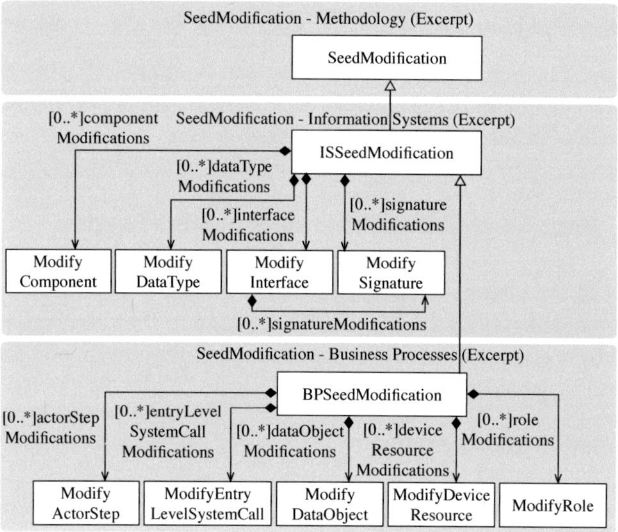

Figure 6.5.: Relationship between the domain-independent `SeedModification` and `SeedModification` in IS [Sta15], and BP

- `SeedModification`: The initial changes to the BP metamodel can be: i) actor roles, ii) device resources used, iii) actor steps, iv) system steps or entry level system calls, and v) data objects as inputs or outputs of the actor steps. Figure 6.5 shows the relationship between the `SeedModification` metaclasses of the methodology, IS [Sta15], and BP.

- `Modification`: The following metaclasses of PCM UsageModel, BPUsageModel, and DataModel can be affected by a change: i) roles, ii) device resources, iii) data objects, and iv) user actions (i.e., acquire device resources, release device resources, actor steps, and system steps). Figure 6.6 shows the relationship between the `Modification` metaclasses of the methodology, IS [Sta15], and BP.

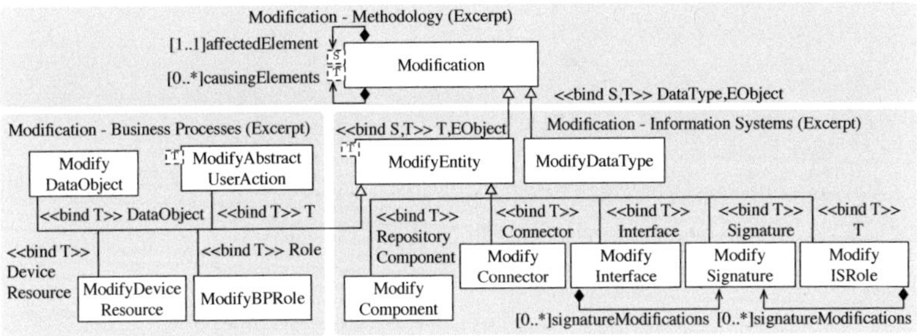

Figure 6.6.: Relationship between the domain-independent `Modification` and `Modification` in IS [Sta15], and BP

- `ChangePropagationStep`: Modifications in IS and BP can be grouped together due to the following causes: i) inter business process change propagation (i.e., changes to the concrete user actions) or ii) change propagation due to data dependency (i.e., changes to data objects, as well as all activities in a BP accessing the affected data objects (i.e., actor steps or system steps)). Figure 6.7 shows the relationship between the `ChangePropagationStep` metaclasses of the methodology, IS [Sta15], and BP.

- `ModificationRepository` contains the domain-specific metaclasses of `SeedModification` and `ChangePropagationStep`, as described in Chapter 5. Figure 6.8 shows the relationship between the `ModificationRepository` metaclasses of the methodology, IS [Sta15], and BP.

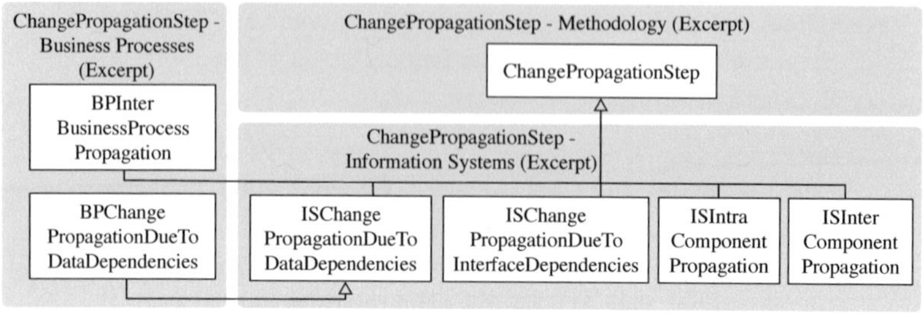

Figure 6.7.: Relationship between the domain-independent `ChangePropagationStep` and `ChangePropagationStep` in IS [Sta15], and BP

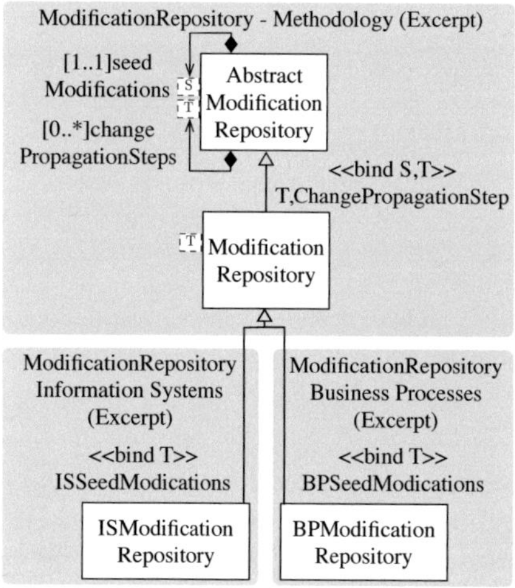

Figure 6.8.: Relationship between the domain-independent `Modification-Repository` and `ModificationRepository` in IS [Sta15], and BP

Example

The previous sections describe the potentially affected model elements by a change. In the Media Store example, a change potentially affects all elements in the model of the software architecture. Examples of the instances of the

IS-specific modification metaclasses are components (e.g., the `Packaging` component), interfaces and their methods (e.g., the `IPackaging` interface), or data types (e.g., the `AudioCollectionRequest` data type). Although model elements that do not have a correspondence in the Media Store code such as connectors can also be affected by a change, they cannot be chosen as seed modification. These model elements are relevant to estimate the change propagation properly (i.e., the change propagation between two components). All other model elements can also be seed modifications in IS.

In the model of the BP design of Media Store, all model elements can be regarded as affected elements. Examples of the instances of the BP-specific modification metaclasses are the actor step `enter username and password`, the system step `download`, or the data object `identity document`. The user of the approach KAMP4BP can also select almost all potentially affected elements as seed modification.

6.2.3. Algorithm of Change Propagation Analysis

This algorithm is composed of a set of change propagation rules. They use the metaclasses of the following metamodels: i) DataModel, ii) OrganizationEnvironmentModel [Hei14], iii) BPUsageModel [Hei14], iv) UsageModel [BKR09], and v) RepositoryModel [BKR09]. The input and output of the algorithms are the instances of the source and the target metaclasses, respectively. If model elements of the instances of the metamodels for IS and BP changes, the corresponding change propagation rules are applied. The rules are defined at the level of the metamodel. In this way, they can be applied to all instances of a metamodel. Each change propagation rule analyzes the change propagation between a source and a target metaclass of the metamodels for IS and BP. Thus, to define the rules instances of each metaclass of the aforementioned metamodels are mapped to a set. In other words, the members of each set represent the elements of metamodel instances of the same type. An example of a set is the set of all data types in a specific instance. In the following, only the sets of the instances of the metaclasses, which are relevant for the change propagation rules, are defined:

- $O = \{o_{o_1}, \ldots, o_{o_n}\}$ is a set of all `DataObjects` in the instances of DataModel.
- $L = \{l_{l_1}, \ldots, l_{l_n}\}$ is a set of all `Roles` in the instances of OrganizationEnvironmentModel.
- $D = \{d_{d_1}, \ldots, d_{d_n}\}$ is a set of all `DeviceResources` in the instances of OrganizationEnvironmentModel.
- $H = \{h_{h_1}, \ldots, h_{h_n}\}$ is a set of all `ActorSteps` in the instances of BPUsageModel.
- $B = \{b_{b_1}, \ldots, b_{b_n}\}$ is a set of all `AcquireDeviceReources` in the instances of BPUsageModel.
- $F = \{f_{f_1}, \ldots, f_{f_n}\}$ is a set of all `ReleaseDeviceReources` in the instances of BPUsageModel.
- $S = \{s_{s_1}, \ldots, s_{s_n}\}$ is a set of all `Signatures` in the instances of RepositoryModel.
- $U = \{u_{u_1}, \ldots, u_{u_n}\}$ is a set of all `OperationSignatures` in the instances of RepositoryModel.
- $P = \{p_{p_1}, \ldots, p_{p_n}\}$ is a set of all `Parameters` in the instances of RepositoryModel.
- $T = \{t_{t_1}, \ldots, t_{t_n}\}$ is a set of all `DataTypes` in the instances of RepositoryModel.
- $E = \{e_{e_1}, \ldots, e_{e_n}\}$ is a set of all `EventTypes` in the instances of RepositoryModel.
- $G = \{g_{g_1}, \ldots, g_{g_n}\}$ is a set of all `EventGroups` in the instances of RepositoryModel.
- $I = \{i_{i_1}, \ldots, i_{i_n}\}$ is a set of all `Interfaces` in the instances of RepositoryModel.
- $J = \{j_{j_1}, \ldots, j_{j_n}\}$ is a set of all `OperationInterfaces` in the instances of RepositoryModel.
- $C = \{c_{c_1}, \ldots, c_{c_n}\}$ is a set of all `EntryLevelSystemCalls` in the instances of RepositoryModel.

- $A = \{a_{a_1}, \ldots, a_{a_n}\}$ is a set of all `AbstractUserActions` in the instances of RepositoryModel.

As `ActorStep`, `AcquireDeviceResource`, `ReleaseDeviceResource`, and `EntryLevelSystemCall` are specific types of `AbstractUserAction`, then $H \cup B \cup F \cup C \subseteq A$. As `OperationInterface` and `EventGroup` are specific types of `Interface`, then $J \cup G \subseteq I$. As `OperationSignature` and `EventType` are specific types of `Signature`, then $U \cup E \subseteq S$.

The relationship between metaclasses of different metamodels can be used to create binary relations over these sets. The relations are defined in the following:

- The relation $HasInnerDeclaration$ is defined over the set O. In this relation, the DataObject $o_{o_i} \in O$ is associated to the DataObject $o_{o_j} \in O$, if the DataObject o_{o_i} contains the DataObject $o_{o_j} \in O$ as inner declaration.
- The relation $HasInput$ is defined over the sets H and O. In this relation, the ActorStep $h \in H$ is associated to the DataObject $o \in O$, if the ActorStep h has the DataObject $o \in O$ as input.
- The relation $HasOutput$ is defined over the sets H and O. In this relation, the ActorStep $h \in H$ is associated to the DataObject $o \in O$, if the ActorStep h has the DataObject $o \in O$ as output.
- The relation $HasResponsibleRole$ is defined over the sets H and L. In this relation, the ActorStep $h \in H$ is associated to the Role $l \in L$, if the ActorStep h has the responsible Role $l \in L$. This relation is left-total and right-unique (i.e., it is a function).
- The relation $HasSuccessorActorStep$ is defined over the set H. In this relation, the ActorStep $h_{h_i} \in H$ is associated to the ActorStep $h_{h_j} \in H$, if the ActorStep h_{h_i} has the ActorStep $h_{h_j} \in H$ as successor. This relation is left-total and right-unique (i.e., it is a function).
- The relation $HasSuccessorEntryLevelSystemCall$ is defined over the sets H and C. In this relation, the ActorStep $h \in H$ is associated to the EntryLevelSystemCall $c \in C$, if the ActorStep h has the EntryLevelSystemCall $c \in C$ as successor. This relation is left-total and right-unique (i.e., it is a function).

- The relation $IsCallToSignature$ is defined over the sets C and U. In this relation, the EntryLevelSystemCall $c \in C$ is associated to the OperationSignature $u \in U$, if the EntryLevelSystemCalls c is a call to the OperationSignature $u \in U$. This relation is left-total and right-unique (i.e., it is a function).
- The relation $OperationSignatureHasParameter$ is defined over the sets U and P. In this relation, the OperationSignature $u \in U$ is associated to the Parameter $p \in P$, if the OperationSignature u has a Parameter $p \in P$.
- The relation $EventTypeHasParameter$ is defined over the sets E and P. In this relation, the EventType $e \in E$ is associated to the Parameter $p \in P$, if the EventType e has a Parameter $p \in P$. This relation is left-total and right-unique (i.e., it is a function).
- The relation $HasDataType$ is defined over the sets P and T. In this relation, the Parameter $p \in P$ is associated to the DataType $t \in T$, if the Parameter p has a DataType $t \in T$. This relation is left-total and right-unique (i.e., it is a function).
- The relation $AcquiresDeviceResource$ is defined over the sets B and D. In this relation, the AcquiresDeviceResource $b \in B$ is associated to the DeviceResource $d \in D$, if the AcquiresDeviceResource b acquires the DeviceResource $d \in D$. This relation is left-total and right-unique (i.e., it is a function).
- The relation $ReleasesDeviceResource$ is defined over the sets F and D. In this relation, the ReleasesDeviceResource $f \in F$ is associated to the DeviceResource $d \in D$, if the ReleasesDeviceResource f releases the DeviceResource $d \in D$. This relation is left-total and right-unique (i.e., it is a function).
- The relation $HasSuccessor$ is defined over the set A. In this relation, the AbstractUserAction $a_{a_i} \in A$ is associated to the AbstractUserAction $a_{a_j} \in A$, if the AbstractUserAction a_{a_i} has the AbstractUserAction $a_{a_j} \in A$ as successor. This relation is left-total and right-unique (i.e., it is a function).

- The relation $HasCorrespondence$ is defined over the sets O and T. In this relation, the DataObject $o \in O$ is associated to the DataType $t \in T$, if the DataObject o has a corresponding DataType $t \in T$.
- The relation $HasReturnType$ is defined over the sets U and T. In this relation, the OperationSignature $u \in U$ is associated to the DataType $t \in T$, if the OperationSignature u has the DataType $t \in T$ as return type. This relation is left-total and right-unique (i.e., it is a function).
- The relation $BelongsToOperationInterface$ is defined over the sets U and J. In this relation, the OperationSignature $u \in U$ is associated to the OperationInterface $j \in J$, if the OperationSignature u belongs to an OperationInterface $j \in J$. This relation is left-total and right-unique (i.e., it is a function).
- The relation $BelongsToEventGroup$ is defined over the sets E and G. In this relation, the EventType $e \in E$ is associated to the EventGroup $g \in G$, if the EventType e belongs to the EventGroup $g \in G$. This relation is left-total and right-unique (i.e., it is a function).

In order to be able to analyze the change propagation in IS and BP, there is a need for change propagation rules in IS and BP and between both IS and BP. Thus, the change propagation rules can be divided into the following groups: i) the change propagation rules in BP, as described in Section 6.2.3.1, ii) the change propagation rules between BP and IS, as described in Section 6.2.3.2, and iii) the change propagation rules in IS, as described in Section 6.2.3.3. The change propagation rules have to be defined based on the aforementioned sets and the relations between them.

6.2.3.1. Change Propagation in Business Process

Seed modifications in BP can be device resources, roles, actor steps, or data objects. A change to an element of these types triggers the corresponding change propagation rule(s). The result of each change propagation rule is a set of newly affected model elements. These model elements are the input for the change propagation rules. Algorithm 3 presents the most relevant change propagation rules needed to calculate the change propagation in BP.

Algorithm 3 Algorithm for the Change Propagation Analysis in the Model of BP design

Input: Model of BP design, seed modifications

1: **Calculate the change propagation from a modified DataObject to the other DataObjects using Algorithm 4**
2: **Calculate the change propagation from modified DataObjects to ActorSteps based on the modified DataObjects as input or output using Algorithm 5**
3: **Calculate the change propagation from a modified Role to the corresponding ActorSteps using Algorithm 6**
4: **Calculate the change propagation from a modified ActorStep to the direct following ActorStep or EntryLevelSystemCall**

Calculate the change propagation from a modified ActorStep, using a DataObject as output, to the direct following ActorStep that has the same DataObject as input using Algorithm 7
Calculate the change propagation from a modified ActorStep, using the DataObject as output, to the direct following EntryLevelSystemCall that uses the corresponding DataType as input using Algorithm 8

5: **Calculate the change propagation from a modified DeviceResource to the corresponding Activities**

Calculate the change propagation from a modified DeviceResource to the corresponding AcquireDeviceResource and ReleaseDeviceResource using Algorithm 9
Calculate the change propagation from a modified AcquireDeviceResource to the following AbstractUserActions that use the same DeviceResource using Algorithm 10

Each phase of Algorithm 3 presents a change propagation rule, which is described in the following as a stand-alone algorithm. Each algorithm is based on the aforementioned sets and relations. Further, other elements such as branches and loops can exist in the model of BP design. Branches and loops can also be nested in each other. Most algorithms of change propagation rules consider these elements. However, the following algorithms present only the basis variant of the change propagation rules without such elements to illustrate the idea of the rules.

As described previously, a data object can be recursively composed of other data objects. It can also be a collection of further data objects. Thus, a change can propagate to the data objects containing an affected data object.

The containment relationship between the data objects can be used for the change propagation analysis. Algorithm 4 presents the change propagation from a modified DataObject to the other DataObjects. The algorithm is based on the idea that the DataObject $o_{o_i} \in O$ in an instance of DataModel (see Section 6.2.1.2) can have the DataObject $o_{o_j} \in O$ as the inner declaration. In other words, o_{o_i} can be composed of other DataObjects (i.e., o_{o_i} is a CompositeDataObject) or can be a CollectionDataObject. In this case, changing o_{o_j} can result in changing o_{o_i}. In general, the composition and the collection relationships can be combined hierarchically. Thus, Algorithm 4 iteratively identifies the potentially affected DataObjects based on the discussed relationships. In each iteration, Y is the set of all DataObjects, which have the affected DataObjects as inner declaration. As sets are duplicate-free, the union of R and Y in each iteration adds only the elements of Y to R, which are not included in R. The relative complement of R in the union of R and Y contains also only the DataObjects, which have not yet been considered. Thus, R is equal to O in the worst case. In other words, Algorithm 4 considers all members of O in this case.

Algorithm 4 Change propagation from DataObject to DataObject

Input: $N \subseteq O$ ▹ Seed modifications
Output: $R \subseteq O$ ▹ Result
$R = N$
while $N \neq \emptyset$ **do**
    $Y = \{o \in O | (\exists n \in N)\, [(o, n) \in HasInnerDeclaration]\}$
    $N = (R \cup Y) \setminus R$
    $R = R \cup Y$
end while

Section 6.2.1.2 describes that an actor step in BP can have inputs or outputs. The inputs or outputs are represented by data objects. If a data object changes, the corresponding actor steps may need to be adapted due to the data flow. Algorithm 5 illustrates the change propagation from a modified DataObject to the corresponding ActorSteps. The ActorStep $h \in H$ in the model of BPUsageModel can have the DataObject $o \in O$ in an instance of DataModel as input or output. Consequently, a change to o can result in a change to h. Based on this data flow, Algorithm 5 identifies the potentially affected ActorSteps.

Algorithm 5 Change propagation from DataObject to ActorStep

Input: $N \subseteq O$ ▷ Seed modifications
Output: $R \subseteq H$ ▷ Result
$R = \{h \in H | (\exists n \in N) [(h, n) \in HasInput \vee (h, n) \in HasOutput]\}$

Actor steps are performed by human actors [Hei+17]. Each human actor takes up at least one role. Consequently, a responsible role can be assigned to several actor steps. If a role changes, the actor steps, for which the corresponding human actors are responsible, may need to be changed. Algorithm 6 presents the change propagation from an affected Role to the ActorSteps with this Role. An actor with the Role $r \in R$ in an instance of OrganizationEnvironmentModel can perform the ActorStep $h \in H$ in an instance of BPUsageModel. Changing the Role r can affect all corresponding ActorSteps h. Thus, Algorithm 6 identifies all ActorSteps, if the responsible Role changes.

Algorithm 6 Change propagation from Role to ActorStep

Input: $N \subseteq L$ ▷ Seed modifications
Output: $R \subseteq H$ ▷ Result
$R = \{h \in H | (\exists n \in N) [(h, n) \in HasResponsibleRole]\}$

As described previously, a BP can be considered as a set of linked activities [Wor99]. Each activity can be an actor step or a system step [Hei+17]. Thus, an actor step can be the successor activity of another actor step. Additionally, each actor step can have an input and an output. The following algorithm considers the change propagation between two connected actor steps, if the first actor step has an output of the same data object as the input of the successor actor step. This heuristic is based on the change propagation due to the data flow, as both actor steps use the same data object. Thus, the successor actor step is assumed to be dependent on the predecessor actor step. Algorithm 6 presents the change propagation from the modified ActorStep $h_i \in H$ in an instance of BPUsageModel to the directly following ActorStep $h_j \in H$, if they use the same DataObject in an instance of DataModel. As there can be a chain of ActorSteps in BP, the algorithm identifies the successor ActorStep of a modified ActorStep based on the aforementioned heuristic in each iteration. Then, it adds the successor ActorStep to the list of ActorSteps that have to be analyzed in the next iteration. As each ActorStep cannot have more than one successor ActorStep [Hei+17], the algorithm can maximally identify one affected ActorStep in each iteration. If the algorithm cannot identify any ActorStep in an iteration, it terminates. Consequently, it considers all ActorSteps in the BPUsageModel in a worst-case scenario. In this way, Algorithm 6 iteratively identifies the potentially affected ActorSteps based on the data flow.

Algorithm 7 Change propagation from ActorStep to ActorStep

Input: $N \subseteq H$ ▷ Seed modifications
Output: $R \subseteq H$ ▷ Result
$R = N$
while $N \neq \emptyset$ **do**
  $N = \{h \in H | (\exists n \in N)(\exists o \in O)[(n, h) \in HasSuccessorActorStep \land (n, o) \in HasOutput \land (h, o) \in HasInput]\}$
  $R = R \cup N$
end while

Similar to the previous case, an actor step can have a successor system step. While the inputs and the outputs of an actor step can be data objects, the inputs and the output of a system step can be data types. As described previously, different types of data can be converted to each other. Thus, a data type in IS can have a corresponding data object in BP. Algorithm 8 is based on this correspondence. It analyzes the change propagation from a modified actor step to the successor system step, if one of the output data objects of the predecessor corresponds to one of the input data types of the successor. It first identifies the successor EntryLevelSystemCall $c \in C$ in an instance of UsageModel of the affected ActorStep $h \in H$ in an instance of BPUsageModel. Then, it finds the corresponding OperationSignature $u \in U$ in an instance of RepositoryModel of the EntryLevelSystemCall h. The algorithm identifies the DataTypes $t \in T$ of the input Parameters $p \in P$ of the OperationSignature u. If one of the output DataObjects $o \in O$ of the affected ActorStep corresponds to one of the identified DataTypes, the algorithm selects the corresponding EntraLevelSystemCall as affected. Thus, Algorithm 8 identifies the potentially affected EntryLevelSystemCalls c based on the aforementioned heuristic. As each actor step cannot have more than one successor system step [Hei+17], the result set of this algorithm is either empty or contains only one system step.

Algorithm 8 Change propagation from ActorStep to EntryLevelSystemCall

Input: $N \subseteq H$ ▷ Seed modifications
Output: $R \subseteq C$ ▷ Result
$R = \{c \in C | (\exists n \in N)(\exists u \in U)(\exists p \in P)(\exists t \in T)(\exists o \in O)[(n,c) \in HasSuccessorEntryLevelSystemCall \land (c,u) \in IsCallToSignature \land (u,p) \in HasParameter \land (p,t) \in HasDataType \land (o,t) \in HasCorrespondence]\}$

AcquireDeviceResource and ReleaseDeviceResource are each the start and the end activity of a sequence of activities, which need a specific device [Hei+17]. Thus, changing the used device can result in changing all AcquireDeviceResources, ReleaseDeviceResources, and activities in between. Algorithm 9 presents the change propagation from an affected device resource to the corresponding activities regarding acquiring and releasing the device resource. The DeviceResource $d \in D$ in an instance of OrganizationEnvironmentModel can be used by the AcquireDeviceResources $b \in B$ and the ReleaseDeviceResources $f \in F$ in BPUsageModel. A change to d can result in further changes to the activities b and f, as they depend on the affected DeviceResource d. Thus, Algorithm 9 calculates the change propagation from a modified DeviceResource to the corresponding AcquireDeviceResources and ReleaseDeviceResources.

Algorithm 9 Change propagation from DeviceResource to AcquireDeviceResource and ReleaseDeviceResource

Input: $N \subseteq D$ ▷ Seed modifications
Output: $R \subseteq (B \cup F)$ ▷ Result
$R = \{b \in B | (\exists n \in N)[(b,n) \in AcquiresDeviceResource]\}$
$R = R \cup \{f \in F | (\exists n \in N)[(f,n) \in ReleasesDeviceResource]\}$

Algorithm 10 identifies the activities (i.e., abstract user actions) that use an affected device resource. AbstractUserActions $a \in A$ in an instance of BPUsageModel can be between AcquireDeviceResource and ReleaseDeviceResource of the same DeviceResource $d \in D$. Further, several blocks of AcquireDeviceResource, ReleaseDeviceResource, and AbstractUserActions in between can be nested in each other. A change to d results in changes to all following AbstractUserActions a that use d. Algorithm 10 iteratively calculates the change propagation from the modified AcquireDeviceResource b to the successor AbstractUserActions a using the same DeviceResource d. In order to be able to consider the hierarchy level of the nested blocks, this algorithm uses a counter. The counter increments, if an AcquireDeviceResource of a DeviceResource of the same type is identified. It counts down, if a ReleaseDeviceResource of a DeviceResource of the same type is identified. While the previous algorithm calculates the change propagation from an affected DeviceResource to AcquireDeviceResource and ReleaseDeviceResource, Algorithm 10 calculates the change propagation to AbstractUserActions in between.

Algorithm 10 Change propagation from AcquireDeviceResource to AbstractUserAction

Require: $N = \{n | n \in D\}$ ▷ seed modification: n is the acquireDeviceResource.
Output: $R \subseteq A$ ▷ Result
$R = \emptyset$
$k = 1$
$X = \{a \in A | (n, a) \in HasSuccessor\}$
while $X \neq \emptyset \land k > 0$ **do**
  if $\{x \in X | x \in B\} \neq \emptyset \land \{d \in D | (\exists n \in N)(\exists x \in X)[(n, d) \in AcquiresDeviceResource \land (x, d) \in AcquiresDeviceResource \land (n, x) \in HasSuccessor]\} \neq \emptyset$ **then**
    $k++$
  end if
  if $\{x \in X | x \in F\} \neq \emptyset \land \{d \in D | (\exists n \in N)(\exists x \in X)[(n, d) \in ReleasesDeviceResource \land (x, d) \in ReleasesDeviceResource \land (n, x) \in HasSuccessor]\} \neq \emptyset$ **then**
    $k--$
  end if
  $Y = X$
  $R = R \cup X$
  $X = \{a \in A | (\exists n \in N)[(n, a) \in HasSuccessor]\}$
end while

6.2.3.2. Change Propagation between Business Processes and Information Systems

As described previously, IS and BP have mutual dependencies. Thus, changes can propagate between IS and BP. Algorithm 11 focuses on the change propagation between both domains. The data flow and different types of the data play an important role in the change propagation analysis, as discussed in the previous sections. Further, a change to a component-based software system can propagate to its interfaces and provided roles. Thus, this type of change affects BP. The following algorithm utilizes the aforementioned dependencies to analyze the change propagation between IS and BP. It contains the most relevant change propagation rules.

Algorithm 11 Algorithm for the Change Propagation Analysis between the Model of IS Architecture and BP Design and vice versa

Input: model of IS architecture and BP design, seed modifications

1: **Calculate the change propagation from a modified data type to the corresponding data object using Algorithm 12**
2: **Calculate the change propagation from a modified data object to the corresponding data type using Algorithm 13**
3: **Calculate the change propagation from a modified data type to the corresponding system steps (EntryLevelSystemCall) using Algorithm 14**
4: **Calculate the change propagation from a modified EntryLevelSystemCall to the corresponding OperationSignature using Algorithm 15**
5: **Calculate the change propagation from a modified OperationSignature to the corresponding EntryLevelSystemCall using Algorithm 16**
6: **Calculate the change propagation from a modified EntryLevelSystemCall to the corresponding OperationInterface using Algorithm 17**

Each phase of Algorithm 11 is a change propagation rule that is described in more detail as a stand-alone algorithm in the following. Each algorithm is based on the aforementioned sets and their relations.

As described previously, the data flow between IS and BP can cause the propagation of change. Thus, if a data type is affected by a change, it can be important to identify the corresponding data objects. Algorithm 12 presents the change propagation from the affected DataObject $o \in O$ in an instance of DataModel to the corresponding DataType $t \in T$ in RepositoryModel. It calculates the change propagation from IS to BP based on the data flow.

Algorithm 12 Change propagation from DataType to DataObject

Input: $N \subseteq T$ ▷ Seed modifications
Output: $R \subseteq O$ ▷ Result
$R = \{o \in O | (\exists n \in N) [(o, n) \in HasCorrespondence]\}$

The described correspondence can be used in opposite direction to calculate the change propagation. Algorithm 13 presents the change propagation from affected DataObject $o \in O$ to the corresponding DataTypes $t \in T$.

Algorithm 13 Change propagation from DataObject to DataType

Input: $N \subseteq O$ ▷ Seed modifications
Output: $R \subseteq T$ ▷ Result
$R = \{t \in T | (\exists n \in N) [(n, t) \in HasCorrespondence]\}$

As described previously, EntryLevelSystemCalls in UsageModel represent system steps in BP [Hei+17]. An EntryLevelSystemCall can be considered as a call to a system service (i.e., a signature) [BKR09]. This signature can have a set of parameters and a return variable of different types. These types are represented by data types [BKR09]. Thus, changing a data type can result in further changes in the corresponding signatures and system steps. Based on the aforementioned data flow, Algorithm 14 first identifies all OperationSignatures $u \in U$ in an instance of RepositoryModel that are called by the EntryLevelSystemCall $c \in C$ in an instance of UsageModel. Then, it identifies all OperationSignatures u that have at least one input parameter or a return type. If the type of one of the parameters or the return type is the same as the affected DataType $t \in T$, the corresponding EntryLevelSystemCall is potentially affected by the change. This case shows the propagation of a change based on the data flow to the provided roles of the IS system model and then to the BP design model. Summarized, Algorithm 14 calculates the potentially changed EntryLevelSystemCalls based on changed DataTypes.

Algorithm 14 Change propagation from DataType to EntryLevelSystemCall

Input: $N \subseteq T$ ▷ Seed modifications
Output: $R \subseteq C$ ▷ Result
$R = \{c \in C | (\exists n \in N)(\exists u \in U)(\exists p \in P)[(c,u) \in IsCallToSignature \wedge ((u,n) \in ReturnType \vee ((p,n) \in HasDataType \wedge (u,p) \in OperationSignatureHasParameter))]\}$

The following algorithm is also based on the correspondence between a system step in BP (i.e., EntryLevelSystemCall in UsageModel) and a signature in IS, which is called by this system step. System steps may be directly affected by a change, for example due to new or changing requirements. Changing a system step can result in further changes in the called signature. Thus, Algorithm 15 calculates the change propagation from BP to IS. The system step (i.e., an EntryLevelSystemCall) $c \in C$ in an instance of UsageModel can be a call to the OperationSignature $u \in U$ in RepositoryModel. Thus, a change to c can result in a change to u. Algorithm 15 identifies the potentially affected OperationSignatures based on this correspondence.

Algorithm 15 Change propagation from EntryLevelSystemCall to OperationSignature

Input: $N \subseteq C$ ▷ Seed modifications
Output: $R \subseteq U$ ▷ Result
$R = \{u \in U | (\exists n \in N)[(n,u) \in IsCallToSignature]\}$

In contrast to the previous algorithm, the direction of the change propagation in the following algorithm is from IS to BP. Based on the aforementioned correspondence between the system steps and the signatures, Algorithm 16 calculates the change propagation from an affected OperationSignature to the corresponding EntryLevelSystemCalls.

Algorithm 16 Change propagation from OperationSignature to EntryLevelSystemCall

Input: $N \subseteq U$ ▷ Seed modifications
Output: $R \subseteq C$ ▷ Result
$R = \{c \in C | (\exists n \in N)[(c,n) \in IsCallToSignature]\}$

The signature called by a system step is contained in an interface. Thus, changing a system system propagates not only to the called signature, but also to the corresponding interface. Algorithm 17 presents the propagation of a change from a modified EntryLevelSystemCall to the corresponding OperationInterface. For this purpose, the algorithm first identifies all OperationSignatures $u \in U$ in an instance of RepositoryModel that are called by the affected EntryLevelSystemCall $c \in C$. Then, it finds all OperationInterfaces j, to which the OperationSignature $u \in U$ belongs.

Algorithm 17 Change propagation from EntryLevelSystemCall to OperationInterface

Input: $N \subseteq C$ ▷ Seed modifications
Output: $R \subseteq J$ ▷ Result
$R = \{j \in J | (\exists n \in N)(\exists u \in U)[(n, u) \in IsCallToSignature \wedge (u, j) \in BelongToOperationInterface]\}$

6.2.3.3. Change Propagation in Information Systems

On the one hand, the seed modification could be in IS. On the other hand, a change can also propagate from BP to IS. In both cases, considering the change propagation in IS is relevant for the maintainability analysis. In addition to the extension of metamodels of modification in KAMP4IS, Algorithm 18 extends the change propagation algorithm of KAMP4IS, proposed in [Sta15; Ros+15b]. The extension involves the change propagation at the level of OperationSignatures. Additionally, it considers the change propagation in DataTypes, EventTypes, and EventGroups. Each phase of Algorithm 18 represents a change propagation rule.

Algorithm 18 Algorithm of the Change Propagation Analysis in IS Architecture Model

Input: Information system architecture model, seed modifications

1: **Apply modified KAMP4IS (see the original version in [Sta15; Ros+15b]) at the level of signatures**
2: **Calculate the change propagation from a modified DataType to the other DataTypes using Algorithm 19**

3: Calculate the change propagation from a modified data type to the corresponding event types using Algorithm 20
4: Calculate the change propagation from a modified DataType to the corresponding EventGroup using Algorithm 21
5: Calculate the change propagation from a modified Signature (i.e., OperationSignature or EventType) to the corresponding interface (i.e., OperationInterface or EventGroup) using Algorithm 22
6: Calculate the change propagation from a modified Interface (i.e., OperationInterface or EventGroup) to its Signatures (i.e., OperationSignature or EventType) using Algorithm 23
7: Calculate the change propagation from a modified EventGroup to the corresponding Components handling or firing this EventGroup. This case is an extension of the change propagation analysis from an affected OperationInterface to the Components providing or requiring this component, as proposed in [Sta15; Ros+15b]
8: Calculate a generalized version of the inter- and intra-change propagation of KAMP4IS [Sta15; Ros+15b] until no new provided or required role is available

Calculate the change propagation from a modified required role of a component to the provided role of the same component (the extension includes the sink and source roles, as well as the operation signatures and the event types)
Calculate the change propagation from a modified provided role of a component to the required role of another component (the extension includes the sink and source roles, as well as the operation signatures and the event types)

Algorithm 18 contains the most relevant change propagation rules. The rules are described as stand-alone algorithms in the following. Each algorithm is based on the aforementioned sets and their relations.

Section 6.2.1.2 describes how the data types can be modeled using PCM. According to this metamodel, a data type can be composed of further data types or a collection of other data types [BKR09]. Thus, if a data type changes and it is contained in a composite or a collection data type, the change can propagate to the data types containing the changed data type. Algorithm 19 uses this correspondence to identify the potentially affected DataTypes iteratively. It is based on the idea that the DataType t_{t_i} in an instance of RepositoryModel can have the DataType t_{t_j} as the inner declaration. In other words, t_{t_i} can be a CompositeDataType or a CollectionDataType. In general, these relationships can be combined recursively. Thus, a change to t_{t_j} can result in a change to t_{t_i}. Algorithm 19 iteratively identifies the DataTypes that are potentially affected by a change to a DataType. In each iteration, the algorithm assigns the DataTypes to set Y that have the changed DataTypes as inner declaration. Then, set N is defined as the relative complement of R in the union of R and Y. In other words, set N contains a subset of set Y. This subset contains the DataTypes that are not already considered, as sets contain only distinct elements. R is equal to T in the worst case, as the union of all sets N resulted from all iterations and the initial N is a subset of or equal to set T. Thus, the algorithm has to consider all members of set T in a worst-case scenario.

Algorithm 19 Change propagation from DataType to DataType

```
Input: N ⊆ T                                              ▷ Seed modifications
Output: R ⊆ T                                             ▷ Result
R = N
while N ≠ ∅ do
    Y = {t ∈ T|(∃n ∈ N) [(t, n) ∈ HasInnerDeclaration]}
    N = (R ∪ Y) \ R
    R = R ∪ Y
end while
```

Similar to the operation signatures in PCM, the event types can also have a parameter. Each parameter has a specific data type. If a data type changes, the change can propagate to the corresponding parameter and, thus, to the event type. Algorithm 20 describes the change propagation from a modified DataType to the EventTypes based on the aforementioned relationship. The EventType $e \in E$ in an instance of RepositoryModel can have the Parameter $p \in P$. The parameter can have the DataType $t \in T$ as its type. If the DataType t changes, the change can propagate to the EventType e. In this way, the following algorithm identifies the potentially affected EventTypes.

Algorithm 20 Change propagation from DataType to EventType

Input: $N \subseteq T$ ▷ Seed modifications
Output: $R \subseteq E$ ▷ Result
$R = \{e \in E | (\exists n \in N)(\exists p \in P)[(e,p) \in EventTypeHasParameter \land (p,n) \in HasDataType]\}$

As described previously, an event type is contained in an event group. Thus, changing a data type can result in further changes in the event type and the corresponding event group. While the previous algorithm identifies the potentially affected EventTypes based on a modified DataType, Algorithm 21 identifies the corresponding EventGroups. The EventGroup $g \in G$ in an instance of RepositoryModel can contain several EventTypes $e \in E$. As described previously, an EventType can have the DataType $t \in T$ as the type of its Parameter. Thus, a change to the DataType t can result in a change to the corresponding EventGroup g. Algorithm 21 uses this relationship to identify the potentially changed EventGroups due to a change to a DataType.

Algorithm 21 Change propagation from DataType to EventGroup

Input: $N \subseteq T$ ▷ Seed modifications
Output: $R \subseteq G$ ▷ Result
$R = \{g \in G | (\exists n \in N)(\exists p \in P)(\exists e \in E)[(p,n) \in HasDataType \land (e,p) \in EventTypeHasParameter \land (e,g) \in BelongsToEventGroup]\}$

If a signature changes, it is desirable to identify the interface containing this signature. For this purpose, Algorithm 22 presents the change propagation from a modified signature to the corresponding interface. The Interface $i \in I$ (i.e., OperationInterface or EventGroup) in an instance of RepositoryModel can contain several Signatures $s \in S$ (i.e., OperationSignature or EventType). If the Signature s changes, the Interface i has to be identified.

Algorithm 22 Change propagation from Signature (i.e., OperationSignature or EventType) to Interface (i.e., OperationInterface or EventGroup)

Input: $N \subseteq S$ ▷ Seed modifications
Output: $R \subseteq I$ ▷ Result
$R = \{i \in I | (\exists n \in N) [(n, i) \in BelongsToOperationInterface) \vee ((n, i) \in BelongsToEventGroup]\}$

Algorithm 23 shows the change propagation from a modified interface to its signatures. A change can also be coarse-grained at the level of interfaces. In this case, it is important to identify the signatures that belong to this interface. Algorithm 23 selects all Signatures (i.e., OperationSignature or EventType) in a changed Interface (i.e., OperationInterface or EventGroup) as affected.

Algorithm 23 Change propagation from Interface (i.e., OperationInterface or EventGroup) to Signature (i.e., OperationSignatures or EventTypes)

Input: $N \subseteq I$ ▷ Seed modifications
Output: $R \subseteq S$ ▷ Result
$R = \{s \in S | (\exists n \in N) [(s, n) \in BelongsToOperationInterface) \vee ((s, n) \in BelongsToEventGroup)]\}$

The last both phases of Algorithm 18 considers an extension of the existing algorithm of the initially developed KAMP4IS [Sta15; Ros+15b]. In PCM, the OperationInterface and EventGroup metaclasses are a specific types of the Interface metaclass. Further, the OperationSignature and EventType metaclasses are specific types of the Signature metaclass. Additionally, the OperationRequiredRole and SourceRole metaclasses are specific types of the RequiredRole metaclass, while the OperationProvidedRole and SinkRole metaclasses are specific types of the ProvidedRole metaclass. Thus, the generalization of the existing algorithms regarding the inter- and intra-change propagation analysis and the change propagation analysis due to interface dependencies enables considering the events in the change propagation analysis. Phases 7 and 8 of Algorithm 18 describe this generalization. As these algorithms are similar to the original ones described in [Sta15], their description is omitted in this thesis.

It is important to note that the aforementioned algorithms regarding the change propagation rules are defined for PCM and its extensions. In particular, their metaclasses and the relationships between them were used to define the rules. Other metamodels require other change propagation rules. Further, the aforementioned change propagation rules are based on heuristics, which are described for each change propagation rule. Other heuristics are also possible, which can result in other change propagation rules. The choice of the appropriate heuristics for a change propagation analysis approach is a trade-off decision based on different influencing factors. Several influencing factors are described in Section 11.4.2 based on the evaluation results.

Example

In this section, the application of the previously described algorithms to Media Store is described. As the Media Store represents a small software system, some described model elements (e.g., events in the software system) or relationships between model elements (e.g., data objects contained in other data objects) do not occur in the program and in the corresponding models. Therefore, only a subset of algorithms can be applied to the Media Store example. In the following, two seed modifications and their impact based on the previously proposed algorithms are described:

Consider that the `download` method in the `IWebGUI` interface is renamed. If the user selects the `download` method as the seed modification, Algorithm 22 in the domain of IS identifies the affected interface containing the changed method. Thus, the `IWebGUI` interface, which contains the `download` method, is identified as affected by the change. This change propagates to the corresponding system step `download`. Algorithm 16 calculates the change propagation between a method in the domain of IS and a system step in the domain of BP. The change propagation terminates, as there are no change propagation rules for the changed model elements and their relationships to other model elements.

The next example illustrates the change propagation due to the data flow. Consider that a new national identification number is introduced. In contrast to the previous national identification number, which is based on numbers, the new one can contain letters. Thus, the seed modification is the data object `Identity Document`. In the following, the application of some change propagation rules on the modified Media Store example is discussed. Algorithm 13 analyzes the change propagation from the data object to the corresponding data type. As the identity document is the input of the actor step `Enter personally identifiable information`, Algorithm 5 calculates the change propagation to this actor step. Further, Algorithm 14 calculates the propagation of the change from the data type to the system step `Register`. Additionally, the change propagation rules of the initial KAMP4IS [Sta15] calculate further change propagation for example from the affected data type to the corresponding interfaces.

6.3. Change Propagation Analysis for Elements of Context Metamodel

Context elements can cause additional effort during the implementation of a change request. Thus, this section proposes the metamodels for context elements and task types, as well as the algorithm for calculating the context task lists. These metamodels and algorithms enable domain experts to consider the effort of changing context elements during the change propagation analysis in IS and BP and can be adapted or extended to further metamodels and algorithms.

6.3.1. Metamodel of Context Elements

There are several reasons for considering context elements. Context elements in BP may cause additional effort, as they have to be changed due to changes to domain elements. Sometimes it could also be important to know, which context elements are affected by a change. The metamodel of context elements in BP contains the following basic elements: training courses, massages, goods, and organizational units. This metamodel can be extended, if required [Ros+17a].

The metamodel of domain elements is the main artifact during the change propagation analysis. Thus, the metaclasses of context metamodel have to reference the corresponding metaclasses of the metamodel of domain elements. Figure 6.9 illustrates a simplified excerpt from the metamodel of context elements.

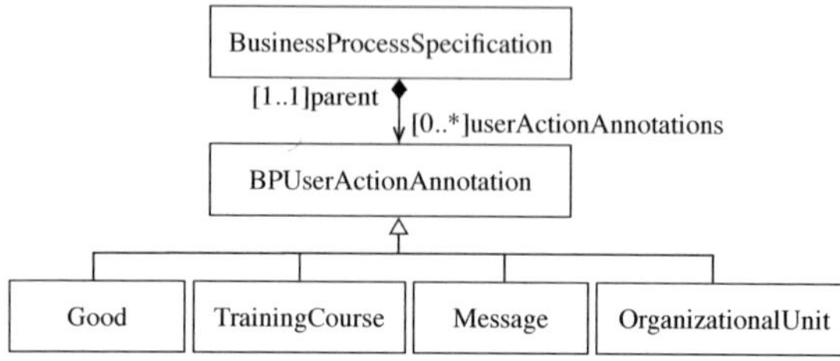

Figure 6.9.: Illustration of context elements of BP - Simplified excerpt

6.3.2. Metamodel of Task Type

No additional task types for the context elements could be identified in BP. However, if new task types are identified, they could be added to this metamodel [HBK18].

6.3.3. Algorithm of Context Task List

Actors can use goods while performing their actor steps. If actor steps change, it could be relevant to consider the goods that are used. Therefore, this algorithm selects the goods that are used by an affected actor step as changed [Ros+17a].

Actor steps can send messages to each other for example due to communication or synchronization [Obj11]. If actor steps change, the change can also affect the sending or receiving messages. Therefore, this algorithm considers messages if the corresponding actor steps change [Ros+17a].

Activities in a BP can be performed by different organizational units. Thus, it could be important to know the organizational units that are affected by a change. This algorithm identifies the affected organizational units [Ros+17a].

If a change affects the actor steps, the involved actors in BP could have to be retrained. For example, changing graphical user interfaces may affect the actors accessing them in their actor steps. Training courses may be necessary in some cases. Therefore, this algorithm suggests training courses if actor steps are affected by a change [Ros+17a].

6.4. Algorithm of Difference Calculation

This algorithm identifies the differences between the following models in BP: *BaseVersion* and *TargetVersion*. In particular, it refines the results of existing generic algorithms to calculate the differences between models. The results of this algorithm are gathered and managed by the algorithm for the derivation of task lists, implemented by the methodology.

Example

Consider that users do not need any registration to access the audio files. This change should only affect the BP design. In other words, the software does not need to be changed. Thus, the actor step `Enter personally identifiable information` and the system step `Register`, as well as the actor step `Enter username and password` and the system step `Login` are removed. The last step of the approach compares the architectures of IS and the design of BP before and after the change. Then, it calculates the differences between both versions. The previously described actor steps and system steps are then the seed modifications for the change propagation algorithms of KAMP4IS and KAMP4BP.

6.5. Conclusions

This chapter proposed an approach to support the co-evolution of IS and BP. For this purpose, the approach uses the mutual dependencies between IS and BP (e.g., the data flow) to analyze the change propagation. As the proposed approach in BP was developed as a further instance of the methodology, it provides further functionality supported by the methodology such as considering users' decisions regarding task list reduction. Further, it allows considering context elements during the co-evolution. Additionally, the before and after comparison is provided by the algorithm of difference calculation. The seed modifications can be defined both in IS at the architecture level or in BP at the level of activities. Based on the seed modifications, the approach identifies the potentially affected model elements of the software architecture in IS and the BP design. Although each of the approaches can also be used in isolation, a holistic view on IS and BP allows a more realistic change propagation analysis. Thus, this contribution answers the *second research question* introduced in Section 1.4.

7. Change Propagation Analysis in Automated Production Systems

Production plants are often designed and implemented for a specific workflow [Fay+15]. Hence, their design and implementation require high initial cost and effort [Lad+13]. Thus, aPS are sustainable systems. They consist of heterogeneous elements from different sub-domains, such as mechanical, electrical/electronic elements and software [Vog+17; Hei+18]. A common standard for the software of the PLC-based aPS is the IEC 61131-3 standard [IEC13]. This standard is used in most aPS systems and is assumed to "be the state of industrial practice in the next 5-10 years" [Vog+15, p. 14]. These heterogeneous elements are from different domains. Thus, one of the main challenges regarding the maintainability is considering the mutual dependencies between these elements. In other words, changing one element from a specific domain can lead to further changes of elements from the same domain or even from other domains. Thus, the involved domains in aPS co-evolve. These factors make the manually effort estimation of changes to aPS very costly and time-consuming [Vog+17; Hei+18; Bus+18c].

In aPS, there are only few approaches addressing the change propagation analysis. Most of these approaches do not provide the automation and a tool support, as described in Chapter 3. Therefore, this chapter presents a model-based approach to automatically analyze the change propagation in aPS. Using metamodels for describing systems in different domains allows a holistic view of the domains involved in aPS. In other words, the approach can analyze the change propagation between heterogeneous elements from the involved domains based on their mutual dependencies. Thus, the approach was designed to answer the *second research question*.

Section 7.1 gives an overview of the approach. The change propagation analysis in mechanical and electrical/electronic elements is presented in Section 7.2. Section 7.3 proposes the change propagation analysis in a PLC software following the IEC 61131-3 standard. Section 7.4 concludes this chapter.

The results of this chapter are based on the results of the Master's thesis of Sandro Koch [Koc17] (i.e., the change propagation analysis in mechanical, electrical/electronic elements of aPS), the Bachelor's thesis of Jannis Rätz [Rät17] (i.e., the change propagation analysis in the control software of aPS), and the practical course [Rät18] (i.e., the change propagation analysis in the behavior of aPS), which were supervised by the author of this dissertation. Further, the results of this chapter regarding the change propagation analysis in mechanical, electrical/electronic elements of aPS and in the control software have been appeared in the papers [Vog+17; Hei+18] and in the paper [Bus+18c], respectively.

7.1. Change Propagation Analysis for Co-evolution of Mechanical, Electrical/Electronic, and Software Elements

To analyze the change propagation in aPS a model-based approach is developed as an instantiation of the methodology proposed in Chapter 5. This approach is mainly composed of two interconnected approaches, namely the Karlsruhe Architectural Maintainability Prediction for automated Production Systems (KAMP4aPS) approach and the Karlsruhe Architectural Maintainability Prediction for International Electrotechnical Commission (KAMP4IEC) approach, which analyzes the change propagation in hardware (i.e., mechanical and electrical/electronic elements) and software of aPS. This section gives an overview of the functionality of this approach.

The idea of the approach is presented in Figure 7.1. It consists of the following steps similar to KAMP4IS and KAMP4BP: i) the preparation phase, ii) the impact phase, and iii) the post-analysis phase [Vog+17; Hei+18; Bus+18c].

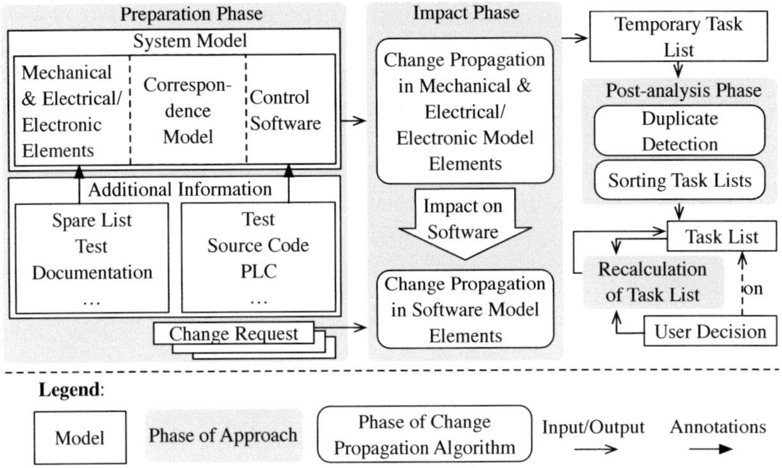

Figure 7.1.: Overview of the KAMP4aPS approach

The input of the approach is prepared in the first phase. It involves the manual preparation of the models for the domain and/or context elements in the plant under study. This phase could be performed by domain experts for example system engineers. The models of domain elements involve models of the hardware (i.e., mechanical, electrical/electronic elements) and the control software. Further, the data flow in the plant has to be modeled. This model allows the change propagation between the hardware and the control software in aPS. The model representing the data flow is referred to as the *correspondence model* in the following [Hei+18]. Although various metamodels allow modeling different elements and aspects of aPS (e.g., software, hardware, or behavior), domain experts can only model elements of a system that have to be analyzed (e.g., only the control software in aPS). In this way, the modeling effort can be reduced. Further, if the effort due to context elements has to be estimated, they can also be considered. Examples of context elements for hardware and software are lists of spare parts, tests, or configuration. The last step in this phase is modeling the seed modifications [Vog+17; Hei+18; Bus+18c]. The impact phase analyzes the change propagation in the domain and context model elements automatically. The PLC software controls the plant. The type of input or output variables in the software corresponds with the electrical signals. The proposed approaches in this section mainly focus on the propagation of changes from hardware (i.e., electrical signals) to software (i.e., types of input and output variables). Thus, if a seed modification affects only the software, the propagation of changes is only analyzed in software. By contrast, changes to hardware can propagate to the software. Thus, if the seed modification is in the hardware, the change propagation in both hardware and software is analyzed. If domain experts modeled context elements, the approach considers them in the change propagation analysis. The output of this phase is a task list consisting of the potentially affected model elements [Vog+17; Hei+18; Bus+18c].

Similar to KAMP4BP, the methodology executes the post-analysis phase of the approach. This phase aims at generating deterministic task lists. For this purpose, it eliminates the duplicates in the task list and sorts the tasks, as described in Section 5.2. If domain experts exclude tasks in the task lists, the methodology considers their decisions. In this case, the methodology iteratively excludes the tasks, which have only excluded causing elements. Reducing task lists based on the decisions of domain experts are discussed in Section 5.2.3 in more detail.

Section 7.2 describes KAMP4aPS for the change propagation analysis in mechanical and electrical/electronic elements. Section 7.3 proposes KAMP4IEC analyzing the change propagation in the control software.

7.2. Change Propagation Analysis in Mechanical and Electrical/ Electronic Elements

This section describes the change propagation analysis in mechanical and electrical/electronic elements. It proposes the instantiation of the methodology to the hardware of aPS to develop the KAMP4aPS approach.

7.2.1. Change Propagation Analysis for Elements of Domain Metamodel

Chapter 5 described the central role of the domain metamodel during the change propagation analysis. This section presents the change propagation analysis based on the domain metamodel of the aPS hardware. In other words, this section describes the instantiation of the mandatory part of the methodology.

7.2.1.1. Metamodel of Domain

This section discusses the metamodel for mechanical and electrical/electronic elements with respect to the three aspects: structure, data flow, and behaviour. Section 7.3.1.1 presents the domain metamodel for the control software.

Structure The structure of mechanical and electrical/electronic elements was metamodeled in a joint work with TUM [Hei+18; Koc17]. Section 2.7 presents the corresponding metamodels in more detail. The developed metamodels are at two different abstraction levels, namely an abstract and a specific metamodel. The abstract metamodel is developed to model a generic plant, while the specific metamodel specializes the abstract metamodel for the xPPU plant. Two variants of KAMP4aPS were developed using both metamodels. Section 11.3 compares the evaluation results of both variants regarding the quality of the change propagation prediction.

Data Flow The propagation of change from mechanical and electrical/electronic elements to the corresponding software can occur using the data flow. In a PLC-controlled plant the control software runs on a PLC [Vog+17]. The sensors and actuators of the plant are connected to the inputs and outputs of the physical interfaces of the PLC. These inputs and outputs correspond to global variables of the PLC software [EMO07]. Figure 7.2 illustrates the connection between the hardware and the corresponding software [Koc17; Hei+18]. This metamodel connects the interfaces of a PLC to the corresponding global variables. In the instance of the hardware metamodel, the cables connected to PLC have to use the same interfaces as PLC. In the instance of the software metamodel, the global variables are used as the main data flow in the PLC software, for example by function blocks. This relationship can be used to analyze the change propagation from the hardware to the PLC software [Koc17; Hei+18].

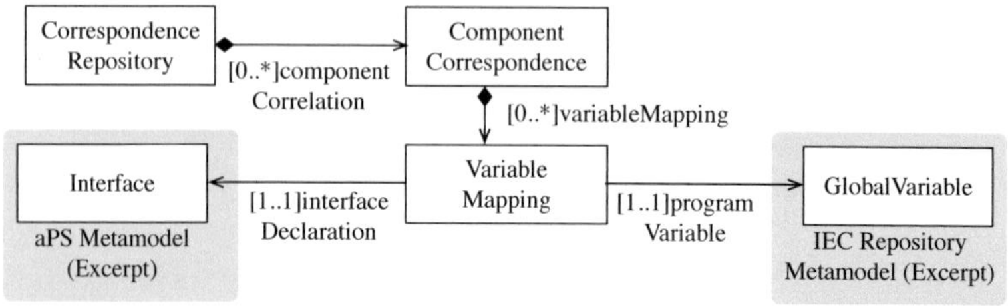

Figure 7.2.: Correspondence model illustrating the relationship between communication interfaces of a PLC and global variables in the control software [Rät18; Koc17; Hei+18]

Behavior Depending on whether a plant is considered as hardware or hardware and software in combination, the behavior of the plant can be considered in different ways: If we only consider the hardware of a plant, the PLC software could determine the behavior of the plant. In this case, the PLC software could be considered as the behavior of the plant. If we consider the plant as both hardware and software, the behavior of the plant can be considered as the interaction between the plant and its operators. The reason for that is that the PLC software waits for the next interaction of the operator, for example pressing the start button [Vog+14a].

This work considers both hardware and software in the process of the change propagation analysis. Thus, the behavior of a plant can be considered as the interaction between the plant and its operators (see Section 7.3.1.1).

Example This paragraph shows the instantiations of the previously described metamodels for the Minimal Plant example introduced in Section 4.1. This section considers only the hardware of a plant. The previous aspects regarding the structure, the behavior, and the data flow for the Minimal Plant example are discussed in the following:

Structure: The abstract and specific metamodels of aPS described in Section 2.7.1 and Section 2.7.2 were used to model the structure of the hardware of the Minimal Plant example. The models show the structure of the same example at two abstraction levels. The structure model of the Minimal Plant example based on the abstract metamodel is illustrated in Section 4.2.1. At a high abstraction level, the conveyor structure can have components for example a frame and a conveyor component. Further, it can have modules such as optical sensor. At a low abstraction level, each specific element such as frame and conveyor belt can be modeled using a specific type of components or modules. An example of that could be the frame and the conveyor belt as two specific types of a component.

Data flow: As described in Section 4.2, the Minimal Plant example consists of an optical sensor in its initial configuration. Using the optical sensor, the presence of a work piece could be recognized. An example of the correspondence model between the hardware and the software is the mapping between the interface for the output of the optical sensor and a global variable as the input of the PLC software.

Behavior: This section considers only the hardware of the plant. Thus, the control software could be used to describe the behavior. An example is the initialization of stack or conveyor. The change propagation in control software is described in Section 7.3.1.1 in more detail.

7.2.1.2. Domain-specific Metamodel of Modification

This metamodel extends the domain-independent metamodel of modification. In other words, it represents the change to the hardware. Its metaclasses reference the metaclasses of the domain metamodel for hardware, which can be affected by a change. In the following, the extension of the metaclasses of the domain-independent metamodel of modification (see Chapter 5) for the abstract metamodel is described. The metaclasses of the domain-independent metamodel of modification were also extended for the specific metamodel. The domain-specific metamodel of modification for the specific metamodel specializes the domain-specific metamodel of modification for the abstract metamodel. For example, the specific metamodel can contain the `Motor` metaclass as a specification of the `Module` metaclass in the abstract metamodel. In this case, the domain-specific metamodel of modification for the specific metamodel contains a metaclass `ModifyMotor` as a specification of the `ModifyModule` metaclass in the domain-specific metamodel of modification for the specific metamodel. While the `ModifyModule` metaclass references the `Module` metaclass, the metaclass `ModifyMotor` references the `Motor` metaclass. As the specification is straightforward, this section presents only the domain-specific metamodel of modification for the abstract metamodel.

- `SeedModifications` in the hardware can be components, modules, interfaces, or structures. Figure 7.3 illustrates the relationship between the `SeedModification` metaclass of the methodology and the corresponding metaclasses for the mechanical and electrical/electronic elements.

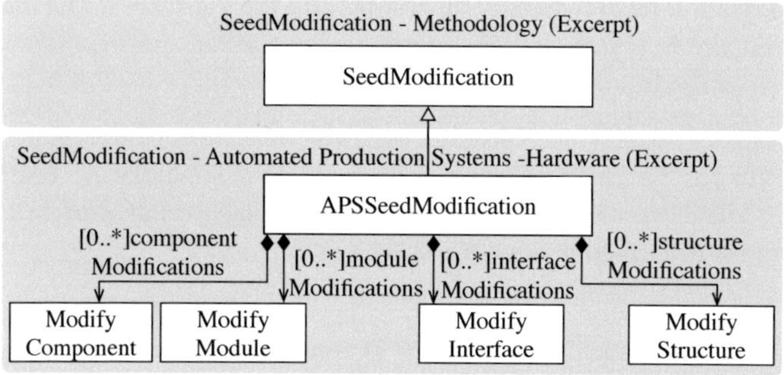

Figure 7.3.: Relationship between the domain-independent `SeedModification` and `SeedModification` in mechanical and electrical/electronic elements

- `Modification`: Components, modules, interfaces, and structures can be potentially changed. Figure 7.4 illustrates the relationship between the `Modification` metaclass of the methodology and the corresponding metaclasses for the mechanical and electrical/electronic elements.

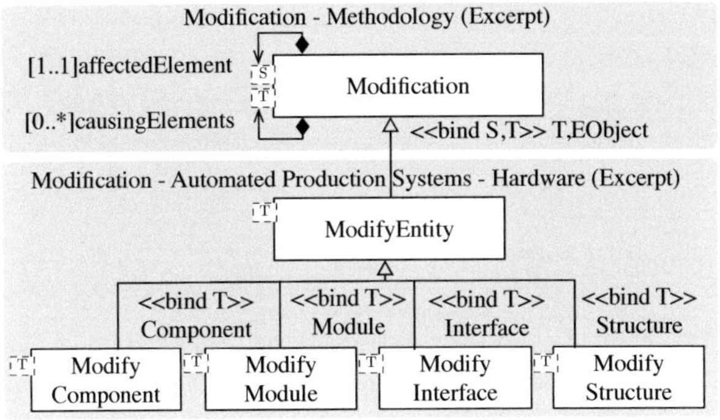

Figure 7.4.: Relationship between the domain-independent `Modification` and `Modification` in mechanical and electrical/electronic elements

- `ChangePropagationStep`: As described previously, a change propagation due to hardware changes can be a common cause for the change propagation in the mechanical and electrical/electronic elements. Figure 7.5 illustrates the relationship between the `ChangePropagationStep` metaclass of the methodology and the corresponding metaclasses for the mechanical and electrical/electronic elements.

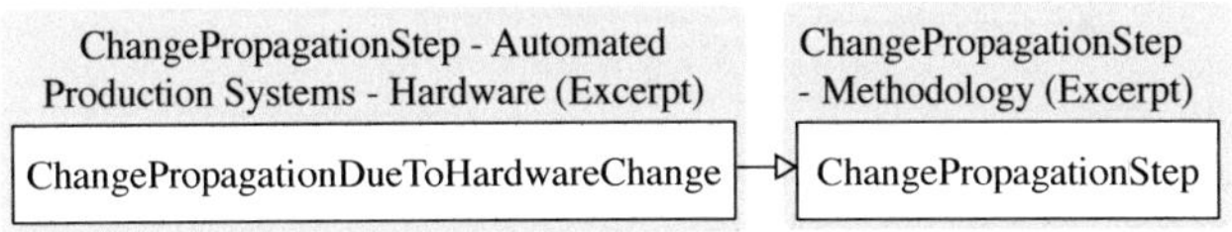

Figure 7.5.: Relationship between the domain-independent `ChangePropagationStep` and `ChangePropagationStep` in mechanical and electrical/electronic elements

- `ModificationRepository` is composed of the metaclasses of the `SeedModification` and `ChangePropagationStep`, as described in Chapter 5. Figure 7.6 illustrates the relationship between the `ModificationRepository` metaclass of the methodology and the corresponding metaclasses for the mechanical and electrical/electronic elements.

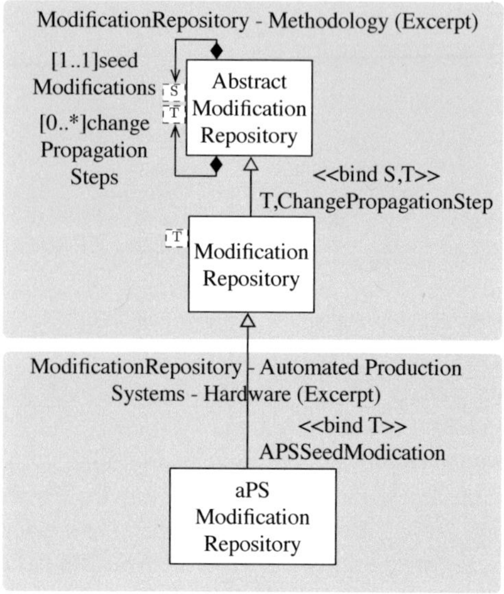

Figure 7.6.: Relationship between the domain-independent `ModificationRepository` and `ModificationRepository` in mechanical and electrical/electronic elements

Example

In the Minimal Plant example, both models of the abstract and specific models can be affected by a change. This depends on the granularity of the created instances of the metamodel. For example, if the model of the Minimal Plant example is created as the instance of the abstract metamodel, the domain expert can select only model elements at a high abstraction levels such as structure or component as changed. In the instance of the abstract metamodel, the conveyor structure, modules such as the conveyor belt, components such as a ramp, or interfaces such as the concrete fixation from motor to frame could be affected by a change. Further, they could be selected by domain experts as seed modifications.

If domain experts use instances of the specific metamodel, they can select the model elements of the instances of the specific metamodel as changed. The metaclasses of the specific metamodel are concrete types of metaclasses of the abstract metamodel. For example, if the model of the Minimal Plant example is an instance of the specific metamodel, domain experts can select the instance of the conveyor or the conveyor belt, instead of the structure or the module.

7.2.1.3. Algorithm of Change Propagation Analysis

There is a need for different change propagation rules depending on the abstraction level of the metamodels representing the domain elements. Despite of the abstraction level of the metamodels, the granularity of the change propagation rules affects the quality of the generated task lists. The change propagation rules are based on the metamodel of the domain elements. Thus, the granularity of the metamodel determines the granularity of the change propagation rules. The more coarse-grained the metamodels of the domain elements, the more coarse-grained the change propagation rules can be specified. However, there could be coarse-grained change propagation rules for a fine-grained metamodel. The following sections describe the change propagation rules for both metamodels at different abstraction levels:

Algorithm of Change Propagation Analysis for the Abstract Metamodel of aPS This algorithm is composed of a set of change propagation rules that are iteratively applied to the model of a plant. These rules can be used for any aPS plant that is modeled based on the abstract metamodel. As the rules are defined for the abstract metamodel, they are coarse granular. In other words, a high number of false positives can occur while analyzing the change propagation in a specific system.

As described previously, the abstract metamodel of the domain elements has a `Component`, an `Interface`, a `Module`, and a `Structure` metaclass. Thus, the change propagation rules are grouped together based on these metaclasses.

To define the change propagation rules, the instances of each metaclass in the abstract metamodel of the domain elements are mapped to a set. In other words, the members of a set represent the instances of a specific type in an instance of the metamodel. The following sets are defined for the change propagation rules:

- $S = \{s_{s_1}, \ldots, s_{s_n}\}$ is a set of all `Structures` in the instances of the abstract metamodel.
- $M = \{m_{m_1}, \ldots, m_{m_n}\}$ is a set of all `Modules` in the instances of the abstract metamodel.
- $C = \{c_{c_1}, \ldots, c_{c_n}\}$ is a set of all `Components` in the instances of the abstract metamodel.
- $I = \{i_{i_1}, \ldots, i_{i_n}\}$ is a set of all `Interfaces` in the instances of the abstract metamodel.

The relationship between metaclasses can be expressed as binary relations over the defined sets:

- The relation $ComponentHasInterface$ is defined over the sets C and I. In this relation, the Component $c \in C$ is associated to the Interface $i \in I$, if the Component c has the Interface i.
- The relation $ComponentIsInStructure$ is defined over the sets C and S. In this relation, the Component $c \in C$ is associated to the Structure $s \in S$, if the Component c is in the Structure s.
- The relation $ComponentIsInModule$ is defined over the sets C and M. In this relation, the Component $c \in C$ is associated to the Module $m \in M$, if the Component c is contained in the Module m.
- The relation $ModuleHasInterface$ is defined over the sets M and I. In this relation, the Module $m \in M$ is associated to the Interface $i \in I$, if the Module m has the Interface i.
- The relation $ModuleIsInStructure$ is defined over the sets M and S. In this relation, the Module $m \in M$ is associated to the Structure $s \in S$, if the Module m is in the Structure s.

- The relation *ModuleIsInModule* is defined over the set M. In this relation, the Module $m_{m_i} \in M$ is associated to the Module $m_{m_j} \in M$, if the Module m_{m_i} is contained in the Module m_{m_j}.

Algorithm 24 iteratively calculates the change propagation in an instance of the abstract metamodel. It starts with the seed modifications. Depending on the type of the seed modifications, the corresponding phases of the algorithm are executed. This results in selecting new model elements as changed. These elements are the new input for Algorithm 24. The algorithm terminates as soon as no new elements are selected in the previous iteration [Hei+18].

Algorithm 24 Algorithm of the Change Propagation Analysis in aPS Architecture Model [Hei+18]

Require: Model of the mechanical and electrical/electronic elements based on the abstract metamodel of structural elements, seed modifications

While there is a new element that is selected as changed

1: Calculate the change propagation from a modified Component using Algorithm 25

2: Calculate the change propagation from a modified Module using Algorithm 26

3: Calculate the change propagation from a modified Interface using Algorithm 27

The rules of Algorithm 24 are described as stand-alone algorithms in the following. Each algorithm is based on the aforementioned sets and their relations.

Changing a Component Algorithm 25 analyzes the change propagation from a modified component to interfaces, structures, and modules. The Component $c \in C$ in an instance of the abstract metamodel can have the Interface $i \in I$. A changc to the Component c can affect the Interface i. The Component c can also be contained in the Module $m \in M$ or in the Structure $s \in S$. Thus, changing the Component c may result in changes in the Module m or in the Structure s. Algorithm 25 identifies the Interfaces, Modules, and Structures that are affected by a change to a component [Hei+18].

Algorithm 25 Change propagation from Component to Module, Interface, and Structure [Hei+18]

Input: $N \subseteq C$ ▷ Seed modifications
Output: $R \subseteq (M \cup I \cup S)$ ▷ Result
$R = \{m \in M | (\exists n \in N) [(n, m) \in ComponentIsInModule]\}$
$R = R \cup \{i \in I | (\exists n \in N) [(n, i) \in ComponentHasInterface]\}$
$R = R \cup \{s \in S | (\exists n \in N) [(n, s) \in ComponentIsInStructure]\}$

Changing a Module Algorithm 26 analyzes the change propagation from an affected module to the corresponding components, interfaces, structures, and modules [Hei+18]. The Module $m_{m_i} \in M$ in an instance of the abstract metamodel can be contained in another Module $m_{m_j} \in M$ or in Structure $s \in S$. If the Module m_{m_i} is changed, the change can propagate to the Module m_{m_j} or to the Structure s. Further, the Module m_{m_i} can also contain the Component $c \in C$ or the Module $m_{m_k} \in M$. In this case, changing the Module m_{m_i} can result in changes to the Component c or the Module m_{m_k}. The module m_{m_i} can also have the Interface $i_{i_l} \in I$. In the case of changing Module m_{m_i}, its interface i_{i_l} can also be changed.

As a change can propagate to all modules contained in the Module m_{m_i} or contain the Module m_{m_i}, the algorithm first identifies all modules iteratively. N is the set of modules, which have to be analyzed in the current iteration of the while loop. In each iteration, the algorithm assigns the modules to set Z. Z contain modules, which contain or are contained in one of the modules of N. To avoid considering a module multiple times, the algorithm assigns only a subset of Z (i.e., $((R \cup Z) \setminus R)$) to N. As set R in the loop contains all potentially affected modules up to the current iteration and sets are duplicate-free, $((R \cup Z) \setminus R)$ contains only modules not yet considered. In the last iteration of the loop, R can contain all modules in the model in the worst case. In other words, R can be equal to M in this case.

Algorithm 26 Change propagation from a Module to Component, Module, Interface, and Structure [Hei+18]

Input: $N \subseteq M$ ▷ Seed modifications
Output: $R \subseteq (M \cup C \cup I \cup S)$ ▷ Result
$R = N$
while $N \neq \emptyset$ **do**
  $Z = \{m \in M | (\exists n \in N)[(n,m) \in ModuleIsInModule \lor (m,n) \in ModuleIsInModule]\}$
  $N = (R \cup Z) \setminus R$
  $R = R \cup Z$
end while
$R = R \cup \{c \in C | (\exists n \in N)[(c,n) \in ComponentIsInModule]\}$
$R = R \cup \{i \in I | (\exists n \in N)[(n,i) \in ModuleHasInterface]\}$
$R = R \cup \{s \in S | (\exists n \in N)[(n,s) \in ModuleIsInStructure]\}$

Changing an Interface Algorithm 27 analyzes the change propagation from a modified interface to components and interfaces. The Module $m \in M$ in an instance of the abstract metamodel can have the Interface $i_{i_j} \in I$. Further, the Component $c \in C$ in the same instance can also have the Interface $i_{i_k} \in I$. Thus, changes in the Interfaces i_{i_j} and i_{i_k} may result in changes in the corresponding Module m and Component c [Hei+18].

Algorithm 27 Change propagation from Interface to Component and Module [Hei+18]

Input: $N \subseteq I$ ▷ Seed modifications
Output: $R \subseteq (C \cup M)$ ▷ Result
$R = \{c \in C | (\exists n \in N)[(c,n) \in ComponentHasInterface]\}$
$R = R \cup \{m \in M | (\exists n \in N)[(m,n) \in ModuleHasInterface]\}$

Changing a Structure A structure can be used to group the components and modules logically. It aims at increasing the abstraction level. An example of a structure in the xPPU is the crane, which is composed of an arm component or a micro switch module [Hei+18]. However, the set of seed modifications should be as small as possible to avoid too many false positives. Choosing a coarse-grained element such as a structure leads to selecting all contained elements as changed, as described in Algorithm 28. This can result in a very large overestimation of the affected model elements (i.e., too many false positives in the task list) and even in changing the whole plant. Although Algorithm 28 provides change propagation rules for an affected structure, selecting coarse-grained elements such as structures should be avoided, if possible. Algorithm 28 selects all contained Components and Modules. The Structure $s \in S$ in an instance of the abstract metamodel can contain the Component $c \in C$ or the Module $m \in M$. Thus, a change in the Structure s can result in changing the Component c or the Module m, which it contains [Hei+18].

Algorithm 28 Change propagation from Structure to Component and Module

Input: $N \subseteq S$ ▷ Seed modifications
Output: $R \subseteq (C \cup M)$ ▷ Result
$R = \{c \in C | (\exists n \in N)\,[(c, n) \in \mathit{ComponentIsInStructure}]\}$
$R = R \cup \{m \in M | (\exists n \in N)\,[(m, n) \in \mathit{ModuleIsInStructure}]\}$

Algorithm of Change Propagation Analysis for the Specific Metamodel of aPS This algorithm is also composed of a set of change propagation rules similar to the change propagation algorithm for the abstract metamodel. These rules were defined for the specific metamodel of the domain elements, as described in Section 2.7.2. The specific metamodel of the domain is created to enable domain experts to create a more fine-grained model of the xPPU plant. In other words, this algorithm cannot be used to analyze the change propagation in any aPS plant. Thus, in order to be able to model an arbitrary plant in a fine-grained way, the specific metamodel of the domain elements has to be extended by the specific elements of the new plant. In general, if the plant is extended by new elements, the specific metamodel of the domain has also to be extended to include the new elements. Additionally, there is a need for new change propagation rules based on the specific metamodel to enable a fine-grained change propagation analysis. This can improve the quality of the change propagation analysis regarding the number of generated false positives. As the specific metamodel of domain elements is very large and heterogeneous, only a subset of all possible rules were defined. If there is sufficient knowledge available about the specific type of component, module, or interface, the change propagation rules can be developed by extending the rules for the abstract metamodel. In general, new change propagation rules for a new specific metamodel can be developed similarly, if required. An example of a specific rule is the change propagation to an interface of a specific component such as a ramp. In this case, the generic algorithms can be extended by a specific change propagation rule to include this knowledge. Another example is changing a sensor. If domain experts know that this change can only propagate to its physical and signal interface, the generic change propagation rule can specialized so that the change propagates only to these interfaces. In other words, the domain-specific knowledge about a specific plant or type of components, modules, interfaces, and structures can improve the results of the change propagation analysis. Thus, the specific rules highly depend on the specific metamodel of the domain elements. As the developed specific rules are a specialization of the generic rules, their descriptions are omitted in this thesis. The results of the change propagation analysis based on both rules are compared in Section 11.3.

Example Some change scenarios were chosen to illustrate the change propagation rules described previously. As the applications of the change propagation algorithms for the abstract metamodel and the specific metamodel are very similar, only the application of the change propagation algorithm for the abstract metamodel is discussed in the following. As the Minimal Plant example is a small example, not all change propagation rules could be covered. Thus, the following change scenario covers a subset of the aforementioned change propagation rules.

So far work pieces are differentiated using their color. In the first change scenario metal work pieces should be detected and sorted out. Thus, the optical sensor should be replaced by an inductive one. As both sensors are modules, Algorithm 26 would be applied in the first iteration of the change propagation analysis. As a module can contain other modules, the analysis identifies all modules that are contained in the affected module. Further, it identifies all modules that contain the affected module. In this example the optical sensor does not contain or is not contained in another module. Therefore, the algorithm does not identify other affected modules. As a module can have interfaces, Algorithm 26 selects the corresponding interfaces of all affected modules. If the sensor has a physical interface for the fixation, Algorithm 26 selects the interface. Additionally, the structures that contain the affected modules are selected. Thus, Algorithm 26 selects the conveyor structure that contains the optical sensor. As a module can contain components, the algorithm selects the contained components in the affected module as changed. Following Algorithm 26, the optical sensor component in the module optical sensor is affected by the change. In summary, the first iteration identifies affected components, interfaces, and structures. In the next iterations,the algorithm of change propagation analysis applies Algorithm 25, Algorithm 27, and Algorithm 28 to the newly affected model elements. If any new model element is identified, all change propagation algorithms for modules, interfaces, components, and structures are applied iteratively [Hei+18].

7.2.2. Change Propagation Analysis for Elements of Context Metamodel

A change to an element in the system's structure or behavior does not only propagate to the other elements in the system's structure and/or behavior, but also to context elements. This results in additional effort during the change implementation. This section proposes the metamodels and algorithms to consider the context elements in the change implementation. Thus, it proposes the instiantiation of the optional part of the methodology to mechanical and electrical/electronic elements of aPS. The following metamodels and algorithms can be extended, if new context elements are identified.

7.2.2.1. Metamodel of Context Elements

This metamodel represents the context elements with respect to the hardware of aPS. In addition to the context elements, this metamodel allows specifying the responsible person roles for conducting a change. In the following, the context elements in the hardware of aPS are described:

- Test Specifications: The main difference between components and modules is that components can be bought by third-party vendors. Thus, they are responsible to test the components. The quality of the components is ensured by the vendors. Therefore, the damaged components are replaced. By contrast, modules are assembled by plant manufacturers using individual components. Thus, plant manufacturers are responsible for the quality of an assembled module. In general, the functionality of the whole plant has to be tested after changing a module or component (referred to in the following as the system test). Figure 7.7 illustrates the test specification [Koc17; Hei+18].

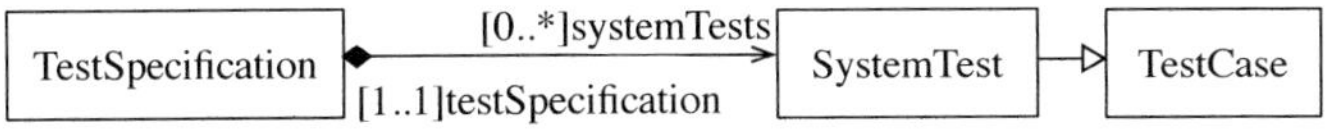

Figure 7.7.: Test specifications for mechanical, electrical/electronic elements [Koc17] based on [Sta15]

- HMI specifications: Changing elements of a plant can lead to changes to the interface between the plant and operators. This can be specialized as the behavior of the plant (see Section 7.3.1.1) or for the sake of simplicity as HMI specification [Koc17; Hei+18].
- Calibration specifications: After changing the elements of the plant, these elements and/or the plant have to be calibrated. If an element needs to be calibrated, calibration specifications can be added to this element [Koc17; Hei+18].
- ECAD specifications: There can also be design descriptions for some elements of the plant. After an element was modified, its design descriptions have to be adapted. This metaclass allows modeling the ECAD design descriptions for elements [Koc17; Hei+18].
- Documentation specifications: There can also be documentation for a plant or its elements. The following types of the documentation can be modeled: maintenance documentation, operator instructions, and training documentation. Training documentation can be either internal or external to the company. Figure 7.8 illustrates the documentation specification [Koc17; Hei+18].
- Stock specifications: There can also be documentation of the elements of a plant that are kept in a warehouse. The information

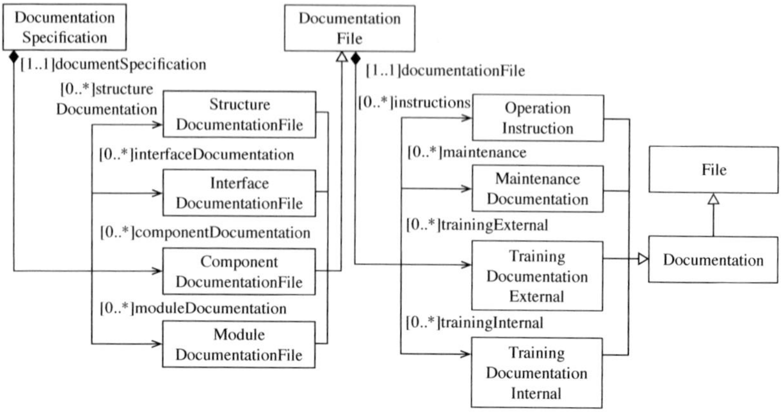

Figure 7.8.: Documentation specifications for mechanical, electrical/electronic elements [Koc17] based on [Sta15]

about the plant elements in the stock can be relevant for the maintainability. However, this metaclass should not be used to specify the entire stock [Koc17; Hei+18].

- Staff specifications: The responsible staff together with their roles for conducting a change can also be documented. Figure 7.9 illustrates an excerpt from the metamodel for specifying the staff. The roles can be extended if required [Koc17; Hei+18].

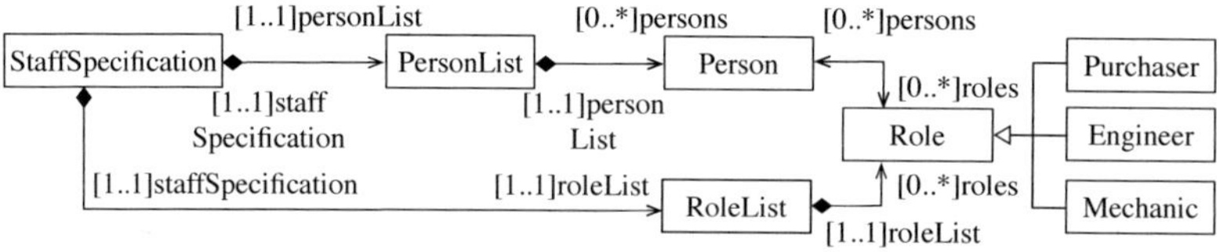

Figure 7.9.: Staff specifications for mechanical, electrical/electronic elements [Koc17] based on [Sta15]

7.2.2.2. Metamodel of Task Type

This metamodel consists of the specific task types in mechanical, electrical/electronic elements of aPS. Examples of these task types are calibration, executing the system test, buying components, or updating the software.

7.2.2.3. Algorithm of Context Task List

If there are context elements for the affected domain elements, they have to be considered. This algorithm allows considering the context elements by a change to a domain element.

As described previously, if elements of a plant are changed, there is a need for system tests. This algorithm considers the system tests after changing the elements of a plant [Koc17; Hei+18].

There could be design descriptions for components, modules, interfaces, or structures of a plant. If these elements are affected by a change, it could be important to consider their design descriptions. Thus, this algorithm extends the task list by the affected design descriptions [Koc17; Hei+18].

The components, modules, interfaces, and structures of a plant can have documentations. Changing these elements may lead to changes in their documentations. This algorithm adds the existing documentations of the affected elements to the task list [Koc17; Hei+18].

There could be back-up elements of the components, modules, interfaces, or structures of a plant in the stock. The documentation of the stock elements can be affected by changing or replacing the elements in a plant. If there are documentations of an affected element in the stock, this algorithm selects these documentations as affected [Koc17; Hei+18].

The interface between the machine and humans can be modeled using the HMI specifications. A change to components, modules, interfaces, or structures of a plant can propagate to the interfaces between the machine and humans. In this case, this algorithm adds the HMI specifications to the task list [Koc17; Hei+18].

Changing elements of a plant can result in the calibration of these elements and/or the whole plant. Calibrations for the elements of a plant can be modeled, if required. This algorithm considers the calibration specifications by changes to a plant and/or its elements [Koc17; Hei+18].

Example

An example of context elements in the Minimal Plant example is the calibration information. If model elements are annotated with this information, the task list contains tasks regarding new calibration of the corresponding plant.

7.2.3. Algorithm of Difference Calculation

This algorithm mainly calculates the differences in the structure of the system models by means of model difference calculation between *BaseVersion* and *TargetVersion.* It identifies the changes to domain elements such as deleted elements from the system model or added elements to the system model by refining the results of existing generic algorithms for difference calculation. The algorithm for the derivation of task lists of the methodology gathers and manages the results of this algorithm.

Example

In the aforementioned change scenario in Section 7.2.1.3, the optical sensor was replaced by an inductive sensor. There are different ways to model the change request in this scenario. The first way is to select the optical sensor as changed. This is already described in Section 7.2.1.3. The second way is to model the system after the change. In other words, the system needs to be modeled with an inductive sensor instead of the optical sensor. The approach can identify the changes between both models. Examples of changes in the resulting task list could be removing the optical sensor and its fixation and adding the new inductive sensor and its fixation.

7.3. Change Propagation Analysis in Control Software

As discussed previously, a PLC-based aPS plant consists of mechanical and electrical/electronic elements, as well as control software [Vog+17]. The control software runs on a PLC. A common standard for the control software is the IEC 61131-3 standard [Vog+17]. This section describes KAMP4IEC as an instantiation of the methodology to the control software following the IEC 61131-3 standard. This allows an automatic change propagation in the control software. Combining KAMP4aPS and KAMP4IEC enables the change propagation from the hardware to the software of aPS.

7.3.1. Change Propagation Analysis for Elements of Domain Metamodel

This section describes the metamodel of the domain elements in a control software, which are programmed according to the standard IEC 61131-1. Further, it presents the instantiation of the mandatory part of the methodology to develop a basis variant of KAMP4IEC.

7.3.1.1. Metamodel of Domain

To automatically analyze the change propagation in a control software, this domain as a sub-domain of aPS needs to be metamodeled. The following sections present the metamodel of the domain elements with respect to the three aspects: structure, data flow, and behavior.

Structure As described in Section 3.7, there are already metamodels of IEC 61131-1. However, most metamodels are very detailed. Consequently, the modeling effort can be too high. Further, some metamodels cover both the structure and the dynamic behavior of the code. KAMP4IEC presents an approach to static change propagation analysis. Thus, it is sufficient, if the underlying metamodel presents only the structure of the control software. To reduce the complexity and modeling overhead of a control software, this section presents a reduced metamodel with focus on the relevant elements to allow the change propagation analysis based on the system's structure. In other words, it presents a metamodel for the domain elements of a control software following the IEC 61131-1 standard at a higher abstraction level. This metamodel can be divided into two further metamodels: i) The **repository** metamodel, which is composed of the software elements that have to be defined only once. After they were defined, other elements of an IEC software can reference these elements. ii) The **system** metamodel describes the composition of an IEC software based on the elements defined in the repository metamodel. In other words, a system metamodel references the metaclasses defined in the repository metamodel. Both metamodels are described in more detail in the following sections [Rät17; Bus+18c]:

Repository Metamodel This metamodel defines all elements in a PLC software following the IEC 61131-1 standard that can be referenced in the System metamodel. These elements could be for example `GlobalVariables`, `FunctionBlocks` and their `Methods` and `Properties`, `Interfaces` and their `AbstractMethods` and `AbstractProperties`, as well as `Functions`. The Repository metaclass contains the metaclasses `GlobalVariables`, `Functions`, `FunctionBlocks`, and `Interfaces`. Figure 7.10 illustrates an excerpt from the Repository metamodel. In the following, the metamodels and their relationships are described in more detail [Rät17; Bus+18c].

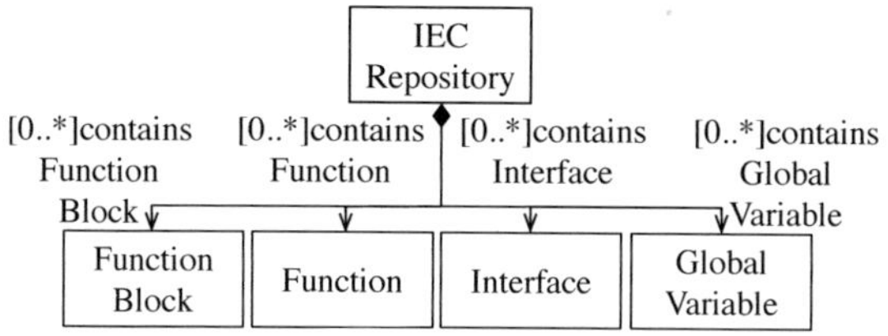

Figure 7.10.: Metamodel of IECRepository - An excerpt

An `Interface` can have `AbstractMethods` and `AbstractProperties`. It can also extend further `Interfaces`. Figure 7.11 illustrates an excerpt from the

Repository metamodel representing the relationship between the `Interface` metaclass and other metaclasses [Rät17; Bus+18c].

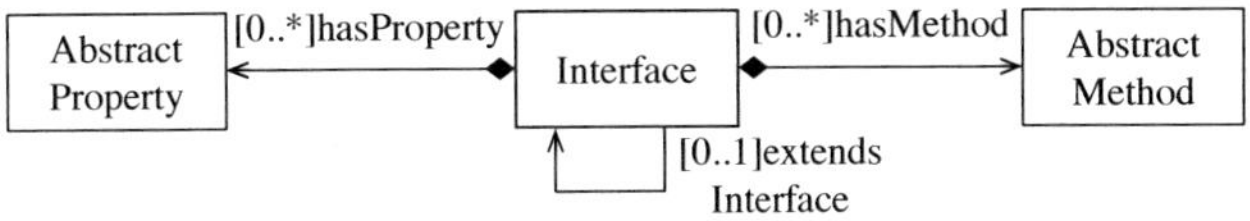

Figure 7.11.: Metamodel of IECRepository involving `Interface` - An excerpt

`FunctionBlocks` can read or write `GlobalVariables`. Further, they can have `Methods` and `Properties`. `FunctionBlocks` can implement `Interfaces` or use objects of them (i.e., instantiating `Interfaces`). Similar to `Interfaces`, `FunctionBlocks` may extend other `FunctionBlocks` or use their instances (i.e., instantiating `FunctionBlocks`). Additionally, `FunctionBlocks` can call `Functions` [Rät17; Bus+18c].

`Methods` can implement `AbstractMethods` and instantiate `FunctionBlocks`. `Methods` can read or write `GlobalVariables` and `Properties` of `FunctionBlocks`. They can also call `Methods` and `Functions` [Rät17; Bus+18c].

`Functions` can call other `Functions`. `FunctionBlocks` can be instantiated within a `Function` [Rät17; Bus+18c].

`Properties` can implement `AbstractProperties`. The type of a `Property` can be a `FunctionBlock` or an `Interface` [Rät17; Bus+18c].

Figure 7.12 illustrates a simplified excerpt from the Repository metamodel, which shows the relationship between a `FunctionBlock` metaclass and other metaclasses [Rät17; Bus+18c].

System Metamodell The system metamodel consists of a `Configuration`, which is composed of a `Program`. A `Program` can define, read, or write `GlobalVariables`. Further, it can instantiate `Interfaces` and `FunctionBlocks`. A `Program` can call `Methods` and `Functions`. It can also read or write `Properties`. In other words, the `Program` metaclass references the metaclasses of the Repository metamodel. In this way, the control software can be modeled using the System metamodel [Rät17; Bus+18c].

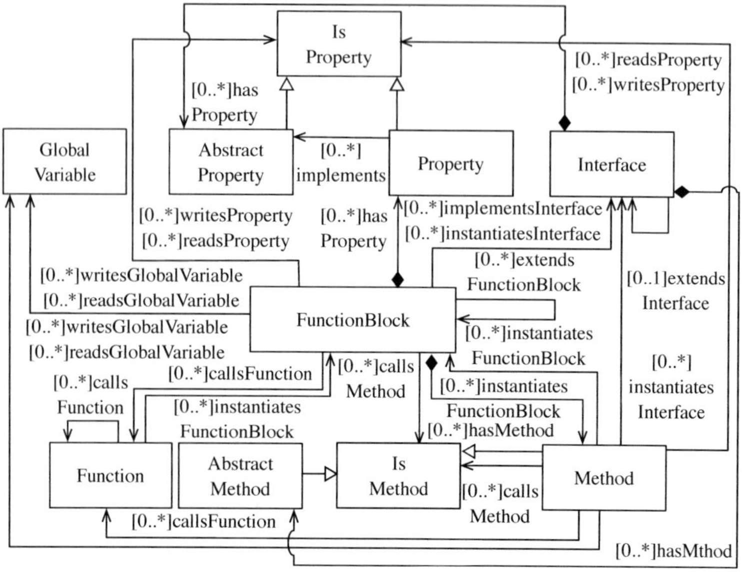

Figure 7.12.: Metamodel of IECRepository involving `FunctionBlock` - An excerpt [Rät17]

Data Flow Section 7.2.1.1 proposed the correspondence metamodel, which allows the change propagation from mechanical and electrical/electronic elements to the PLC software. This change affects the `GlobalVariables`, which serve as seed modifications for further change propagation in the PLC software [Koc17; Hei+18; Rät17; Rät18; Bus+18c].

After a change propagated to `GlobalVariables`, `FunctionBlocks` or `Methods`, reading or writing these `GlobalVariables` can also be affected. The type of `GlobalVariables` and `Properties` can be `FunctionBlocks` or `Interfaces`. Further, the return parameter of `Functions` and `Methods` can be `FunctionBlocks` or `Interfaces` [Rät17]. The metaclass `DerivedType` in Figure 7.13 illustrates the aforementioned data dependencies in a PLC software.

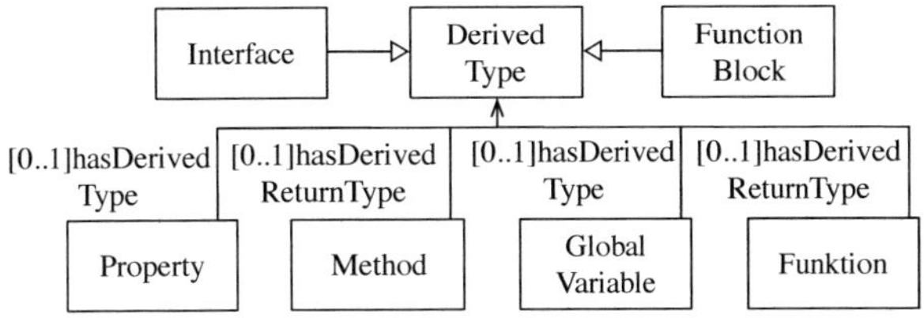

Figure 7.13.: Metamodel of IECRepository involving `DerivedType` - An excerpt [Rät17]

Behavior As described in Section 7.2.1.1, the behavior of a plant can be considered as the interaction between operators and the plant. In this case, a change to the plant can affect the interaction to its operators. For this purpose, this interaction has to be metamodeled. At a high abstraction level, the interaction between operators and the plant can be metamodeled as an ordered sequence of actor steps and system steps. Similar to BP, the actor steps can only be performed by operators, while the system steps can only performed by the plant. A system step is usually controlled by the PLC software. Each system step corresponds to a mode, in which the plant operates automatically [Vog+14a]. Further, the metamodel supports loops or conditions in the behavior of the plant [Rät18]. Figure 7.14 shows an excerpt from the behavior metamodel of the plant.

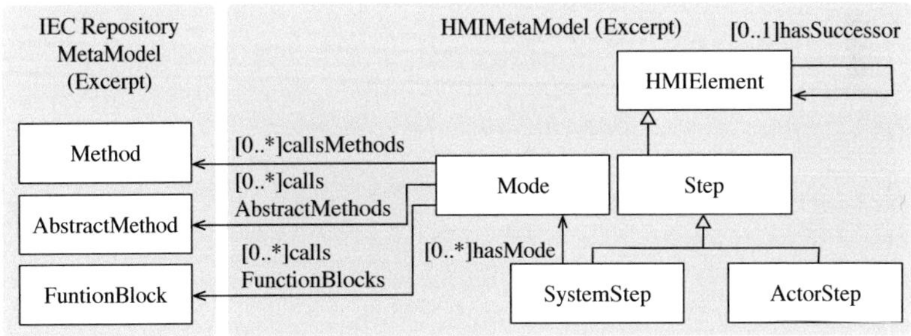

Figure 7.14.: Metamodel of the HMI involving `ActorStep` and `SystemStep` - An Excerpt [Rät18]

Example This section shows the instantiations of the previously described metamodels regarding the structure, the data flow, and the behavior for the Minimal Plant example introduced in Section 4.1. This section considers only the software of a plant.

Structure: The repository and the system metamodels described in Section 7.3.1.1 can be used to model the structure of the software of the Minimal Plant example. This includes a repository model, which contains IEC model elements such as interfaces or function blocks to control the conveyor. Further, it has global variables, for example to read outputs of the optical sensor. The system model contains a configuration, which includes a program. A program describes how an IEC program is composed of the model elements defined in the repository model (e.g., the global variables, which values are read or written by the program).

Data flow: In the IEC program of the Minimal Plant example, the global variables are examples of the data flow. The data flow includes also interfaces and function blocks, as they can be used as a specific type by other model elements such as properties and functions.

Behavior: As mentioned previously, the behavior of a plant could be considered as the interaction of the plant and its operators. For this purpose, the operators of the plant can press different buttons on the operation panel. This results in executing other modes of the plant. An example of the operator interaction with the plant is pressing the start button. Pressing the start button causes the plant to change to the initialization and then in the automatic mode [Vog+14a].

7.3.1.2. Domain-specific Metamodel of Modification

This section describes the application of the domain-independent metamodel of modification introduced in Chapter 5 to the aforementioned metamodel of the PLC software. This allows selecting the changed elements in instances of the aforementioned metamodels.

- `SeedModification`: The initial change can be divided into the changes in the IEC software model and in the HMI model. The initial changes in the model of the IEC software can be i) `GlobalVariable`, ii) `Interface`, iii) `AbstractMethod`, iv)

AbstractProperty, v) FunctionBlock, vi) Method, vii) Property, viii) Function, or ix) Program. Figure 7.15 illustrates the relationship between the domain-independent SeedModification and the specific SeedModifications in the PLC software.

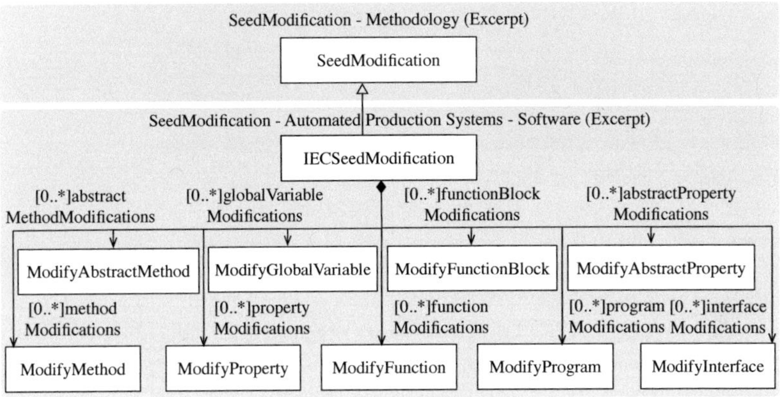

Figure 7.15.: Relationship between the domain-independent SeedModification and the specific SeedModifications in an IEC software [Rät17]

The initial change in an HMI model can be changing an actor step or a system step. Figure 7.16 illustrates the relationship between the domain-independent SeedModification metaclass and the specific SeedModifications regarding the HMI.

- Modification: Similar to the SeedModification, the potentially affected elements can be grouped into two categories - specific Modifications in the IEC software and specific Modifications regarding the HMI. In the IEC software i) GlobalVariable, ii) Interface, iii) AbstractMethod, iv) AbstractProperty, v) FunctionBlock, vi) Method, vii) Property, viii) Function, ix) Program, or x) Configuration can be affected by a change. Figure 7.17 illustrates the relationship between the domain-independent Modification metaclass and the specific Modifications in a PLC software.

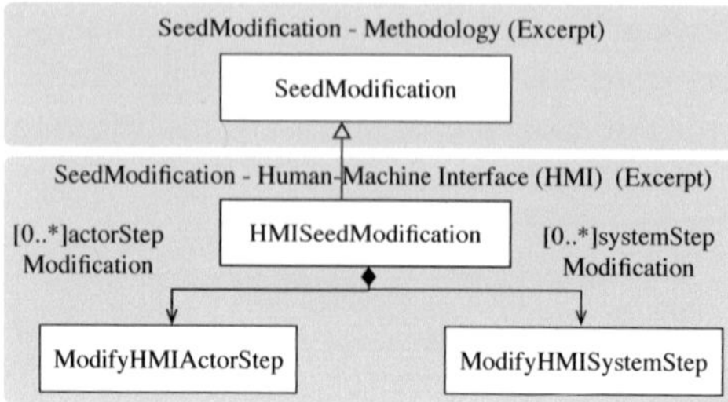

Figure 7.16.: Relationship between the domain-independent `SeedModification` and the specific `SeedModifications` in an HMI [Rät18]

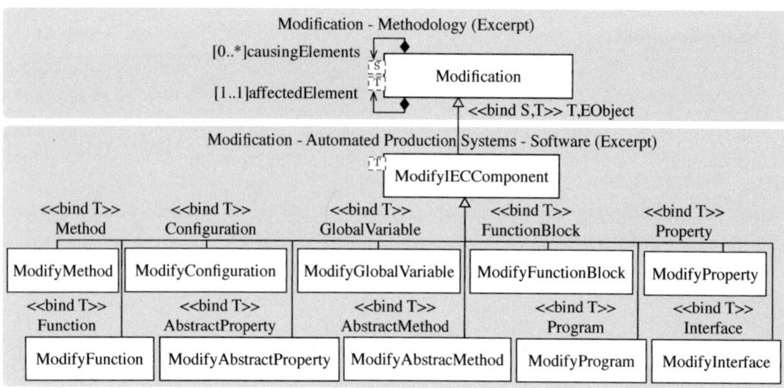

Figure 7.17.: Relationship between the domain-independent `Modification` and the `Modification` of elements in an IEC software [Rät17]

A change can also affect the actor steps and system steps of the HMI. Thus, Figure 7.18 shows the relationship between the domain-independent `Modification` metaclass and the specific `Modifications` regarding the HMI.

- `ChangePropagationStep`: One of the main causes of the change propagation in an IEC software is the data flow. Figure 7.19 illustrates the relationship between the domain-independent

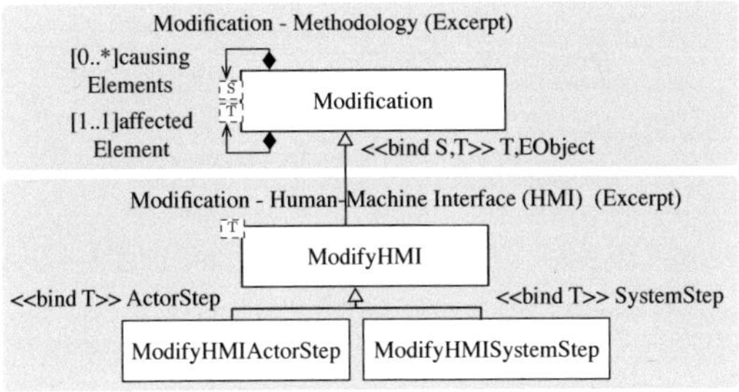

Figure 7.18.: Relationship between the domain-independent `Modification` and the specific `Modifications` in an HMI [Rät18]

`ChangePropagationStep` metaclass and the specific `ChangePropagationSteps` in a PLC software.

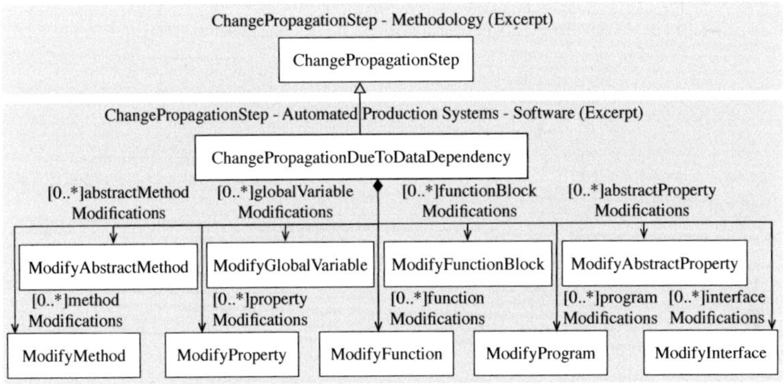

Figure 7.19.: Relationship between the domain-independent `ChangePropagationStep` and `ChangePropagationSteps` in an IEC software [Rät17]

Regardless of the mechanical, electrical/electronic elements or the control software, a change to a plant can affect the HMI. Figure 7.20 illustrates the relationship between the domain-independent `ChangePropagationStep` metaclass and the specific `ChangePropagationSteps` regarding the HMI.

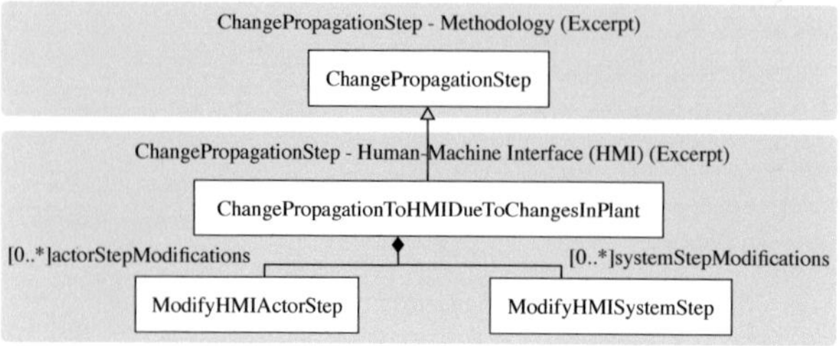

Figure 7.20.: Relationship between the domain-independent `ChangePropagation-Step` and the specific `ChangePropagationSteps` in an HMI [Rät18]

- `ModificationRepository` consists of a `SeedModification` metaclass and `ChangePropagationSteps`, as described in Chapter 5. Figure 7.21 illustrates the relationship between the domain-independent `ModificationRepository` metaclass and the specific `ModificationRepository` in an IEC program.

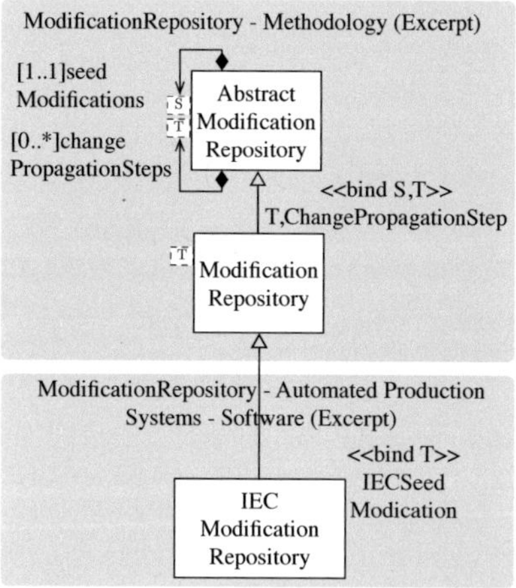

Figure 7.21.: Relationship between the domain-independent `Modification-Repository` and `ModificationRepository` in an IEC software [Rät17]

7.3.1.3. Algorithm of Change Propagation Analysis

To analyze the change propagation, two algorithms were developed each for the model of the PLC software and the HMI. The change propagation algorithms are composed of change propagation rules. The change propagation rules are based on the aforementioned metamodels in Section 7.3.1.1 for a variant of the IEC 61131-1 standard: i) the Repository metamodel, ii) the System metamodel, and iii) the HMI metamodel. To define the change propagation rules the instances of each metaclass of these metamodels have to be mapped to a set. Further, all elements of the instances of these metamodels are mapped to set $M = \{m_{m_1}, ..., m_{m_n}\}$. The relation $References$ is defined over the set M. In this relation, an instance of a metaclass in the Repository, the System, or the HMI metamodel $m_{m_i} \in M$ is associated to another instance $m_{m_j} \in M$, where $m_i, m_j \in N$ and $0 < m_i, m_j < m_n$, if the instance $m_{m_i} \in M$ references the instance $m_{m_j} \in M$. In the following, the instances of each metaclass of the Repository, the System, and the HMI metamodel are mapped to a separate set. In other words, the sets contain the concrete instances of each metaclass. The following sets are the instances of the metaclasses, which are relevant for the change propagation rules:

- $V = \{v_{v_1}, ..., v_{v_n}\}$ is the set of all `GlobalVariables` in the instances of the Repository metamodel.
- $F = \{f_{f_1}, ..., f_{f_n}\}$ is the set of all `Functions` in the instances of the Repository metamodel.
- $B = \{b_{b_1}, ..., b_{b_n}\}$ is the set of all `FunctionBlocks` in the instances of the Repository metamodel.
- $T = \{t_{t_1}, ..., t_{t_n}\}$ is the set of all `Methods` in the instances of the Repository metamodel.
- $P = \{p_{p_1}, ..., p_{p_n}\}$ is the set of all `Properties` in the instances of the Repository metamodel.
- $A = \{a_{a_1}, ..., a_{a_n}\}$ is the set of all `AbstractMethods` in the instances of the Repository metamodel.
- $S = \{s_{s_1}, ..., s_{s_n}\}$ is the set of all `AbstractProperties` in the instances of the Repository metamodel.

- $E = \{e_{e_1}, \ldots, e_{e_n}\}$ is the set of all `Interfaces` in the instances of the Repository metamodel.
- $U = \{u_{u_1}, \ldots, u_{u_n}\}$ is the set of all `Programs` in the instances of the System metamodel.
- $C = \{c_{c_1}, \ldots, c_{c_n}\}$ is the set of all `Configurations` in the instances of the System metamodel.
- $O = \{o_{o_1}, \ldots, o_{o_n}\}$ is the set of all `ActorSteps` in the instances of the HMI metamodel.
- $D = \{d_{d_1}, \ldots, d_{d_n}\}$ is the set of all `SystemSteps` in the instances of the HMI metamodel.
- $Q = \{q_{q_1}, \ldots, q_{q_n}\}$ is the set of all `Modes` in the instances of the HMI metamodel.
- $W = \{w_{w_1}, \ldots, w_{w_n}\}$ is the set of all `HMIElements` in the instances of the HMI metamodel. Thus, it contains for example all actor steps, system steps, loops, or branches.

To better describe the relations over the aforementioned sets and the algorithm of change propagation analysis, super sets of the aforementioned sets are defined as follows: $G = U \cup B \cup T$ is the union set representing the instances of `Programs`, `FunctionBlocks`, and `Methods`. $H = U \cup B \cup T \cup C$ is the union set representing the instances of `Programs`, `FunctionBlocks`, `Methods`, and `Configurations`. $I = U \cup B \cup T \cup F$ is the union set representing the instances of `Programs`, `FunctionBlocks`, `Methods`, and `Functions`. $J = U \cup B \cup T \cup P$ is the union set representing the instances of `Programs`, `FunctionBlocks`, `Methods`, and `Properties`. $K = U \cup B \cup T \cup F \cup A \cup P \cup S \cup V$ is the union set representing the instances of `Programs`, `FunctionBlocks`, `Methods`, `Functions`, `AbstractMethods`, `Properties`, `AbstractProperties`, and `GlobalVariables`. $L = U \cup B \cup T \cup F \cup A \cup P \cup S \cup V \cup E$ is the union set representing the instances of `Programs`, `FunctionBlocks`, `Methods`, `Functions`, `AbstractMethods`, `Properties`, `AbstractProperties`, `GlobalVariables`, and `Interfaces`.

The relationship between metaclasses of different metamodels can be expressed as binary relations over these sets. The following relations refine the aforementioned $References$ relation:

$InterfaceExtendsInterface \subseteq E \times E$, $FunctionBlockInstantiatesInterface \subseteq B \times E$, $ProgramInstantiatesInterface \subseteq U \times E$, $ProgramReadsAbstractProperty \subseteq U \times S$, $MethodCallsFunction \subseteq T \times F$, $FunctionBlockImplementsInterface \subseteq B \times E$, $MethodInstantiatesInterface \subseteq T \times E$, $GlobalVariableHasInterfaceAsType \subseteq V \times E$, $CallsMethod \subseteq Q \times T$, $FunctionHasInterfaceAsReturnType \subseteq F \times E$, $FunctionCallsFunction \subseteq F \times F$, $FunctionHasFunctionBlockAsReturnType \subseteq F \times B$, $ProgramCallsFunction \subseteq U \times F$, $MethodHasInterfaceAsReturnType \subseteq T \times E$, $MethodHasFunctionBlockAsReturnType \subseteq T \times B$, $HasMode \subseteq D \times Q$, $InterfaceHasMethod \subseteq E \times T$, $CallFunctionBlockConstructor \subseteq F \times B$, $MethodInstantiatesFunctionBlock \subseteq T \times B$, $ProgramCallsMethod \subseteq U \times T$, $AbstractMethodHasInterfaceAsReturnType \subseteq A \times E$, $CallsFunctionBlock \subseteq Q \times B$, $FunctionBlockCallsMethod \subseteq B \times T$, $MethodReadsGlobalVariable \subseteq T \times V$, $MethodReadsProperty \subseteq T \times P$, $PropertyHasInterfaceAsType \subseteq P \times E$, $CallsAbstractMethod \subseteq Q \times A$, $PropertyHasFunctionBlockAsType \subseteq P \times B$, $AbstractPropertyHasInterfaceAsType \subseteq S \times E$, $MethodWritesProperty \subseteq T \times P$, $AbstractPropertyHasFunctionBlockAsType \subseteq S \times B$, $MethodCallsMethod \subseteq T \times T$, $ProgramInstantiatesFunctionBlock \subseteq U \times B$, $MethodReadsAbstractProperty \subseteq T \times S$, $FunctionBlockExtendsFunctionBlock \subseteq B \times B$, $FunctionBlockCallsFunction \subseteq B \times F$, $MethodWritesGlobalVariable \subseteq T \times V$, $ProgramReadsGlobalVariable \subseteq U \times V$, $ProgramWritesGlobalVariable \subseteq U \times V$, $ProgramDeclaresGlobalVariable \subseteq U \times V$, $ConfigurationDeclaresGlobalVariable \subseteq C \times V$, $InterfaceHasAbstractMethod \subseteq E \times A$, $ProgramCallsAbstractMethod \subseteq U \times A$, $FunctionBlockCallsAbstractMethod \subseteq B \times A$, $MethodImplementsAbstractMethod \subseteq T \times A$, $MethodCallsAbstractMethod \subseteq T \times A$, $InterfaceHasAbstractProperty \subseteq E \times S$, $ConfigurationInstantiatesProgram \subseteq C \times U$, $GlobalVariableHasFunctionBlockAsType \subseteq V \times B$, $ProgramWritesProperty \subseteq U \times P$, $ProgramWritesAbstractProperty \subseteq U \times S$, $FunctionBlockReadsProperty \subseteq B \times P$, $FunctionBlockWritesProperty \subseteq B \times P$, $FunctionBlockReadsAbstractProperty \subseteq B \times S$, $FunctionBlockWritesAbstractProperty \subseteq B \times S$, $MethodWritesAbstractProperty \subseteq T \times S$, $PropertyImplementsAbstractProperty \subseteq P \times S$, $ProgramReadsProperty \subseteq U \times P$, $FunctionBlockInstantiatesFunctionBlock \subseteq B \times B$, and $HasSuccessor \subseteq W \times W$.

The aforementioned relations are sub-relations of the $References$ relation. A more detailed description of these relations is given in Appendix A.1.

Based on the aforementioned sets and the binary relations, Algorithm 29 analyzes the change propagation in a PLC software. Algorithm 29 identifies set X for each seed modification $n \in N$. X is composed of all model elements of the instances of the Repository and System metamodel, which are affected by a change to one of the seed modifications $n \in N$. The elements $n \in N$ and $x \in X$ are in one of the aforementioned sub-relations of the relation $References$. The predicate of this set defines for which types of n and x, if $n\, References\, x$ or $x\, References\, n$, the change propagates from n to x. Algorithm 29 adds the model elements x to the set of the results R. In other words, R is the set of potentially changed model elements.

A change to the instances of the metaclasses `FunctionBlock` or `Interface` most probably affects several elements in a PLC software. If `FunctionBlocks` or `Interfaces` are affected by a change, Algorithm 29 additionally adds these model elements to the set of the seed modifications (i.e., N). If the seed modification is an instance of the other metaclasses in the PLC software, Algorithm 29 aborts the change propagation after one iteration. This heuristic aims at avoiding generating too many false positives by the algorithm. In this way, Algorithm 29 calculates the change propagation until the set of seed modifications is empty.

After the change propagation in the structure of a PLC software was analyzed, the change propagation to the HMI has to be considered. For this reason, the results of the previous steps have to be analyzed. If model elements are `FunctionBlocks`, `Methods`, or `AbstractMethods`, the change can propagate to a specific mode of the plant. Changing the mode can affect the corresponding system steps. Further, a change can propagate from an affected system step to the successor actor steps. An actor step can also have further actor steps as successor. Changing an actor step can lead to further changes in the successor actor steps.

Similar to the model of BP design, other model elements such as branches and loops can exist in the model of the HMI. Branches and loops can also be nested in each other. Algorithm 29 presents only the basis variant of the change propagation rules without such elements to illustrate the idea of the rules.

Algorithm 29 Change Propagation in IEC Architecture Model [Bus+18c]

Input: $N \subseteq M$ ▷ Seed modifications
Output: $R \subseteq M$ ▷ Result
$R = N$
while $N \neq \emptyset$ **do**
  $X = \{m \in M | (\exists n \in N)[(m, n) \in References \wedge ((n \in V \wedge m \in H) \vee (n \in F \wedge m \in I) \vee (n \in B \wedge m \in K) \vee (n \in E \wedge m \in L) \vee ((n \in A \vee n \in T \vee n \in P) \wedge m \in G) \vee (n \in S \wedge m \in J))]\}$
  $N = (R \cup \{x \in X | x \in B \vee x \in E\}) \setminus R$
  $R = R \cup X$
end while
$Y = \{q \in Q | (\exists n \in (R \cap (B \cup A \cup T)))[(q, n) \in References]\}$
$R = R \cup \{d \in D | (\exists y \in Y)[(d, y) \in HasMode]\}$
$N = R$
$R = R \cup \{o \in O | (\exists n \in (N \cap (O \cup D)))[(n, o) \in HasSuccessor]\}$

Example

Consider that a global variable that represents the output of the optical sensor in the Minimal Plant example is changed due to replacing the optical sensor with an inductive one, as described in Section 7.2.1.3. As the application of Algorithm 29 involves the application of several similar change propagation rules, the application of only a subset of rules to the changed global variable is discussed in the following. The change to the global variable can propagate to the corresponding method regarding transporting the work pieces to the ramp by the conveyor, as this method reads the output of the sensor. Further, KAMP4IEC selects the configuration that contains the affected model elements such as the global variable and the method as changed.

7.3.2. Change Propagation Analysis for Elements of Context Metamodel

Similar to IS, BP, and the hardware of aPS, context elements for the PLC software can cause a higher effort during the implementation of a change request. Considering context elements such as source code files or test cases helps to estimate the change effort more precisely. Such information can be provided by domain experts. The following sections discuss the metamodels and algorithms for considering the effort caused by changing context elements.

7.3.2.1. Metamodel of Context Elements

This metamodel enables domain experts to model the context elements. Examples of context elements in a PLC software are discussed in the following. However, they are not limited to these examples. If other context elements have to be considered during the change propagation analysis, this metamodel can be extended to these elements.

- Test specifications: Aiello et al. propose acceptance tests for validating user stories based on best practices in the Test-Driven Development (TDD) [Aie+07]. There are also test procedures during the design and implementation phase of a PLC software, as proposed in [JT13; Jam15a]. This procedure involves POU-oriented table tests and unit tests to validate the implementation of a PLC software. Table tests are a manual procedure to check the expected values. By comparison, unit tests can cover more advanced testing scenarios. Thus, one of the context elements in an IEC software is the test specification [Rät17; Bus+18c].

  This metamodel enables domain experts to model the test cases in a PLC software as acceptance tests and unit tests. Figure 7.22 illustrate this metamodel. Table tests can be considered as a special form of unit tests. Domain experts can annotate unit test cases for the IEC elements such as methods, functions, or function blocks. The acceptance tests should be annotated for the coarse-grained IEC elements. Examples of such elements are programs, configurations, or function blocks. Thus, this metamodel references the relevant metaclasses of the `Repository` and `System` metamodel [Rät17; Bus+18c].

- Development artifact specifications: Examples of development artifacts are source code files or metadata files, as shown in Figure 7.24. The specific metaclasses of the development artifacts

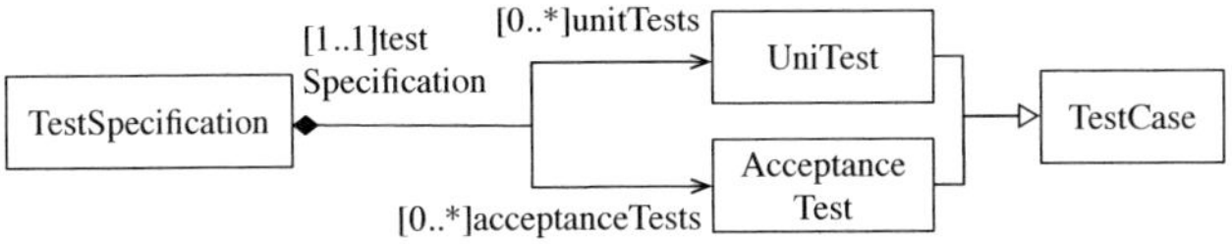

Figure 7.22.: Test specifications for an IEC software [Rät17] based on [Sta15]

reference the corresponding relevant metaclasses of the `Repository` and `System` metamodel [Rät17; Bus+18c].

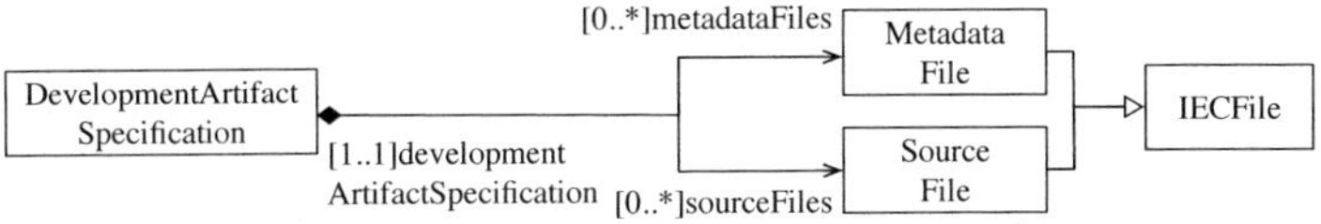

Figure 7.23.: Specification of development artifacts for an IEC software [Rät17] based on [Sta15]

- Staff specifications: Jamro and Trybus [JT13] propose the development phases of a PLC software including modeling, implementation, debugging, as well as deployment and analysis. Additionally, the PLC software should be tested during the modeling and implementation phase. Based on this development process, the metamodel of context elements supports modeling the following roles: developer, test developer, tester, and deployer, as illustrated in Figure 7.24. However, roles during the evolution of a PLC software may not be limited to the proposed roles. Thus, these roles and the corresponding metamodel can be extended. This metamodel allows modeling the responsible persons for various maintenance tasks. The previously defined roles can also be assigned to the responsible persons. A person can be responsible for several roles. Several persons can also have the same role. Each role can be responsible for several IEC model elements in the instances of the `Repository` and `System` metamodel. For example, the instance of the role tester can be assigned to a program or a function block.

This information enables KAMP4IEC to identify the responsible roles and persons to change an artifact [Rät17; Bus+18c].

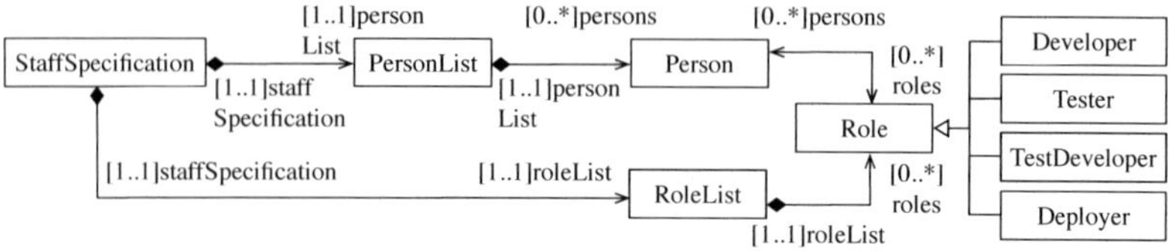

Figure 7.24.: Staff specifications for an IEC software [Rät17] based on [Sta15]

7.3.2.2. Metamodel of Task Type

This metamodel extends the generic metamodel of task types described in Section 5.3.2.2. It contains the specific task types in the evolution of an IEC software based on the context metamodel. Examples of these task types are the implementation of the source code or the deployment of a changed software [JT13; Rät17].

7.3.2.3. Algorithm of Context Task List

The algorithm of context task list identifies the affected context model elements, if a change to the corresponding structural model elements in the IEC `Repository` or `System` model occurs.

As described in the previous section, various IEC model elements can be tested. If model elements in an instance of a PLC software are changed, this algorithm considers testing these elements or the whole software, for example by unit tests or acceptance tests [Rät17].

Further, this algorithm can consider changing various development artifacts needed to implement a change [Rät17].

Example

An example of context elements in the PLC software of the Minimal Plant example is the test specification. In the running example, the global variable representing the value of the optical sensor has to be changed. If the affected method in the change scenario has unit tests, these tests has to be adapted and re-run.

7.3.3. Algorithm of Difference Calculation

If a change affects the structure of a PLC software, this algorithm identifies the differences between *BaseVersion* and *TargetVersion* (i.e., the model of the PLC software before and after the change). This algorithm also refines the results of existing generic algorithms for the difference calculation. Examples of changes to domain elements are adding or removing IEC elements. The algorithm for derivation of task list in the methodology gathers and manages the results of this algorithm.

7.4. Conclusions

This chapter presented an approach to change propagation analysis in aPS. The approach is based on interconnected metamodels representing mechanical and electrical/electronic elements, the control software, as well as the behavior of these systems. Thus, the metamodels provide a holistic view on the system under study comprising heterogeneous elements. The approach is composed of several loosely coupled approaches, which support the change propagation in the aforementioned sub-domains. To develop the change propagation analysis approach for mechanical and electrical/electronic elements two metamodels at two abstraction levels were used [Hei+18]. The abstract metamodel and the corresponding approach can be applied to any plant, while the specific metamodel and the corresponding approach were tailored to a specific plant. A further metamodel, which was mainly specified to model the data flow between the hardware and the software of a plant, enables domain experts to trace the changes from hardware to software. In order to model the control software based on the IEC 61131-3 standard, a further metamodel was presented. The approach based on this metamodel allows analyzing the change propagation in control software. Finally, the behavior of aPS can be considered as a set of linked actor steps and system steps at a high abstraction level (i.e., similar to a BP design [Hei+17]). The system steps reference different modes of a plant, which are controlled by different functionality of the control software. In this way, domain experts can analyze the change propagation from the hardware to the software and from the software to the behavior of a plant. In other words, the aforementioned approaches analyze the propagation of a change based on the mutual dependencies between the heterogeneous elements from different aPS sub-domains. Thus, this contribution answers the *second research question.*

8. Change Propagation Analysis from Requirements to a Specific Domain

During the life cycle of a system the stakeholder needs change [Zha+14]. As the stakeholder needs are directly related to their requirements, it is important to document the relationships both stakeholder needs and requirements [IEE11]. This allows identifying the origin of a change [IEE11]. As stakeholder requirements are met by system requirements, there is a need to maintain further traceability links between them [IEE11]. System requirements have to be traceable to the architectural design [IEE11]. In addition to the forward and backward trace links, there are relationships between individual requirements [Zha+14]. These relationships and trace links are the basis for the change propagation analysis [Zha+14]. As these relationships can be complex, several researchers introduce different types of relationships (e.g., [Poh95; Dur14; Küs13; Zha+14]). Dahlstedt and Persson state in [DP05, p. 95] these relationships "are not problematic per-se, but they influence a number of development activities and decisions". One of these activities is the change management [DP05]. Omitting these relationships and considering the requirements in isolation during the change propagation analysis may result in missing affected elements [DP05]. Thus, considering trace links between requirements, as well as the forward and backward traceability can help to close the gap between changing stakeholder needs and the resulted system during the life cycle of the system.

This chapter introduces an approach to change propagation analysis, which is based on the aforementioned relationships between requirements and from requirements to the system satisfying them. On the one hand, the approach is a further instantiation of the methodology. On the other hand, it can be considered as an extension of an existing approach to change propagation analysis in a specific domain. Thus, it consists of two parts: The generic part of the approach is mainly concerned with the change propagation analysis in requirements and, thus, is independent of a specific domain or a specific approach. The specific part of the approach introduces traceability from changing requirements to the model elements of a system in a specific domain. To avoid semantic repetitions, this chapter abstracts from a specific domain and provides, how the specific part of the approach should be developed in general. Thus, the contribution of this chapter complements the contributions of Chapters 6 and 7 by enabling domain experts to specify seed modifications not only for a system model, but also for its requirements model. This allows considering the evolution of requirements in conjunction with the system satisfying them.

The remainder of this chapter is organized as follows: Section 8.1 gives an overview of how an existing change propagation analysis approach in a specific domain can be extended to support changes to requirements. For this purpose, further metamodels and change propagation algorithms have to be specified, which are presented in Section 8.2. Section 8.3 discusses the design decisions made regarding the identification of context elements. The development of a before and after comparison for requirements is discussed in Section 8.4. Section 8.5 outlines the conclusions of this chapter.

The results of this chapter have been partially developed in a practical research course [HS15]. The corresponding part was supervised by the author of this dissertation. Further, parts of the results of this chapter are based on the Bachelor's thesis of Timo Maier [Mai18], which the author of this dissertation also supervised. Additionally, parts of this chapter have been appeared in the paper [MBR18] and in the paper [HBK18].

8.1. Change Propagation Analysis for Requirements

This section gives an overview of a change propagation analysis approach concerned with requirements changes. This approach can be obtained as an instantiation of the methodology to requirements models. The approaches to change propagation analysis for requirements are mainly designed to trace the changes between requirements and from requirements to system elements. Thus, this chapter presents this approach as an extension of an existing approach, which presents a generalization of the methodology instantiation to a specific domain (i.e., Chapters 6 and 7). The resulting approach can be considered as a change propagation analysis approach consisting three phases: i) In the preparation phase, domain experts model the requirements, the system, and the change requests. ii) The approach automatically analyzes the change propagation in the system model in the impact phase. iii) The post-analysis phase provides further functionality such as sorting or merging the task lists. In other words, it is an abstract view of a domain-specific approach to change propagation analysis such as KAMP4BP or KAMP4aPS. The term *domain-specific approach* refers to this abstract view of the approaches in the following.

Figure 8.1 gives an overview of an approach considering requirements changes. It illustrates the approach as an extension of an existing approach such as KAMP4BP or KAMP4aPS at a high abstraction level. The figure focuses on the first two phases of the approach, as the third phase is mainly provided by the methodology. The change propagation analysis can be considered at the requirements level and/or at the system level. If domain experts are interested in analyzing the change propagation at the requirements level, models representing them are required. These models can be considered as further inputs of the approach and, thus, have to be created in the preparation phase. After the models were created, seed modifications can be the model elements of the requirements or design decisions, and/or the system satisfying them. If at least one of the seed modifications was chosen at the requirements level, the algorithm first identifies the potentially affected requirements and further design decisions. In the next step, the algorithm identifies the model elements of the system, which satisfy the affected requirements or are selected by the affected design decisions. This results in seed modifications at the system level. Based on these model elements, other affected model elements can be identified (e.g., by using KAMP4BP in Chapter 6 or KAMP4aPS in Chapter 7).

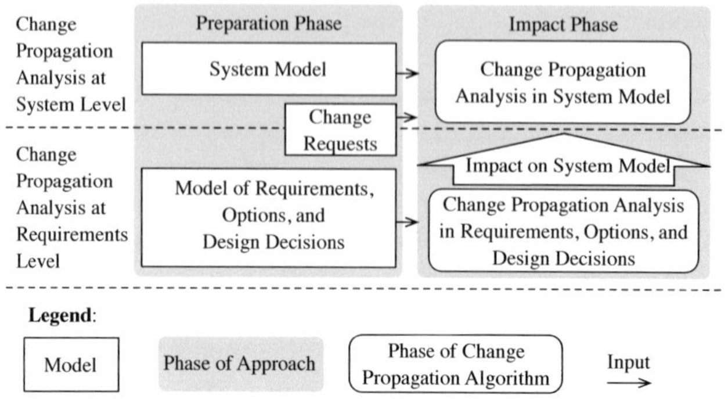

Figure 8.1.: Extension of existing approaches to change propagation analysis to consider requirements, options, and design decisions

8.2. Change Propagation Analysis for Elements of Domain Metamodel

This section presents the metamodels and algorithms, which are required to develop an approach to change propagation analysis at the requirements level.

8.2.1. Metamodel of Domain

This section is concerned with metamodeling the domain under study. However, requirements describe what a system needs and not the concrete system [IEE11]. Additionally, as requirements cannot be considered as a stand-alone domain such as IS or aPS [Hei+18], the previously discussed modeling aspects, namely structure, data flow, and behavior, cannot be applied to requirements. To enable the change propagation from requirements, the *metamodel of domain* has to be interpreted in a broader sense. This assumes only that requirements have to be documented using a formal model. The formal model shall include requirements and their relationships (see the term *conceptual architecture* introduced by Soni et al. as "the system in terms of its major design elements and the relationships among them" [SNH95, p. 1]). Formal models for documenting the requirements and for enabling the upwards and downwards traceability are also introduced by other researchers (see [Zha+14] for various dependency types). The change propagation analysis approach, proposed in this section, is based on the metamodel of Hahn and Schuller [HS15], which is an extension of the metamodel of Durdik [DR13; Dur14] and Küster [Küs13]. This metamodel differentiates between requirements, options, and design decisions. As requirements are independent of a specific implementation [IEE11], the implementation can be considered by using options [HS15]. Options also allow documenting the corresponding rationals [HS15]. Additionally, the metamodel enables domain experts to document their design decisions and their rationals [Dur14]. The main reason for using this metamodel is that it has a modular structure and captures a wide variety of relation types between requirements, options, and design decisions [HS15]. However, using another metamodel, which presents different relationships between requirements, options, design decisions, and/or the system under study is also possible. This metamodel is introduced in more detail in Section 2.5. As it was originally designed for IS, it considers only options for the software architecture using the PCM. To use this metamodel in other domains such as BP and aPS, these options had to be extended for the specific domains. Figure 8.2 examplarily illustrates the relationships between various metamodel files illustrating the generic options and their refinements for the software and hardware of aPS.

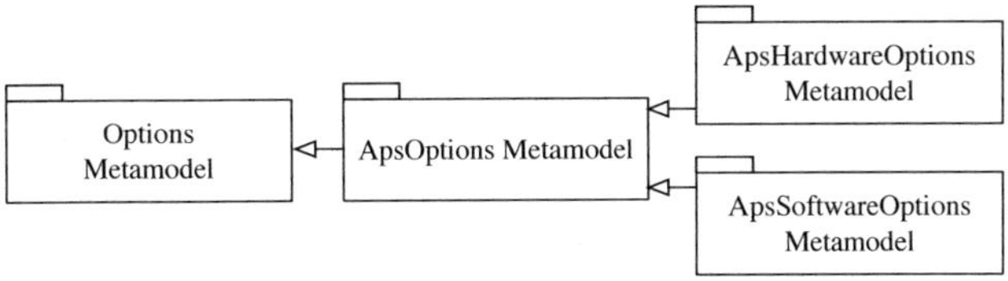

Figure 8.2.: Relationship between the metamodel of options [HS15] and the aPS-specific options [Mai18]

Example

Consider the case, in which it is planned to have only two shapes of work pieces (e.g., cylinder and cuboid) in the Minimal Plant example. A simple requirement can be: "The shape of work pieces shall be identified". This requirement can be implemented in different ways, for example by using different sensor types. In this context, an option can regard one implementation using a specific sensor type. A design decision can select a specific option, which fulfills this requirement.

8.2.2. Domain-specific Metamodel of Modification

This metamodel mainly refers to the model elements in requirements, options, and design decisions, which are potentially affected by a change. As described in Section 5.3.1.2, this metamodel can be organized based on seed modifications, modifications, change propagation steps, and modification repository. To illustrate how the domain-independent metamodel of modification has to be extended to develop a metamodel of modification regarding requirements, options, and design decisions, the corresponding metaclasses of the methodology are illustrated in the following.

- `SeedModification`: As described previously, the goal of considering requirements during the change propagation analysis is primarily to provide domain experts the opportunity to select the affected requirements as initial changes in each domain. In this case, the seed modifications can be: i) requirements, ii) options, or iii) design decisions. Figure 8.3 shows the relationship between the `SeedModification` metaclasses of the methodology and the requirements. Inheriting from seed modifications in other domains enables domain experts to consider the seed modification not only at the level of system elements, but also at the level of requirements, options, and/or design decisions. However, it is important to note that the seed modifications for requirements, options, and design decisions need not necessarily extend the seed modifications of a specific domain. An example of this can be the early design phases of the development, in which the system does not exist. In these phases, domain experts can be interested in the traceability between the requirements, options, and design decisions.

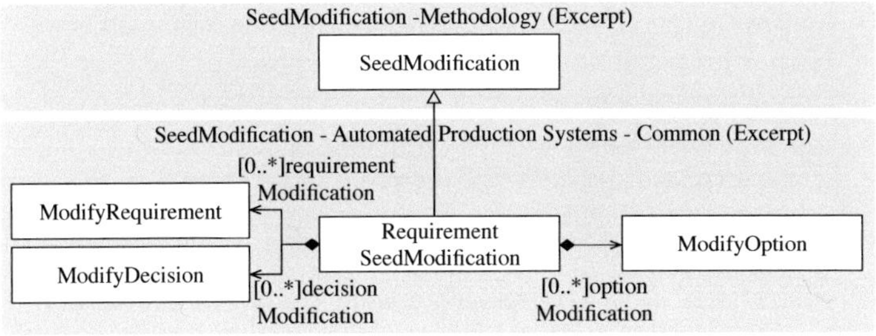

Figure 8.3.: Relationship between the domain-independent `SeedModification` and `SeedModifications` for requirements, design decisions, and options, adapted from [Mai18]

- `Modification`: At the requirements level, requirements, options, or design decisions can be modified in addition to the system elements in a specific domain. Figure 8.4 shows the relationship between the `Modification` metaclass of the methodology and its extensions for the requirements, design decisions, and options.

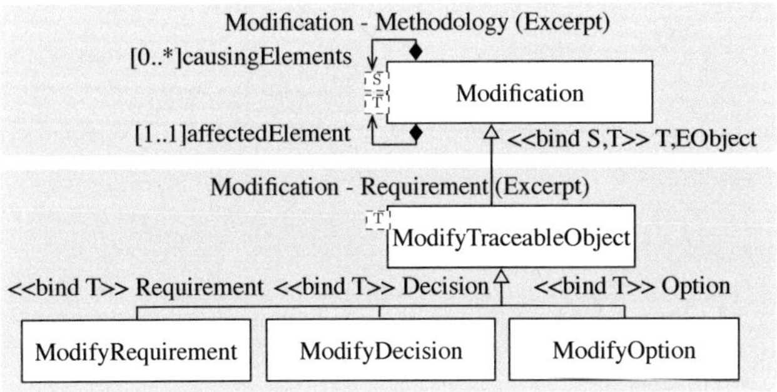

Figure 8.4.: Relationship between the domain-independent `Modification` and `Modifications` for requirements, design decisions, and options, adapted from [Mai18]

- `ChangePropagationStep`: The use of change propagation steps enables domain experts to differentiate between different causes of a change propagation. Thus, the `ChangePropagationStep` of the methodology has to be refined in each instance to include the change propagation steps, which are required in the instance. The common change propagation steps of the methodology instance for the requirements are grouped together to `ChangePropagationDueToSpecificationDependencies`. It consists of changes to requirements, options, and design decisions. As the methodology instance for requirements can be considered as an extension of a domain-specific change propagation analysis approach (e.g., for aPS), the change propagation steps in each domain can refine the common `ChangePropagationDueToSpecificationDependencies` (e.g., due to the specifications for hardware or software in aPS [Mai18]). Thus, the domain-specific change propagation steps due to specifications can refer not only to the modified requirements, options, and design decisions, but also to the system model elements, which are directly affected by them. In other words, these model elements can be considered as the counterparts of the seed modifications for a change propagation analysis at the system level (e.g., an affected component in the aPS hardware or an affected function block in the aPS software). The following sections describe in more detail, how the domain-specific model elements of a system can be derived from affected requirements, options, and design decisions. Figure 8.5 shows the relationship between the `ChangePropagationStep` metaclass of the methodology, its extension for common change propagation steps for requirements, design decisions, and options, and the extension of that for considering requirements changes in a specific domain. However, the latter one can be considered as optional in some cases. An example of these cases is, if domain experts are interested only in the change propagation in requirements, design decision, and options.

- `ModificationRepository` in a specific instance contains the domain-specific metaclasses of `SeedModification` and `ChangePropagationStep`, as described in Chapter 5. As this case is very similar to the extension of the modification repository in the

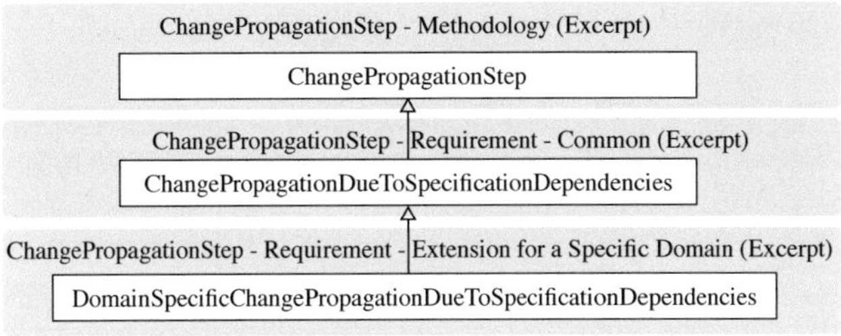

Figure 8.5.: Relationship between the domain-independent `ChangePropagationStep` and `ChangePropagationSteps` for requirements, design decisions, and options [Mai18]

previous chapters regarding KAMP4BP and KAMP4aPS, the metamodel is not further depicted.

Example

In general, requirements, options, and design decisions can be affected by a change. In the previous example, the seed modification can be the requirement regarding the identification of the work pieces' shapes. It can also be an option, which is concerned with a specific implementation to satisfy the requirement. Even the design decision referring to the option, which domain experts have chosen, can be the seed modification. Whether the requirement, the option, or the design decision is the seed modification, depends on the change request and how the change request has to be implemented. For example, the change request may directly involve a specific sensor type as a possible implementation to meet the requirement. In this case, the corresponding option is affected. If domain experts have already modeled different options and have opted for a specific one (i.e., they documented their design decisions), the corresponding design decision can be the seed modification. It is also possible that the requirement has to be changed. For example, the previously described requirement can become obsolete. In this case, the change request initially affects the requirement.

8.2.3. Algorithms of Change Propagation Analysis

This section presents the algorithms for change propagation analysis at the requirements level. If a change request is defined at the requirements level, the change can propagate over the requirements, design decisions, and options to the dependent system elements. This can be done by using the trace links between them (e.g., the traceability metamodel presented in [RJ01]). After the dependent system elements were identified, a domain-specific approach to change propagation analysis can be used to identify further system elements (e.g., KAMP4BP or KAMP4aPS). Therefore, to develop a change propagation analysis at the requirements level (i.e., the seed modifications can be requirements, options, and design decisions), three phases can be differentiated:

- Trace links between requirements, options, and design decisions can be used to identify the affected requirements, options, and design decisions. This phase can be considered as common, as it does not depend on a specific domain. This phase is described in Section 8.2.3.1 in more detail.
- The next phase is concerned with identifying model elements at the system level, which are directly affected by a change to requirements, options, or design decisions. This depends on the relationships between the domain-specific model elements and requirements, options, or design decision. For example, an option can be concerned with introducing a new component in a software system to fulfill a certain requirement. Thus, changing the requirement can trigger a change in the option and in the specific component in the software system. In contrast to the previous phase, this phase depends on requirements, options, or design decisions on the one hand, and the system in a specific domain satisfying them on the other hand. Section 8.2.3.2 describes the change propagation rules for this phase.
- The component in the previous example can be considered as the seed modification for a change propagation analysis at the system level. This phase identifies the affected model elements in a system based on this seed modification. An example of a corresponding

approach for the aforementioned seed modification can be KAMP4IS.

Sections 8.2.3.1 and 8.2.3.2 propose the change propagation analysis for the first two phases, while Chapters 6 and 7 introduce the change propagation analysis in the third phase.

8.2.3.1. Change Propagation Analysis for Requirements, Options, and Design Decisions

This section presents the change propagation rules, which are independent of a specific domain. To utilize the trace links between requirements, options, and design decisions, some prerequisites have to be fulfilled, which are described in the following in more detail. Requirements, design decisions, and options can be formulated in different ways (e.g., unambiguously or vaguely). Similar to the paradigms in IS (e.g., CBSE), there are guidelines for formulating the requirements. In order to be able to use the trace links between requirements and the system satisfying them for a change propagation analysis, the formulated requirements must have certain characteristics. The IEEE 29148 standard summarizes the characteristics and criteria of the individual requirements and the sets of requirements, as well as the language to formulate them [IEE11].

According to the IEEE 29148 standard, the individual requirements refer only to necessary capabilities and are independent of a specific implementation. Additionally, the requirements have to be formulated unambiguously and must not have any conflicts to the other requirements. Each requirement refers to only one requirement and is complete at the same time. Further, the requirements are feasible regarding the technology. Each requirement has to be upwards and downwards traceable. In order to ensure the verifiability of the requirements, they further need to be measurable. According to this standard, a set of requirements has to have the following characteristics: "complete", "consistent", "affordable", and "bounded" [IEE11, p. 11f]. A more detailed description of the previously described characteristics and criteria is given in the standard [IEE11].

The standard specifies further how to formulate good requirements [IEE11]. One of the important criteria is that requirements are concerned with *what* a system needs. The requirements must not be formulated vaguely. The standard also excludes general and ambiguous terms. Examples of ambiguous terms are "vague pronouns" or "negative statements" [IEE11, p. 12].

If requirements do not fulfill the previously described characteristics and criteria, the results of a change propagation analysis may be useless (e.g., a change propagation analysis based on conflicting requirements). Thus, the following change propagation rules assume that the requirements already meet the characteristics and criteria of the IEEE 29148 standard [IEE11]. However, the metamodels provided by Durdik [DR13; Dur14], Küster [Küs13], and Hahn and Schuller [HS15] allow documenting several possible relationships between requirements, design decisions, and options. This also includes relationships, which are excluded by the IEEE 29148 standard such as "conflicts with". Thus, the following change propagation rules omit these relationships. In other words, the following rules assume that formal models of requirements, options, and design decisions exist, which follow the aforementioned guidelines.

Similar to the previous approaches, the change propagation rules are defined for all instances of a metamodel. The relevant metamodels for the following rules are Requirements, Options, and Decisions metamodel (see Section 2.5). To define the rules the instances of the relevant metaclasses of these metamodels are mapped to a set. These sets are defined in the following:

- $Q = \{q_{q_1}, \ldots, q_{q_n}\}$ is the set of all `Requirements` in the instances of the Requirements metamodel.
- $O = \{o_{o_1}, \ldots, o_{o_n}\}$ is the set of all `Options` in the instances of the Options metamodel.
- $D = \{d_{d_1}, \ldots, d_{d_n}\}$ is the set of all `DesignDecisions` in the instances of the Decisions metamodel.
- $G = O \cup D$ is the union set representing the instances of `Options` and `DesignDecisions`.

The relationship between metaclasses of different metamodels can be used to create binary relations over these sets. These relationships are based on different relation types, defined by Relations metamodel (see Section 2.5). The relations are defined in the following:

- The relation *RequirementHasDependent* is defined over the set Q. In this relation, the Requirement $q_{q_i} \in Q$ is associated to the Requirement $q_{q_j} \in Q$, if the Requirement q_{q_j} is dependent on the Requirement $q_{q_i} \in Q$.
- The relation *OptionHasDependent* is defined over the set O. In this relation, the Option $o_{o_i} \in O$ is associated to the Option $o_{o_j} \in O$, if the Option o_{o_j} is dependent on the Option $o_{o_i} \in O$.
- The relation *DecisionHasDependent* is defined over the set D. In this relation, the DesignDecision $d_{d_i} \in D$ is associated to the DesignDecision $d_{d_j} \in D$, if the DesignDecision d_{d_j} is dependent on the DesignDecision $d_{d_i} \in D$.
- The relation $TriggerOf$ is defined over the sets Q and G. In this relation, the Requirement $q \in Q$ is associated to the Option or DesignDecision $g \in G$, if the Requirement q is the trigger of the Option or DesignDecision g.
- The relation *ResolvedBy* is defined over the sets Q and G. In this relation, the Requirement $q \in Q$ is associated to the Option or DesignDecision $g \in G$, if the Requirement q is resolved by the Option or DesignDecision g.
- The relation *CouldBeResolvedBy* is defined over the sets Q and G. In this relation, the Requirement $q \in Q$ is associated to the Option or DesignDecision $g \in G$, if the Requirement q could be resolved by the Option or DesignDecision g.

The following algorithms define the change propagation rules based on the aforementioned sets and relations. These algorithms can be applied to requirements, options, and design decisions. Thus, they are independent of a specific domain.

A requirement, an option, or a design decision can have dependent requirements, options, or design decisions, respectively. If a requirement changes, the dependent requirements can be affected. This heuristic can also be applied to options and design decisions. Algorithm 30 presents the change propagation from requirements to requirements, from options to options, and from design decisions to design decisions. For this purpose, it uses *RequirementHasDependent*, *OptionHasDependent*, and

$DecisionHasDependent$ relations. Depending on, whether a model element of the input $n \in N$ is a member of the Requirement set Q, the Option set O, or the Decision set D, the algorithm applies the corresponding relation to the model element. If the input model element $n \in N$ has a dependent requirement, option, or design decision model element, the algorithm assigns the dependent model element to set Z in each iteration. As sets do not contain any duplicates, $(R \cup Z) \setminus R$ contains only members of set Z, which are not already contained in the result set R. The result set R can be equal to either Q, D, or O in the worst case. In this case, the algorithm iteratively assigns set N all members of either Q, D, or O. Thus, the maximum number of iterations of the while loop is whether $|Q|$, $|D|$, or $|O|$ (i.e., the cardinality of the sets).

Algorithm 30 Change propagation from Requirement, Option, or DesignDecision to Requirements, Options, or DesignDecisions, respectively

Input: $N \subseteq (Q \cup O \cup D)$ ▷ Seed modifications
Output: $R \subseteq (Q \cup O \cup D)$ ▷ Result
$U = Q \cup O \cup D$
$R = N$
while $N \neq \emptyset$ **do**
  $Z = \{u \in U | (\exists n \in N)[(n, u) \in RequirementHasDependent \vee (n, u) \in OptionHasDependent \vee (n, u) \in DecisionHasDependent]\}$
  $N = (R \cup Z) \setminus R$
  $R = R \cup Z$
end while

While the previous algorithm considers the relationships within requirements, options, and design decisions, the following algorithm is based on the relationships between them. This is based on $TriggerOf$, $ResolvedBy$, and $CouldBeResolvedBy$ relations. These relations are defined to describe the relationships between a requirement on the one hand and options and design decisions on the other hand. These relations consider the cases, in which a requirement can be the trigger of certain options and design decisions or it is (or could be) resolved by certain options and design decisions. Thus, the dependent options and design decisions can be affected by a change to the requirement. These relations are used by Algorithm 31 to calculate the change propagation. The algorithm checks for a model element representing the requirement $q \in Q$, whether it is a trigger of the design decision $d \in D$ or the option model element $o \in O$. Additionally, it checks, whether the requirement q is (or could be) resolved by the design decision model element d or the option model element o. The set of results R contains design decisions and/or options, for which at least one of the predicates in R is true.

Algorithm 31 Change propagation from Requirement to Options and DesignDecisions

Input: $N \subseteq Q$ ▹ Seed modifications
Output: $R \subseteq (O \cup D)$ ▹ Result
$G = O \cup D$
$R = \{g \in G | (\exists n \in N) [(n, g) \in TriggerOf \lor (n, g) \in ResolvedBy \lor (n, g) \in CouldBeResolvedBy]\}$

Algorithms 30 and 31 use trace links in a forward direction to calculate the change propagation. This heuristic is based on the goal of the change propagation analysis to identify the dependent model elements at the system level. Using both forward and backward directions can result in a high overestimation of the results. However, if domain experts are interested in identifying all requirements, options, design decisions, and model elements of the system, which can be directly or indirectly related to the seed modifications, both directions can be utilized.

8.2.3.2. Tracing a Change from Requirements, Options, and Design Decisions to Domain-Specific Model Elements

The previous section was concerned with the change propagation within and between the requirements, options, and design decisions. This section identifies the elements of a system model in a specific domain, which are directly affected by a change to requirements, options, and design decisions. As the development of this step is very similar for different domains, this section abstracts from a specific domain and the possible systems within it. The term *domain* in this section can regard IS, BP, or aPS. Further, it is assumed that a formal model of requirements, options, and design decisions exist, which the system under study satisfies. For this purpose, set $V = \{v_{v_1}, \dots, v_{v_n}\}$ is defined as the set of all model elements of interest in a system model in a specific domain. The model elements of this set for a specific instance of the methodology depend on the domain, for which requirements, options, and design decisions have to be considered. For example, if domain experts in aPS are interested in the change propagation analysis for the PLC software at the requirements level, this set contains model elements of the PLC metamodel such as instances of `GlobalVariables`, `Functions`, `FunctionBlocks`, or `Methods`. This set can also contain model elements of `Components`, `Interfaces`, `Modules`, or `Structures`, as well as their refinements such as a specific sensor type, if the focus of the change propagation analysis is the aPS hardware. Other examples are the domain-specific model elements in IS (e.g., `DataType`) and BP (e.g., `DataObject`).

As the domain and the systems within it are considered in a broader sense, this section abstracts from the type of the relationship between requirements, options, and design decisions on the one hand and the system satisfying them on the other hand. Thus, the relation $References$ is defined over the sets O and V. In this relation, the Option $o \in O$ is associated to $v \in V$, if the Option o references v. As described previously, v is the set of all elements of a system model in a specific domain such as `GlobalVariables` in IEC. $References$ can be considered as a generic relation, which has to be further refined in a specific context by other relations such as $IntroduceNew$, $Change$, or $Remove$. Additionally, more fine-grained relationships can be used. Various types of such relationships in IS (e.g., merging or splitting components) are given by Relations metamodel, introduced in Section 2.5.

In particular, if options are changed, the model elements, which are directly referenced by them, have to be identified. Algorithm 32 uses the aforementioned $References$ relation to identify the model elements of a system, which are directly affected due to the changed option. Thus, it has to be refined to be able to consider specific relation types in a domain. The specifications of the relation $References$ are not necessarily binary relations, as they can be defined over several sets. For example, $MergesComponents$ relation can be defined over the set of options and further sets representing the components before the merge process. In these cases, the algorithm has to be further adapted.

Algorithm 32 Change propagation from Option to domain-specific model elements

Input: $N \subseteq O$ ▷ Seed modifications
Require: $R \subseteq V$ ▷ Result
$R = \{v \in V | (\exists n \in N) [(n, v) \in References]\}$

As described previously, there can be more than one option realizing a requirement. If domain experts opt for a specific option, the aforementioned metamodels proposed by [HS15; Dur14; Küs13] enable them to document their decision using the Decisions metamodel, as described in Section 2.5. To document the selected option by a decision, the Selected relationship can be used. This relationship is presented by the binary relation *Selects*. The relation *Selects* is defined over the sets D and O. In this relation, the Design Decision $d \in D$ is associated to the Option $o \in O$, if the Design Decision d selects the option o.

During the evolution, domain experts can opt for other options. This can be considered as a change to the existing decisions. Changing a decision can result in changing the selected options, which can result in further changes in the dependent system elements realizing the options. This change propagation is considered by Algorithm 33. It uses the previously described relationships to identify the affected model elements of a system $v \in V$, after the decision $d \in D$ changes. This change propagation is based on the option $o \in O$, which is selected by the design decision d (i.e., *Selects* relation) and realized by the system model element v (i.e., *References* relation).

Algorithm 33 Change propagation from Decision to domain-specific model elements

Input: $N \subseteq D$ ▷ Seed modifications
Require: $R \subseteq V$ ▷ Result
$R = \{v \in V | (\exists o \in O) (\exists n \in N) [(o, v) \in References \wedge (n, o) \in Selects]\}$

Example

Consider the previously described change requests affecting the option, the design decision, and the requirement. As described previously, *References* is a generic relation and shall be refined in a specific development. The refinement of this relation in this example is *IntroduceNew*, which is concerned with the usage of a new sensor type.

If the option regarding a specific sensor is changed, Algorithm 32 identifies the affected model elements of the Minimal Plant example (i.e., the specific sensor type in this example), which is introduced by the option.

If domain experts opt for another option, the corresponding design decision changes. Algorithm 33 identifies the affected model elements of the system via the selected option.

In the case of the obsolete requirement, Algorithm 31 identifies the affected options and design decisions, which are triggered by or are (or could be) solved by the affected requirement. Depending on, whether the algorithm identifies the affected options and/or design decisions, the result triggers Algorithm 32 and/or Algorithm 33. Both algorithms result in affected model elements of the Minimal Plant example, which are introduced by the affected option.

8.3. Change Propagation Analysis for Elements of Context Metamodel

In this chapter, requirements are discussed as a possible usage context of the methodology. As described in Chapter 5, context elements involve technical and organizational artifacts such as documentations and tests [Ros+15b; Sta15]. Considering these model elements at the requirements level or at the domain level (i.e., system's structure and behavior) is a design decision. This thesis is based on the idea of [MT10] considering the architecture of a system as its main artifact. Thus, context elements were considered at the level of the domain. Consequently, the change propagation analysis for the elements of context metamodel could be omitted during the instantiation of the methodology for the requirements. However, there is also possible to consider context elements at the requirements level. Considering context elements at the requirements level results in developing the required metamodels and algorithms.

8.4. Algorithm of Difference Calculation

Similar to the other instantiations of the methodology, an algorithm for calculating the differences between two models can be developed. A use case for this algorithm is, if the models of requirements, options, and design decisions have been evolved over time. In this case, domain experts can be interested in identifying the dependent requirements, options, design decisions, or other artifacts. The difference calculation may result in identifying the changed, removed, or added requirements, options, or design decisions, which can be used to identify the dependent model elements of the system under study. The algorithm for derivation of task lists in the methodology gathers and manages the results.

8.5. Conclusions

This chapter was concerned with requirements, options, and design decisions as change triggers. The proposed approach builds on a domain-specific approach to change propagation analysis. It utilizes the different types of relationships between requirements, options, design decisions, and the dependent system elements to analyze the change propagation. In this way, it enables domain experts to analyze the impact of a change to the models of both requirements and the system satisfying them.

In particular, the approach presented in this chapter consists of two parts: The first part is independent of the approaches to change propagation analysis in a certain domain. The second part forms a connecting link between the domain-independent change propagation analysis for requirements, options, or design decision, and the domain-specific approach to change propagation analysis. To analyze the change propagation in the dependent system, a further approach such as KAMP4BP or KAMP4aPS has to be used. Thus, the contributions of Chapters 6 and 7 are complemented by the contribution of this chapter, as domain experts can specify the change request for both systems and requirements. Summarized, this contribution partially answers the *second research question.*

9. A Language for Change Propagation Rules

There are several methods to construct an approach to change propagation analysis (e.g., based on change propagation rules or information retrieval). The approaches proposed in this thesis are based on change propagation rules, which define the propagation of a change between two system elements. In particular, the rules use metamodels defining different element types as metaclasses and their relations. Hence, the rules depend on a specific metamodel and are applied to all instances of this metamodel. Consequently, changing the metamodel can result in changing the change propagation rules. As a metamodel can evolve continuously, maintaining the change propagation rules can be considered as a main task in the life cycle of change propagation analysis approaches. It is desirable to keep this maintenance task at a minimum [Bus+18b].

A further aspect in the development of a change propagation analysis approach is concerned with the role of a domain expert. As described previously, the role of a domain expert is concerned with the maintenance of the system under study in a specific domain. Although domain experts in a specific domain can also have programming knowledge, they are not necessarily programming experts. Additionally, a change propagation analysis approach is written in a specific programming language, usually in a GPL. This assumes programming knowledge for domain experts. It is desirable for domain experts to focus on the maintainability properties of the system under study, and not on the concrete implementation of the change propagation analysis approach. In other words, domain experts should be able to focus on the relations between the metaclasses, which are involved in change propagation rules. In addition to the modularity of the change propagation analysis approach, the programming knowledge of domain experts also plays an important role. For example, domain experts may have a limited knowledge of a GPL, in which the change propagation rules have to be implemented. One way is to delegate the implementation tasks regarding the change propagation rules to their colleagues, who have more programming knowledge. However, this solution is time-consuming and can lead to failure for example due to the lack of shared knowledge. Further, the change propagation rules can be added, removed, or adapted over time. Thus, the described solution makes the maintainability of change propagation rules difficult. Summarized, domain experts should be able to describe at least several common patterns of change propagation rules [Bus+18b].

For the aforementioned reasons, there is a need for a DSL, which allows focusing on the relevant information regarding the maintainability analysis. In a model-based and rule-based approach, this information includes the metaclasses and their relations. The term *domain* in the term DSL regards the application domain (i.e., in this case the change propagation analysis). In the context of this thesis, this definition of domain is only used in the acronym DSL. The change propagation rules can range from very simple to very complex. In contrast to a GPL, the DSL does need to cover all possible change propagation rules. The main requirement of the DSL is the ability to be applicable to several common patterns of the rules. To facilitate the task of implementing the change propagation rules, the DSL has to provide a reduced set of language elements. In other words, there is a trade-off between the size of the subset of rules, to which the DSL can be applied and its complexity. In other words, the benefit of a DSL (compared to a GPL) is the reduced set of language elements for a specific domain [Bus+18b].

This chapter addresses the aforementioned issues and presents Change Propagation Rule Language (CPRL) as a DSL to describe the change propagation rules. This language enables domain experts to specify several common patterns of change propagation rules. Using the language allows a flexible adaptation of the rules and facilitates their reuse. Further, it provides features to integrate the change propagation rules, which are written in Java. These features can be used to specify complex change propagation rules, which cannot be written in the proposed language. However, the use of this language can be considered as optional. In other words, domain experts do not need to use the language, if they are programming experts in Java. In addition to Java, further interfaces to other languages such as OCL or Xtend can be provided. This allows domain experts to specify change propagation rules in various languages. However, the use of a dedicated

DSL for change propagation rules can improve the implementation tasks and the maintainability of the rules [Bus+18b; Löp18].

CPRL abstracts from the heterogeneity of elements from different domains by considering the metaclasses and the references between them. Thus, the contribution of this chapter complements the contribution of Chapter 5 to partially answer the *first research question*.

Section 9.1 addresses the problems of using a GPL to specify the frequently used patterns of change propagation rules. Based on these problems and patterns, the requirements for the corresponding DSL are proposed in Section 9.2. Section 9.3 presents the language design based on the aforementioned requirements. The main limitations of the language and the assumptions during the development are discussed in Section 9.4. Section 9.5 briefly summarizes the contributions of this chapter.

A former version of the language has been appeared in the Master's thesis of Inna Belyantseva [Bel18]. The results of this chapter are mainly based on the Bachelor's thesis of Martin löper [Löp18]. Both theses were supervised by the author of this dissertation. A former version of the language was also presented in the paper [Bus+18b]. Thus, the content of this chapter has been appeared in the aforementioned works.

9.1. Problem Statement

This section describes the problems and shortcomings while using a GPL to specify the change propagation rules. In the following, the problems are illustrated using excerpts of a metamodel in IS [Rat13] in Section 9.1.1 and a simplified metamodel in BP based on [Hci14] in Section 9.1.2. Section 9.1.3 discusses the problems arising during the usage of a GPL for specifying the change propagation rules.

9.1.1. Event Example – Forward Reference

Figure 9.1 illustrates the relationship between an event group and the corresponding event types in IS. This metamodel is an excerpt from the event-based communication developed by Rathfelder [Rat13]. Event types

```
public static List<EventType> lookUpEventTypeWithEventGroup(Collection<
     EventGroup> modifiedEventGroup){
  List<EventType> eventTypes = new LinkedList<EventType>();
  for (EventGroup eventGroup : modifiedEventGroup)
    eventTypes.addAll(eventGroup.getEvent());
  return eventTypes; }
```

Listing 9.1: Java code for the lookup in the *Event Example* - Simplified

can be sent and received by components. Event groups contain at least one event type. Similar to the concept of interfaces in CBSE, event groups are contracts between the components sending the events and the components processing them [Rat13].

If an event group is changed (e.g., removed), the contained event types can also be affected. A change propagation rule should describe this change propagation. Listing 9.1 illustrates a possible Java code for this change propagation rule. This code searches for event groups, which are affected by a change. Then, it navigates along a **forward reference** to identify the contained event types.

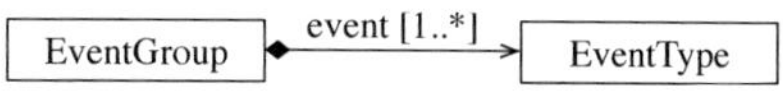

Figure 9.1.: Relationship between an event group and its event types - A simplified excerpt from PCM [Rat13]

9.1.2. Actor Example – Backward Reference

Figure 9.2 presents the relationship between an actor and its roles in an organization in BP. This is a slightly modified example from the organization environment metamodel developed by Heinrich [Hei14]. This example considers the human actors as resources. In this metamodel, each human resource takes up one or more roles in an organization [Hei14].

If a role in an organization is changed, the affected human actors need to be identified. This can be specified by a change propagation rule as illustrated in the Java code example in Listing 9.2. The Java code iterates over all actor resources and their roles in the model. If the role is affected

```java
public static List<ActorResource> lookUpActorResourceWithRole(IS ISModel,
    Collection<Role> modifiedRole) {
  List<ActorResource> actorResources = new LinkedList<ActorResource>();
  for (ActorResource actorResource : ISModel.getContainsActorResources())
    for (Role role : actorResource.getRole())
      if (modifiedRole.contains(role))
        actorResources.add(actorResource);
  return actorResources; }
```

Listing 9.2: Java code for the lookup in the *Actor Example* - Simplified

by the change, the code adds the corresponding actor resource to the list of affected actor resources. This code represents a change propagation rule along a **backward reference**.

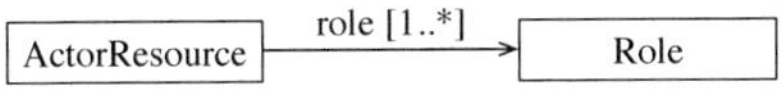

Figure 9.2.: Relationship between an actor resource and the corresponding roles - An excerpt from a simplified metamodel based on BPUsagemodel [Hei14]

9.1.3. Discussion

In the previous sections two change propagation rules along a forward and along a backward reference are illustrated. However, a rule can also be along a chain of forward and backward references. Figure 9.3 gives a simplified excerpt from the PCM involving interfaces, signatures, and entry level system calls [BKR09]. Detailed information on the involving metamodels is given in Section 2.3 and Section 2.4. It is conceivable that changes to operation interfaces can affect the corresponding entry level system calls. Beginning from the affected `OperationInterfaces` in all models, the change propagation rule has to search along a forward reference for `OperationSignatures` involved. Then, it has to search along a backward reference to identify all `EntryLevelSystemCalls` referencing the affected `OperationSignatures`. This change propagation rule is a combination of a forward and backward navigation. In general, a change propagation rule can also be composed of a chain of forward and backward navigation. The corresponding code, thus, can involve redundant technical code. The recurring code can also be grouped together (i.e., a method). However, both solutions could be prone to errors [Bus+18b].

Figure 9.3.: Relationship between an operation interface and the corresponding signatures and entry level system calls - An excerpt from a simplified metamodel based on the PCM [BKR09]

The recurring technical code could also be a source of error during the evolution of the metamodel. As described previously, the change propagation rules are described for a concrete metamodel. Any change to the underlying metamodel results in further changes in the change propagation rules. This results in changing the recurring technical code for describing the rules in a GPL. Thus, maintaining change propagation rules is a time-consuming and error-prone task [Bus+18b].

A prerequisite for implementing change propagation rules in a specific GPL is programming skills in that GPL. A further prerequisite is the knowledge of the software architecture of the change propagation analysis approach [Bus+18b]. In other words, these factors (i.e., coding still in general) influence the code quality and the maintainability of the change propagation rules.

It is desirable to have a change propagation rule language, which hides the technical aspects (e.g., technical recurring code of a GPL) from the domain expert. The language should ease specifying and maintaining the change propagation rules by focusing on the metaclasses and their relations. In this way, the language has to increase the reusability of the change propagation rules [Bus+18b].

9.2. Requirements for Change Propagation Rule Language

As described previously, domain experts may not be the developers of the change propagation analysis approach at the same time. Maybe, they have less experience in the GPL, in which the change propagation analysis approach is written. Thus, the first requirement is to separate the concerns between both roles. The language shall cover the common and important change propagation rules, such as the selection of the model elements or the traceability along the forward or backward references. The current version of the language is based on KAMP4IS, KAMP4BP, KAMP4aPS, and KAMP4IEC to identify the common and important categories of change propagation rules [Bus+18b; Bel18; Löp18].

The language shall have a succinct and unambiguous syntax. It aims at reducing the effort for creating and maintaining change propagation rules. The language shall be declarative. A declarative language hides the implementation details of model traversal for example in a backward navigation. The language shall allow the validation of rules. In other words, domain experts can specify only valid references between the elements. This can be achieved by using an explicit parser and grammar with the type system. Further, the language shall hide the cardinality of references from domain experts. This also aims at reducing the work for maintaining the change propagation rules [Bus+18b].

9.3. Language Design

A DSL can be categorized based on the following characteristics (see Section 2.1): i) internal vs. external, ii) imperative vs. declarative, iii) visual vs. textual, and iv) executable vs. non-executable DSL [MHS05; Fow10; Löp18]. CPRL represents a declarative language, as domain experts need only to specify the change propagation over a set of metaclasses (i.e., a backward change propagation between two metaclasses). One of the requirements of the CPRL was to reduce the amount of code, which is necessary by a GPL. This can be achieved by abstracting from the technical code using an explicit grammar and code generation. Thus, CPRL is developed as an external DSL. Further, CPRL is designed as a textual language. It is a non-executable DSL. From the CPRL code Java code can be generated.

Figure 9.4 illustrates a simplified model of CPRL. Different language elements of the presented model illustrate the identified categories during the analysis of the change propagation rules of KAMP4IS, KAMP4BP, KAMP4aPS, and KAMP4IEC [Löp18; Bel18]. This section gives an overview on these language elements and their relationships. The following subsections describe each language element in more detail.

A **rule file** contains a **rule file header** containing a set of configurations (e.g., **imports**) and a set of **blocks**. Each block contains a set of change propagation **rules**. A block can be a **standard block**. In this context, a block is used to group rules. A block can also be defined recursively. The rules in a **recursive block** are evaluated recursively until they identify new affected model elements. In the context of the language, a **rule** identifies for a set of input model elements a set of output model elements. In other words, a rule selects a set of output model elements, which are potentially affected by the change. For this purpose, a rule is composed of a first lookup followed by a set of **lookups**. The input of each lookup is the output of the previous lookup. A **lookup** can either filter model elements (i.e., hereinafter referred to as **selection**) or enable the navigation between model elements (i.e., hereinafter referred to as **navigation**). The first lookup in a rule is referred to as **rule source**. The input of the rule source is the set of model elements, which are affected by the change. The blocks and the rules are evaluated in the specified order. A **navigation** can either be a forward navigation or a backward navigation. In a **forward navigation**, the lookup searches for the instances of the affected metaclasses along a forward reference in the metamodel. In a **backward navigation** the search direction is reversed. A **selection** can be either at the type level (i.e., hereinafter referred to as **type selection**) or at the instance level (i.e., hereinafter referred to as **instance selection**). A lookup can also be a **rule call**, which is a call to an already specified rule to increase the reuse of existing rules [Löp18]. The following sections describe the relevant language elements of CPRL in more detail [Löp18].

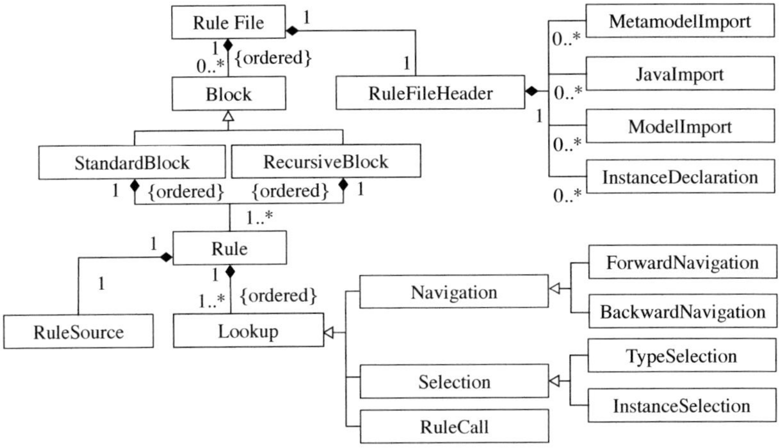

Figure 9.4.: A reduced and simplified illustration of the relevant elements of CPRL as class diagram, adapted from [Bus+18b; Löp18]

9.3.1. Rule File

The rule file represents the root element of the language. As described previously, a rule file is composed of a header and a set of blocks, which are described in the following in more detail [Löp18].

9.3.1.1. Rule File Header

The file header contains a set of metamodel imports, Java imports, model imports, and instance declarations. In this way, the rules defined afterwards can reference the external elements (e.g., metamodels) and further model elements.

In particular, the import can be done either at the level of metamodel or model. At the level of metamodel, importing a metamodel allows accessing all instances of the metamodel. At this level, a metamodel, a metaclass, or a structural feature can be referenced.

At the level of models, importing models allows accessing a specific instance or a set of instances with specific properties. The properties represent the structural features. However, model elements cannot be identified in the same way as metaclasses, as model elements cannot be uniquely identified in general (i.e., there is not any attribute in general, which can be used to identify an instance uniquely.). Thus, an instance declaration can be generally performed using the evaluation of a predicate.

The predicate can be declared for example by integrating a code block. In this case, all instances for which the predicate is evaluated to true can be identified. To implement the code block Xbase is embedded into the grammar of CPRL. The use of an existing expression language reduces the CPRL grammar. The compiler generates then Java code.

9.3.1.2. Blocks of Change Propagation Rules

A rule file is composed of a set of blocks. Blocks can be standard or recursive. The standard blocks group the change propagation rules based on the semantics of the change propagation (e.g., inter-component change propagation or change propagation due to hardware change). The rules in a standard block are evaluated only once in the specified order. A recursive block allows evaluating the rules at least once. The evaluation of the change propagation rules in an iteration results in new affected elements, to which the rules of the recursive block can be applied. In this case, the rules are evaluated again. The rules are evaluated, until no new model elements are identified in an iteration. An example of the application of a recursive block is the analysis of the change propagation within the composition of model elements. In this example, model elements can be recursively composed of other model elements. To specify change propagation rules for hierarchically composed model elements, recursive blocks can be used. The blocks and the contained rules are evaluated in the order specified by domain experts.

9.3.2. Rule

The approaches presented in this thesis are based on change propagation rules. Thus, rules are the main elements of CPRL. A rule has an input and an output. The input of a rule is a subset of model elements, which are affected so far. This subset of model elements has to fulfill a specific predicate (e.g, a specific type). After the input is selected, a rule defines a change propagation along references to a set of specific model elements. This set presents the output of the rule. Both input and output of a rule are typed [Löp18].

In general, change propagation rules can be defined at the level of metamodel or at the level of models. If the change propagation rules are defined at the level of metamodel, they can be applied to all instances of the metamodel. Defining the change propagation rules at the level of models allows domain experts to specify fine-grained change propagation rules. These change propagation rules can be used, for example, if the metamodel is defined at a high abstraction level or if domain experts need to differentiate between specific instances of a metaclass. However, they may not be generalizable to the other instances of the same metamodel, as they are tailored to a specific metamodel instance.

A rule is composed of a name, a rule source, and a set of lookups. The name is also a unique identifier for the rule. In the following, the rule source and lookups are described in more detail [Löp18].

9.3.2.1. Roule Source

The rule source selects the model elements, to which the rule has to be applied (i.e., input). The model elements are of a specific source type or its subclasses. This type represents the type of the rule input. A rule source can be a metaclass rule source, an instance rule source, or an external rule source.

In a metaclass rule source, a metaclass is referenced. This rule source selects all model elements that have the same type as the metaclass or one of its subclasses.

In an instance rule source, an instance of a metaclass is referenced. Instance declaration is described in Section 9.3.1.1.

The external rule source aims at reusing the existing rules. In this case, a specific rule can be referenced. Note that the rules must not reference each other in a way that they cause a circular dependency. If a rule references another rule, the referenced rule is applied to the model elements and its output is used as the input of the current rule. The source type is the type of the output of the referenced rule.

9.3.2.2. Lookups

Lookups are the basic units defining the propagation of a change between two sets of elements. The first set is the input of the lookup and the second set is its output. The concatenation of a set of lookups in a rule allows identifying the affected elements based on the rule sources. In this concatenation, the output of each lookup, which is not the last lookup, is the input of the next lookup. The output of the last lookup represents the output of the rule. The output of the rule is added to the list of affected elements. In other words, the outputs of the lookups in between are forwarded to the next lookup and are not added to the list of the affected model elements. This is the main difference between a rule and a lookup. Further, the output type of a lookup in between has to have the same input type of the next lookup.

There are different types of lookups: i) selection, ii) navigation, and iii) rule call. In the following, different lookup types are described in more detail [Löp18].

Selection of Model Elements The selection specifies which model element has to be considered in a rule. Thus, the use of the selection narrows down the set of model elements in a rule. There are different selection types: i) type selection, ii) instance selection, or iii) instance selection using predicates.

The type selection allows identifying model elements of a specific type. It can be a general type selection or a subtype selection. The general type selection allows selecting any types, while the selection type in the subtype selection has to be a subtype of the input.

The instance selection references an instance, which is already declared. The instance selection using predicates is a special case of the instance selection, which does not require the declaration of the instance in advance.

In this case, the instances can be selected using a code block (i.e., predicate) in the rule.

Navigation between Model Elements The use of navigation allows identifying the model elements of the output set based on the model elements of the input set. This lookup type navigates along the reference between the model elements of the input and the output. It identifies for the input set of affected model elements the output set of potentially affected model elements. The navigation direction and the navigation condition determine the affected model elements.

The navigation direction specifies along which references the model elements have to be determined. It can be either forward or backward. Each navigation direction defines the available navigation conditions. Forward and backward navigation are described in the following in more detail [Löp18].

In a forward navigation, the target for the navigation along a structural feature has to be defined. In particular, the target of a forward navigation can be a structural feature, a metaclass, or an instance, as illustrated in Listing 9.3. If the target is a structural feature, the lookup determines all model elements based on the value of a structural feature. In other words, the lookup identifies all model elements (i.e., the output), to which the input model elements reference using the value of the specific structural features. Additionally, the identified model elements have the type or a subtype of output. If the target is a metaclass, the lookup identifies all model elements, which are instances of the given metaclass or its subtypes. If the target is an instance of a metaclass, the set of instances has to be defined previously using the instance declaration (see Section 9.3.1.1). In this case, the output is a subset of this set.

In a backward navigation, the source for the navigation along a structural feature has to be defined. In particular, the source of a backward navigation can be a metaclass, a metaclass together with a structural feature, or an instance, as illustrated in Listing 9.4. If the source is a metaclass, the lookup identifies all model elements, which are instances of the given metaclass or its subtypes. It is also conceivable that the source has more than one structural feature with the same type as or a subtype of the input. In this

```
forward navigation = "->" forward navigation target
forward navigation target = forward navigation metaclass target
                          | forward navigation instance target
                          | forward navigation structural feature target
forward navigation metaclass target = "metaclass(" metaclass reference ")"
forward navigation instance target = "instance(" instance declaration
     reference ")"
forward navigation structural feature target = "feature(" structural
     feature reference ")"
```

Listing 9.3: An excerpt from the grammar of CPRL for forward navigation in EBNF

```
backward navigation = "<-" backward navigation source
backward navigation source = backward navigation metaclass source
                           | backward navigation instance source
backward navigation metaclass source = "metaclass(" metaclass reference [","
      structural feature reference] ")"
backward navigation instance source = "instance(" instance declaration
     reference ")"
```

Listing 9.4: An excerpt from the grammar of CPRL for backward navigation in EBNF

case, the specific structural feature can be used in addition to the metamodel. If the target is an instance of a metaclass, the set of instances has to be defined previously based on the instance declaration. In this case, the output of the rule is a subset of this set.

Further, it can be important to select causing elements to identify, how the change propagates in a system model. For this reason, the causing element marker can be used to select navigation (i.e., causing elements) in a change propagation rule. The causing elements in a rule cause that a specific element is affected by a change. If no navigation in a rule is marked, the first navigation is by default the causing element. If an affected model element has not been added to the task list, the model element and its causing element will be added. Otherwise only the causing element has to be updated.

Rule Call As described previously, rule calls are used to increase the reusability of the change propagation rules. If a rule is called as a part of another rule, the output of the referenced rule is returned to the other rule. In this context, a rule call can be seen as a call to a stateless helper function. Thus, rule calls can be used to avoid code duplicates.

9.3.2.3. Example

Section 9.1 describes various issues regarding the recurring technical code in a GPL during the implementation of the common change propagation rules. Listing 9.5 illustrates the application of the language to two examples from Section 9.1 involving the change propagation each along the forward and backward reference. These examples show that the rules in CPRL have less technical code. In Listing 9.5, the metamodels for IS and BP are imported as `is` and `bp`, respectively.

The first two rules illustrate two alternatives for a forward navigation, depicted in Figure 9.1. Instead of invoking the generated method `getEvent`, the rules focus on the metamodel in IS. The first rule shows a forward navigation based on the structural feature `event`, while the second rule illustrates a forward navigation based on the metaclass `EventType`. Using a metaclass in a change propagation rule causes that the rule considers all structural features between both metaclasses. By contrast, the first alternative allows selecting a specific structural feature between two metaclasses unambiguously.

The next two rules show two possible alternatives to navigate along a backward reference. The third rule is an example of a backward navigation, which source is a metaclass. In this rule, the affected metaclass is specified, which allows considering all structural features in between. By contrast, the fourth rule specifies both the metaclass and the structural feature in the backward navigation. The last rule specifies the change propagation for the third example, illustrated in Figure 9.3. It consists of a forward navigation based on a specific structural feature and a backward navigation using a metaclass and a structural feature.

This example illustrates two benefits of a DSL: i) less technical code in the case of the concatenation of forward and backward navigation and ii) omitting the cardinality. This example shows that domain experts do not need to specify the cardinality in the

```
rule EventTypeWithEventGroup: metaclass(is::EventGroup) -> feature(event);
rule EventTypeWithEventGroup: metaclass(is::EventGroup) -> metaclass(
     is::EventType);
rule ActorResourceWithRole: metaclass(bp::Role) <- metaclass(bp::ActorStep);
rule ActorResourceWithRole: metaclass(bp::Role) <- metaclass(
     bp::ActorStep,role);
rule EntryLevelSystemCallWithOperationInterface: metaclass(
     is::OperationInterface) -> feature(signatures__OperationInterface) <-
     metaclass(
     is::EntryLevelSystemCall,operationSignature__EntryLevelSystemCall);
```

Listing 9.5: CPRL rules for the example - two alternatives for forward navigation (i.e., the `EventTypeWithEventGroup` rule) and backward navigation (i.e., the `ActorResourceWithRole` rule)

CPRL explicitly. In other words, no distinction is made between the syntax of the structural features `signatures__OperationInterface` and `operationSignature__EntryLevelSystemCall`. If domain experts want to implement the change propagation rule in Java, they have to differentiate between the return types of the generated methods invoked. In this example, while the generated method `getOperationSignature__EntryLevelSystemCall()` returns one element, the generated method `getSignatures__OperationInterface()` returns a collection of elements.

9.4. Assumptions and Limitations

CPRL was designed to specify several common (i.e., not all) change propagation rules. The design of the current version of CPRL is based on the categories of change propagation rules identified during the analysis of KAMP4IS, KAMP4BP, KAMP4aPS, and KAMP4IEC. These change propagation analysis approaches and the corresponding rules were developed independent of the language (i.e., before CPRL were developed). In general, CPRL supports change propagation rules using the forward and the backward navigation based on a metamodel or its instances. These rules can be executed either sequentially or recursively. The language provides also other features such as selecting model elements at different levels in an inheritance hierarchy. The use of CPRL can be considered as optional. For example, if domain experts are experienced in Java programming, they do not need to use the proposed language. Further, interfaces to the other programming languages (e.g., OCL or Xtend) should also facilitate implementing the change propagation rules. Additionally, other declarative languages such as VQL can also be used [Löp18].

The design of CPRL is based on sets of model elements. For example, predicates use the elements of these sets. This property aims at hiding the technical code regarding the loops for selecting only a subset of model elements. Additionally, CPRL can be regarded as local, as it allows access to only variables in the current loop in the case of nested loops. Thus, the navigation condition for a specific instance is based on the attributes of this instance. Recursive blocks in CPRL are based on model elements, which are identified in the past iterations (i.e., the sets cannot be defined by users). A recursive block is executed repeatedly until the change propagation rules contained in the block do not identify further model elements. Further, the user cannot define new attributes in a lookup or add attributes to model elements. However, as described previously, the features not provided yet by CPRL can be written using imperative code in Java. These features not supported yet are not conceptual restrictions of the language and can be implemented as future work [Löp18; Bus+18b].

9.5. Conclusions

This chapter presented a declarative language to describe change propagation rules. The main goal of the development of the language was to support relevant and common patterns of change propagation rules. The development of the language was based on our experience that specific patterns of change propagation rules are reused. The main pattern of the rules was the navigation along or against a reference between two metaclasses, which were called forward and backward referenc e, respectively. Thus, the language aims at abstracting from the recurring technical code needed to specify these patterns of rules in a GPL. This leads to less time to develop rules and the reduction of errors. Further, the use of a dedicated language provides support to domain experts, who are not the developers of the change propagation analysis approach or have a little programming experience in a GPL. Additionally, the language supports sequential and recursive execution of rules at the metamodel or model level. As the language is a DSL with a reduced set of language elements, not all possible rules can be specified in the language. To address this issue, the generated code resulted from the code written in the DSL can be extended by integrating imperative code in Java. Summarized, this chapter complements the contribution of the maintainability analysis methodology (see Chapter 5), as it abstracts from the heterogeneity of elements from different domains by considering metaclasses and references between them. In this way, it partially answers the *first research question.*

10. Categories of Change Triggers in Business Processes

A software system continuously changes through its life cycle [MG10]. Patterns of change trigger aims at better predicting and managing possible future changes. For this purpose, several patterns of change triggers were developed in IS. Maybe the most important pattern was proposed by Swanson in [Swa76]. This pattern involves three dimensions categorizing various maintenance activities. Due to this categorization, a maintenance activity can be *corrective*, *adaptive*, or *perfective*. Several researchers use or adapt his categorization in different ways.

IS are used in several BP [Ros+17a; Hei+17]. Thus, the activities of BP can be generally considered as system steps and actor steps [Hei+17]. While system steps present the activities performed by IS, actor steps are the activities, which are performed by humans [Hei+17]. Actor steps and system steps in BP depend on each other and affect each other mutually. Consequently, a change in an actor step and/or in a system step can result in further changes in other actor steps and/or system steps. In general, a change in BP can lead to further changes in the IS used by the BP and vice versa [Ros+17a]. In other words, changes in BP can be considered as one of the main change triggers in IS and vice versa [Cha+01]. In contrast to existing work in IS regarding the categorization of change triggers, there is no comprehensive category of change triggers in the domain of BP. To identify the categories of change triggers a literature review was conducted in BP. This section gives an overview on the design and the results of this review. Section 10.1 presents the terminology used for the literature review. Section 10.2 gives an overview of the research methodology. The findings of the study are provided in Section 10.3. Based on these findings, a categorization scheme for change triggers in BP was developed. Section 10.4 presents this categorization. The validity discussion about the research method is given in Section 10.5. The last section summarizes the contributions of this chapter.

The content of this chapter is based on the results of the diploma thesis of Angelika Kaplan, which the author of this dissertation supervised [Kap17]. A follow-up study on this topic was also conducted, which has been appeared in the papers [Kap+18a; Kap+18b]. Thus, most content of this chapter was appeared in the aforementioned works.

10.1. Terminology

There are several definitions for change triggers in BP, which are implicitly or explicitly described in the existing literature. For example, Karthik and Reddy define a change trigger as "the initiated change is the primary cause of the propagation and the effect of that change becomes the cause of the subsequent stage" [KR16, p. 5]. This definition implicitly introduces a chain of change, which plays an important role in the impact analysis. Another definition of change triggers is proposed by Nwokeji et al. as the "event or circumstance that can bring about changes in an enterprise" [Nwo+18, p. 1]. For this review, the definition of change trigger was generalized and extended to "an event that can influence the operational process. Change triggers can be regarded as reasons, which initiate a change process. They affect the activities of a BP (i.e., manually, semi-automatically, or automatically) and the actors involved. A change trigger can be a unique event during the operating time of a BP or can occur recurrently" [Kap17, p. 131]. In this context, categories for change triggers "aggregate similar reasons or events and group them based on their semantics" [Kap17, p. 131].

10.2. Research Method

To identify change triggers in BP the following **main research question** was originally defined: "Which categories of change triggers can be identified in BP" [Kap+18a, p. 1]? During the conduction of the pilot study, two general categories of papers could be identified: the empirical and non-empirical studies. However, most papers fall into the latter one. Additionally, the reviewed papers addressed several sub-domains of BP (e.g., Business Process Flexibility (BPF)). Due to both findings, two (follow-up) secondary research questions were defined to structure the results of the review. They also aim at improving the classification of change triggers. In addition to the main research question, both questions were answered during the literature review. **First secondary research question**: "In which sub-domains of BP can change triggers be identified" [Kap17, p. 52]? **Second secondary research question**: "Is there any empirical evidence for change triggers provided in a paper" [Kap17, p. 52]?

Figure 10.1 presents the approach during the literature review. To develop a review protocol a pilot study was conducted iteratively. The goal of the pilot study was to evaluate the plan during the study. Based on its results, the review protocol of the review was defined.

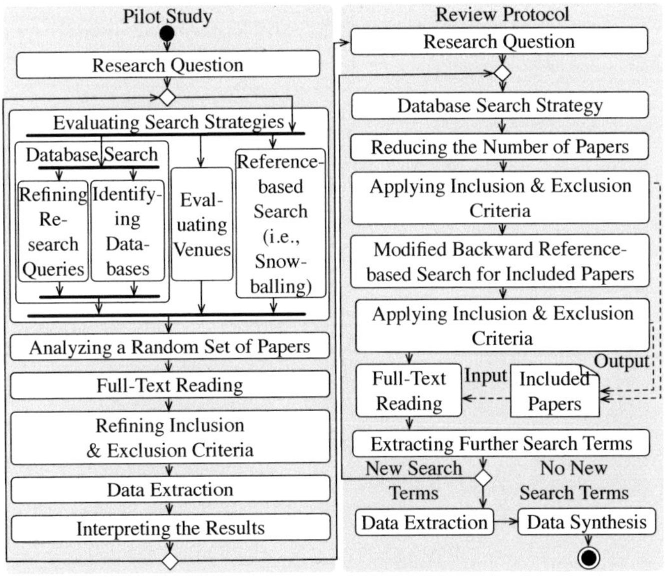

Figure 10.1.: Overview of the review process involving the pilot study and the review protocol as an activity diagram [Kap+18a, p. 2]

10.2.1. Pilot Study

The pilot study consists of four iterations. The first both iterations can be considered as a keyword and a descriptor-based approach to identify the appropriate search queries. However, the results of these iterations showed that the number of search results was very high. Further, the search results did not contain any relevant papers regarding categories of change triggers. Thus, the third iteration used structured and generalized search queries. Based on the results of the third iteration, the search and the analysis strategy were refined in the last iteration. The following subsections describe the pilot study in more detail [Kap17].

1. Iteration

The goal of the first iteration of the pilot study was the identification of the best search strategy. Thus, several strategies were evaluated in this iteration:

- Database: The main and the secondary research questions involve several domains. Thus, the database strategies recommended by Kitchenham [Kee07] had to be adapted to multidisciplinary databases.
- PICO(C): The PICO(C) strategy, which originates from the medical technique, can be used to identify research questions and search strategies [Kee07]. The acronym PICO(C) stands for *Population* (or *Problem*), *Intervention*, *Comparison*, *Outcome*, and *Context* [Kee07]. However, this strategy cannot be used for the research question in this review, as the main research question cannot be mapped to the attributes of the PICO(C) strategy.
- Reference search: This search strategy is based on the initially included papers. However, as there were not any primary included papers, a snowball search (i.e., a forward and backward reference search) could not be used in this iteration. Thus, the first step is to show that such publications exist.

- Manual screening of a set of selected venues: A further method to reduce the number of publications is the manual screening of a set of selected venues. However, this method had also to be excluded due to the multidisciplinary nature of the main research question. Another important prerequisite for this method is the period, in which the research papers were published. However, no information is available regarding the period, in which the relevant papers with focus on the main research question were published. Thus, this was a further reason for excluding this method. Additionally, screening of only a set of selected venues can result in biased results.

As described previously, the database search was the main search strategy in the first iteration. The first task of this strategy was to build the search queries. In other words, a keyword-based and a descriptor-based approach were used. The terms in these queries were derived from the terminology used in IS. The following search queries were used: "business process" "change propagation", "business process" "change impact", business process evolution, business process co-evolution information system, "business process" "change type", "business process" "change categories", business process information system change, business process software change, business process modification, enterprise architecture change impact, enterprise architecture change propagation, and business process maintenance. Google Scholar (GS) with default preferences was used as the main database, as it is a multidisciplinary bibliographic database. To reduce the number of hits, the exact match was used for some queries. In this way, an AND concatenation can be avoided. Classification scheme (e.g., methods proposed in [BRT93]) could not be used in the search strategy due to the multidisciplinary nature of the main research question [Kap17].

The aforementioned search queries resulted in a high number of hits (i.e., in some cases more than 3000000 hits). To improve the search queries, random subsets of the results were analyzed. The analysis showed that there is only a little overlap of the query results. However, these subsets did not result in any relevant publications regarding the categories of change triggers. Thus, the search queries had to be improved in the next iterations [Kap17].

2. Iteration

In the second iteration, the search queries were generalized. The new queries were comprised the domain specification (i.e., business process or workflow), changes and the corresponding change aspects (i.e., in this case triggers and their synonyms), as well as synonyms of change categories. Other examples of change aspects are effects or implementations of changes. However, only change triggers are relevant for the main search query. Thus, *change aspect* refers to change triggers in the following. Applying the previous criteria resulted in the following types of search queries [Kap17]:

- ("business process" OR workflow) AND change AND (taxonomy OR classification OR class OR classes OR dimension OR typology OR topology OR type OR types OR category OR categories)
- ("business process" OR workflow) AND ("change category" OR "change categories" OR "category of change" OR "categories of change") and ("business process" OR workflow) AND ("change type" OR "change types" OR "type of change" OR "types of change")

The multidisciplinary bibliographic databases were expanded to the following list: GS, SpringerLink, ACM DL, Web Of Science (WOS), Scopus, Bielefeld Academic Search Engine (BASE), and Association for Information System research electronic Library (AISeL). However, the number of hits was still too high (e.g., in some cases more than 400000 hits).

Similar to the previous iteration, random subsets of the results were reviewed. This aimed at improving the search queries to identify the relevant papers as efficiently as possible. The result of the review was a few numbers of research papers with focus on changes, however, neglecting the change aspect [Kap17].

3. Iteration

The results of the first two iterations showed that there is a need for generalized search queries with a well-defined structure. In other words, they must not depend on BP sub-domains such as BPF or on a specific sub-domain of a BP such as health care systems. Similar to the previous iteration, the change aspect in the search query was specified as the trigger of the change in this iteration. Other change aspects such as impact were omitted [Kap17].

In this iteration, the results of two types of search queries were analyzed. As a result, a search query is the cross product of the following search terms: i) research domain under study (i.e, "business process" and "workflow"), ii) "change", iii) synonyms of the change aspect (i.e., "trigger"), and optional iv) synonyms of the classification scheme (e.g., "category"). While the first three search terms are mandatory, the latter one is optional. Thus, the first type of the search queries consists of three search terms, while the second one consists of four terms. Synonyms of each search term were used in a search query. This iteration used the same bibliographic databases as in the previous iteration. The number of search terms in a search query is limited in some databases (e.g., a search query in IEEE Xplore can consist of a maximum of 15 search terms). For this reason, AND and OR concatenations could not be used for all databases. Thus, explicit cross products of the search terms were built [Kap+18a].

Both types of search queries still resulted in a high number of hits (e.g., in some cases more than 300000 hits). Similar to the previous iterations, various random subsets of the results were reviewed. However, they did not contain relevant papers (i.e., papers with focus on categories of change triggers). Thus, there was still a need for improving the search queries. The logical connection between the second and the third search term in a search query is AND. In this case, the AND concatenation does not result in a strong connection between both terms. To improve the search query, this concatenation has to be adapted. Following approaches can be used to adapt the search queries: i) The second and the third search terms can be combined to one search term (i.e., a phrase search such as "change trigger*" or "trigger* for change*"). ii) Alternatively, both search terms can be concatenated using proximity operators (e.g., change* NEAR/5 trigger*). The application of both approaches and the evaluation of their results showed that most bibliographic databases do not support the proximity operators. Thus, the first approach was applied to improve the search query in the next iteration [Kap+18a].

4. Iteration

As discussed in the previous iteration, the search queries contain a phrase search consisting of the term "change" and the synonyms of "trigger" (e.g., "change trigger*"). This iteration aims at identifying the best search query in terms of relevant papers. Thus, the following types of search queries were evaluated in this iteration to refine the search query [Kap+18a]:

- The first type of search queries consists of two search terms: the research domain under study (i.e., "business process" and "workflow") and the phrase search consisting of "change" and synonyms of "trigger" (e.g., "change trigger").
- The second type of search queries consists of three search terms: in addition to the search terms of the previous type, this type also consists of synonyms of classification (e.g., "category").

To identify the best search query, random subsets of the results of both search queries were evaluated. The results of the first search query contained more relevant papers. Thus, this search query was used during the study. Additionally, the full text of the random sets of papers had to be read to decide whether the papers contain categories of change triggers. A further benefit of the full-text reading was extracting further synonyms for each search term. Further, the search queries had to be adapted due to the specific search characteristics of each database [Kap+18a].

Search Strategies The resulting search strategies of the pilot study are described in the following [Kap17; Kap+18a]:

- **Bibliographic databases:** The main search strategy was the use of bibliographic databases. Following bibliographic databases were used in the review: i) **GS** is a multidisciplinary database. One of the results of the pilot study was that the results of GS searches contain papers of other databases such as AISeL, IEEE Xplore, and SpringerLink search. The search results of ii) **Scopus** and iii) **WOS** contained only a few papers. iv) **BASE** is also a multidisciplinary database. This database provides options to include the search results of other databases such as AISeL and Springer Open Choice. In other words, ACM DL, IEEE Xplore, AISeL, and SpringerLink were omitted, as GS, Scopus, WOS, and BASE contained their search results.

- **Reference-based search:** After a set of included papers has been identified, a reference-based search was used as the second strategy (i.e., forward and backward snowballing). However, this strategy was considered as inefficient to answer the main research question. Wohlin defined the efficiency as "the number of included papers in relation to the total number of candidate papers examined" [Woh14, p. 7]. Thus, this strategy was conducted only in one iteration.
- **Selected venues:** As described previously, this strategy was excluded due to three main reasons: i) The research questions were general and multidisciplinary. ii) There were not any initial included papers. iii) Considering only a set of selected venues can lead to biased results.

Reading Strategies While the previous section deals with the search strategy, this section considers the reading strategies to extract the data and to answer the research questions [Kap17; Kap+18a].

- **Bibliographic databases:** For the papers resulted from the database searches, the title, the abstract, and the conclusion were read. Further, a local-reading method for the relevant sections containing the search terms was conducted. Additionally, the inclusion of a paper required skimming the whole paper. After a paper was included, the relevant data had to be extracted. For this reason, the whole paper was read intensively.
- **Modified reference-based search:** Local reading the relevant sections could not be applied to this search strategy, as search terms are required for this method. However, as these papers were identified by reference, there are not any search terms for these papers. Consequently, the title, the abstract, and the conclusion of the papers were analyzed in the first step. In the second step, the whole paper was skimmed. If the paper was included, its content was intensively analyzed in the next phase.

- **Empirical studies:** To identify the empirical studies, the same approach was applied as in the database search. Further, the method design was analyzed.

10.2.2. Review Protocol

The results of the pilot study led to the review protocol. Based on the Kitchenham's guidelines [Kee07] the study was conducted iteratively and incrementally. This section describes the review protocol in more detail [Kap17; Kap+18a].

10.2.2.1. Research Question

As described in Section 10.2, the goal of the review was to answer the main research question: "Which categories of change triggers can be identified in BP" [Kap+18a, p. 1]? The goal of the pilot study was to evaluate the plan of the review. The resulting search queries were formulated generally. This allowed answering the secondary research questions regarding the BP sub-domains and the empirical evidence.

10.2.2.2. Search and Data Extraction Process

As described previously, the main search strategy was the database search. Based on the results of the pilot study (see the fourth iteration of the pilot study) generic search queries composed of two main search terms were formulated: i) the domain under study (i.e., "business process" and "workflow") and ii) the phrase search consisting of two search terms: the term "change" and synonyms of the term "trigger". The search query can be considered as a cross product of both search terms. During the review, further synonyms of trigger were found. The cross product allows defining a new search query by simply combining the first search term with the new synonyms of the second search term. Table 10.1 illustrates the terms of the phrase search composed of the synonyms of the term "trigger" and the term "change".

synonyms of "trigger"	phrase search for "change" and synonyms of "trigger"
trigger	"change trigger*" "trigger* for change*" "trigger* of change*" "trigger event*"
reason	"change reason*" "reason* for change*" "reason* of change*"
force	"change force*" "force* for change*" "force* of change*"
driver	"change driver*" "driver* for change*" "driver* of change*"
cause	"change cause*" "cause* for change*" "cause* of change*"
need	"need for change" "need to change"
origin	"origin* for change*" "origin* of change*"
source	"source* for change*" "source* of change*"
lever	"change lever*" "lever* for change*" "lever* of change*"

Table 10.1.: Synonyms for the phrase search involving the term "change" and synonyms of the term "trigger" [Kap17; Kap+18a; Kap+18b]

As described previously, GS, WOS, Scopus, and BASE were used in the database search phase. The search queries were adapted to the syntactical characteristics of each database.

10.2.2.3. Analysis Strategies

Despite conducting a pilot study, the number of database hits was still in some cases too high. While the number of hits of WOS, Scopus, and BASE for any search query was not more than 170, the number of GS hits for some search queries was more than 17000. For this reason, analyzing all papers resulted from the database search was not feasible. Thus, the main goal of this phase was to find a strategy to analyze only a subset of hits and, thus, to identify the relevant papers efficiently (see [Woh+00] for the definition of the efficiency). To address this issue, the first 20 papers for all search queries of all databases were analyzed. As the number of hits for GS was much higher than WOS, Scopus, and BASE, the following two methods were used to systematically find subsets of search results for GS: i) the decomposition of the second search term (i.e., the phrase search) and ii) the use of a modified search strategy, if the number of hits for the new search queries was still too high. A further goal of these methods is to avoid the ranking bias of the publications by the databases. For example, higher citation of a paper can improve its ranking. For this reason, GS can rank older publications higher than the recent ones. Both methods are presented in the following in more detail [Kap17; Kap+18a].

Decomposition of the second search term According to this method, the more hits of a search query by GS, the more papers for this query have been analyzed. Depending on the number of the initial GS hits two categories of the search queries can be built: i) The number of hits for the search queries in the first category is less than 1000. ii) The number of hits for the search queries in the second category is more than 1000. In the first category, the first 20 papers of the search results were analyzed. The search queries in the second category were decomposed into further search queries based on the second part of the search query (i.e., the phrase search). This method replaced the asterisk character (i.e., *) in these queries with the equivalent characters explicitly. In this way, the search query was replaced with several search queries. In the next step, the first 20 papers in the result of each search query were analyzed. An example of the application of this method is for the query part "reason* for change*". The number of results for the corresponding search query was about 2180. This method decomposed this query part into the following query parts: "reason for change", "reasons for change", "reason for changes", and "reasons for changes". For each query, the first 20 papers were analyzed.

Modified search strategy As described previously, the older a publication, the higher GS can rank it due to more citations. This method aims at avoiding the ranking bias of these publications. Similar to the previous method, this method was applied to the search queries with a high number of hits by GS. Depending on the number of hits of the search queries, their results were divided into three categories:

- If the number of hits for a search query was less than 500, the first 20 papers were analyzed.
- If the number of hits for a search query was between 500 and 1000, the first 20 papers were analyzed. Then, the papers were sorted by time. Additionally, the first 20 papers published between 2011 and 2016 were analyzed.
- In all other cases, the method in the second case was applied. Additionally, the first 20 papers published between 2006 and 2011 were analyzed.

Tables A.1 to A.9 in Appendix A.2 present the search queries for each database and the number of hits. They also show which methods were applied to each search query.

10.2.2.4. Inclusion and Exclusion Criteria

The following sections describe the inclusion and exclusion criteria for the main and the secondary research questions.

Criteria for the main research question This section presents the inclusion criteria for the main research question. The criteria were based on the content and the bibliographical data of the papers:

- An included paper has to be in one of the sub-domains of BP. In other words, the title, the abstract, the keywords (or the descriptors), or the introduction must contain information regarding BP. Typical indicators for such information are terms such as Change Management (CM), process management, Business Process Change (BPC), Business Process Modeling (BPM), or BPF.
- An included paper has to explicitly contain the terms indicating categories of change triggers. Examples of typical terms for categories are *class/es*, *category/ies*, or *type/s*. Other change aspects such as change impact were omitted. A paper can also contain more

than one change aspect. In this case, only papers are included, which explicitly describe change triggers. Although all BP sub-domains are considered (e.g., BPF or workflow management), the categories of change triggers have to be generic (e.g., independent of a specific sub-domain).

- Only research papers from conferences, journals, symposiums, workshops, and magazines were analyzed.

The exclusion criteria for the study were as follows:

- Papers, which are not in any sub-domain of BP, were excluded.
- Duplicates and redundant information were excluded. Note that duplicates are also papers with identical semantic contents and contributions. Examples of this are papers, which were published both in a conference and in a journal as an extended version. In this case, only the journal papers were included.
- Papers, which are shorter than 7 pages (e.g., short papers), were excluded.
- Papers, which were not free available, were excluded.
- Grey literature were excluded. Examples are technical reports, theses, presentation slides, white papers, books, or book chapters.
- Papers, which are not written in English, were excluded.

Additional criteria for the secondary research question regarding empirical studies The inclusion and exclusion criteria for the main and the secondary research questions were the same. The following inclusion criteria were only considered for the secondary research question regarding empirical studies:

- The title or the abstract has to indicate that an empirical study was conducted. The abstract should describe the method design. Otherwise, the corresponding sections regarding the method design were reviewed.
- The results of the paper have to originate in a cooperation with an organization (i.e., industry).

Data item	Description
Study ID	Unique reference ID for the paper
Title	Title of the Study
Year	Calender year of the publication
Sub-domain	Research context or domain
Venue	Conference, journal, symposium, workshop, or magazine
Name	Name of the specific venue
Category	Change trigger categories in BP as quotation from the paper
Study type	Empirical or non-empirical study
Research method	Research design of an empirical study
Change trigger	Change triggers in empirical studies as quotation from the paper

Table 10.2.: Data extraction format [Kap17, p. 63]

10.2.2.5. Data Extraction Format

After including a paper, it has been intensively analyzed regarding the research questions. Table 10.2 presents the data extraction format during the review.

10.3. Findings

This section presents the results of the literature review. The goal of the review was to answer the main research question and, then, the secondary research questions. Thus, the papers were analyzed regarding these aspects (i.e., categories of change triggers in BP, the corresponding BP sub-domains, and the empirical evidence). A descriptive (i.e., non-quantitative) data synthesis was conducted for each included paper to extract data according to Table 10.2. The data synthesis deals with collecting and summarizing the results of the papers included [Kee07]. Section 10.3.1 presents the papers identified during the review to answer the main research question. Section 10.3.2 shows the identified papers regarding the secondary research questions [Kap17; Kap+18a].

10.3.1. Publications on Categories of Change Triggers in Business Processes

The papers were analyzed with regard to the inclusion and exclusion criteria. The included papers contain terms, which explicitly indicate the change trigger and a categorization. After a paper has been included, a full-text reading was conducted. To answer the first secondary research question, the corresponding BP sub-domain (e.g., BPF) for each paper was also extracted. Further, a paper can be either empirical or non-empirical. Tables 10.3 and 10.4 give an overview of the study results.

Overall, only one of the included papers was an empirical study (see [P1] in Table 10.3). The paper is written in the sub-domain of Organizational Change (OC) and CM. The results of this paper were gathered through interviews in 28 organizations within six months. The interviews aimed at identifying the factors for the successful management of changes. In general, two categories of change triggers were identified: 1) "external drivers" (e.g., due to changing "customers requirements" or other stakeholders, "regulatory demand", "market competition", or "shareholders") and 2) "internal drivers" (e.g., "improving operational efficiency", "quality of products and services", or process) [OT07, p. 3]. Further, the paper states that internal and external drivers influence each other. In other words, the internal drivers are rather "a manifestation of external drivers for change" [OT07, p. 3].

Other included papers (i.e., [P2] to [P10]) were non-empirical papers. Table 10.4 gives an overview of these papers and the proposed categories of change triggers in BP. In the following, the proposed category of each paper is briefly proposed [Kap17].

[P2] can be categorized in the sub-domain of workflow management technologies (i.e., automatically performed BP activities). The paper states that an effective reacting to changes is the main challenge of Workflow Management Systems (WfMS). For this reason, a set of six criteria is used to classify the change. The first criterion considers the reasons for change. The reasons for change can be grouped into the change triggers due to developments 1) "outside the system" (i.e., environment) and 2) "inside the system" (i.e., problems identified inside the system) [AJ00, p. 2]. If the development is outside the system, the change can be due to 1.1) "changing business context" (i.e. due to "Business Process Reengineering (BPR)", "changing marketplace", or

Ref.	Title	Year	Categories	Sub-domain
[P1]	A new Framework for Managing Change [OT07]	2007	1. Internal drivers 1.1. Improving operational efficiency 1.2. Need to improve the quality of products and services 1.3. Process improvement 2. External drivers 2.1. Customer requirement 2.2. Demand from other stakeholders (e.g., government) 2.3. Regulatory Demand 2.4. Market competition 2.5. Shareholders/city	OC CM

Table 10.3.: Overview of empirical papers including categories of change triggers in BP [Kap17, p. 133][Kap+18a]

"demands of individual customers"), 1.2) "changing legal context" (e.g., due to "new legislature"), or 1.3) "changing technological contexts" (e.g., due to "new technology" or changing "technical infrastructure") [AJ00, p. 2]. If the development inside the system causes the change, its reason can be either 2.1) "logical design errors" (e.g., "deadlocks or missing data") or 2.2) "technical problems" (e.g., "failing components") [AJ00, p. 2].

[P3] is concerned with the sub-domain OC. This paper presents internal (e.g., due to "personnel, culture, or technology") and external change triggers (e.g., due to "customers, competition, or regularity environment") as a possible way to classify the need for change [VVL03, p. 4].

[P4] can be considered in the sub-domain of BPF. The authors present a taxonomy for BPF, which is based on the taxonomy proposed in [RSS06]. One aspect of this taxonomy considers the origin of change, which can be either 1) "internal business policies" (e.g., due to management strategies and decisions) or 2) "external business regulations" (e.g., due to legislature, norms, or contracts) [GV06, p. 4].

[P5] is in the sub-domain of IT/Business Alignment (IT/BA). The authors propose a new framework in this paper. The framework provides classification along several dimensions (e.g., "nature of change", "origin of change", or "nature of impact of a change") [NCG08, p. 5]. The origin of change can be in its turn either 1) "internal" or 2) "external" [NCG08, p. 5].

[P6] is also in the sub-domain of IT/BA and Change Management System (CMS). The paper presents an approach to adapt the execution environment, if the corresponding BP changes. The authors distinguish between two change triggers in BP: 1) automatically triggered changes (e.g., due to 1.1) "quality indicators" (e.g., "performance") and 1.2) "reasons for inefficiencies" of "user behavior") and 2) manually triggered changes (e.g., due to 2.1) changing "technologies", 2.2) changing "environment", or 2.3) changing "goals of a company") [THF08, p. 3].

[P7] and [P10] give an overview on approaches to change engineering. Due to the lack of method design, these papers could not be considered as empirical studies. Based on the results of the literature review they present two categories of reasons for change: 1) "emergent changes arising from the properties of the product" (e.g., due to 1.1) correcting errors during the design, 1.2) changes, if products do not fulfill the safety requirements, 1.3) changes, if products do not fulfill the functional requirements, and 1.4) quality problems of products (e.g., "poor design or incorrect manufacture and assembly instructions")) and 2) "initiated changes" (e.g., due to 2.1) "customers", 2.2) "marketing", 2.3) supporting maintenance tasks of a product, 2.4) supporting production, 2.5) changes arising from suppliers, 2.6) "product engineering", 2.7) management policies of companies, and 2.8) legislature) [Jar+11, p. 7],[KR16].

[P8] is in the sub-domain of Service-Oriented Computing (SOC). The authors present in this paper a framework for change management in LCS. Further, a classification for top-down changes is proposed: 1) "business-centric changes" (e.g., due to "commercial purpose" such as improvement of a BP) and 2) "regulation-centric changes" (i.e., "complying with new regulation") [Liu+11, p. 6].

In the sub-domain of BPM, [P9] presents the problem arising from changing BP over time. The authors distinguish between triggers "from external factors" (e.g., due to new technology or legislature) and "from internal factors" (e.g., errors during the design) [KKF12, p. 5].

Table 10.4 summarizes the results. It shows that several papers distinguish between external and internal factors of change triggers. Additionally, the categorizations presented in several papers are hierarchically structured. Both patterns were also used to develop a comprehensive categorization, which is presented in the next section. Further, the generalized search query and the modified analysis method allow considering several sub-domains of BP [Kap17; Kap+18a].

Ref.	Title	Year	Categories	Sub-domain
[P2]	Dealing with Workflow Change: Identification of Issues and Solutions [AJ00]	2000	1. Developments outside the system 1.1. Changing business context 1.2. Changing legal context 1.3. Changing technological context 2. Developments inside the system 2.1. Logical design errors 2.2. Technical problems	WfMS
[P3]	Integrated Enterprise Transformation: Case Application in Engineering Project Work in the Belgian Armed Forces [VVL03]	2003	1. Internal change trigger 2. External change trigger	OC
[P4]	Compliant and Flexible Business Processes with Business Rules [GV06]	2006	1. Internal business policy change 2. External business regulation change	BPC BPF
[P5]	Conceptual Dependencies between two Connected IT Domains: Business/IS Alignment and IT Governance [NCG08]	2008	1. Internal origin of change 2. External origin of change	IT/BA

Ref.	Title	Year	Categories	Sub-domain
[P6]	Life Cycle for Change Management in Business Process Using Semantic Technologies [THF08]	2008	1. Automatically based on 1.1. Measurement of key performance indicators or quality indicators 1.2. Reasons for inefficiencies 2. Manually due to 2.1. Technology changes 2.2. Changes in the environment 2.3. Changes in the goals of company	CMS IT/BA
[P7]	Engineering Change: An Overview and Perspective on the Literature [Jar+11]	2011	1. Changes starting a chain of changes: 1.1. Emergent (e.g., error correction, safety, change of function, or product quality problems) 1.2. Initiated (e.g., customers or legislators)	EC
[P8]	Efficient Change Management in Long-term Composed Services [Liu+11]	2011	1. Top-down change 1.1. Business-centric changes 1.2. Regulation-centric changes	LCS/ SOC CM
[P9]	Timeline Visualization for Documenting Process Model Change [KKF12]	2012	1. Triggers (or reasons) for change from external factors 2. Triggers (or reasons) for change from internal factors 3. Triggers for evolutionary changes	BPM
[P10]	Engineering Changes in Product Design - A Review [KR16]	2016	1. Emergent changes (Product itself due to the error during the design process) 2. Initiated changes (External source)	ECM

Table 10.4.: Overview of non-empirical papers involving categories of change triggers in BP [Kap17, p. 135f][Kap+18a]

10.3.2. Empirical Studies to Change Triggers in Business Processes

Although the main goal of the review was to identify the categories of change triggers in BP, the search and analysis strategies were general enough to answer the secondary research questions. The focus of the research question, which this section is concerned, is, whether there is any empirical study regarding change triggers in BP. In contrast to the main contribution of the review, which regards to the categories of change triggers in BP, this question deals with individual change triggers in BP from industry. In other words, the included papers must have a practical relevance or had to be conducted in cooperation with industry. Table 10.5 summarizes the empirical studies and the change triggers discussed. The empirical studies in these papers are based on face-to-face communication, phone interview, semi-structured interviews, and questionnaires. These papers present the change triggers and not categories of them. Thus, the change triggers are fine-grained and at a low abstraction level [Kap17].

Ref.	Title	Year	Change Trigger	Sub-domain
[P11]	New Organisation Structures for Global Business: An Empirical Study [WB98]	1998	- IT, the WWW, and communication technologies advances - Homogenisation of global branding and manufacturing - Increasingly successful global organisation - Customer-demanded advances in levels of service of transportation goods - Increased normality of cross-country and cross-continent trade goods - Governmental encouragement and subsidies for industrial investment - The proliferation of free-trade zones and trade-blocks - Changes in political boundaries - Increases in air leisure and business travel - Increasingly global focus of media and politics - Globalisation - Alternative organizational strategies	OC

Ref.	Title	Year	Change Trigger	Sub-domain
[P12]	Organisational Change: The Australian Experience [SL00]	2000	- To become more competitive - To improve productivity/efficiency - To reduce costs - To increase capacity - To improve management efficiency - To improve occupational health and safety - To improve management/ employee communication - To improve customer service - To improve workplace culture - To improve product/service - To improve input from employees - To improve sales	OC
[P13]	The Triangular Model for Dealing with Organizational Change [Ala07]	2007	Social/economic transformation	OC
[P14]	Implementation of Organizational Changes in Estonian Companies [Ala+08]	2008	Trigger event: - Leaving the centrally planned Soviet Union to reorient to European market at the beginning of 1990. - Introduction of western standards - Increasing the efficiency (cf.[Ala07])	CM

Table 10.5.: Overview of the empirical papers containing change triggers in BP (i.e., without any categorization) [Kap17, p. 138f]

10.4. Categorization of Change Triggers in Business Processes

The previous sections proposed change triggers in BP based on empirical studies, as well as their categorizations in empirical and non-empirical papers. This section presents a new categorization based on the data extracted in the previous sections. Further, there is a need for a scheme or concept to build a new categorization. The concept used for this categorization is presented in the following section:

10.4.1. W-Questions

This section describes the underlying schema and concept to build a new categorization. This schema is based on the W-questions. The W-questions are used to structure the results of the previous sections (see Sections 10.3.1 and 10.3.2) and to develop a new comprehensive categorization based on these results. The W-questions are described in the following [Kap17; Kap+18a]:

- *Why* refers to the corresponding change aspect in BP (i.e., *change trigger*).
- *Who* or *What* describes the *participation* in a change (i.e., the *role*).
- *Where* relates to the *origin* of a change.
- *When* or *how* presents further *properties* and the *characteristics* of a change trigger.

Based on the W-questions a categorization scheme was developed, which is composed of three components. The components regard each the W-questions *who*, *where*, and *when* [Kap17; Kap+18a].

10.4.2. Category of Change Triggers in Business Processes

As described previously, the answer of the first question (i.e., *why?*) presents the change trigger. Other questions regard the dimensions of the categorization. Thus, the categorization of change *triggers* in BP is composed of three components at the highest abstraction level: *participation* (i.e., to answer the question *who*?), *origin* (i.e., to answer the question *where*?), and *characteristics* (i.e., to answer the question *when?* or *how*?). Table 10.6 presents the category of change triggers in BP based on the W-questions. The category is composed of four abstraction levels, as illustrated in Table 10.6. The abstraction levels are presented by layers: The first layer presents the highest abstraction level. The fourth layer is the specification of the proposed categorization. Consequently, a component (e.g., *participation*) can be specialized in further subcomponents (i.e., *initiators*, *reluctant participants*, and *further participants*) in the next higher layer. In other words, a change trigger can be described using different components of the category and at different abstraction levels. A change can also cause a chain of further changes [Jar+11]. Thus, a further goal of the category proposed in Table 10.6 is the support of change triggers in a chain of changes. The following sections discuss the components of the category in more detail [Kap17; Kap+18a].

10.4.2.1. Component 1 - Participation

The first component in the highest abstraction level is the component *participation*. The second layer of Table 10.6 shows that a participant in a change trigger can have either an *initiator* (e.g., [P7,P10]), a *reluctant* (e.g., [P7]), or a *further* role (e.g., passive). The initiators and the reluctant participants are opposed to each other (see the change model of Lewin [Lew47]). These participants have an active role during the change, while other participants have a passive role in a change process. As all three roles have the same refinements at low abstraction levels, only the initiator role is described in more detail. Both *legal* and *non-legal entities* can initiate a change process. The legal entities can be persons or person groups. At a lower abstraction level, they can be *internal* or *external stakeholders* (e.g., [P1,P7]). In this context, the terms internal and external regard the structure of an organization. Examples for internal stakeholders are employees or managers. [EKS08] discusses different roles such as project leader in the sub-domain of BP management in more detail. By contrast, examples for external stakeholders are customers, suppliers, or creditors. Further discussion on the stakeholder analysis is given by [Jar+11]. As the categorization proposed in this thesis is general, these components were not further specialized. The non-legal entities can be considered as methods or systems, which provide decision support, communication medium (e.g., [P13]), or technical support for internal stakeholders (e.g., [P2]). Examples for this subcomponent are reports, conferences, or meetings [Kap17; Kap+18a].

10.4.2.2. Component 2 - Origin

This section discusses the *origin* of a change trigger [Kap17; Kap+18a]. A change can have an *external* or an *internal* origin (cf. systems the-

Layer 1	Layer 2	Layer 3	Layer 4
partici-pation	initiators	legal entities	internal and external stakeholder
		non-legal entities	control and monitoring systems key performance indicator further systems (e.g., hardware, software, infrastructure) methods of communication
	reluctant participants	– " –	– " –
	further participants	– " –	– " –
origin	internal origin	person-related influence	skills and expert knowledge culture and ethical reasons leadership style internal stakeholder requirements
		business domain (process and structure)	business strategy, business goals business rules quality and performance organizational structure and further events
		technology and IT	logical design errors in business process model inefficient business model design (e.g., performance, benchmarking) hardware failure and technical problems safety
	external origin	person-related regulations	external stakeholder requirements
		socio-economics	demography culture and ethical reasons
		politics	national legislation international agreements and conventions
		further regulations	standards and norms certification, seal/label (seal guarantees)
		economy	inflation globalization characteristics of economic systems
		location	climate natural disaster and hazards competing conditions referred to economic system
		technology	data communication and IT infrastructure data storage and processing IT security hardware evolution new production methods, working techniques and methods, materials

Layer 1	Layer 2	Layer 3	Layer 4
charac-teristics	degree of urgency	reactive proactive	
	degree of intensity	low medium high	
	degree of complexity	low medium high	
	degree of prediction	predictable unpredictable	
	degree of hierarchy	top-down change bottom-up change hybrid change	

Table 10.6.: Categories of change triggers in BP [Kap17, p. 169],[Kap+18a, p. 6]

ory [Ber68]). Most identified papers consider this categorization as the main category of change triggers in BP (e.g., [P1,P5,P9]). The system theory was also applied to *economy* (e.g., organization), *sociology* (e.g., social constructs), *technology* (e.g., hardware), or a combination of those (e.g., *socio-economics*). The subcomponents of internal origin also reflect the described concept (i.e., the third layer in Table 10.6). To develop a comprehensive categorization of change triggers in BP, the structure of the categorization has to be extended to include more components. Thus, the components internal and external have three and seven subcomponents in the next higher abstraction level, respectively.

The internal origin can be the *influences of a person*, the *business domain (i.e., process and structure)* and the *technology and IT* at a lower abstraction level. The first subcomponent can be considered as the influences of a person or a person group who causes a change in BP. In particular, these influences could be due to the *expert knowledge* (e.g., the new knowledge of actors can influence a BP by improving it), *culture and ethical reasons* (e.g., organizational culture [P3]), *leadership style* [P13], or *requirements of the internal stakeholders* (e.g., [P7]).

The second subcomponent (i.e., business domain) can be understood as the organizational factors triggering a change. At a lower abstraction level, a business domain can be *business strategies*, *goals*, and *rules* (e.g., [P4]). These components involve the business policies and expertise. Examples of that are business rules [BRG01]. Its goal is defined by [BRG01] as "to assert business structure or to control or influence the behavior of the business". They aim at improving the products and services in organizations. As they aim at regulating BP, they can trigger a change (e.g., [P8]). Other subcomponents of the business domain are *quality attributes* such as *performance* (e.g., [P6]) and *further events*. Quality attributes regard the quality of services and products provided by BP, as well as workflows. In this case, if the quality attributes are not satisfied, they can trigger a change in BP. Further events include events such as fire blights or a new organizational form (e.g., [P13]). An example of an organizational form can be corporation.

The last subcomponent of change triggers with an internal origin is *technology* and *Information Technology (IT)*. They regard all technical systems, which aim at supporting BP. This subcomponent also involves models. In this way, comparison of the results in the real word and the results obtaining from the model can be an indicator for the design in the real world. A poor design can trigger a change in BP for example by replanning the corresponding BP (e.g., [P2]). Hardware problems (e.g., [P2]) or safety issues (e.g., [P7]) can be further triggers in this category.

The external origin has seven subcomponents at the next lower abstraction level. As described previously, this classification is based on economy, sociology, technology and the combinations of them.

Regulations are one of the most important change triggers, as they constrain the frame of the BP (e.g., [P6,P8]). The *person-related regulations* define regulations, which are caused by persons. In other words, the *requirements of external stakeholders* influence the corresponding BP (e.g., [P1]). *Politics* can also trigger a change in BP. It involves subcomponents such as *national* (e.g., [P2,P10]) and *international laws*, *conventions*, and *agreements* (e.g., [P4]). In other words, the location of a company and the aforementioned subcomponents intertwine. *Further regulations* can also be reasons for change. Examples of these regulations are *standards* and *norms* (e.g., [P4,P7]), such as quality standard DIN EN ISO 8402 [ISO92], DIN EN ISO 9000 to 9004 [Bra09], environmental standard ISO 14000, Eco-Management and Audit Scheme (EMAS) [Bra10], certification and seal/label (i.e., seal guarantees). *Economic factors* can also affect a BP. An example of this can be *inflation* or *globalization* (e.g., [P11]). *Locations* such as *competing conditions regarding economic systems* (e.g., [P1,P3]) play also an important role as change triggers. *Technology* as a further change trigger can be refined based on several concepts such as Moore's Law [Moo65] or Metcalfe's Law [MB76]. These refinements relate to the technological evolution and development. This includes the *IT infrastructure* of an organization. The *security* of a BP can also act as a change trigger (i.e., attacking an IS, which supports a workflow). Additionally, *new technologies or production techniques*, as well as *materials* (e.g., [P10]) are also sources of change. The aforementioned methods include methods for the management and operational business.

10.4.2.3. Component 3 - Characteristics

The *characteristics* present the properties of a change [Kap17; Kap+18a]. In contrast to both previous components, there are only three refinement layers for characteristics.

The *degree of urgency* (e.g., [P7], [P10]) presents the need for an immediate action. This can occur either *proactive* or *reactive*. Proactive changes relate to preventive measures. They can also be innovation drivers due to their creative nature. Reactive changes are change triggers in an organization referring to measures which have to be taken due to internal or external events. In contrast to proactive change, they are forced. Hammer and Champy describe in [HC93] that these changes can cause a radical redesign.

The *degree of intensity* regards the impact of change triggers in a chain of changes, which cause further change triggers (cf. degree of complexity). It answers the last *W-question* (i.e., *When?* or *How?*). The impact caused by these changes can be classified as high, medium, or low. This task has to be done by domain experts. However, the classification is not always straightforward.

Similar to the previous category, the *degree of complexity* is concerned with the effects of a change trigger over a long period of time (e.g., [P7]). Consequently, the change triggers caused by the original change trigger have to be considered for the analysis. The categorization of a change trigger regarding this component requires the documentation of the change process (cf. [P9]).

The *degree of prediction* (e.g., [P7]) presents the probability of the occurrence of a change trigger. This can be *predictable* or *unpredictable*. The *degree of prediction* can be used for change triggers that aim at improving the BP.

The *degree of hierarchy* (e.g., [P13]) addresses the categorization of the change triggers, which occur in the hierarchical structure of an organization. Its refinements namely *top-down changes* (e.g., [P8]), *bottom-up changes*, and *hybrid/middleware changes* can be used for sociological, economic, and technological contexts and all process types. The top-down changes present the changes, which originate from the management level. BPR is an example of such changes. By contrast, the bottom-up changes are initiated by employees.

This section proposed a comprehensive category for change triggers in BP. As the categorization is not limited to a specific sub-domain or sector of BP, it can be regarded as a generic categorization. It is based on the system theory and the W-questions (see Section 10.4.1), which show several aspects of a change trigger. Consequently, the components of the category at a high abstraction level reflect the W-questions. Thus, it allows the categorization of change triggers based on different components (i.e., criteria such as participation and origin) [Kap17; Kap+18a].

10.4.3. Benefits of an Explicit Category of Change Triggers

This section discusses the benefits of a comprehensive category of change triggers in BP:

i) As described previously, BP consist of a set of actor steps and system steps [Hei+17]. The system steps allow invoking the services of an IS [Hei+17]. Thus, both IS and BP influence each other and change together during their life cycles [Ros+17a]. For this reason, IS and BP have to be considered together in the process of the change propagation analysis [Ros+17a]. Thus, a comprehensive category of change triggers in BP cannot only aim at managing the future changes in BP, but also in IS [Kap+18a].

ii) This category can be used to develop a checklist for possible future risks, changes, and requirements [Kap+18a].

iii) The proposed category abstracts from a specific sub-domain of BP. Thus, it presents a generic category, which can be used in different organizations and BP. Further, a change trigger can be categorized along several components [Kap+18a].

10.4.4. Design Decisions and Assumptions

This section presents the design decisions and the assumptions during the development of the proposed category [Kap17; Kap+18a].

The structure of the category presented in Table 10.6 is hierarchically organized. This structure is proposed by several papers (e.g., [P2]). Consequently, a change trigger can be categorized in a specific or generic manner along a component (e.g., participation). Different components are independent of each other. Thus, the proposed category can easily be extended due to its hierarchical structure and the independence of its components.

The initial categorization scheme had five layers. However, the categorization was too complex due to the last layer, as the level of specialization was too high. Thus, the fourth and fifth levels were merged to avoid a complex categorization scheme.

In order to be able to apply the categorization to any BP, it was developed regardless of a specific sub-domain of BP. Thus, the category can be considered as generic.

The category allows the categorization of a change trigger along different components (i.e., participation, origin, or properties) or subcomponents at several abstraction levels.

10.5. Threats to Validity

This section discusses the threats to validity during the conduction of the study [Kap17; Kap+18a].

The main search strategy was the database search, as suggested by Evidence-Based Software Engineering (EBSE) guidelines such as [Kee07]. As described previously, the PICO(C) strategy was not applicable to the proposed research questions. The search queries were derived from the main research question. However, the generic search queries also allowed answering the secondary research questions.

During the data extraction phase, new synonyms of the search terms were extracted. These synonyms were used to build cross products of the search terms for new search queries. This method was used to have a complete set of synonyms.

The search queries had to be adapted to the syntactic characteristics of different databases. Although the search strategy and the search query were adapted during the pilot study, they still resulted in a high number of hits (i.e., the number of hits was more than 52000). Consequently, analyzing all hits could not be conducted feasibly. Thus, the evidence is limited to the analyzed subset of all papers obtained during the database search.

Biased ranking was also an aspect of the search results. Consequently, older publications have more citations and can be considered as more relevant in the search results. To avoid this bias, a method has been developed to identify the recently published papers.

Another finding during the database search strategy regards the search queries, for which GS showed more than 1000 hits. In these cases, GS only allowed access to the first 1000 results. Thus, this can be considered as a limitation for all systematic studies.

During the pilot study, the initial inclusion and exclusion criteria were refined. The reasons for this were avoiding the subjective bias, a better reproducibility of the results, the diversity of the contents, and the multidisciplinary nature of the research questions.

10.6. Conclusions

This chapter presented a comprehensive category of change triggers in BP. For this purpose, a pilot study was iteratively conducted to identify the research method. The resulting search strategy was chosen to answer the main research question and the secondary ones. The process was based on the guidelines of Kitchenham [Kee07] and was conducted iteratively and incrementally. The review protocol and in particular the search and read strategies were designed to handle a high number of research publications, as well as their diversity. A further goal was to avoid the bias of the publications. The resulting publications were mainly divided into empirical studies and non-empirical papers.

The resulting category was designed to answer the following W-questions regarding different aspects of a change trigger: i) *Who* or *What* refers the *participation* in a change. ii) *Where* refers the *origin* of a change. iii) *When* or *how* refers the *characteristics* of a change trigger. Thus, the new category comprises several dimensions (i.e., components) to address the aforementioned aspects. The dimensions were, further, refined in four layers, which represent different abstraction levels. Further, the category can be considered as generic, as it was developed regardless of a specific organization or a sub-domain of BP. Thus, it can be applied to different BP and organizations. Summarized, this category contributes to the evaluation of the change propagation analysis approach in BP (see Section 11.2). During the evaluation, several change scenarios were designed to cover different dimensions of the category.

11. Evaluation

As a contribution of this thesis a maintainability analysis methodology was presented to facilitate the development of modular change propagation analysis approaches in a specific domain involving heterogeneous elements. The resulting approaches are based on metamodels and use change propagation rules to describe the dependencies between the metaclasses. This chapter discusses the evaluation of the methodology and the resulting approaches.

This chapter is structured as follows: Section 11.1 discusses the relevancy and comprehensiveness of the methodology by evaluating its instances in IS, BP, and aPS. In Section 11.2, the instance of the methodology in BP is evaluated using two community case studies. The instance of the methodology in aPS is evaluated using the community case study xPPU. The results of this evaluation are presented in Section 11.3. Section 11.4 summarizes the results of the evaluation and the influencing factors during the instantiation of the methodology. Further, it discusses the threats to validity.

11.1. Maintainability Analysis Methodology

The maintainability analysis methodology, introduced in Chapter 5, can be considered as a generic guideline for the development of the change propagation analysis approaches. It aims at improving the development process by providing generic metamodels and algorithms for various change propagation analysis approaches (i.e., its instances). Additionally, the methodology provides guidelines for the development of a change propagation analysis approach in a specific domain in terms of modular metamodels and algorithms. Thus, the methodology aims at facilitating the reuse of not only the metamodels and algorithms, but also the underlying concepts and best practices needed during the development. To develop a change propagation analysis approach, the methodology has to be instantiated in a specific domain. As described previously, the resulting approach is also referred to as an instance of the methodology. Thus, this section discusses the applicability of the methodology to different domains. The content of this section has been appeared in the paper [HBK18].

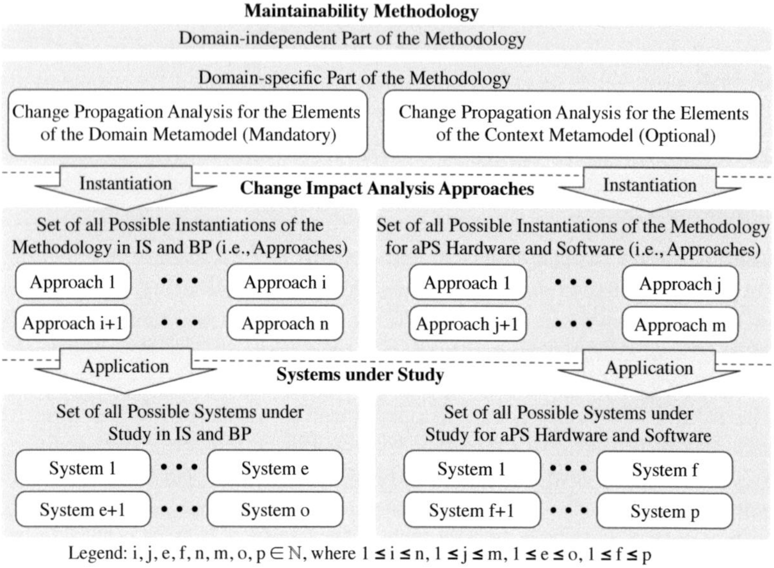

Figure 11.1.: Schematic illustration of the relationships between the maintainability analysis methodology, its concrete instances, and the application of the instances to specific systems

Figure 11.1 illustrates the relationships between the maintainability analysis methodology, its instances, and the application of the instances to specific systems. As described in Chapter 5, the output of each instance is an automatically generated task list. It is conceivable that there can be more than one instance of the methodology in a specific domain (see the first both layers of Figure 11.1). One influencing factor for both different instances and the generated task lists is the granularity of the metamodels in a domain. For example, Chapter 7 shows the use of two metamodels at two different abstraction levels in aPS. While the abstract metamodel allows modeling any plant, the specific metamodel is tailored to the xPPU. In this way, two different change propagation analysis approaches have been developed for aPS. Another influencing factor is the granularity of the change propagation rules. The rules can specify the change propagation in a fine-grained or in a coarse-grained manner. Additionally, the rules may cover all possible relationships between all metaclasses or only a few important relationships. The evaluation of KAMP4BP together with KAMP4IS in the following section shows the effect of different change propagation rules on the generated task lists. There are also other factors such as whether the optional parts of the methodology are implemented or not due to their relevance in a specific case. These factors lead not only to several instances of the methodology in a specific domain, but also affect the quality of the generated task lists of the instances.

During this thesis, one instance of the methodology in the domain of BP and two instances of the methodology in the domain of aPS were developed. The instance of the methodology in BP has four variants, which slightly differ regarding the change propagation rules. Thus, the goal of this section is not to evaluate the quality of the output of each individual instance. This section discusses the applicability of the methodology to different domains based on the developed instances. It is important to note that other instances of the methodology are also conceivable. In other words, this section focuses on the first both layers of Figure 11.1 (i.e., the maintainability analysis methodology and the resulting instances). The quality of the results of the developed instances (i.e., the latter both layers of Figure 11.1) is evaluated in the next sections of this chapter (see Sections 11.2 and 11.3).

Section 11.1.1 presents the goals, questions, and metrics of the evaluation. After the instances of the methodology have been developed, the applicability of the methodology regarding the reusability of each element of the methodology in the respective instance was evaluated. An overview of the results is given in Section 11.1.2. Section 11.1.3 discusses the assumptions and limitations.

11.1.1. Evaluation Goals, Questions, and Metrics

The Goal Question Metric (GQM) plan [Bas92; BCR94] was used to evaluate the methodology. The **Goal** is to evaluate the relevance and the comprehensiveness of the methodology by instantiating it in different domains. For this reason, the methodology has been instantiated in several domains. These instances were analyzed for the evaluation [HBK18].

Question 1 aims at evaluating the relevance of the methodology: In how many instances each element of the methodology is used? As described previously, not all elements of the methodology have to be instantiated in a domain. This highly depends on the development phase of the system under study, the development effort for the instance, and the desired granularity of the results. The more often an element of the methodology was instantiated, the more relevant it can be considered. To answer this question, **Metric 1** is defined as the ratio, R, of the number of instances in which an element is used, U, to the number of all instances, N. This metric can be obtained as $R = \frac{U}{N}$ [HBK18].

To evaluate the comprehensiveness of the methodology, **Question 2** is formulated: Can any common metamodel or algorithm be extracted from the instances, which were not already considered by the methodology? The term *common metamodel or algorithm* regards any metamodel or algorithm, which occurs in more than one instance. These metamodels and algorithms are considered as *common* in the evaluation, only if they are necessary to develop the change propagation analysis approaches in these domains. The less common metamodels or algorithms not considered by the methodology, the more comprehensive the methodology can be considered. Thus, **Metric 2** is the number of the missing common metamodels or algorithms in the methodology [HBK18].

In the following, an overview of the selected domains is given: The methodology was instantiated to the domain of BP, as BP can be regarded as a set of actor steps and system steps at a high abstraction level [Hei+17]. Thus, a change to BP or to the IS used can propagate not only in each domain, but also to the other domain [Ros+17a]. In this way, the co-evolution of IS and BP can be considered [HBK18].

The evolution of a plant in aPS involves the evolution of its heterogeneous elements, which can be mechanical and electrical/electronic elements or the control software [Vog+17]. Thus, the co-evolution of different sub-domains can be considered in this domain. The wide range of the heterogeneous elements in this domain necessitates the need for an automated change propagation analysis approach. This approach aims at identifying most elements during the change propagation analysis phase [HBK18].

The seed modification can be selected either at the level of the system elements or requirements. In the former case, domain experts select system elements as seed modification based on the change request. In the latter case, the affected requirements have to be identified based on the change request. Maybe requirements cannot be considered as a stand-alone domain. However, changing requirements causes further changes in the systems implementing them. Considering requirements is particularly important at the early stages of the development process and to keep the requirements and the corresponding systems consistent with each other during the evolution [HBK18].

11.1.2. Evaluation Results

Table 11.1 gives an overview of the evaluation results to answer **Question 1** and **Question 2**. In the evaluation, instances of the methodology for IS, BP, aPS, and requirements have been considered. One instance of the methodology was developed each in IS [Sta15; Ros+15b] and BP [Ros+17a]. For hardware elements of aPS (i.e., electrical/electronic elements), two instances of the methodology regarding two abstraction levels of the domain metamodel have been developed and considered. For software elements of aPS (i.e., PLC software according to the IEC 61131-3 standard), one instance of the methodology has been created. As described in the previous chapters, to allow modeling the change triggers at requirements level, the instances of the methodology in IS, BP, and aPS were extended by instantiation of the methodology to requirements. In other words, the instances of the methodology regarding requirements complement the other instances of the methodology in each domain. In order to answer the evaluation questions regarding requirements, the instances of the methodology in each domain were omitted to focus only on the instances of methodology regarding

		Domain: / Metamodels & Algorithms:	IS	BP	aPS HW	aPS SW	Req	Metric 1
Domain-independent		Domain-independent Metamodel of Modification	✓	✓	✓	✓	✓	1.0
	Task List Algorithm	Algorithm for Derivation of Task Lists	✓	✓	✓	✓	✓	1.0
		Duplicate Elimination Algorithm	✓	✓	✓	✓	✓	1.0
		Task List Sorter Algorithm	✓	✓	✓	✓	✓	1.0
	Task List Reduction	Metamodel of Task List Reduction	✓	✓	✓	✓	✓	1.0
		Algorithm of Task List Reduction	✓	✓	✓	✓	✓	1.0
Domain-specific	Change Propagation for Elements of Domain Metamodel	Metamodel of Domain	✓	✓	✓	✓	✓	1.0
		Domain-specific Metamodel of Modification	✓	✓	✓	✓	✓	1.0
		Algorithm of Change Propagation Analysis	✓	✓	✓	✓	✓	1.0
	Change Propagation for Elements of Context Metamodel	Metamodel of Context Elements	✓	✓	✓	✓	x	0.8
		Metamodel of Task Types	✓	x	✓	✓	x	0.6
		Algorithm of Context Task List	✓	✓	✓	✓	x	0.8
		Algorithm of Difference Calculation	✓	✓	✓	✓	✓	1.0
Metric 2	How many common elements in different instances were missing in the methodology?		0	0	0	0	0	

Legend: ✓:used, x : not used, aPS HW: mechanical and electrical/electronic elements in aPS, aPS SW: PLC software in aPS following the IEC 61131-3 standard

Table 11.1.: Commonalities of the methodology instantiations [HBK18, p. 5]

requirements. Further, the evaluation abstracts from different requirements instances regarding different domains (i.e., IS, BP, aPS hardware, or aPS software) by considering only the conceptual elements. Thus, N (i.e., the number of all instances) is 5 [HBK18]. The implementation of the domain-specific elements of the methodology in BP, aPS, and requirements was given in Chapters 6 to 8. Thus, this section only summarizes the results during the instantiations of the methodology.

Question 1 is concerned with, how often the metamodels and algorithms of the methodology are used in its instances. The third column of Table 11.1 contains the metamodels and algorithms of the methodology. The next five columns present the instances of the methodology in IS, BP, hardware elements of aPS, software elements of aPS, and requirements. Each cell in these columns states whether the corresponding instance uses or implements a metamodel or a certain algorithm of the methodology. As described in Chapter 5, the elements of the methodology have to be considered as conceptual. Thus, different programming languages, tool, and techniques can be used to instantiate the methodology. For example, a metamodel of the methodology can be in its instances a metamodel, `Enum`, or GPL code. An algorithm of the methodology can be in its instances GPL or DSL code. Thus, the evaluation of the methodology abstracts from the technical implementation by considering the concepts. The last column contains the values of Metric 1 as the number of the implementation or the use of each methodology element in the instances to the number of all instances [HBK18].

As the instances of the methodology are change propagation analysis approaches containing the domain-independent metamodels and algorithms of the methodology, the number of instances, in which they occur (i.e., U) is 5. In other words, Metric 1 is 1.0 for the domain-independent metamodels and algorithms of the methodology. However, as the domain-independent metamodels and algorithms are always provided by the methodology, they are not considered in the following. All elements of the mandatory part of the methodology regarding the domain under study (i.e., metamodel of the domain, domain-specific metamodel of modification, and algorithm for change propagation) were implemented in all instances. The value of U for these elements of the methodology in its instances is 5. Metric 1 is 1.0 for these metamodels and this algorithm of the methodology [HBK18].

The instances for IS, aPS hardware, and aPS software implement all optional elements regarding the change propagation analysis in the context elements. However, the requirements instances do not implement the metamodels regarding context elements and task types, and the corresponding algorithm of context task list. This can be considered as a design decision, as context elements such as test cases can be considered either at the system level or at the requirements level. In the instances used for the evaluation, these methodology elements were developed at the system level, as this thesis considers the architecture of a system as its main artifact (see the definition of the system's architecture in [MT10]). In this example, the specification of requirements does not consider test cases. However, the corresponding system can be tested whether it satisfies the requirements. Other instances of the methodology considering context elements at requirements level are also possible [HBK18].

The BP instance implements a metamodel for the context elements and the corresponding algorithm for the context task list. However, the metamodel for the task type could not be implemented in BP. Summarized, the value of Metric 1 is 0.8 for the metamodel of context elements and the algorithm of context task list. The value of Metric 1 is 0.6 for the metamodel of task types. However, these elements of the methodology were considered as optional. All instances implement the algorithm of difference calculation. Thus, the value of Metric 1 for this element is 1.0 [HBK18].

Most optional elements of the methodology can be used to consider the impact of context elements in a domain. However, this depends on the relevance of their impact during the change propagation analysis. In other words, although considering these elements can lead to more precise results of the change propagation analysis, they need not necessarily be implemented in a domain. Thus, if they do not exist in an instance, they do not affect the relevance of the methodology. Further, the mandatory part of the methodology considering the change in the domain under study was implemented in all instances. Thus, the methodology can be considered as sufficiently relevant [HBK18].

Question 2 aims at counting the number of common metamodels and algorithms in the instances of the methodology, which are missing in the methodology. The last row of Table 11.1 presents the values of this metric. No common relevant metamodel or algorithm could be found in the instances, which the methodology does not consider. Thus, the value of Metric 2 is 0 for all instances. Consequently, the methodology can be considered as sufficiently comprehensive [HBK18].

11.1.3. Assumptions and Limitations

As discussed previously, the methodology offers a generic guideline to develop the change propagation analysis approaches in different domains involving heterogeneous elements. Thus, there cannot be a unique instance of the methodology in a domain. The outputs of different instances can vary regarding the precision and recall. For example, an imprecise prediction of the change propagation can be sufficient in some cases (e.g., prior to the development of the system). Another example considers the cases, in which domain experts accept the existence of a few false negatives to avoid having too many false positives in the task list. These factors can affect the quality of the outputs of the instances. However, the quality of the output of individual instances is independent of the quality of the methodology. Thus, the evaluation discusses the existence of the elements specified by the methodology and not the concrete implementation of them.

In the evaluation, only instances of the methodology for IS, BP, aPS, and requirements have been considered. Maybe, the methodology is also applicable to other domains, which were not discussed in this section. The application of the methodology to these domains may differ from the presented results. Further, except for the hardware elements of aPS only one instance of the methodology has been developed in other domains. As described previously, these instances may differ from the presented instances. Thus, the results may not be transferable to all possible instances. However, the evaluation shows the relevance of the instantiation of different methodology elements in order to develop an approach to change propagation analysis in a specific domain. Omitting parts of the methodology (e.g., the optional parts) can result in false negatives in the output of the instances.

11.2. Change Propagation Analysis in Business Processes

This section presents the evaluation of KAMP4BP, discussed in Chapter 6. As described previously, KAMP4BP can be considered as an instance of the methodology in the domain of BP. As the domains of IS and BP interweave, the evaluation results of KAMP4BP also include the results of KAMP4IS.

For the evaluation of this approach two community case studies were used. These case studies are described in Sections 11.2.1 and 11.2.2. At the beginning of the chapter, Figure 11.1 illustrated the relationships between the maintainability analysis methodology, its concrete instances, and the application of the instances to specific systems. The evaluation presented in this section corresponds to the application of an instance of the methodology in the domain of IS and BP to two systems (see the latter both layers of Figure 11.1). Section 11.2.3 discusses the goals, questions, and metrics of the evaluation.

KAMP4BP is a scenario-based approach. Thus, the change scenarios of the evaluation were developed based on the categories of change triggers in BP, presented in Chapter 10. These scenarios and the results of the application of the approach to two case studies are proposed in Sections 11.2.4 and 11.2.5. The results of all change scenarios are summarized in Section 11.2.6. Section 11.2.7 gives an overview of assumptions and limitations.

The content of this section is based on and extends the results of the Bachelor's thesis of Maximilian Peters [Pet18], in which the evaluation scenarios and different cases for the case studies were developed. This Bachelor's thesis was supervised by the author of this dissertation. A former version of the evaluation has been appeared in the paper [Ros+17a]. Thus, most content of this section was appeared in the aforementioned works.

11.2.1. CoCoME Case Study

The hybrid cloud-based Common Component Modelling Example (CoCoME) [HRR16] was used to evaluate the KAMP4BP approach [Ros+17a]. CoCoME is a component-based software system [Her+08]. It has been set up in a GI Dagstuhl research seminar as a community case study [Her+08; Hei+15]. Further, CoCoME presents a common case study for the approaches in the context of evaluation, as its complexity can be considered as appropriate [Hei+15]. The availability of several development artifacts makes the use of CoCoME as a common case study well suited [Hei+15]. Applying several approaches to a community case study as an evaluation subject allows comparing their evaluation results [Ros+17a].

CoCoME is a trading system similar to a supermarket chain [Her+08; Hei+15]. Thus, it is commonly comprehensible [Hei+15]. CoCoME supports processes such as sale or administrative tasks [Her+08; Hei+15].

As a trading system CoCoME consists of a set of stores. The stores are connected to an enterprise server. Each store has a store server, which controls the cash desk line in the store. A cash desk line consists of a set of cash desks. A cash desk comprises hardware resources (e.g., barcode scanner), which are connected to the cash desk computer [Her+08; Ros+17a].

The following sections describe the model of the software architecture of CoCoME and the corresponding BP.

11.2.1.1. Model of Software Architecture

The software architecture of CoCoME is composed of a set of composite components, as illustrated in Figure 11.2 [Her+08; HRR16; Ros+17a]:

- The composite component `TradingSystem::Inventory` consists of two further composite components: `::Application` and `::Data`. The `::Application` component provides operations for the data query and sale booking. The communication and access to the database are organized using the `::Data` component [Her+08; HRR16].
- The composite component `WebService::Inventory` allows the frontend to access information regarding the enterprise (e.g., the set of all stores connected to an enterprise). This component acts as a wrapper between the presentation layer and the business logic layer [Her+08; HRR16].

- The composite component `TradingSystem::CashDeskLine` presents the physical hardware resources of cash desks (e.g., barcode scanner) [Her+08; HRR16].
- The composite component `WebService::CashDeskService` allows the frontend to access the cash desk components. Similar to the component `WebService::Inventory`, this component is also a wrapper between the presentation layer and the business logic layer [Her+08; HRR16].
- The composite component `WebFrontend::Web` presents the presentation layer [Her+08; HRR16].

The PCM model of the CoCoME used for the evaluation represents the software architecture comprising the components, interfaces, data types, and event groups. This model represents the system at the abstraction level of signatures and event types. The interfaces of the whole system was created based on the following heuristic: These interfaces contain only the signatures that are used by at least one of the following BP models.

11.2.1.2. Model of Business Processes

CoCoME supports several processes (e.g., the sale or reporting process) [Her+08; HRR16]. In the following, an overview of the relevant processes is given [Her+08; HRR16]:

- The main process of CoCoME is the `sale process`. It describes the process of buying products by customers on the cash desks in a store [Her+08].
- The `manage express checkout process` is an extension of the `sale process`. It describes the sale process, if the customer buys only a few numbers of products. In this case, the buying process is accelerated [Her+08].
- Buying new products for a store is described in the `order products process` [Her+08].

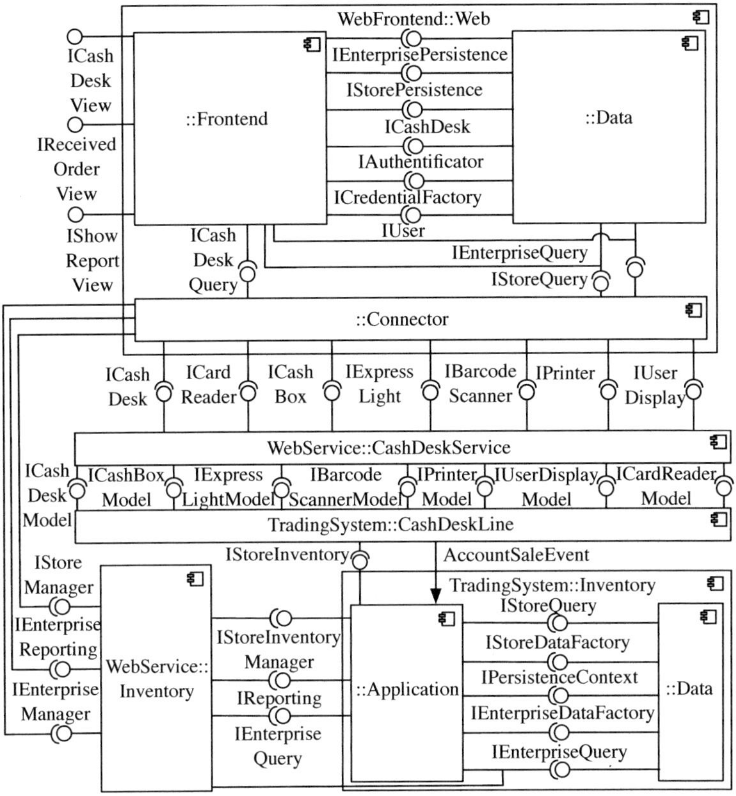

Figure 11.2.: Component diagram of CoCoME [HRR16; Ros+17a]

- After receiving the ordered products, the new products have to be inventoried. This process is defined by the `receive ordered products process` [Her+08].
- The `show stock reports process` defines creating and displaying stock reports in a store [Her+08].
- The `show delivery reports process` describes creating reports about the mean times of the deliveries [Her+08].

- Changing the price of single products is defined in the `change price process` [Her+08].

11.2.2. mRUBiS Exemplar

modular Rice University Bidding System (mRUBiS) has been initially developed at the Rice University and INRIA. It was set up for evaluating design patterns, as well as analyzing the scalability of application servers and their performance [1]. Since then it was extended for example to serve as an exemplar for self-healing and self-optimization [Vog18]. mRUBiS is the modularization variant of Rice University Bidding System (RUBiS). Thus, mRUBiS is a component-based software system.

RUBiS represents an auction web site. It is developed based on eBay.com. RUBiS supports main processes of an auction web site such as selling, browsing, and bidding. Further, following actor roles can interact with RUBiS: visitors, buyers, and sellers. Visitors can browse the web site. However, they need to register, if they want to buy or sell items [2].

11.2.2.1. Model of Software Architecture

The software architecture of mRUBiS can be considered as a set of composite components [AM], as illustrated in Figure 11.3:

- The composite component `QueryService` provides services for searching items in the database.
- The composite component `PersistenceService` allows storing business objects (e.g., users, items, or bidding).
- The composite component `InventoryService` manages the inventory (e.g., query the number of available instances of a specific item).
- The composite component `AuthenticationService` allows authenticating users.

[1] `https://cs.nyu.edu/~totok/professional/software/rubis/rubis.html`
[2] `http://rubis.ow2.org/`

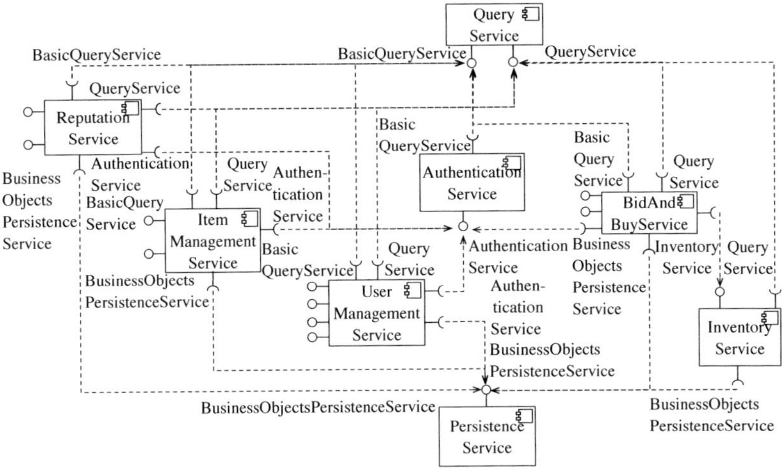

Figure 11.3.: Component diagram of mRUBiS [AM]

- The composite component `ReputationServices` manages rating users.
- The composite component `BidAndBuyService` provides the ability to bid on items and to buy items immediately.
- The composite component `UserManagementService` provides services for managing users (e.g., registering a new user or querying the user information).
- The composite component `ItemManagementService` allows managing items (e.g., registering an item).

The PCM model of the mRUBiS used for evaluation represents the software architecture comprising components, interfaces, and data types. This architecture model differs slightly in terms of interfaces, as well as components and their interfaces from the original architecture, depicted in Figure 11.3. The model represents the system at the abstraction level of signatures.

11.2.2.2. Model of Business Processes

As mRUBiS presents an auction web site based on eBay.com, several processes can be defined. In the following, relevant processes of mRUBiS are discussed. These processes have been developed in the Bachelor's thesis of Maximilian Peters [Pet18], which has been supervised by the author of this dissertation.

- The `user registration process` describes registering new users on mRUBiS in order to be able to buy or sell items.
- The process of authenticating registered users is described by the `authentication process`.
- If users want to place items on mRUBiS for sale, they have to register them beforehand. It is defined by `item registration process`.
- mRUBiS allows its users to search for items. If users find an item, they can reserve it. The `item query process` describes this process.
- Bidding on mRUBiS is described by the `bidding process`.
- The `buy now process` describes buying items immediately without bidding on them.
- The `reputation process` defines rating sellers by buyers.

11.2.3. Evaluation Goals, Questions, and Metrics

The GQM plan [Bas92; BCR94] was used to evaluate KAMP4BP. **Goal 1** evaluates the quality of the automatically generated task list in comparison to a reference task list. In other words, the goal is to evaluate the quality of the results. The reference task list is a manually created task list. This task list is based on the code, the IS architecture model, and the model of the BP design. It contains model elements that have to be changed in order to implement a change. The generated task list contains the model elements, which the approach automatically identifies. Note that the users' decisions regarding task list reduction were not considered to avoid influencing the results. In other words, the tasks in a task list, which refer to the elements not affected by the change, were not eliminated. By comparing both a generated task list and the corresponding reference task list a task in the generated task list can be categorized into three different groups: i) True positive tasks (t_p): These tasks are contained in both the generated task list and the reference task list. ii) False positive tasks (f_p): These tasks are contained only in the generated task list, but not in the corresponding reference task list. iii) False negative tasks (f_n): These tasks are missing in the generated task list, but can be found in the corresponding reference task list [Ros+17a].

To avoid considering the same model element at different abstraction levels, the model elements were considered at the lowest abstraction level. For example, the signatures of an interface were considered instead of the whole interface. Another example is the collection data type. In this case, the contained data types were considered [Ros+17a].

The first and the second question aim at evaluating the quality of the generated task list regarding the ratio of true positives, false positives, and false negatives. **Question 1.1** is defined as: How precise is the automatically generated task list in comparison to the reference task list? **Metric 1.1** quantifies the first question as: $precision = \frac{t_p}{t_p + f_p}$ [Pow08]. Thus, this metric relates to the number of true positives and the number of false positives. **Question 1.2** is formulated as: How complete is the automatically generated task list in comparison to the reference task list? **Metric 1.2** measures the completion of the generated task lists as: $recall = \frac{t_p}{t_p + f_n}$ [Pow08]. In other words, this metric relates to the number of true positives and the number of false negatives [Ros+17a].

The second goal addresses the well-known benefit of an automated approach regarding decreasing the effort of the change propagation analysis. **Goal 2** evaluates the coverage of the automatically generated task list in comparison to the number of all model elements. Thus, **Question 2** is whether KAMP4BP can reduce the number of model elements needed to be considered during the change propagation analysis phase. The first metric aims at relating the number of true positives (t_p) to the number of all model elements (n). **Metric 2.1** calculates the ratio: $r_t = \frac{t_p}{n}$. The second metric aims at relating the number of model elements referenced by the generated task list ($l = t_p + f_p$) to the number of all model elements (n). **Metric 2.2** calculates $r_g = \frac{l}{n}$. The effort reduction can be calculated by comparing both metrics [Ros+17a].

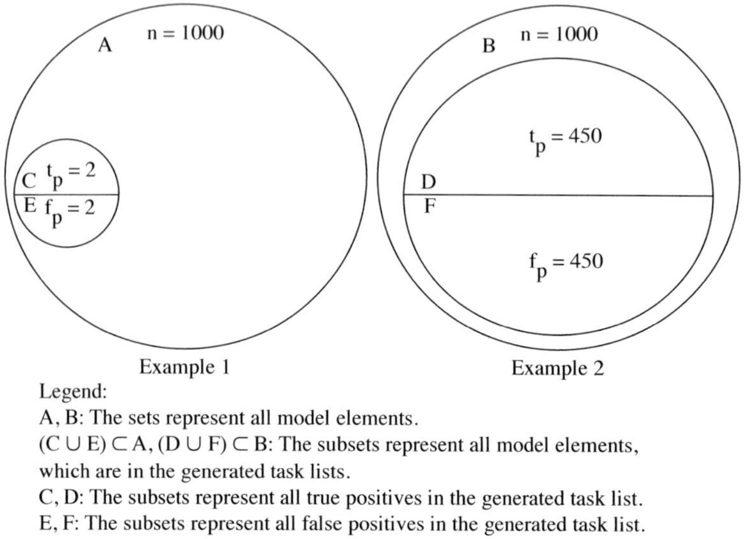

Figure 11.4.: Comparison of the precision metric using two examples

Figure 11.4 illustrates the problem arising by using only the precision metric and the need for the r_t and the r_g metrics. Consider the first example, where the number of all model elements is 1000 (i.e., $n = 1000$). Further, the generated task list contains four elements (i.e., $l = 4$). Two elements from four elements are false positives (i.e., $f_p = 2$). The remaining two elements are true positives (i.e., $t_p = 2$). No model element from the reference task list is missing (i.e., $f_n = 0$). The value of the precision metric is 50%, even though the approach significantly reduced the number of model elements, which need to be considered (i.e., the number of model elements in the generated task list is four).

In the second example, the number of all model elements is the same as the first example (i.e., $n = 1000$). However, the generated task list contains 900 model elements (i.e., $l = 900$), from which only 450 model elements are true positives (i.e., $t_p = 450$). In other words, the remaining model elements are false positives (i.e., $f_p = 450$). Similar to the first example, no false negative exists (i.e., $f_n = 0$). The value of the precision metric is again the same (i.e., 50%), even though the domain expert has to analyze almost all model elements. In this case, the approach cannot support the domain expert during the change propagation analysis approach.

These two examples show two different cases regarding the change propagation analysis, in which the values of the precision metric are the same. Thus, they make the need for further metrics clear. These metrics have to be used to differentiate between the aforementioned cases. The goal of these metrics is to determine whether the approach can reduce the number of model elements, which domain experts need to consider. In other words, the metrics aim at determining the cases, in which the approach can support the domain expert during the change propagation analysis. For this purpose, the r_t and r_g metrics were used in this evaluation in addition to the precision and recall metrics.

Sections 11.2.4 and 11.2.5 discuss the evaluation of KAMP4BP using different change scenarios based on CoCoME and mRUBiS. For each change scenario, four cases were differentiated [Pet18]:

- **1st case:** In the first case, all change propagation rules proposed in the initial KAMP4IS [Sta15; Ros+17a] and the extended KAMP4IS (see Section 6.2.3.3), as well as in KAMP4BP (see Section 6.2.3.1), and between KAMP4IS and KAMP4BP (see Section 6.2.3.2) are considered.
- **2nd case:** In the second case, the propagation of change from a modified data type that is not a seed modification, to several other model elements such as interfaces, signatures, and entry level system calls is omitted.
- **3rd case:** In the initial variant of KAMP4IS, the change propagation in a component and between two components (i.e., the change propagation due to inter- and intra-component dependencies [Sta15]) is determined iteratively. This case considers the change propagation due to inter- and intra-component dependencies only in one iteration, as described in the following using an example.

- **4th case:** This case combines both the second case and the third case.

To discuss the third case, Figure 11.5 illustrates the change propagation based on the inter- and intra-component dependencies in a small example. In this example, there is at least one component-internal dependency [Sta15; Ros+15b] between the provided role of each component and its required role. Further, the seed modification is *Interface I1* (i.e., *Iteration 0* in Figure 11.5). In the first iteration, the approach selects the required role of *Interface I1*, *Component2*, and the corresponding provided role of *Interface I2*. In each iteration, the approach identifies the corresponding required role of an affected provided role, as well as, the component, and its corresponding provided role.

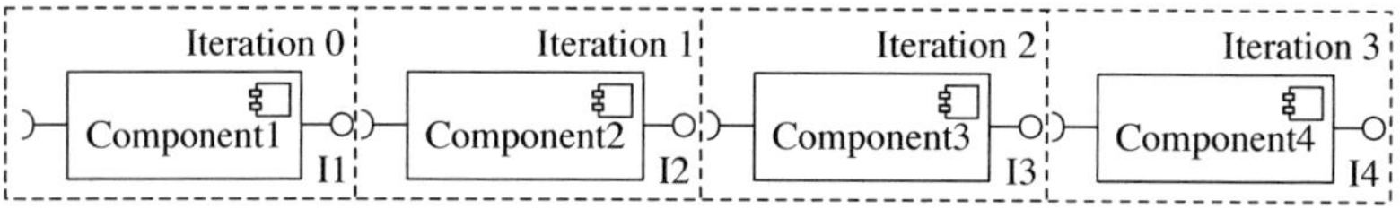

Figure 11.5.: Schematic illustration of the change propagation due to inter- and intra-component dependencies in different iterations – Seed modification: Interface I1 (based on [Sta15; Pet18])

The second and the third case consider the effects of two change propagation rules, which are aforementioned in each case. These change propagation rules were developed during the training phase of the change propagation algorithm (see [Sta15; Ros+17a]). However, the observations show that these rules are only used in a small set of scenarios. The main reasons for this observation are the programming style and the abstraction level. For example, if the programmers often use chains of method calls, the rules regarding the inter- and intra-component change propagation are needed. If these rules are not needed, the use of them can result in more false positives in the results. The goal of these four cases is to analyze the effect of these change propagation rules on the generated task lists. Additionally, they allow analyzing the influencing factor regarding the change propagation rules on the instances of the methodology and their results.

In the following evaluation, the change propagation due to the inter- and intra-component dependencies is used to only select the potentially affected components. In other words, the interfaces and signatures, which were resulted due to the inter- and intra-component dependencies, were considered only as the cause for selecting affected components. Consequently, they were not further considered in the evaluation of the change propagation and the analysis of the task lists. This is due to the black-box principle of components [Reu16].

11.2.4. Change Scenarios and Evaluation Results for CoCoME

As described in Chapter 6, to adequately analyze the change propagation IS need to be considered in conjunction with BP. KAMP4BP is a model-based and scenario-based approach. Thus, KAMP4BP is evaluated using different change scenarios. The change scenarios used for the evaluation are based on the category of change triggers discussed in Chapter 10. In other words, they present equivalence classes for change triggers. Table 11.2 shows the coverage of the categories of change triggers by the change scenarios of CoCoME. Further, the chosen change scenarios are also equivalence classes of the relevant metaclasses of PCM [BKR09], BPUsageModel [Hei+17], and DataModel [Ros+17a] regarding the maintainability. Additionally, the change scenarios were chosen with the focus of mutual dependencies between the BP and the corresponding IS. The following change scenarios and evaluation cases are based on the change scenarios and evaluation cases of a Bachelor's thesis, which the author of this dissertation supervised [Pet18].

The following sections discuss the change scenarios for CoCoME.

11.2.4.1. Change Scenario 1: Self-checkout

In some CoCoME stores, customers spend a lot of time waiting in queues. The result of a customer satisfaction survey is introducing self-checkout machines to reduce the wait times in cashier-assisted checkouts of CoCoME. Thus, the management decides to introduce new self-checkout machines.

Layer 1	Layer 2	Layer 3	Coverage Scenarios
participation	initiators	legal entities	1, 4, 5, 9, 10
		non-legal entities	7
	reluctant participants	legal entities	8
		non-legal entities	6
	further participants	legal entities	3
		non-legal entities	2
origin	internal origin	person-related influence	5
		business domain (process and structure)	8
		technology and IT	4
	external origin	person-related regulations	1
		socioeconomics	9
		politics	10
		further regulations	7
		economy	6
		location	3
		technology	2
characteristics	degree of urgency	reactive	1, 3, 6, 10
		proactive	2, 4, 5, 7, 8, 9
	degree of intensity	low	5, 9
		medium	1, 2, 4, 6, 7, 10
		high	3, 8
	degree of complexity	low	1, 3, 4, 5, 10
		medium	2, 7, 9
		high	6, 8
	degree of prediction	predictable	1, 2, 4, 5, 6, 7, 8, 9, 10
		unpredictable	3
	degree of hierarchy	top-down change	1, 2, 3, 4, 6, 8, 9, 10
		bottom-up change	5
		hybrid change	7

Table 11.2.: Application of categories of change triggers in BP to CoCoME based on [Pet18]

The customers can scan the products themselves. After scanning the products, they can also perform the payment process themselves. One cashier can attend several self-checkout lanes.

Evaluation Cases: / Metric:	1st Case: All Rules	2nd Case: All Rules without Data Type Change Propagation	3rd Case: 1 Iteration by Inter- and Intra-component Propagation	4th Case: All Rules without Data Type Change Propagation and 1 Iteration by Inter- and Intra-component Propagation
Precision	71.22%	71.22%	71.22%	71.22%
Recall	100.00%	100.00%	100.00%	100.00%
r_g	18.53%	18.53%	18.53%	18.53%
r_t	13.20%	13.20%	13.20%	13.20%

Table 11.3.: Results of the 1st change scenario in CoCoME

Table 11.3 summarizes the results for the aforementioned four cases. The initially selected model elements were the affected roles and device resources in BP. The change mainly propagates to the activities, which need the affected resource. Further, the change affects the actor steps performed by the actor roles to be changed. The false positives in this scenario are mainly the system steps (i.e., the entry level system calls) in the sale process, as these system steps are still needed for the sale process. The recall is 100%, as no model elements from the reference task list were missing in the generated task list. The precision is 71.22% for all generated task lists in all cases. This change scenario affects 13.20% of all model elements (i.e., r_t), as it involves several activities in different BP design models. r_g shows that 18.53% of the model elements can be found in the generated task list. The difference between both metrics r_t and r_g is due to false positives. The reason for the generation of the false positives is that the model of the BP design is at a high abstraction level. Thus, the change request has also to be mapped to seed modifications at a high level of abstraction (i.e., rolls and device resources). In other words, a fine-grained metamodel and model can help to improve the results in this scenario. However, the comparison between r_t and r_g shows that the generated task list can reduce the effort of change propagation analysis, as only a fraction of all model elements need to be considered by software architects and/or process designers.

This change scenario affects only BP. In other words, IS remains unchanged, as the same functionality has to be provided before and after the change. As the aforementioned four cases consider different change propagation rules regarding IS, the values of the metrics in all four cases are equal.

11.2.4.2. Change Scenario 2: RFID

A new technology based on Radio-Frequency IDentification (RFID) should replace the barcode technology. An internal study of CoCoME shows that the new technology can speed up the scanning process. Thus, the management of CoCoME decides to introduce the RFID technology. For this purpose, RFID tags replace the barcode of products. Further, cashiers have to use RFID readers instead of barcode scanners.

Evaluation Cases: / Metric:	1st Case: All Rules	2nd Case: All Rules without Data Type Change Propagation	3rd Case: 1 Iteration by Inter- and Intra-component Propagation	4th Case: All Rules without Data Type Change Propagation and 1 Iteration by Inter- and Intra-component Propagation
Precision	32.96%	77.19%	33.08%	78.57%
Recall	100.00%	100.00%	100.00%	100.00%
r_g	35.60%	15.20%	35.47	14.93%
r_t	11.73%	11.73%	11.73%	11.73%

Table 11.4.: Results of the 2nd change scenario in CoCoME

Table 11.4 summarizes the results for the aforementioned four cases. As seed modification, the data object *barcode* and the corresponding device resource in BP were selected. This data object has a corresponding data type *barcode*. Thus, this model element is also affected by the change. As the model element *barcode* is referenced by several other model elements (e.g., data types and interfaces), the change propagates to many model elements. As presented in Table 11.4, the generated task list with all change propagation rules includes many false positives, as many model elements depend on the seed modifications. Thus, this scenario can be considered as a fundamental change in CoCoME. Consequently, the precision value for the first case is 32.96%.

One reason for this observation is that a change to the data object *barcode* and the corresponding data type *barcode* leads to several false positives due to data dependencies. The newly added false positives to the generated task list lead to other false positives due to the application of the change propagation rules to these model elements. Examples of such false positives could be interfaces and signatures, as well as other data types and data objects. One option to reduce the number of false positives is omitting the corresponding rules. These rules recursively identify data types and data objects based on the modified data types and data objects. The results for omitting these rules are shown in the third column of Table 11.4. This option reduces the number of model elements in the generated task list by more than 50% compared to the total number of model elements in the generated task list resulted by all change propagation rules. Thus, this option excludes all model elements such as signatures and interfaces, which use data types referencing the *barcode* data type.

Another option to reduce the number of false positives is to reduce the number of iterations in the inter- and intra-component change propagation, as illustrated in the fourth column of Table 11.4. This option does not significantly reduce the number of elements in the generated task list, as it can be seen by comparing the values of precision and r_g metrics. Thus, the reduction of the number of elements in the generated task list in the fourth case (i.e., combining the second and the third case) is mainly due to omitting the rules for the data type propagation. The recall values of all four cases show that the generated task lists contain all model elements of the reference task list.

r_t shows that this change scenario affects 11.73% of all model elements. r_g shows the ratio of the number of model elements which software architects and/or process designers need to consider based on the generated task list to all model elements. In the first case, r_g is 35.60%, which means that the task list contains 35.60% of all model elements in the first case. After the reduction of the propagation of false positives due to data dependencies, r_g is 15.20%. The third case shows that the reduction of the number of iterations improves the results slightly (i.e., r_g is 35.47%). In addition to omitting the change propagation in data types, the reduction of the number of iterations (i.e., the fourth case) also reduces the number of model elements in the generated task list slightly (i.e., r_g is 14.93%) in comparison to the second case. Thus, the results show, even though the generated task list for this change scenario contains a high number of false positives, it reduces the number of model elements to be considered significantly even in the first case (i.e., 35.60% of all model elements). The cases, in which the data type propagation is omitted, contain considerably less model elements than in the first case.

Additionally, the approach provides the functionality to explicitly exclude the false positives (i.e., decision supporting by reducing task lists in Section 5.2.3.1). For this purpose, the causing elements for each model element in the generated task list are given. In other words, the traceability allows identifying the cause of the false positive propagation. The causing elements enable the software architects and/or process designers to reproduce the change propagation between model elements. Thus, software architects and/or process designers can exclude the cause of the false positive propagation. The approach uses this information to calculate a new task list. However, this functionality is not used during the evaluation to avoid biasing the results.

11.2.4.3. Change Scenario 3: Excess Demand

A shortage of a desired product occurs in one of CoCoME stores, which leads to temporary customers dissatisfaction and drop in sales in this store. Both CoCoME managers and customers want to solve the problem as soon as possible. The management of CoCoME decides to adapt the local good transportation from other stores as one of the fastest way to solve the problem. To adapt CoCoME the according signatures regarding dispatching products need to be changed.

Evaluation Cases: / Metric:	1st Case: All Rules	2nd Case: All Rules without Data Type Change Propagation	3rd Case: 1 Iteration by Inter- and Intra-component Propagation	4th Case: All Rules without Data Type Change Propagation and 1 Iteration by Inter- and Intra-component Propagation
Precision	50.00%	50.00%	100.00%	100.00%
Recall	100.00%	100.00%	100.00%	100.00%
r_g	0.80%	0.80%	0.40%	0.40%
r_t	0.40%	0.40%	0.40%	0.40%

Table 11.5.: Results of the 3rd change scenario in CoCoME

Table 11.5 summarizes the results for the aforementioned four cases. This change scenario mainly covers the effects of a change to signatures. As r_g shows, the generated task list contains only a small fraction of all model elements (i.e., 0.80% of all model elements in the first two cases). In other words, the change affects only a small set of all model elements. However, the precision value of the task list is 50.00% for the first two cases. This scenario is very similar to the example illustrated in Figure 11.4. This example regards cases with a low value of precision and r_g at the same time. The reason for this observation is that the precision metric considers only true positives and false positives in the generated task list. Thus, it neglects the number of all model elements. The comparison between r_g and r_t for the first two cases shows that the software architects and/or process designers need only consider 0.80% of all model elements using the generated task list. In other words, the generated task list reduces the effort of the change propagation analysis considerably despite the low precision value. As the data flow does not cause the propagation of false positives in this scenario, there is no difference between the values of the metrics in the first two cases.

In contrast to the previous scenarios, the signature dependencies cause the propagation of false positives. Thus, reducing the number of iterations of inter- and intra-component change propagation reduces the number of false positives significantly. The effect of omitting the corresponding rule can be seen in the last two columns of Table 11.5. As the generated task lists include no false positives in these cases, the precision is 100.00%. The generated task list in the third case contains only half as many elements as the generated task lists in the first two cases (i.e., the value of r_g for the third case is 0.40%). Further, no model element from the reference task list is missing in any of the generated task lists. In other words, the recall value for all cases in this scenario is 100%.

11.2.4.4. Change Scenario 4: Refactoring

The interfaces of software architecture of CoCoME were designed according to the provided processes. To separate different concerns, the managers together with the software architects of CoCoME decide to split the implementation of a provided interface into several interfaces [Ros+17a]. This change should improve the maintainability of CoCoME software.

Evaluation Cases: / Metric:	1st Case: All Rules	2nd Case: All Rules without Data Type Change Propagation	3rd Case: 1 Iteration by Inter- and Intra-component Propagation	4th Case: All Rules without Data Type Change Propagation and 1 Iteration by Inter- and Intra-component Propagation
Precision	100.00%	100.00%	100.00%	100.00%
Recall	100.00%	100.00%	100.00%	100.00%
r_g	5.73%	5.73%	5.73%	5.73%
r_t	5.73%	5.73%	5.73%	5.73%

Table 11.6.: Results of the 4th change scenario in CoCoME

Table 11.6 summarizes the results for the aforementioned four cases. This change initially affects one of the interfaces provided by CoCoME. Changing an interface results in change propagation to all its signatures. Further, changes to the signatures of a provided interface propagate to the corresponding system steps. A change to an interface results also in changing the components providing or requiring this interface. All model elements referenced in the generated task list are true positives. Further, no model element from the reference task list is missing in the generated task list. Thus, the precision and the recall values of the generated task lists for all cases in this scenario are both 100%. Further, r_t and r_g values are equal (i.e., they are 5.73%).

As neither the data dependencies, nor the inter- and intra-component dependencies cause the change propagation in this change scenario, there is no difference between the discussed four cases.

11.2.4.5. Change Scenario 5: Inventory Improvement

A new employee in the inventory suggests CoCoME to improve the registration of the ordered products. For this purpose, the corresponding system step in the BP regarding the registration of the ordered products needs to be adapted.

Evaluation Cases: / Metric:	1st Case: All Rules	2nd Case: All Rules without Data Type Change Propagation	3rd Case: 1 Iteration by Inter- and Intra-component Propagation	4th Case: All Rules without Data Type Change Propagation and 1 Iteration by Inter- and Intra-component Propagation
Precision	100.00%	100.00%	100.00%	100.00%
Recall	100.00%	100.00%	100.00%	100.00%
r_g	0.40%	0.40%	0.40%	0.40%
r_t	0.40%	0.40%	0.40%	0.40%

Table 11.7.: Results of the 5th change scenario in CoCoME

Table 11.7 summarizes the results for the aforementioned four cases. In this scenario, the change propagates to the corresponding signatures of the system step. The component, which provides the interface including the affected signature, needs also to be changed. Thus, this change affects only a few model elements of CoCoME (i.e., r_t is 0.40%). In this change scenario, there are neither false positives nor false negatives in the generated task lists. Thus, precision and recall values for all four cases are 100%. Further, the generated task lists and the reference task list contain the same model elements. In other words, the values of r_t and r_g are equal.

In this scenario, there is no difference between the four cases, as the data dependency is not the reason for the change propagation. Further, the change does not propagate along inter- and intra-component dependencies.

11.2.4.6. Change Scenario 6: Scalability

Due to globalization and economic growth the management of CoCoME plans to expand the stores and to extend the range of the offered products. However, the current database cannot scale. For this purpose, CoCoME plans to replace the component handling the data persistence as one of the first steps. However, this change involves several further changes as hiring new employees. Thus, the long-term consequences of this change can be very high.

Evaluation Cases: / Metric:	1st Case: All Rules	2nd Case: All Rules without Data Type Change Propagation	3rd Case: 1 Iteration by Inter- and Intra-component Propagation	4th Case: All Rules without Data Type Change Propagation and 1 Iteration by Inter- and Intra-component Propagation
Precision	100.00%	100.00%	100.00%	100.00%
Recall	100.00%	100.00%	100.00%	100.00%
r_g	0.13%	0.13%	0.13%	0.13%
r_t	0.13%	0.13%	0.13%	0.13%

Table 11.8.: Results of the 6th change scenario in CoCoME

Table 11.8 summarizes the results for the aforementioned four cases. This change scenario deals with changing the internal of a component without changing its interfaces. CoCoME has a component-based software architecture. For this reason, the change request can be implemented by only changing the corresponding component. The change does not propagate to other components and interfaces. Thus, r_g and r_t are each 0.13%. As the generated task lists and the reference task list contain the same model elements, the precision and recall values are each 100%. As this change does not affect any data types, interfaces, and signatures, the generated task lists in all four cases contain the same model elements.

11.2.4.7. Change Scenario 7: Encryption

One of the outcomes of an internal workshop with managers and employees of CoCoME is the current login of employees is not secure. CoCoME plans secure login for employees to accomplish the required security standards. For this purpose, a corresponding data type needs to be changed.

Evaluation Cases: / Metric:	1st Case: All Rules	2nd Case: All Rules without Data Type Change Propagation	3rd Case: 1 Iteration by Inter- and Intra-component Propagation	4th Case: All Rules without Data Type Change Propagation and 1 Iteration by Inter- and Intra-component Propagation
Precision	76.92%	90.91%	76.92%	90.91%
Recall	100.00%	100.00%	100.00%	100.00%
r_g	1.73%	1.47%	1.73%	1.47%
r_t	1.33%	1.33%	1.33%	1.33%

Table 11.9.: Results of the 7th change scenario in CoCoME

Table 11.9 summarizes the results for the aforementioned four cases. In this scenario, a data type is initially changed. The change mainly propagates to the other model elements due to the data dependency. Similar to the RFID scenario (see Section 11.2.4.2) the data flow results in further false positives in this scenario. Thus, the precision value in the first case is 76.92%. This value is calculated without considering the number of all model elements in the generated task list, as the precision refers only to the number of true positives and false positives (see Figure 11.4). The relation between the number of true positives in the task list to the number of all model elements can be seen by the r_g value (i.e., 1.73% in the first case). As the affected data type is referenced by a small number of model elements, the change propagation affects only a small fraction of all model elements (i.e., r_t is 1.33%). The comparison between the r_t and the r_g values in the first case shows that the generated task list considerably reduces the number of model elements, which domain experts have to consider during the change propagation analysis. As the data flow is the reason for the propagation of false positives, omitting the corresponding rules in the second case reduces the number of false positives. The precision value in the second case is 90.91%. The generated task list in this case contains 1.47% of all model elements (i.e., r_g). As the inter- and intra-component dependencies do not result in the propagation of change in this scenario, the generated task lists in the first and the third case contain the same model elements. The generated task list in the last case also contains as many elements as in the generated task list in the second case (i.e., r_g is 1.47% in both cases). No element is missing in the generated task lists. Thus, the recall value is 100.00% in all cases.

11.2.4.8. Change Scenario 8: Managerial Roles

To manage the stores efficiently, the management of CoCoME plans to combine several store manager roles into one store manager role. The goal of cutting some management jobs is to save costs. Thus, one manager is responsible for several stores. As this change affects the role hierarchy and the management of CoCoME, short-term and long-term consequences of this change can be high.

Evaluation Cases: / Metric:	1st Case: All Rules	2nd Case: All Rules without Data Type Change Propagation	3rd Case: 1 Iteration by Inter- and Intra-component Propagation	4th Case: All Rules without Data Type Change Propagation and 1 Iteration by Inter- and Intra-component Propagation
Precision	80.00%	80.00%	100.00%	100.00%
Recall	100.00%	100.00%	100.00%	100.00%
r_g	4.00%	4.00%	3.20%	3.20%
r_t	3.20%	3.20%	3.20%	3.20%

Table 11.10.: Results of the 8th change scenario in CoCoME

Table 11.10 summarizes the results for the aforementioned four cases. The role *store manager* is initially affected in this change scenario. Additionally, the corresponding interface has also to be refactored in order to be extensible for possible future responsibilities of the changed role. The second seed modification belongs to the refactoring activities, as the new merged manager role has to perform the tasks of each store manager. This change affects 3.20% of all model elements in both IS and BP of CoCoME. The precision of the task list in the first both cases is 80.00%. As all model elements in the reference task list can also be found in the generated task list, the recall value for the first both cases is 100.00%. The propagation of false positives is due to inter- and intra-component change propagation, as the comparison between the first and the third case shows. Further, the data type does not cause the change propagation in this scenario. For this reason, the generated task lists in the last two cases contain the same model elements as in the reference task list. Thus, the precision and recall values are 100.00% for these cases. Further, r_t and r_g values are equal (i.e., 3.20%). Although the precision values of the first two cases were 80.00%, the values of the r_g metric show that the generated task list contains only a small subset of all model elements. The reason for this observation was illustrated in Figure 11.4. Summarized, the generated task lists can significantly reduce the number of model elements that have to be manually analyzed by domain experts.

11.2.4.9. Change Scenario 9: Receipt

An increasing number of customers pay with credit cards. As the bank statements provide the list of transactions, it is not economically to print receipts for each sale. To reduce costs, the cashier shall hand out receipts only upon request (i.e., only if the client asks for a receipt).

Evaluation Cases: / Metric:	1st Case: All Rules	2nd Case: All Rules without Data Type Change Propagation	3rd Case: 1 Iteration by Inter- and Intra-component Propagation	4th Case: All Rules without Data Type Change Propagation and 1 Iteration by Inter- and Intra-component Propagation
Precision	100.00%	100.00%	100.00%	100.00%
Recall	100.00%	100.00%	100.00%	100.00%
r_g	0.53%	0.53%	0.53%	0.53%
r_t	0.53%	0.53%	0.53%	0.53%

Table 11.11.: Results of the 9th change scenario in CoCoME

Table 11.11 summarizes the results for the aforementioned four cases. The seed modification involves the actor steps regarding handing out the receipts in the corresponding BP. As the actor steps are referenced by a few numbers of other model elements, the change propagates only to a small fraction of the model elements of the BP design. For this reason, the r_t value is 0.53%. In this scenario, the change propagates to actor steps with a data dependency to the affected actor step. As the change affects only the BP design of CoCoME, the generated task lists in all cases contain the same model elements. Further, the generated task lists and the reference task list also include the same model elements. Thus, the precision and recall values are each 100.00%. Additionally, r_t and r_g values are equal.

11.2.4.10. Change Scenario 10: Transparency

Due to a new transparency law for the employees in an organization, CoCoME plans to improve the right to access information about its stores. To implement the law CoCoME changes the corresponding interface for accessing stock information.

Evaluation Cases: / Metric:	1st Case: All Rules	2nd Case: All Rules without Data Type Change Propagation	3rd Case: 1 Iteration by Inter- and Intra-component Propagation	4th Case: All Rules without Data Type Change Propagation and 1 Iteration by Inter- and Intra-component Propagation
Precision	70.59%	70.59%	100.00%	100.00%
Recall	100.00%	100.00%	100.00%	100.00%
r_g	2.27%	2.27%	1.60%	1.60%
r_t	1.60%	1.60%	1.60%	1.60%

Table 11.12.: Results of the 10th change scenario in CoCoME

Table 11.12 summarizes the results for the aforementioned four cases. This change initially affects the interface, which provides access to stock information. The change propagates from the affected interface and its signatures to all interfaces and signatures referencing them. This can result in further changes in the system steps of the BP design models. Additionally, affecting an interface results in changing the components providing or requiring it. Thus, the change propagation in one iteration based on the inter- and intra-component dependencies reduces the number of false positives. As the change request does not affect any data types and data objects, the data flow does not result in the propagation of false positives. This can also be seen by comparing the values of r_g of all cases in Table 11.12. The comparison shows that the generated task lists in the first two cases contain the same number of model elements. Thus, the values of the precision and r_g metrics are 70.59% and 2.27%, respectively. Accordingly, the task lists in the latter both cases contain the same model elements, as the last case combines the second and the third case (i.e., r_t and r_g values are 1.60% in both cases). As the comparison between the generated task lists and the reference task list does not result in any false negatives, the values of recall are 100.00% in all cases.

Layer 1	Layer 2	Layer 3	Coverage Scenarios
participation	initiators	legal entities	1, 2, 7 8, 9
		non-legal entities	5
	reluctant participants	legal entities	4
		non-legal entities	6
	further participants	legal entities	3
		non-legal entities	10
origin	internal origin	person-related influence	1
		business domain (process and structure)	2
		technology and IT	3
	external origin	person-related regulations	7
		socioeconomics	9
		politics	4
		further regulations	8
		economy	6
		location	10
		technology	5
characteristics	degree of urgency	reactive	3, 4, 6 7, 10
		proactive	1, 2, 5 8, 9
	degree of intensity	low	1, 5, 9
		medium	2, 4, 6, 7, 8
		high	3, 10
	degree of complexity	low	1, 2, 3 4, 5, 8, 9
		medium	7, 10
		high	6
	degree of prediction	predictable	1, 2, 4 5, 8, 9
		unpredictable	3, 6, 7, 10
	degree of hierarchy	top-down change	2, 3, 4, 6 7, 8, 9, 10
		bottom-up change	1
		hybrid change	5

Table 11.13.: Application of categories of change triggers in BP to mRUBiS based on [Pet18]

11.2.5. Change Scenarios and Evaluation Results for mRUBiS

This section shows the change scenarios and the evaluation results of KAMP4BP using a further evaluation subject, namely mRUBiS. Similar to Section 11.2.4, KAMP4BP was evaluated using a set of change scenarios based on mRUBiS. As the change scenarios cover the categories of change triggers in BP (see Chapter 10), they represent equivalence classes of change scenarios. Table 11.13 shows the coverage of the categories of change triggers by the change scenarios of mRUBiS. In comparison to CoCoME, mRUBiS is a smaller software system and has fewer components. Consequently, the BP of mRUBiS contains fewer activities. These BP do not use any resource devices and data objects. The chosen change scenarios cover other relevant metaclasses of PCM [BKR09], BPUsageModel [Hei+17], and DataModel [Ros+17a] regarding the maintainability. Similar to Section 11.2.4, the scenarios were chosen with focus on the mutual dependencies between the IS and the corresponding BP. The following change scenarios and evaluation cases are based on the change scenarios and evaluation cases of a Bachelor's thesis, which the author of this dissertation supervised [Pet18].

The following sections discuss the change scenarios for mRUBiS.

11.2.5.1. Change Scenario 1: User Registration

An employee of mRUBiS suggests changes in users' registration process to improve registering new users. After this modification, users can also register via phone or email.

Evaluation Cases: / Metric:	1st Case: All Rules	2nd Case: All Rules without Data Type Change Propagation	3rd Case: 1 Iteration by Inter- and Intra-component Propagation	4th Case: All Rules without Data Type Change Propagation and 1 Iteration by Inter- and Intra-component Propagation
Precision	100.00%	100.00%	100.00%	100.00%
Recall	100.00%	100.00%	100.00%	100.00%
r_g	0.83%	0.83%	0.83%	0.83%
r_t	0.83%	0.83%	0.83%	0.83%

Table 11.14.: Results of the 1st change scenario in mRUBiS

Table 11.14 summarizes the results for the aforementioned four cases. The change request initially affects the actor step regarding the registration of users. As the user registration activity has to be performed either way, the software system remains unchanged. The change propagation rules regarding data dependencies, as well as inter- and intra-component dependencies mainly refer to the change propagation in the software architecture. Thus, they do not affect the generated task lists in this change scenario. Consequently, the generated task lists in all cases contain the same model elements as in the reference task list. Thus, the precision and recall values are 100.00%. In other words, r_t and r_g values are equal. The change affects only a small set of all model elements (i.e., r_t is 0.83%).

11.2.5.2. Change Scenario 2: Performance

To improve the performance of the processes of mRUBiS (i.e., as one of the main quality attributes), the managers decide to parallelize the software system. For this purpose, they want to deploy mRUBiS components on different platforms. To have a high degree of parallelization, it is preferable to have more small components instead of few large components that contain a majority of business logic. Thus, the components have to be decomposed.

Evaluation Cases: / Metric:	1st Case: All Rules	2nd Case: All Rules without Data Type Change Propagation	3rd Case: 1 Iteration by Inter- and Intra-component Propagation	4th Case: All Rules without Data Type Change Propagation and 1 Iteration by Inter- and Intra-component Propagation
Precision	77.78%	77.78%	77.78%	77.78%
Recall	100.00%	100.00%	100.00%	100.00%
r_g	7.44%	7.44%	7.44%	7.44%
r_t	5.79%	5.79%	5.79%	5.79%

Table 11.15.: Results of the 2nd change scenario in mRUBiS

Table 11.15 summarizes the results for the aforementioned four cases. The refactoring begins with the component providing inventory services. This interface can be divided into two further interfaces. Thus, the component providing this interface needs also to be divided into two components. As this interface is required by other interfaces, the change propagates to these interfaces. This results in the propagation of false positives. The precision of the first case is 77.78%. As the change does not affect any data types, the precision of the second case is also 77.78%. The false positives are created during the first iteration of inter- and intra-component change propagation. Thus, reducing the number of iterations does not change the number of false positives (i.e., the precision value is 77.78% in the third case). Consequently, combining the second and the third case (i.e., the fourth case) does not influence the generated task list. In this scenario, no model element from the reference task list is missing. Thus, the recall of all four cases is 100%. In this scenario 5.79% of all model elements are actually affected by the change. Due to false positives the generated task list contains 7.44% of all model elements.

11.2.5.3. Change Scenario 3: Privacy

Due to design flaws clients of mRUBiS can access private data of sellers. However, buyers should only see seller ratings according to the requirements of the system. Thus, the user interface for the clients has to be changed.

Evaluation Cases: / Metric:	1st Case: All Rules	2nd Case: All Rules without Data Type Change Propagation	3rd Case: 1 Iteration by Inter- and Intra-component Propagation	4th Case: All Rules without Data Type Change Propagation and 1 Iteration by Inter- and Intra-component Propagation
Precision	100.00%	100.00%	100.00%	100.00%
Recall	100.00%	100.00%	100.00%	100.00%
r_g	3.31%	3.31%	3.31%	3.31%
r_t	3.31%	3.31%	3.31%	3.31%

Table 11.16.: Results of the 3rd change scenario in mRUBiS

Table 11.16 summarizes the results for the aforementioned four cases. The change affects the interface regarding displaying sellers' information. This change affects only a signature of an interface and therefore the component providing it. Thus, the change affects only a small number of all model elements (i.e., r_t is 3.31%). The change does not affect any data types. Additionally, the change does not propagate due to inter- or intra-component dependencies. Thus, the generated task lists in the four cases contain the same model elements. Further, they do not contain any false positives in four cases. As no model element from the reference task list is missing, the recall value is 100%. The values of r_t and r_g are equal.

11.2.5.4. Change Scenario 4: Additional Information

Due to a new law, users have to provide a Completely Automated Public Turing test to tell Computers and Humans Apart (CAPTCHA) for human authentication during the registration and authentication. The BP of mRUBiS must be adapted due to the new law. However, this change results in higher overhead of users' registration and authentication.

Evaluation Cases: / Metric:	1st Case: All Rules	2nd Case: All Rules without Data Type Change Propagation	3rd Case: 1 Iteration by Inter- and Intra-component Propagation	4th Case: All Rules without Data Type Change Propagation and 1 Iteration by Inter- and Intra-component Propagation
Precision	73.33%	73.33%	73.33%	73.33%
Recall	100.00%	100.00%	100.00%	100.00%
r_g	12.40%	12.40%	12.40%	12.40%
r_t	9.09%	9.09%	9.09%	9.09%

Table 11.17.: Results of the 4th change scenario in mRUBiS

Table 11.17 summarizes the results for the aforementioned four cases. In this change scenario the seed modifications are the corresponding system steps of the user registration and authentication interface. This change propagates from the affected system steps in BP to the corresponding interfaces in IS and then to the components implementing these interfaces. As the seed modifications originate in BP, reducing the number of iterations by the inter- and intra-component change propagation does not influence the results. Further, the change does not affect any data types. Consequently, the generated task lists of all four cases contain the same model elements. As this change affects 9.09% of all model elements (i.e., r_t), it can be considered as a fundamental change to the system. The value of r_g for all cases is 12.40%. In other words, the generated task lists contain a few model elements more than the reference task list for all cases in this scenario. However, the precision value is 73.33%, as this metric considers only true positives and false positives in the generated task list (see Figure 11.4). As no affected model element is missing in the generated task lists, the recall values for all four cases are 100%.

11.2.5.5. Change Scenario 5: New Technology

The software of mRUBiS uses third party libraries. The vendors of the libraries provide updates (i.e., a new version of the libraries is available.). Therefore, the implementation of the affected components has to be changed.

Evaluation Cases: / Metric:	1st Case: All Rules	2nd Case: All Rules without Data Type Change Propagation	3rd Case: 1 Iteration by Inter- and Intra-component Propagation	4th Case: All Rules without Data Type Change Propagation and 1 Iteration by Inter- and Intra-component Propagation
Precision	100.00%	100.00%	100.00%	100.00%
Recall	100.00%	100.00%	100.00%	100.00%
r_g	0.83%	0.83%	0.83%	0.83%
r_t	0.83%	0.83%	0.83%	0.83%

Table 11.18.: Results of the 5th change scenario in mRUBiS

Table 11.18 summarizes the results for the aforementioned four cases. The seed modification is the component that is based on the previous version of the libraries. mRUBiS has a component-based software architecture. Therefore, in this scenario only the implementation of the component is affected by the change. The provided and required interfaces remain unchanged. The generated task lists and the reference task list contain the same model elements in all cases. The reason for that is that no data types and interfaces are affected by the change. Thus, the precision and recall values are 100%. Further, r_t and r_g have the same values in all cases (i.e., 0.83%).

11.2.5.6. Change Scenario 6: Organizational Growth

mRUBiS plans to expand its services into other countries. After the international expansion, the database is the bottleneck in the system due to a high number of registrations. Thus, the corresponding interface has to be exchanged. It is assumed that the expansion has high long-term consequences.

Evaluation Cases: / Metric:	1st Case: All Rules	2nd Case: All Rules without Data Type Change Propagation	3rd Case: 1 Iteration by Inter- and Intra-component Propagation	4th Case: All Rules without Data Type Change Propagation and 1 Iteration by Inter- and Intra-component Propagation
Precision	70.00%	70.00%	70.00%	70.00%
Recall	100.00%	100.00%	100.00%	100.00%
r_g	16.53%	16.53%	16.53%	16.53%
r_t	11.57%	11.57%	11.57%	11.57%

Table 11.19.: Results of the 6th change scenario in mRUBiS

Table 11.19 summarizes the results for the aforementioned four cases. This change scenario initially affects an interface. The change propagates to interfaces and signatures, which depend on the affected interface and its signatures. This leads to changing all components requiring or providing the affected interfaces. Thus, the generated task lists contain 16.53% of all model elements. As this change affects 11.57% of all model elements, it has a high impact on the models of IS and BP. In this scenario, the data type does not cause the change propagation. Thus, omitting the corresponding rules does not affect the results, as it can be seen by comparing the first and the second case. Further, the false positives were generated during the first iteration of inter- and intra-component change propagation. Consequently, the task lists in the first and the third case are the same. As all cases generate the same task list, thc precision values of the generated task lists in all cases are 70.00%. The recall values of all cases are 100%, as no model element from the reference task list is missing in the generated task lists.

11.2.5.7. Change Scenario 7: Search Query

mRUBiS conducts a customer satisfaction survey to improve its services. Based on this survey, the managers decide to extend the search possibilities due to customers' feedback. This involves searching the products in several price intervals.

Evaluation Cases: / Metric:	1st Case: All Rules	2nd Case: All Rules without Data Type Change Propagation	3rd Case: 1 Iteration by Inter- and Intra-component Propagation	4th Case: All Rules without Data Type Change Propagation and 1 Iteration by Inter- and Intra-component Propagation
Precision	44.44%	44.44%	44.44%	44.44%
Recall	100.00%	100.00%	100.00%	100.00%
r_g	7.44%	7.44%	7.44%	7.44%
r_t	3.31%	3.31%	3.31%	3.31%

Table 11.20.: Results of the 7th change scenario in mRUBiS

Table 11.20 summarizes the results for the aforementioned four cases. The seed modifications are the corresponding signatures for searching products. In this scenario, the change propagates to components and signatures in the IS, as well as system steps in the BP. The interface, in which the signatures occur, is required by several other interfaces. Thus, the change propagation results in selecting several components, which are not actually affected by the change. Consequently, the precision value of the results is 44.44%. As no model element from the reference task list is missing in the generated task lists, the recall value is 100.00% for all cases. 3.31% of all model elements are affected by this change request (i.e., r_t). Although the generated task list contains only a small fraction of all model elements (i.e., r_g is 7.44%), the precision value is low. This scenario is also very similar to the example illustrated in Figure 11.4. The main reason for this observation is that the precision neglects the number of all model elements and relates only to the number of true positives and false positives in the generated task lists. In other words, the comparison between r_t and r_g values shows that the approach can significantly reduce the number of all model elements that need to be considered despite the low precision values. As this change does not affect any data types, the results of the first and the second case are equal. Further, reducing the number of iterations does not improve the precision of the results, as the false positives are generated in the first iteration. Consequently, the task lists of all cases contain the same model elements.

11.2.5.8. Change Scenario 8: Encryption

So far, users' passwords are stored as plain-text. Due to a new law and to improve the security software architects of mRUBiS plan to store the hashes of users' passwords.

Evaluation Cases: / Metric:	1st Case: All Rules	2nd Case: All Rules without Data Type Change Propagation	3rd Case: 1 Iteration by Inter- and Intra-component Propagation	4th Case: All Rules without Data Type Change Propagation and 1 Iteration by Inter- and Intra-component Propagation
Precision	38.10%	75.00%	38.10%	75.00%
Recall	100.00%	100.00%	100.00%	100.00%
r_g	52.07%	26.45%	52.07%	26.45%
r_t	19.83%	19.83%	19.83%	19.83%

Table 11.21.: Results of the 8th change scenario in mRUBiS

Table 11.21 summarizes the results for the aforementioned four cases. The seed modification is the data type representing users' passwords. As several data types are composed of this data type, the change propagates due to data dependencies to the other data types. Further, the data dependencies result in the propagation of change to the other model elements such as signatures or components. Data dependencies also cause several false positives. Thus, the precision of the task list in the first case is 38.10%. For this reason, neglecting the propagation of change from one data type to the other data types improves the precision of the results considerably. Thus, the precision of the task list in the second case is 75.00%. As the inter- and intra-component dependencies do not cause further false positives, the generated task lists in the first and in the third case contain the same model elements. Thus, the results in both cases have the same precision. Additionally, combining the second and the third case in the fourth case results in the same task list as in the second case. As no element of the reference task list is missing in the generated task list, the recall is 100% in all cases. Further, this change scenario represents a scenario with a high impact, as it affects 19.83% of all model elements (i.e., r_t). Due to false positives in the generated task lists, the value of r_g is 52.07% in the first and in the third case and 26.45% in the second and in the fourth cases. Thus, the generated task lists (especially the second and the fourth case) can considerably reduce the number of model elements, which domain experts need to consider during the analysis of the change propagation. Note that this scenario (especially the first and the third case) is also similar to the example depicted in Figure 11.4.

11.2.5.9. Change Scenario 9: Accessibility

The managers of mRUBiS plan to change the interface for the user registration. This decision aims at improving the accessibility and the usability of mRUBiS, especially for disabled persons.

Evaluation Cases: / Metric:	1st Case: All Rules	2nd Case: All Rules without Data Type Change Propagation	3rd Case: 1 Iteration by Inter- and Intra-component Propagation	4th Case: All Rules without Data Type Change Propagation and 1 Iteration by Inter- and Intra-component Propagation
Precision	100.00%	100.00%	100.00%	100.00%
Recall	100.00%	100.00%	100.00%	100.00%
r_g	2.48%	2.48%	2.48%	2.48%
r_t	2.48%	2.48%	2.48%	2.48%

Table 11.22.: Results of the 9th change scenario in mRUBiS

Table 11.22 summarizes the results for the aforementioned four cases. The seed modification is the interface for the user registration, which propagates to the corresponding signature and system step. This change does not cause any false positives or false negatives. As no data types are affected by the seed modifications, omitting the corresponding rules does not affect the generated task list. As this change only impacts one of the interfaces provided by the software system, reducing the number of iterations in the inter- and intra-component change propagation does not affect the generated task list in this scenario. Thus, the generated task lists in all cases and the reference task list contain the same model elements. In this scenario, 2.48% of all model elements are affected (i.e., r_g and r_t values).

11.2.5.10. Change Scenario 10: Competition

In some regions, new organizations cause drop in sales of mRUBiS. Thus, the BP of mRUBiS has to be changed in these regions due to competition. mRUBiS plans to offer direct sales only in these regions. However, the software system is not affected by the change, as it is further used in the other regions.

Evaluation Cases: / Metric:	1st Case: All Rules	2nd Case: All Rules without Data Type Change Propagation	3rd Case: 1 Iteration by Inter- and Intra-component Propagation	4th Case: All Rules without Data Type Change Propagation and 1 Iteration by Inter- and Intra-component Propagation
Precision	100.00%	100.00%	100.00%	100.00%
Recall	100.00%	100.00%	100.00%	100.00%
r_g	2.48%	2.48%	2.48%	2.48%
r_t	2.48%	2.48%	2.48%	2.48%

Table 11.23.: Results of the 10th change scenario in mRUBiS

Table 11.23 summarizes the results for the aforementioned four cases. This change scenario affects the role *bidder*, which leads to changing the actor steps corresponding to this role. In other words, this scenario is only concerned with actor steps performed by bidders. As this change does not affect the software system (i.e., neither the change propagation due to data dependencies nor the inter- and intra-component change propagation), the generated task lists in all four cases and the reference task list include the same model elements. Thus, the precision and recall values are 100.00%. This change affects 2.48% of all model elements (i.e., t_t and r_g values).

11.2.6. Summary of Evaluation Results

This section presents the summary of the evaluation results regarding both case studies, namely CoCoME and mRUBiS. Figure 11.6 summarizes the values of r_t in comparison to the values of the precision metric for the first case (i.e., applying all change propagation rules). Along each axis a bloxplot is added to summarize the values of r_t and the values of precision for the first case. The boxplot regarding the precision value shows that 75% of all precision values in this case were higher than 70.44%. The precision values were 100% in 9 of 20 change scenarios. Thus, the median is 78.89% and the upper quartile is 100%. On average, the precision value is 79.27%. This diagram can be used for the comparison between the boxplot regarding the r_t values and the boxplots regarding the r_g values in different cases, as described in the following.

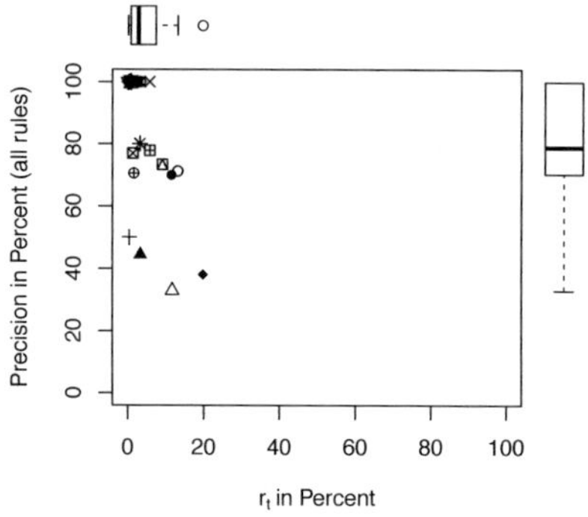

Figure 11.6.: Comparing the evaluation results of r_t and precision while applying all change propagation rules

Figure 11.7 compares the relation between the precision and r_g for all cases. Each change scenario has the same symbol in all scatter diagrams. Each scatter diagram has been extended by two boxplots. The vertical boxplot summarizes the values of the precision in each case, while the horizontal boxplot summarizes the values of r_g. In this way, the values of each metric can be compared between different cases. The comparison between the precision values and the r_t values in Figure 11.6, as well as the precision values and the r_g values in Figure 11.7 shows that there is a tendency towards the number of affected model elements by a change scenario and its precision value. The outliers in the first case (see Figure 11.6) result from the second scenario of CoCoME and the eighth scenario of mRUBiS with a precision value of 32.96% and 38.10%, respectively. The generated task lists of these change scenarios contained the most affected model elements. In other words, the r_g values are 35.60% and 52.07%, respectively. In these scenarios, the change affects a majority of the model elements (i.e., r_t values are 11.73% and 19.83%, respectively). However, it cannot be concluded that a high number of affected model elements always results in a low precision. For example, although the r_t value in the first CoCoME scenario is 13.20%, the precision value is rather high (i.e., 71.22%). Further, the comparison between the precision, r_t, and r_g values shows although the precision values are rather low in some cases, the application of KAMP4BP significantly reduces the number of model elements need to be considered. This can be seen even for the outliers in the first case based on the r_t, and r_g values. The reason for lower precision and lower r_g in some cases has been already illustrated in Figure 11.4. Additionally, the generated task list contains the least amount of false positives for change requests, which affect only a small number of model elements.

Omitting the change propagation from data types improved the average of the precision values in the aforementioned scenarios (i.e., the mean value for the scenarios in this case is 84.02%). The lower quartile is 72.28% in this case. This means, that 75% of all precision values in this case were higher than 72.28%.

In the third case, the change propagation due to inter- and intra-component dependencies has been conducted in only one iteration. This is based on the heuristic that the effects of a change in a component-based software remain locally. Although this case contains the same outliers as in the first case, it can reduce the number of model elements in the generated task lists in several scenarios. This can also be seen by the corresponding boxplots regarding the precision and r_g in Figure 11.7. In this case, the mean value of the precision metric over all scenarios is 84.24% and the generated task list contains on average 8.68% of all model elements (i.e., r_g). Further, 75% of all precision values were higher than 72.28%.

In the last case, the algorithm of change propagation iterates only one iteration over the inter- and intra-component dependencies while omitting the change propagation within data types. Thus, this case combines the second and the third case. As shown in Figure 11.7, this also improves the precision values (i.e., the precision is 89.06% on average). Improving the mean value of precision correlates with reducing the mean value of r_g (i.e., r_g is 6.35% on average). In this case, 75% of all precision values were higher than 77.08%. The outlier of the last case regarding the precision value is caused by the

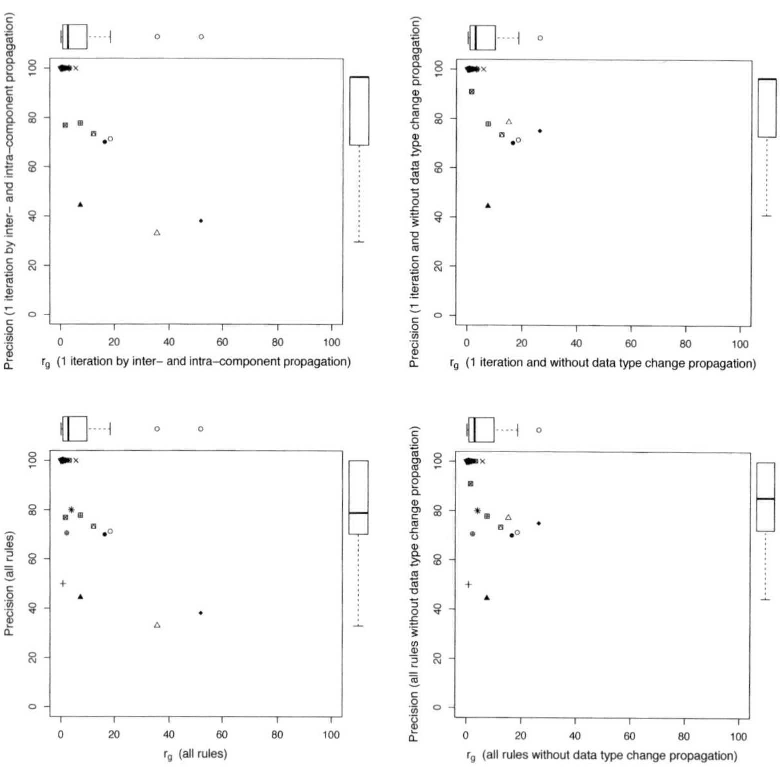

Figure 11.7.: Comparing the evaluation results of tuples (r_g, precision) for the aforementioned four cases. Each change scenario has the same symbol in all diagrams

seventh change scenario of mRUBiS with a precision value of 44.44%. The reason for the low precision is the concatenation of the following change propagation rules: i) the change propagation from a modified signature to the interface containing the signature and ii) the change propagation from the affected signatures to all components requiring these signatures. As the signature is not implemented or used in the most components marked as affected, these components were considered as false positives. Neither omitting the change propagation within a component, nor reducing the number of iterations due to inter- and intra-component dependencies can improve the precision in this change scenario. However, the r_t value shows that only a small number of model elements are affected in this change scenario. The comparison between the r_t and r_g values shows that the generated task list references only a small number of model elements. Thus, it can improve the change propagation analysis despite the low precision value. The precision metric relates only to the number of true positives and the number of false positives in a task list. It neglects the number of all model elements. For this reason, despite the low r_g and r_t values, the precision value for this scenario is rather low.

11.2.7. Assumptions and Limitations

Although the goal of the evaluation was to evaluate the quality of the generated task list by KAMP4BP [Ros+17a], the change propagation rules of the initial KAMP4IS [Sta15; Ros+15b] and their extensions strongly influence the evaluation results of KAMP4BP (KAMP4IS was evaluated in [Sta15]). The reason is that KAMP4BP extends KAMP4IS. Further, if a change propagation rule of KAMP4IS results in false positives in the initial stages of the change propagation analysis (e.g., the second scenario of CoCoME in Section 11.2.4.2), these false positives result in further false positives in the later stages of the change propagation analysis. Therefore, the consequences of two change propagation rules in IS were exemplary discussed in the evaluation of KAMP4BP. Although precision values of the second and the third case are higher than in the first case, the recall values in these scenarios are 100%.

As discussed previously, the corresponding rules for the second and the third case can be used in a small number of scenarios depending on the programming style and can result in more false positives. However, there could be change scenarios, in which omitting the change propagation from the data types affected by an initially changed data type, as well as the inter- and intra-component change propagation leads to false negatives. No realistic change scenario could be found in CoCoME and mRUBiS without changing the case studies to illustrate the problem. However, mRUBiS can be modified in order to construct an example for a change scenario illustrating this problem. Buyers can leave a comment for an item in mRUBiS. The description of the comment is realized as STRING. In this way, any description is allowed. However, consider that the description is a composed data type and a user changes the composed data type description. Considering both change propagation rules would result in identifying all affected model elements. However, this would also result in generating a high number of false positives. Omitting both change propagation rules would result in missing an affected method invocation in the task list. However, this reduces the number of false positives significantly. One can argue that changing a signature has a little impact. Thus, missing this signature in the task list can be accepted. In general, omitting such rules can have a high impact on the generated task list. There are several solutions for the previous example. One solution can be developing change propagation rules at a low abstraction level (e.g., maybe at the instance level for the specific scenarios). However, the resulting change propagation analysis approach cannot be generalized to other systems. In other words, the change propagation rules may need to be adapted for other systems. Another example is a case, in which a signature in an interface does not contain any affected data types as parameters or return type and has to be renamed as a result of the change request. Such affected model elements cannot be easily identified using aforementioned change propagation rules. One heuristic could be to use the implementation of such interfaces or their signatures. According to this heuristic, if the implementation of an interface or a signature has to be changed, the corresponding interface or signature is also affected by a change. However, this can lead to the propagation of the internal changes in a component to its interfaces. In this way, a component can no longer be considered as a black box. Such heuristics also violate the information hiding principle and can cause a high number of false positives in the results. Using component internal dependencies as suggested by Stammel [Sta15; Ros+15b] can help to identify such interfaces or signatures, only if the providing interface or signature of a component has a dependency to an affected requiring interface or signature. In this case, the corresponding rules for inter- and intra-component change propagation have to be used not only to identify the components, as used in previously described change scenarios, but to identify all potentially affected interfaces and signatures, as originally proposed by Stammel [Sta15]. The latter solution finds such interfaces and signatures, but highly overestimate the results in IS projects. One possible solution for all other cases (e.g., no dependencies to any affected model element) can be a heuristic regarding name search. Another possible solution is to use the coarse-grained elements in a software architecture such as interfaces instead of more fine-grained entities such as signatures. In other words, if the generated task list contains interfaces, they can indicate that the whole interfaces (i.e., not only individual signatures) need to be considered during the change propagation analysis. Which heuristics and which change propagation rules have to be used for a specific change propagation analysis approach or a whole software system highly depend on the coding style and have to be evaluated individually. Summarized, these examples show that although there are only a few change scenarios for these change propagation rules, omitting them may result in false negatives. Although omitting these change propagation rules improves the precision values of the results, there is a trade-off decision between the number of false positives and false negatives. In general, domain experts have to decide which case is suitable for a specific change propagation analysis. This depends on several factors, such as the implementation overhead of the change propagation analysis approach or the abstraction level of the metamodels, models, and rules. The influencing factors are described in Section 11.4.2.

As discussed at the beginning of the section, the goal of this evaluation was to evaluate KAMP4BP. KAMP4IS was evaluated in an empirical study (cf. [Sta15]). Thus, the evaluation of KAMP4IS is out of scope of the evaluation of this thesis. The aforementioned examples and the corresponding four cases in the evaluation results aim at illustrating the effects of the evaluation results of KAMP4IS on KAMP4BP.

KAMP4BP provides generic change propagation rules. In general, there can be BP schema and the corresponding instances. Thus, the algorithm and the rules can be adapted to a specific BP schema. This can highly improve the prediction results. As discussed previously, the generalization can suffer in these cases.

11.3. Change Propagation Analysis in Automated Production Systems

This section presents the evaluation of KAMP4aPS and KAMP4IEC, discussed in Chapter 7. While KAMP4aPS considers the change propagation in mechanical and electrical/electronic elements (i.e., hardware) in aPS, KAMP4IEC automatically calculates the change propagation in the PLC software. These approaches can be considered as instances of the methodology in the domain of aPS. As described in Chapter 7, a change in mechanical and electrical/electronic elements of aPS can result in further changes in the PLC software. However, not every change in the hardware will cause a change in the PLC software. Thus, to develop a comprehensive set of representative change scenarios, which cover all relevant equivalence classes of model elements, the change propagation in the hardware and the software of aPS was evaluated separately.

For the evaluation of these approaches a community case study was used. This case study is described in Section 11.3.1. At the beginning of the chapter, Figure 11.1 illustrated the relationships between the maintainability analysis methodology, its concrete instances, and the application of the instances to specific systems. The evaluation presented in this section corresponds to the application of several instances of the methodology in the domain of aPS to a system (see the latter both layers in Figure 11.1). Sections 11.3.2 and 11.3.3 discuss the goals, questions, and metrics of the evaluation of KAMP4aPS and KAMP4IEC, respectively. These sections also present the change scenarios and the results of the application of the approaches to each scenario. Section 11.3.4 gives an overview of the assumptions and limitations.

The content of this section is based on the results of a Master's thesis [Koc17] and a Bachelor's thesis [Rät17], which the author of this dissertation supervised. A follow-up version of the KAMP4aPS evaluation was appeared in the paper [Hei+18]. The evaluation of KAMP4aPS, which is presented in the following, is based on and extends the evaluation of the paper [Hei+18]. The evaluation of KAMP4IEC is based on and extends the evaluation of the paper [Bus+18c] and the Bachelor's thesis [Rät17]. Thus, most content of this section was appeared in the aforementioned works.

11.3.1. xPPU Case Study

The xPPU is illustrated in Figure 11.8. It is an extension version of the PPU. It was established as a community demonstrator for industrial manufacturing plants within the priority programme SPP 1593 [Hei+18; Vog+17; Bou+17]. The PPU case study "is limited in size and complexity but provides a valuable trade-off between problem complexity and evaluation effort" [Vog+14a, p. 1]. Similar to CoCoME, the engineering artifacts and documents of PPU are available [Vog+17] [3]. Further, a set of change scenarios are defined for the community case study [Vog+14a].

The xPPU presents a lab-size plant, which mainly comprises a stack, a crane, a stamp, and a conveyor. The stack serves as a store for work pieces. The crane picks the work pieces from the stack and transports them to other positions of the plant (e.g., stamp). In this process, different types of work pieces can be differentiated (e.g., due to their material) [Vog+17; Bou+17; Vog+14a].

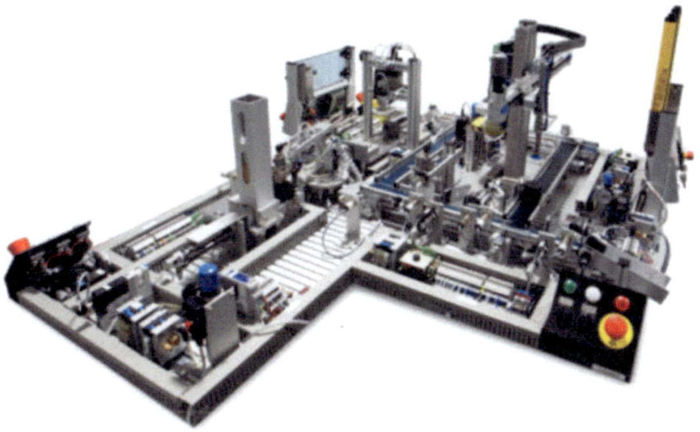

Figure 11.8.: xPPU as a lab-sized demonstrator for aPS [Hei+18, p. 3]

[3] https://www.ais.mw.tum.de/en/research/equipment/ppu/

11.3.2. Change Propagation Analysis in Mechanical and Electrical/Electronic Elements

This section discusses the evaluation of KAMP4aPS, which is presented in Chapter 7. KAMP4aPS was developed as an instance of the methodology and considers the change propagation in mechanical and electrical/electronic elements of aPS. In the following, *mechanical and electrical/electronic elements* and *hardware* are used interchangeably. Changes in the hardware can cause further changes in the PLC software [Hei+18].

The xPPU plant comprises mechanical and electrical/electronic elements, as well as a PLC software. The mechanical and electrical/electronic elements of the xPPU were used to evaluate the KAMP4aPS approach [Vog+17]. The following sections describe the study design, as well as the change scenarios and the corresponding results.

11.3.2.1. Evaluation Goals, Questions, and Metrics

A GQM plan [Bas92; BCR94] was used to evaluate KAMP4aPS. Similar to KAMP4BP in Section 11.2.3, **Goal 1** evaluates the quality of the automatically generated task lists in comparison to the manually created reference task lists. The reference task lists were developed based on the knowledge of the Automatisierung und Informationssysteme (AIS) group of the TUM. The generated task lists were automatically created by KAMP4aPS. Similar to the evaluation of KAMP4BP, users' decisions regarding task list reduction were not considered. After comparing a generated task list and the corresponding reference task list, a task can be considered as either true positive (t_p), false positive (f_p), or false negative (f_n). The focus of **Question 1.1** is the precision of the generated task list: How precise is the automatically generated task list in comparison to the reference task list? **Metric 1.1** is defined as: $precision = \frac{t_p}{t_p + f_p}$ to consider the number of true positives and the number of false positives [Pow08]. In contrast to the first question, **Question 1.2** considers the completeness of the generated task list: How complete is the automatically generated task list in comparison to the reference task list? **Metric 1.2** is defined as: $recall = \frac{t_p}{t_p + f_n}$ to consider the number of true positives and the number of missing model elements in the generated task list (i.e., false negatives) [Pow08]. Metric 1.1 and

Metric 1.2 regard two cases. In the first case, both domain and context elements are considered, while the second case considers only domain elements. Context elements not only involve the organizational and technical artifacts but also aim at documenting the tacit knowledge of domain experts. Thus, context elements in the following examples were chosen with regard to the aforementioned aspects. Additionally, the following scenarios were designed to involve different context elements (if possible) to be able to evaluate the effects of different context elements. Further, the context elements were modeled at a low abstraction level and annotated on as many model elements as possible. However, it is conceivable that documenting the tacit knowledge cannot always be possible or the granularity of the documentation can vary from scenario to scenario or from aPS to aPS. Additionally, context elements can be added or removed over time. Further, different domain experts may extend the model of domain elements with other context elements, as they can consider other context elements as more relevant for the change effort estimation. For these reasons, the precision and the recall metrics are given in the following change scenarios for both cases with context elements and without context elements.

Similar to the evaluation of KAMP4BP, the next goal addresses whether KAMP4aPS can reduce the effort needed in the change propagation analysis. Thus, **Goal 2** evaluates the coverage of the automatically generated task list in comparison to the number of all model elements. As Goal 1 neglects the number of all model elements in the evaluation results, this goal aims at considering the number of all model elements while analyzing the change propagation. **Question 2** is defined as: Can KAMP4aPS reduce the number of model elements in a domain, which have to be considered by an aPS expert during the change propagation analysis phase? **Metric 2.1** can be defined as $r_t = \frac{t_p}{n}$. It is the ratio of the number of true positives (t_p) to the number of all model elements (n). **Metric 2.2** is the ratio of the number of the model elements in a domain referenced by the generated task list ($l = t_p + f_p$) to the number of all model elements (n): $r_g = \frac{l}{n}$. Metric 2.1 and Metric 2.2 regard only the model elements in a domain. To answer this question, the values of both metrics have to be compared.

To calculate precision, recall, r_t and r_g, true positives and false positives have to regard only the affected model elements in the task lists and not how they are affected. During the analysis of the evaluation results, task types should be ignored. Hence, tasks, which reference the same model element but have different task types, have to be considered only once.

In the evaluation of KAMP4BP, the effects of different change propagation rules on the generated task list were shown. In the evaluation of KAMP4aPS, the effects of two aPS metamodels on the generated task list should be discussed. The next question aims at evaluating an appropriate abstraction level of metamodels and the corresponding change propagation rules for the change propagation analysis in aPS. **Question 2.2** is also: Which influences has the abstraction level of the metamodel on the quality of the generated task lists compared to the corresponding reference task list? To answer this question an instance of both metamodels at different abstraction levels is created. Further, corresponding change propagation rules were created for each abstraction level, as described in Section 7.2.1.3. For each change scenario, all calculated metrics for both models at two abstraction levels were compared.

11.3.2.2. Change Scenarios and Evaluation Results

For evaluating KAMP4aPS, three change scenarios for the hardware of the xPPU were chosen based on the abstract aPS metamodel, introduced in Section 2.7.1. The abstract aPS metamodel is composed of `structure`, `component`, `module`, and `interface` metaclasses. The following change scenarios cover changing the micro switch `module`, the ramp `component`, and the physical `interface` of ramp. As a structure acts as a container to organize other model elements (i.e., `modules` and `components`), the following change scenarios do not cover changes to structure. Additionally, as modules can contain other modules and components, changes to structures are similar to changes to modules. Another reason for omitting changes to structures is that a change to a structure represents a change propagation at a very high abstraction level. A seed modification at a high abstraction level may result in a high overestimation of the results. Thus, the set of seed modifications should be chosen as small as possible [Hei+18; Ros+17a]. The change scenarios with `component`, `module`, and `interface` as seed modifications represent the equivalent classes of relevant model elements regarding the change propagation.

To evaluate KAMP4aPS, two models of the xPPU were created manually. The first model is based on the abstract metamodel, whereas the second model is based on the specific metamodel. Both metamodels were based on the AML models provided by the AIS group of the TUM. While the abstract metamodel can be used to model any plants, the specific metamodel is tailored to the xPPU [Hei+18]. On the one hand, to use the specific metamodel for the other plants, it has to be extended to dedicated elements in these plants. On the other hand, as the representation of the plant elements in the abstract metamodel is very abstract, it is expected that a change propagation analysis based on the corresponding model can lead to results with a low precision [Boh02]. In the following, the effect of the granularity of the metamodel on the results is also discussed. For this purpose, the change scenarios were also modeled for both xPPU models. The results of the change propagation analysis are discussed for both models. In general, the domain expert has to decide on the granularity of the metamodel. Different factors such as the metamodeling and the implementation overhead, as well as the precision of the results can affect this design decision. These factors are discussed in Section 11.4.2 in more detail.

Change Scenario 1: Module This change scenario is based on the scenario 13 of the xPPU technical report [Vog+14a]. This scenario describes changing the sensor `modules` for better detecting the position of the crane in the xPPU. Prior to the change, the position of the crane is detected by three micro switches. Each micro switch acts as a binary sensor detecting whether the crane is in a certain position. Thus, the crane position can be detected only in three positions exactly. The ability to detect the position of the crane should be improved. For this purpose, the micro switches should be replaced by a single potentiometer. In contrast to a micro switch, the potentiometer can detect the position of the crane continuously. In this scenario, three micro switch `modules` are affected initially. A micro switch module contains a micro switch `component`, a fixture `component`, and a communication `interface`. Thus, this change scenario shows that not only the micro switches and the potentiometer are affected by the change, but also the connected elements [Hei+18].

Metric: \ Model Abstraction:	Abstract Model	Specific Model
Precision (regarding domain and context elements)	57.14%	95.24%
Precision (regarding domain elements)	44.90%	95.65%
Recall	100.00%	100.00%
r_g	42.61%	20.00%
r_t	19.13%	19.13%

Table 11.24.: Results of the 1st change scenario for the xPPU

Table 11.24 illustrates the evaluation results for both models in the first change scenario. Regardless of the abstraction level of both metamodels, no model element of the reference task list was missing in the generated task lists (i.e., the recall value is 100.00% for both models). Thus, only the precision values for both cases with context element and without context elements are given. Table 11.24 shows that the change propagation analysis based on the abstract model results in a high number of false positives (i.e., the precision value regarding the domain and context elements is 57.14%), whereas the generated task list based on the specific model contains only a few numbers of false positives (i.e., the precision value regarding the structural and context elements is 95.24%). Calculating the precision values by considering only the domain elements for both abstract and specific models also lead to similar results. In this case, the precision value for the abstract model is slightly lower (i.e., 44.90%) than the precision value of the case with context elements (i.e., 57.14%). For the specific model, both precision values are almost equal (i.e., 95.24% for the case with context elements and 95.65% for the case without context elements). The reason for generating many false positives for the abstract model is that the change propagation rules could not differentiate between different types of plant elements. Examples of this are the instances of the `component` and `module` metaclasses from the abstract metamodel. In this example, a valve and a ramp are both components. Further, the model does not distinguish between different types of sensors (e.g., micro switches, optical sensors, or inductive ones) and motors, as they are all considered as instances of the `module` metaclass. Therefore, the analysis cannot stop iterating over new model elements and change propagation rules, as soon as the type of the model element does not match. By contrast, the change propagation rules for the specific model can distinguish between different types of model elements. Thus, they can analyze the change propagation and identify the affected model elements more precisely.

The r_t value shows that 19.13% of all domain model elements are affected in this change scenario. Thus, this scenario can be considered as a fundamental change in the model. As there are only a few false positives in the generated task list based on the specific model, the r_g value for the specific model is also 20.00%. However, the generated task list based on the abstract model contains 42.61% of all model elements due to the high overestimation described previously.

Change Scenario 2: Component This change scenario is based on the scenario 1 of the xPPU technical report [Vog+14a]. This scenario describes changing the mechanical `component` ramp for increasing the capacity. Before the change, the xPPU has regular ramps with a total capacity of three work pieces. In this change scenario, the regular ramps should be replaced by another ramp with more capacity. Thus, a new Y-shaped ramp with a capacity of six work pieces was selected. The ramp `component` is contained in the conveyor `structure` and has an `interface`. Via this `interface` the ramp `component` can be connected to the frame of the plant. Thus, replacing the ramp affects the frame and the fixation `interface` [Hei+18].

Metric: / Model Abstraction:	Abstract Model	Specific Model
Precision (regarding domain and context elements)	27.78%	100.00%
Precision (regarding domain elements)	25.00%	100.00%
Recall	100.00%	100.00%
r_g	28.87%	7.22%
r_t	7.22%	7.22%

Table 11.25.: Results of the 2nd change scenario for the xPPU

Table 11.25 summarizes the results for both models in the second scenario. The change affects only 7.22% of all model elements actually (i.e., r_t). No element is missing in the generated task lists for both the abstract and the specific model. Thus, the recall value for both cases is 100.00%. Similar to the first change scenario, only the precision values for both cases with context element and without context elements are discussed in the following.

Similar to the first scenario, the change propagation analysis for the abstract model overestimates the affected model elements. This results in a low precision for the abstract model (i.e., the precision value for the cases with context elements is 27.78%.). Considering only the domain elements also leads to similar results regarding the precision value (i.e., the precision value is 25.00%.). The r_g value for this model shows that the change propagation selects only 28.87% of all model elements as changed, despite the low precision. This effect (i.e., lower precision and lower r_g at the same time) is already illustrated in Figure 11.4. The reason for this effect is that the precision considers only the number of true positives and false positives. In contrast to precision, r_g relates to the number of all selected model elements (i.e., true positives and false positives) and the number of all model elements.

Similar to the first change scenario, the results of the change propagation analysis based on the specific model are precise (i.e., the precision value in this case is 100.00%). Thus, the generated task list and the reference task list contain the same model elements of the specific model.

Change Scenario 3: Interface This change scenario is not based on the xPPU technical report due to the small dimension of the change and was, thus, developed separately. This scenario describes changing the physical interface of the ramp component for improving the friction. This scenario was chosen due to its change propagation characteristics. In the xPPU, an `interface` connects the ramp to only one main element of the plant, namely the frame. Thus, if the change propagation rules were not designed accurately, the result of the change propagation analysis may also contain all elements connected to the frame. In this change scenario, the `interface` modification affects the connected ramp and frame [Hei+18].

Metric: \ Model Abstraction:	Abstract Model	Specific Model
Precision (regarding domain and context elements)	11.61%	100.00%
Precision (regarding domain elements)	8.57%	100.00%
Recall	100.00%	100.00%
r_g	36.08%	3.09%
r_t	3.09%	3.09%

Table 11.26.: Results of the 3rd change scenario for the xPPU

Table 11.26 illustrates the evaluation results for both models in the case of changing an interface. As described previously, the r_t value shows that the change affects only a small number of all model elements (i.e., 3.09%). Similar to the previous change scenarios, no model element from the reference task list was missing in the generated task lists for both models. Thus, this scenario considers only the precision metric for the discussed cases (i.e., with and without context elements). However, the generated task list for the abstract model contains 36.08% of all model elements (i.e., r_g). This shows that the change propagation analysis cannot differentiate between different types of model elements. Thus, it overestimates the results to avoid overlooking model elements (i.e., false negatives). The overestimation results in a precision value of 11.61% for the abstract model for the case with context elements. The case without context elements results in slightly lower precision value (i.e., 8.57%). In contrast to the abstract model, the change propagation analysis for the specific model does not contain any false positives. Therefore, the precision of the generated task list for the specific model is 100.00%.

11.3.2.3. Summary of Evaluation Results

This section summarizes the evaluation results of KAMP4aPS based on the xPPU models at two abstraction levels. In the previously described change scenarios, no model element from the reference task lists is missing in the generated task lists by KAMP4aPS regardless of the abstraction level of the models. However, the abstraction of the metamodel influences the resulting instances (i.e., models) and the granularity of the change propagation rules (i.e., as the rules distinguish between different types of model elements). They influence the precision of the evaluation results. In particular, the change propagation algorithm for the abstract metamodel iterates over all change propagation rules, until the algorithm does not identify new model elements in the current iteration. The corresponding change propagation rules for an abstract metamodel are also defined at an abstract level. In other words, they cannot consider the specific types of the metaclasses such as `components` or `modules`. The benefit of this is that the abstract metamodel and the corresponding change propagation rules can be applied to any plant. However, they overestimate the results by generating a high number of false positives. By contrast, the change propagation analysis based on the specific metamodel generates only a few numbers of false positives in the previously described change scenarios. The corresponding change propagation algorithm consists of a set of change propagation rules, which were tailored to the specific metamodel. Thus, extending the specific metamodel requires new change propagation rules. Summarized, there is a trade-off design decision between the abstraction level of the metamodel and the corresponding change propagation rules on the one hand and the effort of developing and changing the metamodel, the corresponding change propagation rules, and the precision of the results on the other hand. This is discussed in Section 11.4.2.

11.3.2.4. Assumptions and Limitations

In the evaluation of KAMP4aPS, two metamodels at two abstraction levels were considered. The specific metamodel was designed based on the xPPU. As the xPPU is a community case study, the corresponding metamodel contains typical elements of a plant such as cranes and sensors (i.e., the specializations of `structure`, `module`, `component`, and `interface`) [Hei+18; Vog+14a]. To use the metamodel and the change propagation rules for another plant, the specific metamodel has to be extended to the elements of the plant under study. More fine-grained abstraction levels of the metamodel are also conceivable. For example, different sensors from different vendors could be metamodeled separately. If the metamodel is too fine-grained or tailored to a specific plant, it cannot be generalized adequately. In the sensor example, if a plant uses other sensors or even the same sensors from other vendors, the metamodel has to be extended or refactored and the corresponding change propagation rules have to be adapted. The specific metamodel was chosen, as it contains typical plant elements [Hei+18]. Further, more metaclasses and relations between the metaclasses in a metamodel correlate with more change propagation rules. This increases the effort of implementing the change propagation analysis approach.

As described previously, the task types during the analysis of duplicates in the task list were ignored. In other words, the true positives and false positives regard only the affected elements in the task lists and not how they are affected. For example, the tasks *Add component table* and *Change component table* were considered only once, as both refer to the element *table*. Thus, considering these tasks as two different tasks can result in other values of the metrics. Another influencing factor on the results is the technical and organizational artifacts that have to be considered. Considering other technical and organizational artifacts can lead to other values of the metrics especially the precision and recall metrics. For this purpose, the evaluation considers not only domain elements together with context elements, but also domain elements without context elements. As the value of the recall metric was 100.00% for all change scenarios, only the precision metric regarding both cases were calculated. The values of the precision metric regarding the domain and context elements are similar to the values of the precision metric regarding only the domain elements in the discussed change scenarios.

As described previously, the evaluation compares the results for two models at two abstraction levels. For this purpose, the models contained the same elements. An example of this is the simple motor. It is represented as a specific element type in the specific metamodel, while it can be modeled only as a component using the abstract metamodel. Thus, the modeling effort for both models was the same.

11.3.3. Change Propagation Analysis in Control Software

This section presents the evaluation results of KAMP4IEC, which is proposed in Section 7.3. KAMP4IEC can be considered as a further instance of the methodology. It analyzes the change propagation in a PLC software, which is developed based on the IEC 61131-3 standard. To evaluate the approach, the PLC software of the xPPU was used. The following sections describe the goals, questions, and metrics of the evaluation, as well as the change scenarios and the corresponding results.

11.3.3.1. Evaluation Goals, Questions, and Metrics

A GQM plan [Bas92; BCR94] was used for the evaluation of KAMP4IEC. Similar to the evaluation of KAMP4BP and KAMP4aPS, **Goal 1** evaluates the quality of the automatically generated task lists in comparison to the manually created reference task lists. The reference task list is based on the PLC software and the corresponding model based on the metamodels for the IEC 61131-3 programs. It references model elements regarding the program elements that have to be modified to implement the change. The generated task list is automatically created by the approach. Similar to the previous evaluations the decision of users regarding task list reduction was not considered. After comparing a generated task list and the corresponding reference task list, a task can be considered as either true positive (t_p), false positive (f_p), or false negative (f_n). **Question 1.1** is concerned with the precision of the generated task list: How precise is the automatically generated task list in comparison to the reference task list? **Metric 1.1** relates to the number of true positives and the number of false positives as: $precision = \frac{t_p}{t_p + f_p}$ [Pow08]. **Question 1.2** deals with missing elements in the generated task list: How complete is the automatically generated task list in comparison to the reference task list? **Metric 1.2** relates to the number of true positives and the number of false negatives as: $recall = \frac{t_p}{t_p + f_n}$ [Pow08].

Similar to KAMP4BP, the next goal addresses whether the use of KAMP4IEC decreases the effort of the change propagation analysis. Thus, **Goal 2** evaluates the coverage of the automatically generated task list in comparison to the number of all model elements. **Question 2** is defined as: Can KAMP4IEC reduce the number of model elements, which domain experts need to consider during the change propagation analysis phase? To answer this question, two metrics were defined, similar to the previous evaluations. **Metric 2.1** is the ratio of the number of model elements referenced by the reference task list (t_p) to the number of all model elements (n): $r_t = \frac{t_p}{n}$. **Metric 2.2** is the ratio of the number of model elements referenced by the generated task list ($l = t_p + f_p$) to the number of all model elements (n): $r_g = \frac{l}{n}$. The effort reduction can be observed by comparing the values of both metrics. Comparing both metrics allows analyzing whether KAMP4IEC can reduce the effort of the change propagation analysis.

11.3.3.2. Change Scenarios

To evaluate KAMP4IEC, a set of change scenarios were identified. The change scenarios can be considered as equivalence classes of model elements, which are relevant for the change propagation analysis. Thus, the change scenarios cover all relevant metaclasses. Additionally, they cover the change propagation rules, which were defined based on the relations of the metaclasses. The first three change scenarios analyze the impact of changing a hardware part of a plant on the PLC software. These scenarios are partially developed based on the evolution scenarios of the xPPU [Vog+14a]. The other change scenarios were designed to cover the remaining relevant IEC metaclasses and the remaining change propagation rules.

If the change propagation algorithm for the PLC software (see Algorithm 29) identifies affected function blocks and interfaces in the model of software, it adds these model elements to the set of seed modifications to calculate further change propagation. Thus, changing function blocks or interfaces can have a high impact on the results of the algorithm. For this purpose, several change scenarios were designed to consider changes to function blocks or interfaces.

This section describes the change scenarios. The following section discusses the results of the evaluation. The evaluation scenarios and results are based on and extend the scenarios and results of the KAMP4IEC evaluation appeared in [Rät17; Bus+18c].

Change Scenario 1: Structure The first change scenario was designed based on one of the evolution scenarios of the xPPU [Vog+14a]. This scenario deals with removing the stamp of the xPPU. Consequently, the seed modifications are the input and output global variables, as well as the function block realizing the stamp functionality. This change scenario covers the following seed modifications in the IEC repository model: `GlobalVariable` and `FunctionBlock`.

Change Scenario 2: Module This change scenario corresponds to the first change scenario of the hardware (see Section 11.3.2.2). It considers replacing three micro switch modules for the detection of the crane positions with a single potentiometer. This scenario is also based on one of the evolution scenarios of the xPPU [Vog+14a]. The sensors are connected to the PLC. Consequently, the input and output of the PLC are presented in the model as global variables. In this scenario, the corresponding global variables for the input of the micro switches have to be changed. This change scenario covers the following seed modification in the IEC repository model: `GlobalVariable`.

Change Scenario 3: Component This scenario deals with removing the binary start button of the plant and adding a rotary one. The goal is switching between different production modes. The global variable corresponding to the binary start button has the type `BOOL`. Thus, the type of the corresponding global variable has to be changed from `BOOL` to `INT`. This change scenario covers the following seed modification in the IEC repository model: `GlobalVariable`.

Change Scenario 4: Function Block In this change scenario, a function block and its methods have to be renamed. The function block mainly provides the functionality to control the conveyor in the xPPU. This function block is instantiated by a further function block. Additionally, the methods of this function block are called by the methods of another function block. This change scenario covers the following seed modification in the IEC repository model: `FunctionBlock`.

Change Scenario 5: Function Block This change scenario was designed to analyze the effects of refactoring a function block, which implements the functionality of the crane in the xPPU. The refactoring involves splitting the function block into further function blocks due to separation of concerns. Similar to the previous scenario, a further function block instantiates the affected function block and several of its methods call the methods of the affected function block. This change scenario covers the following seed modification in the IEC repository model: `FunctionBlock`.

Change Scenario 6: Function Block This change scenario is concerned with changing a function block, which mainly provides the functionality of the stack in the plant. Similar to the previous both scenarios, this function block is instantiated by a further function block, which methods call the methods of the affected function block. The change has also a refactoring nature without changing the functionality of the function block. This change scenario covers the following seed modification in the IEC repository model: `FunctionBlock`.

Change Scenario 7: Function Block This change scenario analyzes the effect of changing a function block, which is accessed by several IEC elements. For this scenario, the PLC software has to be changed to contain a new function block. This function block implements an existing interface. It is also extended by another function block. Additionally, the return type of a function is the new function block. Further elements of the PLC software contain, access, or extend the new function block. Thus, the impact of deleting this function block has to be analyzed. This change scenario covers the following seed modification in the IEC repository model: `FunctionBlock`.

Change Scenario 8: Function For this change scenario, a new helper function `CheckGreaterEquals` was added to the PLC software. `CheckGreaterEquals` provides the functionality to compare two values. The helper function is accessed by several IEC elements. It is also called by another functions and function blocks. Several elements of the PLC software contain or call the helper function. This change scenario analyzes the effect of deleting `CheckGreaterEquals` on the PLC software. Thus, this change scenario covers the following seed modification in the IEC repository model: `Function`.

Change Scenario 9: Interface In this change scenario, a new interface was added to the PLC software. The new interface is accessed by several other IEC elements. It extends an existing interface. A function block in the PLC software implements the new interface. There are also other IEC elements using this interface (e.g., a global variable of the interface type). This scenario analyzes the impact of deleting this interface. Thus, this change scenario covers the following seed modification in the IEC repository model: `Interface`.

Change Scenario 10: Interface This change scenario should represent a fundamental change to the PLC software. In this change scenario, an interface, which is implemented by several function blocks, has to be changed. The change mainly involves renaming the interface and its methods. Thus, this change scenario covers the following seed modification in the IEC repository model: `Interface`.

Change Scenario 11: Interface In this change scenario, the effects of a change to a further interface has to be analyzed. Compared to the previous scenario, this interface is implemented by a function block and is instantiated by another function block. Additionally, the function block implementing this interface has to implement not only its abstract methods, but also its abstract properties. Further, the methods of the interface are called by another function block. Thus, this change scenario covers the following seed modification in the IEC repository model: `Interface`.

Change Scenario 12: Method In this scenario, the return type of an abstract method of an interface was changed from `BOOL` to `Enum`. A function block implements this abstract method. Further, this method is called or contained by other IEC elements. Thus, this change scenario covers the following seed modification in the IEC repository model: `AbstractMethod`.

Change Scenario 13: Property This change scenario considers the effect of changing a return type of an abstract property of an interface from `BOOL` to `INT`. A property of a function block implements this abstract property. Further, this method is called directly or indirectly by other IEC elements.

Thus, this change scenario covers the following seed modification in the IEC repository model: `AbstractPrperty`.

Change Scenario 14: Program In this scenario, the main program is renamed. Thus, this change scenario covers the following seed modification in the IEC system model: `Program`.

11.3.3.3. Evaluation Results

Table 11.27 illustrates the evaluation results of KAMP4IEC. The rows present the change scenarios described previously. The second and the third column each contain the values of the precision and the recall metrics. Additionally, two further ratios were calculated (i.e., r_t and r_g). r_t is the ratio of the model elements, which are actually changed (i.e., true positives) to all model elements, while r_g presents the ratio of all model elements in the generated task list by KAMP4IEC to all model elements. As the scenarios analyze the impact of changing different model elements, the number of all model elements slightly varies from scenario to scenario. Some scenarios have more model elements than in the original xPPU model. Consequently, they are more complex than the original xPPU model. These change scenarios were constructed to be able to cover as many dependencies and change propagation rules as possible.

Metric: / Change Scenario:	Precision	Recall	r_t	r_g
Change Scenario 01: Structure (Hardware)	89.19%	100.00%	14.22%	15.95%
Change Scenario 02: Module (Hardware)	100.00%	100.00%	5.15%	5.15%
Change Scenario 03: Component (Hardware)	100.00%	100.00%	2.15%	2.15%
Change Scenario 04: Function Block (Software)	75.00%	100.00%	7.76%	10.34%
Change Scenario 05: Function Block (Software)	83.33%	100.00%	10.78%	12.93%

Change Scenario: \ Metric:	Precision	Recall	r_t	r_g
Change Scenario 06: Function Block (Software)	80.95%	100.00%	7.33%	9.05%
Change Scenario 07: Function Block (Software)	100.00%	100.00%	4.98%	4.98%
Change Scenario 08: Function (Software)	100.00%	100.00%	2.13%	2.13%
Change Scenario 09: Interface (Software)	100.00%	100.00%	3.73%	3.73%
Change Scenario 10: Interface (Software)	87.65%	100.00%	30.60%	34.91%
Change Scenario 11: Interface (Software)	97.83%	100.00%	19.40%	19.83%
Change Scenario 12: Method (Software)	100.00%	100.00%	2.15%	2.15%
Change Scenario 13: Property (Software)	100.00%	100.00%	1.72%	1.72%
Change Scenario 14: Program (Software)	100.00%	100.00%	0.86%	0.86%

Table 11.27.: Evaluation results of the approach to change propagation analysis for the control software regarding precision, recall, r_t, and r_g

Table 11.27 shows that no model element from the reference task lists was missing in the generated task lists. In other words, the value for the recall metric was 100.00% for the previously discussed change scenarios. To avoid false negatives, the change propagation rules overestimate the results. This leads to a high recall value by the generated task list. This was motivated by the overall goal during the development of the approach regarding accepting more false positives in order to avoid false negatives. Additionally, Table 11.27 shows that the precision values of the first, fourth, fifth, sixth, tenth, and eleventh change scenarios are not 100.00%. In other words, only the generated task lists of these scenarios contain false positives. As discussed previously, this is due to the trade-off design decision between different factors influencing the recall and the precision values (see Section 11.4.2). In particular, avoiding more false negatives corresponds with accepting more false positives. As the change propagation rules were designed to avoid as many false negatives as possible, they generate false positives in the results. In principle, the change propagation rules could also be adapted to generate fewer false positives by omitting the less likely change scenarios. However, the generated task lists may contain false negatives. Additionally, the change scenarios with lower precision values present fundamental changes to the PLC software, as it can be seen by the r_t values in Table 11.27. Thus, if a change results in false positives in an iteration, the false positives can result in further false positives. In general, the approach provides the functionality to avoid the propagation of change by considering users' decisions (see Section 5.2.3). In such cases, aPS experts can exclude the cause of a false positive propagation. However, this functionality was not used to avoid biasing the evaluation results. Despite the precision value, r_t and r_g show that KAMP4IEC generates only a few false positives for the aforementioned change scenarios. Furthermore, the comparison between r_t and r_g shows that the approach reduces the effort of the change propagation analysis, as aPS experts have to analyze only a subset of all model elements using the generated task lists.

11.3.4. Assumptions and Limitations

Similar to the previously described approaches, the change propagation rules of KAMP4IEC are based on a predefined metamodel (see Section 7.3.1.1). This metamodel covers the relevant IEC elements for the change propagation analysis. IEC elements, which are not contained in the metamodel (e.g., data types that are defined by users) can be partially mapped to the existing metaclasses. Another solution is extending the metamodel and the change propagation rules to cover the new metaclasses and their relationships [Bus+18c].

As there are different dialects for IEC 61131-3, it was not feasible to provide metamodels and change propagation analysis approaches for all existing dialects. The metamodel, which was developed for KAMP4IEC, is based on the dialect of CodeSys V3.1. This dialect is very similar to the original standard and additionally provides Object-Oriented Programming (OOP). Using the OOP extension enables domain experts to modularize the PLC software. However, the PLC programs, which were developed using other dialects may require an adapted version of the proposed metamodel. One solution is to change these programs to use the OOP extensions. Another solution is to adapt the proposed metamodel and the change propagation rules to the IEC dialect used for a specific program [Bus+18c].

11.4. Discussion of Evaluation Results and Influencing Factors

Section 11.4.1 describes the relation between the evaluation results and the research questions, introduced in Section 1.4. Additionally, Section 11.4.2 presents the influencing factors on the results of the methodology instances. A discussion on validity is given in Section 11.4.3.

11.4.1. Discussion of Evaluation Results

This section describes, to which extent the evaluation results answer the research questions proposed in the introduction chapter (see Section 1.4).

One of the main contributions of this thesis is the development of a maintainability analysis methodology. For this purpose, the idea of a model-based and architecture-based approach, which was originally developed in IS [Sta15], was generalized to a domain-independent methodology. Thus, the comprehensiveness of the methodology and the relevance of the methodology's elements were evaluated by instantiating the methodology in different domains comprising heterogeneous elements. The instantiations of the methodology to these domains resulted in model-based and architecture-based approaches to change propagation analysis in the respective domain. The evaluation of the methodology regarding the comprehensiveness shows, although the domains are different and contain heterogeneous elements, the methodology provides comprehensive concepts to develop model-based and architecture-based approaches in these domains. The evaluation of the methodology regarding the relevance of the methodology's elements shows that the mandatory part of the methodology regarding the change effort caused by systems' structure and behavior in a domain had to be instantiated in all considered domains to obtain a complete approach to change propagation analysis. For this purpose, metamodels of the system's architecture were used, which represent the structure of the heterogeneous elements in these domains. Further, the optional part of the methodology regarding the change effort caused by context elements can also be considered in a domain, if the change effort resulted from organizational and technical artifacts in this domain can considerably contribute to the effort of implementing the change. Thus, the evaluation shows that the methodology provides relevant concepts for the development of a model-based and architecture-based change propagation analysis approach in different domains comprising heterogeneous elements. Summarized, the development of the methodology as a generalization of a change propagation analysis approach in IS on the one hand and the evaluation regarding its comprehensiveness and the relevance of its elements on the other hand answer the *first research question* (see Section 1.4).

While the previous paragraph discussed the applicability of the elements of the methodology during the development of a model-based and architecture-based approach in different domains comprising heterogeneous elements, this paragraph is concerned with the evaluation of the resulting approaches in each domain. These approaches analyze the change propagation using the dependency analysis based on mutual dependencies of heterogeneous elements in different domains. For this purpose, these approaches were applied to several community case studies as representative case studies in the respective domain. During the evaluation, the precision, the recall, and the fraction of model elements in the task lists to all model elements were evaluated. Additionally, different influencing factors were varied such as the abstraction levels of the used metamodel or different sets of change propagation rules. These factors leaded to different instances of the methodology in each domain. The evaluation results show that the output (i.e., task lists) of the instances reduced the effort of the change propagation analysis for domain experts by considerably reducing the set of all model elements, which have to be analyzed by domain experts. Additionally, the results show that considering mutual dependencies between heterogeneous elements from different domains (e.g., IS and BP) or sub-domains of a domain (e.g., aPS) provide domain experts a holistic change propagation analysis across different domains. The evaluation results for two metamodels at different abstraction levels in aPS shows that fine-grained metamodels representing several types of elements and their relationship can improve the results of the change propagation analysis approach. Considering different change propagation rules in BP allowed analyzing the effects of rules, which were designed due to different programming style, on the results of the change propagation analysis. In general, considering more semantics (e.g., the metaclasses of a metamodel and their relationships) can improve the results of the change propagation analysis. The importance of considering semantics during the change propagation analysis is also discussed by other researchers such as Bohner [Boh02]. However, there are different influencing factors, which can result in different approaches to change propagation analysis and affect their results. These influencing factors are discussed in the following section. Additionally, extending the architectural model of a system by organizational and technical artifacts can result in more comprehensive task lists due to considering the tacit knowledge of domain experts. Summarized, the evaluation shows that the effects of a change can be identified based on the architecture of a system and the design of a process by considering the mutual dependencies between heterogeneous elements from different domains. Hence, this answers the *second research question* (see Section 1.4).

As described previously, the methodology is based on the idea of the dependency analysis between heterogeneous architectural elements from different domains. Thus, the instances of the methodology mainly use architectural models and the dependencies between their elements to analyze the change propagation. The development of a methodology to construct model-based and architecture-based approaches on the one hand and the evaluation of the instances of this methodology in different domains on the other hand show that an architectural model is a suitable abstraction to identify the change effort across different domains. Thus, these contributions answer the *overall research question* (see Section 1.4).

The evaluation shows that there is not a unique instance of the methodology in a specific domain. There are different influencing factors, which result in different instantiations of the methodology. Thus, the following section discusses these influencing factors in more detail.

11.4.2. Influencing Factors on Results of Change Propagation Approaches

In Sections 11.2 and 11.3, different instances of the methodology are applied to three community case studies in different domains. The instances varied from the change propagation rules (see Section 11.2) to the abstraction level of the metamodels (see Section 11.3). These and other factors affect the results of the generated task lists regarding the precision, the recall, and the ratio of the number of model elements in the generated task list to all model elements. The previous sections explicitly described some influencing factors and their effects in the corresponding change scenarios. This section summarized the relevant influencing factors. These factors can also be considered as guidelines to instantiate the methodology in a specific domain.

In addition to the influencing factors described in the following, there are also factors, which are derived from the **overall objectives** of a change propagation analysis approach. For example, the goal of a change propagation analysis is not always identifying all affected elements of the system in advance. The goal can also be a rough estimation of the affected elements, for example to refine the architecture design of the system or to weigh a possible implementation against another one regarding their effects. Thus, it is important to consider the overall objectives in advance.

11.4.2.1. Metamodel of Domain

The metamodel of the domain is used to describe the system under study in a specific domain. It contains the relevant metaclasses and their relationships. According to Stachowiak [Sta73], a model is created to fulfill a certain purpose for certain subjects (i.e., in this context, subjects are domain experts who are responsible for maintaining the system) in a certain period. As described by this characteristic, the properties of the metamodel and the corresponding model cannot be generally specified and must be relevant to domain experts and especially for the purpose. The choice of the relevant properties depends on the context and the usage of the model. One of these properties is the granularity of the metamodel. This property is concerned with the level of abstraction. In other words, the main question is, which elements of the system under study a metaclass represents. For example, in KAMP4aPS two metamodels at two abstraction levels were considered. The abstract metamodel is composed of four metaclasses. In this metamodel, the metaclass `component` represents all parts of a plant, which can be bought from a third-party vendor. Each metaclass from the abstract metamodel was further refined in the specific metamodel. This metamodel provides refined metaclasses for a `component` metaclass such as `arm` or different sensor types [Hei+18]. The choice of the metamodel affects the resulting change propagation rules. In the abstract metamodel, the change propagation rules can only differentiate between the relationship between four types of model elements, namely `structures`, `modules`, `components`, and `interfaces`. In the `component` example, the change propagation rules for the abstract metamodel cannot differentiate whether a `component` is an `arm` or a `sensor`. As shown in Section 11.3.2.2, the evaluation results for the specific metamodel are more precise than those for the abstract metamodel. However, which metamodel and in particular which properties of the resulting model seem relevant to domain experts (i.e., subjects) for the maintainability analysis (i.e., purpose) cannot be determined in advance. Nevertheless, there are some factors influence the choice of the properties. In the following, relevant influencing factors on this design decision are described in more detail.

One of the influencing factors aims at the period in the previously described characteristic. This corresponds to the phases of the development life cycle. While the system does not exist in the early phases (e.g., concept, planning, or design), the late phases are mainly concerned with the maintenance [Lar04]. In other words, a concrete system exists in the late phases of the development process. If a change propagation analysis approach is used in the early phases, the metamodel of the domain may be designed at a very coarse-grained manner, as the concrete system and the model elements could not be specified at that time. Thus, a coarse-grained metamodel can support modeling the system at an abstract level of abstraction. This model can be used during the design phase to reason about the possible future changes and their effects. In this way, the system can be incrementally designed and developed with regard to the maintainability. A change propagation analysis approach can also be applied in an iterative and incremental development process [Lar04].

One can argue that a comprehensive metamodel can be designed in advance, which contains all possible types of system elements at a fine-grained abstraction level. This argument cannot be accepted in general, as some domains such as aPS can involve a wide variety of artifacts, which differ in their properties. From which properties can be abstracted during the development of the metamodel is a design decision (e.g., whether the granularity of a component, a sensor, a sensor type such as an optical sensor, or even a specific optical sensor from a certain vendor is sufficient). This design decision also corresponds to the context, the usage, and the purpose of the metamodel, as well as the effort of designing the metamodel, which represents a further relevant influencing factor. Metamodeling all possible parts at a fine-grained level of abstraction is a time-consuming and error-prone task. Further, a fine-grained metamodel, which is composed of several thousand metaclasses, is difficult to use. In the aPS example, it may be possible that proprietary parts have to be explicitly designed for a plant. Thus, not all possible parts can be known in advance. Additionally, only a small fraction of a comprehensive metamodel can be relevant to model the systems. This corresponds to another influencing factor, which is concerned with how many systems have to be modeled using a specific metamodel. If the metamodel is used to model only one system, omitting the elements, which are not used, lowers the cost during the metamodeling phase.

Another influencing factor is concerned with how long a system and the correspondence metamodel and model are in operation. If a system is in operation for decades (e.g., some aPS plants [Vog+17; Hei+18]), a fine-grained metamodel, which may be tailored to the system, improves the change propagation analysis. For this purpose, the system under study has also to be modeled at a fine-grained level of abstraction.

As described previously, a fine-grained metamodel increases the effort and the cost of the development. If the metamodel does not allow modeling the coarse-grained parts of a system, it increases the modeling effort. In this case, it is possible that the metamodel cannot be used at the early phases of development, in which parts of the system are not yet known at a fine-grained level of abstraction.

The evolution of the system is a further influencing factor. If the metamodel is designed at a very fine-grained level of abstraction and is tailored to certain systems, the systems and the metamodel, as well as the corresponding models have to co-evolve. This factor should also be considered in an iterative and incremental development process. Additionally, this restricts the use of the metamodel for other systems, as the metamodel has to be adapted and extended for further systems.

The result of the change propagation analysis (i.e., the purpose) is a major influencing factor during the design of the metamodel. Section 11.3.2.2 shows that a fine-grained metamodel improves the results of the analysis significantly. The previously described factors are a subset of all factors influencing the design of the metamodel. Depending on these influencing factors, the context, and the usage of the metamodel, different metamodels can be developed.

After a metamodel has been developed or selected, its instances have to be created reflecting the system under study. Several influencing factors affect the choice of the appropriate model for a certain purpose. These factors are very similar to the factors influencing the design of the metamodel, described previously. One difference is that the granularity of the metamodel limits the granularity of the resulting models. In other words, if the metamodel was designed at a high abstraction level such as the abstract model of aPS, the resulting models may have many elements. However, the types of elements are either `component`, `module`, `interface`, or `structure` in this example. Further, adapting or extending a metamodel to include future element types (i.e., the evolution of the metamodel) can result in changing all its instances. Thus, the choice of a metamodel and the appropriate instance for the change propagation analysis is a trade-off decision, which can be influenced by the previously described factors.

11.4.2.2. Algorithm for Change Propagation Analysis

The previous section discussed different influencing factors on a metamodel design. Further, it discussed the effects of the granularity and the quality of a metamodel on the corresponding change propagation rules using the abstract and the specific metamodel of aPS. This section assumes that a metamodel and its appropriate instance have already been developed or selected. Thus, it discusses different factors influencing the choice of the change propagation rules.

Similar to the metamodels, one of the important influencing factors is the granularity of the change propagation rules. If the change propagation rules consider many change propagation cases, which also cover the rare change propagation situations, the analysis can result in a high overestimation of the affected elements (i.e., too many false positives). Section 11.2 illustrates this factor based on four cases. It considers the effects of two change propagation rules on the results, which consider change propagation situations depending on the programming style. Although they resulted in false positives in several change scenarios in the evaluation, omitting them can lead to false negatives in general, even if they did not occur in the change scenarios of the evaluation.

If the change propagation rules consider only a few change propagation cases, which occur in most change scenarios, the analysis can result in an underestimation of the affected elements (i.e., false negatives). On the one hand, an underestimation may result in missing relevant model elements for the change propagation analysis. Elements are considered to be important for the change propagation analysis for example if the effort of changing them is high. Thus, these model elements have to be contained in the generated task lists. In other words, if task lists do not contain elements, which cause a high change impact, domain experts have to manually analyze the change propagation in the system models. On the other hand, a high overestimation of the results may cause that the generated task list contains almost all model elements in the worst case. In other words, a high overestimation increases the effort of the change propagation analysis, as domain experts may have to manually analyze all system models in the worst case. In some cases an overestimation and in other cases an underestimation can be accepted by domain experts. However, a high overestimation or a high underestimation may distort the results. Whether an overestimation or an underestimation is acceptable, depends on the overall objectives of the analysis and cannot be generally determined in advance. Additionally, the overestimation and the underestimation affect each other. Avoiding the underestimation of the results can lead to an overestimation, as domain experts need to develop change propagation rules considering rare change propagation situations.

Another important influencing factor is the development costs of the change propagation analysis approach. Considering many change propagation rules at a fine-grained abstraction level corresponds to a detail analysis of the system (e.g., at the later phases of the development process or if the approach needs to be tailored to a system) or similar systems (e.g., at the early phases or if the approach shall be applied to many systems). Thus, the generalizability of the approach and the phases of the development process are two further influencing factors. Further, the rules depend on the overall objectives of the change propagation analysis approach, as discussed previously. In the previous approaches, the change propagation rules are developed with regard to avoiding the underestimation of the results. However, the change propagation rules can be principally adapted or extended according to the scenario or system under study. Additionally, if domain experts can accept an underestimation, the change propagation rules considering rare change propagation situations can be omitted. This can significantly reduce the false positive generation (e.g., the four cases in the evaluation of KAMP4BP).

If a metamodel presents a system at a fine-grained abstraction level and the change propagation rules are also developed at a fine-grained abstraction level, the generated task lists contain a few numbers of false positives and false negatives (e.g., the specific variant of KAMP4aPS). However, the development costs of these change propagation analysis approaches are higher than the costs of the approaches generating a vague estimation. Further, to apply such approaches to the other systems, the metamodel and the change propagation rules have to be adapted or extended. One reason to develop such fine-grained approaches is, if the system is in operation for a long period. To sum up, the choice and the granularity of change propagation rules are a trade-off decision, which can be influenced by several factors.

11.4.2.3. Seed Modifications

The previous two sections described the influencing factors on the choice of the metamodel, the resulting model, and the change propagation rules. If the metamodel, the model, and the change propagation rules have been fixed, the choice of the seed modification affects the results. The reason for this is that a change request can be implemented in different ways [Sta15; Ros+15b]. Using different seed modifications can result in different task lists. On the one hand, using different seed modifications can support domain experts to compare different possible implementations. On the other hand, a change propagation analysis approach cannot be considered as a black box, as domain experts should know the granularity of the used metamodel and the change propagation rules. In this way, they can identify the valid seed modifications, which are supported by the change propagation analysis approach.

11.4.3. Threats to Validity

In the previous sections, the evaluation results of KAMP4BP, KAMP4aPS, and KAMP4IEC were proposed. These approaches were developed as instances of the methodology. They are model-based and rule-based approaches, which analyze the propagation of changes in different scenarios. Thus, this section addresses the threats to validity of these instances of the methodology as model-based and rule-based approaches regardless of the domain under study. However, examples from each approach are used to illustrate the discussed threats. The following classes of threats to validity are based on [Run+12].

11.4.3.1. Internal Validity

Internal validity deals with "a causal relationship between outcomes and intervention/treatment" [Run+12, p. 39]. The proposed change propagation analysis approaches are based on models. In other words, the metaclasses and their relationships affect not only the resulting models, but also the change propagation rules, as the rules consider these relationships to trace the propagation of changes. The choice of the metamodel essentially affects the change propagation rules. For this purpose, the most metamodels used for the previous approaches were created by domain experts. For example, the metamodel of BP was derived from BPMN [Hei+17]. Another example is the aPS metamodels, which were created based on the AML models provided by the domain experts from the AIS group of the TUM [Hei+18]. The quality of the resulting models is also one of the most important influencing factors, as they can vary in different factors such as precision and granularity. Further, different domain experts could model the same element differently. For example, aPS experts can model a motor either as a `component`, which was bought from a third-party vendor, or as a `module`, which is composed of other parts (e.g., `components` or `modules`). For this purpose, the generated task lists were compared with the reference task lists, which were created manually. The comparison considers only elements, which occurred both in the system under study and its model. Additionally, there is not only one way to implement a change. In other words, there could be more than one possible set of seed modifications and one possible reference task list for a change scenario. However, it was assumed that different task lists involve similar model elements [Ros+17a; Hei+18].

11.4.3.2. External Validity

External validity addresses "the domain to which study finding can be generalized" [Run+12, p. 39]. The authors also state in [Run+12, p. 19] that "for descriptive research questions, the case study may be feasible if representativeness of a sampling based study may be sacrificed for better realism in a case study." In other words, the application of the proposed approaches to other case studies or even to other scenarios may lead to other results. However, a case study "investigates a contemporary phenomenon in depth and within its real-life context, especially when the boundaries between phenomenon and context are not clearly evident" [Yin08, p. 18]. Thus, this can be applied to "many, if not most, research studies in software engineering" [Run+12, p. 19].

To evaluate the proposed approaches three community case studies were used. They are composed of typical elements of the systems in each domain and provide typical functionality [Hei+18]. Thus, it can be assumed that other systems in each domain have a similar structure [Hei+18]. Using community case studies, it is possible to compare different research approaches [HRR16]. As it was not feasible to consider all possible change scenarios for the evaluation, the change scenarios were chosen to cover the relevant metaclasses of each metamodel for the change propagation analysis. The application of the instances of the methodology to other change scenarios results in other task lists, which can lead to different values of the considered metrics in this evaluation. The evaluation results show that instances of the methodology can be developed and applied to a set of change scenarios to consider the mutual dependencies between different domains or sub-domains of a domain to obtain more comprehensive task lists. Further, a literature review has been conducted to systematically identify categories of change triggers in BP [Kap+18a]. Thus, the change scenarios in BP were also developed with focus on this comprehensive categorization. However, if the change triggers are considered from other view points, they can also be assigned to other subcategories. In aPS, the change scenarios were also chosen to represent the common changes in this domain [Hei+18]. The change scenarios for the PLC software also cover all change propagation rules.

As the change scenarios in the evaluation cover the relevant metaclasses at a fine-grained level, the complex scenarios can be considered as a composition of the fine-grained changes. Nonetheless, other case studies and more change scenarios in future can support to draw conclusions from the results of the evaluation.

11.4.3.3. Construct Validity

Construct validity "shows that the correct operational measures are planned for the concepts being studied" [Run+12, p. 39]. The proposed approaches are model-based and scenario-based. The goal of the evaluation for each instance of the methodology was to evaluate the quality of the results of the change scenarios in each domain. As not all possible change scenarios can be analyzed, the choice of representative change scenarios is an important aspect. Thus, the change scenarios in BP are based on a comprehensive category of change triggers resulted from a literature review (see Chapter 10). The change scenarios in aPS show common changes in this domain [Vog+14a; Hei+18]. Further, the change scenarios were chosen to cover all important equivalence classes of model elements. These classes represent the metaclasses of the metamodels in each domain, which are relevant for the change propagation analysis. Further, the models in aPS were created manually based on the AML models, which have been already used to model the xPPU [Hei+18].

11.4.3.4. Reliability

This validity discussion, also known as conclusion validity, describes "to what extent the data and the analysis are dependent on the specific researchers" [Run+12, p. 72]. To evaluate KAMP4BP two community case studies were used to lower the risk of biased results. Further, a comprehensive category of change triggers in BP was determined in a literature review.

In aPS, the researchers from the AIS group of the TUM were involved in the construction of the metamodels by providing the AML models and the selection of the appropriate change scenarios. The description of some change scenarios was already proposed in the previous work of the AIS group [Vog+14a]. Additionally, statical metrics were used to quantify the results [Hei+18].

12. Conclusion

This chapter summarizes the contributions of this thesis and the evaluation and gives an overview of possible future work.

12.1. Summary

This thesis presented a generic methodology, which generalizes the idea of a model-based and architecture-based approach to change propagation analysis in IS (i.e., [Sta15]). The methodology uses the systems' structure as the main artifact for the change propagation analysis. Thus, it can be considered as a guideline to develop change propagation analysis approaches for different domains comprising heterogeneous elements. Chapter 5 gave an overview of the characteristics of the systems and the domains, in which the methodology can be instantiated. As the methodology abstracts from a specific implementation, tool, and technology, it provides a generic guideline. To abstract from the heterogeneity of elements, the methodology uses modeling concepts. These concepts allow for a dependency analysis between different types of elements. In this way, the methodology answers the *first research question.* Additionally, the systems' structure and behavior can be extended with further information regarding organizational and technical artifacts in a project (e.g., similar to [Sta15]), which enable domain experts to derive more complete lists of affected elements. This is based on the idea that changing these artifacts can considerably contribute to the effort resulted by a change request. To develop a change propagation analysis approach, the methodology can be instantiated in a specific domain. The instances of the methodology in different domains analyze the effects of an initial change request on the systems' structure and behavior based on a dependency analysis. In this thesis, the instances of the methodology were used to analyze the complex co-evolution of IS and BP, as well as the co-evolution of heterogeneous elements in aPS.

The instance of the methodology in BP was developed as an extension of the original approach to change propagation analysis in IS (i.e., [Sta15]). IS are used in several BP, for example, to support customers to achieve their goals [Cha+01]. Thus, considering IS or BP in isolation and without their mutual dependencies can lead to underestimation of the change effort. Hence, composing the change propagation analysis approaches in IS and BP provides domain experts a holistic view on a system and its behavior. They allow for analyzing the propagation of a change not only in one domain, but also between both domains. Thus, this contribution answers the *second research question.*

To analyze the change propagation in mechanical and electrical/electronic components, as well as control software of aPS, several loosely-coupled approaches were developed. Each approach was developed as an instance of the methodology and is concerned with the maintainability analysis of a sub-domain of aPS. For this purpose, several metamodels representing heterogeneous elements from different sub-domains were used. These metamodels give domain experts a holistic view on the system under study. One of these metamodels represents the data flow between hardware and control software in aPS. Thus, the composition of the corresponding approaches for hardware and control software allows analyzing the propagation of a change from the hardware of a plant to its control software. Additionally, metamodeling the behavior of aPS as a linked list of actor steps and system steps enables the traceability of a change from the control software to the behavior of a plant. Summarized, the approaches allow analyzing the change propagation in each sub-domain of aPS and between them to answer the *second research question.*

Domain experts have to define seed modifications for each change request either at the level of system elements or requirements. However, the previously described instances of the methodology support seed modifications, which are defined for system models. To address this issue, these instances were extended to enable domain experts to specify seed modifications at requirements level. Using this extension, the propagation of a change can be analyzed in requirements and design decisions, as well as to the model of the system satisfying them. Thus, this contribution aims at closing the gap between the changing needs of stakeholders and requirements on the one hand and the resulting system one the other hand. Thus, it complements the last both contributions.

As the methodology and its instances are based on the dependency analysis methods, they can be considered as rule-based approaches. To support domain experts to specify change propagation rules, Chapter 9 proposed a language for these rules. The language aims at providing a set of language elements to cover the relevant and common patterns of change propagation rules. Examples of these patterns are navigation along or against the direction of a reference between two metaclasses or their instances. The language can be considered as declarative, as it abstracts from the technical code, for example, needed for traversing models. A further benefit of using a dedicated language for change propagation rules is that the domain experts do not need any in-depth information about the implementation of the change propagation analysis approach. Thus, a main requirement of the language was to differentiate between the tasks of the roles of domain experts and developers of change propagation analysis approaches. The language complements the maintainability analysis methodology by abstracting from the heterogeneity of elements in different domains. Thus, it partially answers the *first research question.*

As IS and BP can influence each other mutually, a subset of all possible changes has its source in BP. To systematically determine and analyze the category of change triggers in BP, a literature review was conducted. The new comprehensive category allows for categorization of change requests along different dimensions (i.e., participation, origin, or characteristics of a change request) and at different abstraction levels. Additionally, this category can be used as a guideline to design BP and IS with regard to possible future changes. It can also be used to facilitate requirements elicitation and managing future changes and risks. As the category was developed independently of a specific organization or a sub-domain of BP, it can be considered as generic. This category contributes to the evaluation of the methodology's instance in BP.

One of the main contributions of this thesis was to analyze, how a change propagation analysis approach in IS can be generalized to a domain-independent approach, which is applicable to other domains with heterogeneous elements. For this purpose, the methodology was developed and instantiated in different domains. Thus, the methodology was evaluated regarding the relevance of different elements of it and its completeness. For this purpose, the elements of the methodology were analyzed, whether they were needed in different instantiations. Additionally, different instantiations were analyzed regarding missing elements in the methodology.

The instances of the methodology were analyzed regarding the quality of their results. Its instances in IS and BP were applied to two case studies: the community case study CoCoME and the exemplar mRUBiS. The instances developed to analyze the change propagation in mechanical and electrical/electronic components, as well as the control software of aPS were evaluated using the hardware and the software of the community case study xPPU. The community case studies were used for the evaluation, as they allow comparing the evaluation results of different approaches. The evaluation of the instances focused on the precision, recall, and coverage of their outputs (i.e., generated task lists). To this end, different change scenarios were developed. The change scenarios for BP are based on the aforementioned category of change triggers in this domain. A further prerequisite for the choice of the scenarios was to cover all equivalence classes of model elements, which are relevant for maintainability. For each change scenario, a further list of actually affected model elements was created manually. The output of the instances for each change scenario was compared to the corresponding list, which was created manually. Thus, the precision, recall, and coverage metrics regard this comparison. Further, different metamodels and models (i.e., for the evaluation of the instance in aPS), as well as change propagation rules (i.e., for the evaluation of the instance in BP) were developed. Based on these metamodels, models, and rules different influencing factors during the development of instances, as well as their outputs were extracted and discussed.

12.2. Outlook

This section discusses the potential future work that addresses the possible extensions and improvements of the aforementioned approaches, as well as the limitations of them.

So far, only one instance of the methodology was developed for each domain or sub-domain, except for the aPS hardware. In order to analyze the applicability of the methodology in different domains, the methodology can be instantiated in each domain in different ways. The instances can be developed based on the influencing factors, described in Section 11.4.2. These instances can be used to systematically analyze the effects of the influencing factors. Thus, it is possible to develop a guideline based on this experience for the development of the possible future instances of the methodology. The effects of different influencing factors not only on the development of individual instances, but also on their results regarding precision and completeness can be systematically analyzed.

In order to analyze the applicability of the methodology, it was instantiated in IS, BP, aPS both at system level and requirements level. However, the application of the methodology is not limited to these domains. In other words, the methodology can be instantiated in other domains, which fulfill the characteristics described in Section 5.1. The instantiation of the methodology to new domains enables a broader analysis of the applicability of the different methodology's parts.

The methodology is mainly based on an approach to change propagation analysis, developed in IS [Sta15]. This approach was evaluated using an empirical study. The study has shown that an automated approach helps less-experienced users to estimate more complete and precise change effort. The approaches in this thesis were developed to show that a generalization of this architecture-based and model-based approach can be applied to heterogeneous elements from different domains. Thus, the instances of the methodology developed in this thesis were evaluated using community case studies. In this way, it was, further, shown that an architecture-based and model-based approach originally developed in IS can be extended to other domains comprising heterogeneous elements. However, future empirical studies can show, to what extent the use of an automated approach can help domain experts during the analysis of change propagation in different domains. The setup of these empirical studies can be chosen similar to the previous work conducted by Stammel [Sta15]. Hence, users can be assigned to one of the following three groups: i) The less-experienced users of a treatment group, who use the tool. ii) The less-experienced users of a control group, who analyze the change propagation manually. iii) The experienced users of an expert group, who analyze the change propagation manually. The results of these groups and the time required to perform the tasks can be compared to draw further results regarding the benefits of an automated approach.

A further possible work could also be concerned with the scalability analysis of the automated approaches proposed in this thesis. For this purpose, different types of dependencies between model elements such as forward references or loops can be utilized. In addition to these types, different number of model elements and different rule types can be used. Further, the time needed to create models can be compared to the frequency of the future change requests and the time needed to analyze the change propagation both manually and automatically. Additionally, other factors can also be considered such as the time needed to develop the corresponding instances of the methodology at different abstraction levels (see Section 11.4.2). In this way, it can be estimated, when the effort to create an automated approach to change propagation analysis could pay off.

The approach to change propagation analysis in BP (see Chapter 6) was developed using a generic metamodel for BP (i.e., [Hei+17]). Thus, the corresponding change propagation rules are also developed generically. In order to improve the precision of the results, fine-grained metamodels representing specific IS and BP can be defined. A modeling language, which is tailored to a specific context or system allows for defining more fine-grained change propagation rules. This enables domain experts to estimate the change propagation more precisely. However, this approach cannot be applied to any systems. Additionally, the development time and costs can be higher than a generic approach due to more fine-grained metamodeling and code development.

Similar to IS, there are different programming languages and their dialects to develop control software. Different programming languages and their dialects include language elements and features, which a metamodel of the language can represent. Considering these language elements can enable domain experts to analyze the change propagation more precisely. The metamodel proposed in this thesis is mainly based on the CodeSys V3.1. dialect for the IEC 61131-3 standard. Thus, it is conceivable to develop further metamodels representing other programming languages and/or their dialects in the future. In order to develop complete change propagation analysis approaches, change propagation rules in addition to metamodels have to be specified. In this way, the change propagation analysis approach can cover a wider range of control software.

The output of the approaches presented in this thesis is a set of potentially affected model elements. Thus, a possible future work could be to use this output for analyzing the costs of a change request. A more fine-grained output can help to estimate costs more precisely. For this purpose, the costs of changing different system elements should be known in advance. Costs can be estimated in different ways (e.g., in person-months).

Domain experts have to select seed modifications in the model based on the change requests. Thus, a further future work could be an automated identification of seed modifications based on the change requests. How the seed modifications can be identified automatically, depends on the change requests. For example, an extension of a natural language processing approach (e.g., [JM09]) can be used to analyze a text containing the change requests.

The approaches proposed in this thesis need models representing the architecture of a system. In IS, different reverse engineering approaches exist, which extract the software architecture from code (e.g., [Kro12]) and extend it with technical and organizational artifacts (e.g., [Ros+17c]). These approaches use heuristics to extract architecture-related information. The idea of these approaches can also be applied to other domains to derive models of the system's architecture automatically. An example for such approaches is a process mining approach (e.g., [Aal16]). A further example could be an automated approach to extract architecture models from control software. It is also possible to develop an approach to change propagation analysis based on a metamodel, which the output of a specific reverse engineering approach is based on.

The approaches proposed in this thesis can be further extended to include versioning systems' architecture based on their models during the development and the evolution of these systems. This idea can also be extended by considering technical and organizational artifacts. The results can, then, be used for further analysis such as future decision-making processes.

The change propagation rule language can be extended with regard to described limitations in Section 9.4. An example of a possible extension could be to allow users to define and to change the set of affected model elements in a recursive block. A further example of a technical extension is to reference change propagation rules, which are defined in different rule files to improve the reusability of the rules.

A possible future work could also be the evaluation of the change propagation rule language. For this purpose, experts in different programming languages can describe the change propagation rules in the corresponding languages. The results can be compared to the results of the experts, who specified the change propagation rules in CPRL with regard to different aspects such as lines of code or scalability. Additionally, an empirical study can be conducted. The participants could be experts in a programming language and domain experts, who are not experienced in the programming language. The focus of the study could be on how a change propagation rule language can help less-experienced domain experts to describe the rules.

Chapter 5 highlighted the importance of considering the system's structure and design in interrelated domains during the maintainability analysis to obtain holistic change propagation analysis approaches. These approaches can help to identify the change effort across different domains comprising heterogeneous elements. Hence, the methodology and its instances aim at providing a domain-spanning change propagation analysis based on system's structure and design.

A. Appendix

A.1. Relations between IEC Model Elements

This section gives a detailed description of the binary relations, which are defined in Section 7.3.1.3. The relations are defined over the sets representing the instances of different metaclasses in Repository and System metamodel for IEC, as well as the instances of HMI metamodel. The sets are also defined in Section 7.3.1.3.

- The relation $ProgramInstantiatesInterface$ is defined over the sets U and E. In this relation, the Program $u \in U$ is associated to the Interface $e \in E$, if the Program u instantiates the Interface e.
- The relation $FunctionBlockInstantiatesInterface$ is defined over the sets B and E. In this relation, the FunctionBlock $b \in B$ is associated to the Interface $e \in E$, if the FunctionBlock b instantiates the Interface e.
- The relation $FunctionBlockImplementsInterface$ is defined over the sets B and E. In this relation, the FunctionBlock $b \in B$ is associated to the Interface $e \in E$, if the FunctionBlock b implements the Interface e.
- The relation $InterfaceExtendsInterface$ is defined over the set E. In this relation, the Interface $e_{e_i} \in E$ is associated to the Interface $e_{e_j} \in E$, if the Interface e_{e_i} extends the Interface e_{e_j}.
- The relation $GlobalVariableHasInterfaceAsType$ is defined over the sets V and E. In this relation, the GlobalVariable $v \in V$ is associated to the Interface $e \in E$, if the GlobalVariable v has the Interface e as type.

- The relation $GlobalVariableHasFunctionBlockAsType$ is defined over the sets V and B. In this relation, the GlobalVariable $v \in V$ is associated to the FunctionBlock $b \in B$, if the GlobalVariable v has the FunctionBlock b as type.
- The relation $FunctionHasInterfaceAsReturnType$ is defined over the sets F and E. In this relation, the Function $f \in F$ is associated to the Interface $e \in E$, if the Function f has the Interface e as return type.
- The relation $FunctionHasFunctionBlockAsReturnType$ is defined over the sets F and B. In this relation, the Function $f \in F$ is associated to the FunctionBlock $b \in B$, if the Function f has the FunctionBlock b as return type.
- The relation $CallFunctionBlockConstructor$ is defined over the sets F and B. In this relation, the Function $f \in F$ is associated to the FunctionBlock $b \in B$, if the Function f calls the constructor of the FunctionBlock b.
- The relation $MethodInstantiatesInterface$ is defined over the sets T and E. In this relation, the Method $t \in T$ is associated to the Interface $e \in E$, if the Method t instantiates the Interface e.
- The relation $MethodHasInterfaceAsReturnType$ is defined over the sets T and E. In this relation, the Method $t \in T$ is associated to the Interface $e \in E$, if the Method t has the Interface e as return type.
- The relation $MethodHasFunctionBlockAsReturnType$ is defined over the sets T and B. In this relation, the Method $t \in T$ is associated to the FunctionBlock $b \in B$, if the Method t has the FunctionBlock b as return type.
- The relation $MethodInstantiatesFunctionBlock$ is defined over the sets T and B. In this relation, the Method $t \in T$ is associated to the FunctionBlock $b \in B$, if the Method t instantiates the FunctionBlock b.
- The relation $InterfaceHasMethod$ is defined over the sets E and T. In this relation, the Interface $e \in E$ is associated to the Method $t \in T$, if the Interface e has the Method t.

- The relation *AbstractMethodHasInterfaceAsReturnType* is defined over the sets A and E. In this relation, the AbstractMethod $a \in A$ is associated to the Interface $e \in E$, if the AbstractMethod a has the Interface e as return type.
- The relation *AbstractMethodHasFunctionBlockAsReturnType* is defined over the sets A and B. In this relation, the AbstractMethod $a \in A$ is associated to the FunctionBlock $b \in B$, if the AbstractMethod a has the FunctionBlock b as return type.
- The relation *PropertyHasInterfaceAsType* is defined over the sets P and E. In this relation, the Property $p \in P$ is associated to the Interface $e \in E$, if the Property p has the Interface e as type.
- The relation *PropertyHasFunctionBlockAsType* is defined over the sets P and B. In this relation, the Property $p \in P$ is associated to the FunctionBlock $b \in B$, if the Property p has the FunctionBlock b as type.
- The relation *AbstractPropertyHasInterfaceAsType* is defined over the sets S and E. In this relation, the AbstractProperty $s \in S$ is associated to the Interface $e \in E$, if the AbstractProperty s has the Interface e as type.
- The relation *AbstractPropertyHasFunctionBlockAsType* is defined over the sets S and B. In this relation, the AbstractProperty $s \in S$ is associated to the FunctionBlock $b \in B$, if the AbstractProperty s has the FunctionBlock b as type.
- The relation *ProgramInstantiatesFunctionBlock* is defined over the sets U and B. In this relation, the Program $u \in U$ is associated to the FunctionBlock $b \in B$, if the Program u instantiates the FunctionBlock b.
- The relation *FunctionBlockInstantiatesFunctionBlock* is defined over the set B. In this relation, the FunctionBlock $b_{b_i} \in B$ is associated to the FunctionBlock $b_{b_j} \in B$, if the FunctionBlock b_{b_i} instantiates the FunctionBlock b_{b_j}.
- The relation *FunctionBlockExtendsFunctionBlock* is defined over the set B. In this relation, the FunctionBlock $b_{b_i} \in B$ is associated to

the FunctionBlock $b_{b_j} \in B$, if the FunctionBlock b_{b_i} extends the FunctionBlock b_{b_j}.

- The relation *MethodCallsFunction* is defined over the sets T and F. In this relation, the Method $t \in T$ is associated to the Function $f \in F$, if the Method t calls the Function f.
- The relation *FunctionBlockCallsFunction* is defined over the sets B and F. In this relation, the FunctionBlock $b \in B$ is associated to the Function $f \in F$, if the FunctionBlock b calls the Function f.
- The relation *ProgramCallsFunction* is defined over the sets U and F. In this relation, the Program $u \in U$ is associated to the Function $f \in F$, if the Program u calls the Function f.
- The relation *FunctionCallsFunction* is defined over the set F. In this relation, the Function $f_{f_i} \in F$ is associated to the Function $f_{f_j} \in F$, if the Function f_{f_i} calls the Function f_{f_j}.
- The relation *MethodReadsGlobalVariable* is defined over the sets T and V. In this relation, the Method $t \in T$ is associated to the GlobalVariable $v \in V$, if the Method t reads the GlobalVariable v.
- The relation *MethodWritesGlobalVariable* is defined over the sets T and V. In this relation, the Method $t \in T$ is associated to the GlobalVariable $v \in V$, if the Method t writes the GlobalVariable v.
- The relation *ProgramReadsGlobalVariable* is defined over the sets U and V. In this relation, the Program $u \in U$ is associated to the GlobalVariable $v \in V$, if the Program u reads the GlobalVariable v.
- The relation *ProgramWritesGlobalVariable* is defined over the sets U and V. In this relation, the Program $u \in U$ is associated to the GlobalVariable $v \in V$, if the Program u writes the GlobalVariable v.
- The relation *ProgramDeclaresGlobalVariable* is defined over the sets U and V. In this relation, the Program $u \in U$ is associated to the GlobalVariable $v \in V$, if the Program u declares the GlobalVariable v.

- The relation $ConfigurationDeclaresGlobalVariable$ is defined over the sets C and V. In this relation, the Configuration $c \in C$ is associated to the GlobalVariable $v \in V$, if the Configuration c declares the GlobalVariable v.
- The relation $InterfaceHasAbstractMethod$ is defined over the sets E and A. In this relation, the Interface $e \in E$ is associated to the AbstractMethod $a \in A$, if the Interface e contains the AbstractMethod a.
- The relation $ProgramCallsAbstractMethod$ is defined over the sets U and A. In this relation, the Program $u \in U$ is associated to the AbstractMethod $a \in A$, if the Program u calls the AbstractMethod a.
- The relation $ProgramCallsMethod$ is defined over the sets U and T. In this relation, the Program $u \in U$ is associated to the Method $t \in T$, if the Program u calls the Method t.
- The relation $FunctionBlockCallsAbstractMethod$ is defined over the sets B and A. In this relation, the FunctionBlock $b \in B$ is associated to the AbstractMethod $a \in A$, if the FunctionBlock b calls the AbstractMethod a.
- The relation $FunctionBlockCallsMethod$ is defined over the sets B and T. In this relation, the FunctionBlock $b \in B$ is associated to the Method $t \in T$, if the FunctionBlock b calls the Method t.
- The relation $MethodImplementsAbstractMethod$ is defined over the sets T and A. In this relation, the Method $t \in T$ is associated to the AbstractMethod $a \in A$, if the Method t implements the AbstractMethod a.
- The relation $MethodCallsMethod$ is defined over the set T. In this relation, the Method $t_{t_i} \in T$ is associated to the Method $t_{t_j} \in T$, if the Method t_{t_i} calls the Method t_{t_j}.
- The relation $MethodCallsAbstractMethod$ is defined over the sets T and A. In this relation, the Method $t \in T$ is associated to the AbstractMethod $a \in A$, if the Method t calls the AbstractMethod a.

- The relation *InterfaceHasAbstractProperty* is defined over the sets E and S. In this relation, the Interface $e \in E$ is associated to the AbstractProperty $s \in S$, if the Interface e has the AbstractProperty s.
- The relation *ProgramReadsProperty* is defined over the sets U and P. In this relation, the Program $u \in U$ is associated to the Property $p \in P$, if the Program u reads the Property p.
- The relation *ProgramWritesProperty* is defined over the sets U and P. In this relation, the Program $u \in U$ is associated to the Property $p \in P$, if the Program u writes the Property p.
- The relation *ProgramReadsAbstractProperty* is defined over the sets U and S. In this relation, the Program $u \in U$ is associated to the AbstractProperty $s \in S$, if the Program u reads the AbstractProperty s.
- The relation *ProgramWritesAbstractProperty* is defined over the sets U and S. In this relation, the Program $u \in U$ is associated to the AbstractProperty $s \in S$, if the Program u writes the AbstractProperty s.
- The relation *FunctionBlockReadsProperty* is defined over the sets B and P. In this relation, the FunctionBlock $b \in B$ is associated to the Property $p \in P$, if the FunctionBlock b reads the Property p.
- The relation *FunctionBlockWritesProperty* is defined over the sets B and P. In this relation, the FunctionBlock $b \in B$ is associated to the Property $p \in P$, if the FunctionBlock b writes the Property p.
- The relation *FunctionBlockReadsAbstractProperty* is defined over the sets B and S. In this relation, the FunctionBlock $b \in B$ is associated to the AbstractProperty $s \in S$, if the FunctionBlock b reads the AbstractProperty s.
- The relation *FunctionBlockWritesAbstractProperty* is defined over the sets B and S. In this relation, the FunctionBlock $b \in B$ is associated to the AbstractProperty $s \in S$, if the FunctionBlock b writes the AbstractProperty s.

- The relation *MethodReadsProperty* is defined over the sets T and P. In this relation, the Method $t \in T$ is associated to the Property $p \in P$, if the Method t reads the Property p.
- The relation *MethodWritesProperty* is defined over the sets T and P. In this relation, the Method $t \in T$ is associated to the Property $p \in P$, if the Method t writes the Property p.
- The relation *MethodReadsAbstractProperty* is defined over the sets T and S. In this relation, the Method $t \in T$ is associated to the AbstractProperty $s \in S$, if the Method t reads the AbstractProperty s.
- The relation *MethodWritesAbstractProperty* is defined over the sets T and S. In this relation, the Method $t \in T$ is associated to the AbstractProperty $s \in S$, if the Method t writes the AbstractProperty s.
- The relation *PropertyImplementsAbstractProperty* is defined over the sets P and S. In this relation, the Property $p \in P$ is associated to the AbstractProperty $s \in S$, if the Property p implements the AbstractProperty s.
- The relation *ConfigurationInstantiatesProgram* is defined over the sets C and U. In this relation, the Configuration $c \in C$ is associated to the Program $u \in U$, if the Configuration c instantiates the Program u.
- The relation *CallsMethod* is defined over the sets Q and T. In this relation, the Mode $q \in Q$ is associated to the Method $t \in T$, if the Mode q calls the Method t.
- The relation *CallsAbstractMethod* is defined over the sets Q and A. In this relation, the Mode $q \in Q$ is associated to the AbstractMethod $a \in A$, if the Mode q calls the AbstractMethod a.
- The relation *CallsFunctionBlock* is defined over the sets Q and B. In this relation, the Mode $q \in Q$ is associated to the FunctionBlock $b \in B$, if the Mode q calls the FunctionBlock b.

- The relation *HasMode* is defined over the sets D and Q. In this relation, the SystemStep $d \in D$ is associated to the Mode $q \in Q$, if the SystemStep d has the Mode q.
- The relation *HasSuccessor* is defined over the set W. In this relation, the HMIElement $w_{w_1} \in W$ (e.g., an actor step) is associated to the HMIElement $w_{w_2} \in W$ (e.g., a system step), if the HMIElement w_{w_1} has the HMIElement w_{w_2} as successor.

A.2. Supplementary Material for the Literature Review

Chapter 10 describes the review protocol of the literature review to identify categories of change triggers in business processes. The literature review was mainly based on the results of a database search method, which also described in Chapter 10 in more detail. This section presents the supplementary material for the study. This includes the search query for each database, the number of hits for each query, and the corresponding time span. The following tables also provide the relevant database settings. The content of this chapter is based on the results of a diploma thesis, which the author of this dissertation supervised [Kap17]. The supplementary material for a follow-up study is given in [Kap+18b].

Database	Adapted Search Queries for Search Term "trigger"	#Hits
GS	("business process" OR workflow) AND ("change trigger" OR "change triggers")	504
WoS	TOPIC: (("business process" OR workflow) AND change* AND trigger*) Timespan: All years. Search language=Auto	54
Scopus	ALL (("business process" OR workflow) AND ("change* trigger*"))	18
BASE	("business process" OR workflow) AND ("change trigger" OR "change triggers")	9
GS	("business process" OR workflow) AND ("trigger for change" OR "trigger for changes" OR "triggers for change" OR "triggers for changes")	362
Scopus	ALL (("business process" OR workflow) AND "trigger* for change*")	4
BASE	("business process" OR workflow) AND ("trigger for change" OR "trigger for changes" OR "triggers for change" OR "triggers for changes")	5
GS	("business process" OR workflow) AND ("trigger of change" OR "trigger of changes" OR "triggers of change" OR "triggers of changes")	143
Scopus	ALL (("business process" OR workflow) AND "trigger* of change*"	8
BASE	("business process" OR workflow) AND ("trigger of change" OR "trigger of changes" OR "triggers of change" OR "triggers of changes")	5
GS	("business process" OR workflow) AND ("trigger event" OR "trigger events")	~4790
WoS	TOPIC: (("business process" OR workflow) AND trigger* AND event*) Timespan: All years. Indexes: SCI-EXPANDED, SSCI.	46
Scopus	ALL (("business process" OR workflow) AND "trigger* event*")	30
BASE	("business process" OR workflow) AND ("trigger event" OR "trigger events")	12

Table A.1.: Overview of search queries including the search term "trigger" [Kap17, p. 68]

Databse	Adapted Search Queries for Search Term "reason"	#Hits
GS	("business process" OR workflow) AND ("change reason" OR "change reasons")	383
WoS	TOPIC: (("business process" OR workflow) AND change* reason*) Timespan: All years. Indexes: SCI-EXPANDED, SSCI.	102
Scopus	ALL (("business process" OR workflow) AND "change* reason*")	6
BASE	("business process" OR workflow) AND ("change reason" OR "change reasons")	–
GS	("business process" OR workflow) AND ("reason for change" OR "reason for changes" OR "reasons for change" OR "reasons for changes")	~2180
	("business process" OR workflow) AND ("reason for change")	751
	("business process" OR workflow) AND ("reason for changes")	148
	("business process" OR workflow) AND ("reasons for change")	~1040
	("business process" OR workflow) AND ("reasons for changes")	414
Scopus	ALL (("business process" OR workflow) AND "reason* for change*")	18
BASE	("business process" OR workflow) AND ("reason for change" OR "reason for changes" OR "reasons for change" OR "reasons for changes")	14
GS	("business process" OR workflow) AND ("reason of change" OR "reason of changes" OR "reasons of change" OR "reasons of changes")	177
Scopus	ALL (("business process" OR workflow) AND "reason* of change*")	2
BASE	("business process" OR workflow) AND ("reason of change" OR "reason of changes" OR "reasons of change" OR "reasons of changes")	14

Table A.2.: Overview of search queries including the search term "reason" [Kap17, p. 69]

Database	Adapted Search Queries for Search Term "force"	#Hits
GS	("business process" OR workflow) AND ("change force" OR "change forces")	712
WoS	TOPIC: (("business process" OR workflow) AND change* force*) Timespan: All years. Indexes: SCI-EXPANDED, SSCI.	60
Scopus	ALL (("business process" OR workflow) AND "change* force*")	38
BASE	("business process" OR workflow) AND ("change force" OR "change forces")	–
GS	("business process" OR workflow) AND ("force for change" OR "force for changes" OR "forces for change" OR "forces for changes")	~1630
	("business process" OR workflow) AND "force for change"	898
	("business process" OR workflow) AND "force for changes"	27
	("business process" OR workflow) AND "forces for change"	809
	("business process" OR workflow) AND "forces for changes"	32
Scopus	ALL (("business process" OR workflow) AND "force* for change*")	44
BASE	("business process" OR workflow) AND ("force for change" OR "force for changes" OR "forces for change" OR "forces for changes")	21

Database	Adapted Search Queries for Search Term "force"	#Hits
GS	("business process" OR workflow) AND ("force of change" OR "force of changes" OR "forces of change" OR "forces of changes")	~1,450
	("business process" OR workflow) AND "force of change"	277
	("business process" OR workflow) AND "force of changes"	12
	("business process" OR workflow) AND "forces of change"	~1190
	("business process" OR workflow) AND "forces of changes"	31
Scopus	ALL (("business process" OR workflow) AND "force* of change*")	11
BASE	("business process" OR workflow) AND ("force of change" OR "force of changes" OR "forces of change" OR "forces of changes")	21

Table A.3.: Overview of search queries including the search term "force" [Kap17, p. 70]

Database	Adapted Search Queries for Search Term "driver"	#Hits
GS	("business process" OR workflow) AND ("change driver" OR "change drivers")	~1180
	("business process" OR workflow) AND "change driver"	349
	("business process" OR workflow) AND "change drivers"	951
WoS	TOPIC: (("business process" OR workflow) AND change* driver*) Timespan: All years. Indexes: SCI-EXPANDED, SSCI.	29
Scopus	ALL (("business process" OR workflow) AND "change* driver*")	69
BASE	("business process" OR workflow) AND ("change driver" OR "change drivers")	14
GS	("business process" OR workflow) AND ("driver for change" OR "driver for changes" OR "drivers for change" OR "drivers for changes")	~1830
	("business process" OR workflow) AND "driver for change"	671
	("business process" OR workflow) AND "driver for changes"	47
	("business process" OR workflow) AND "drivers for change"	~1180
	("business process" OR workflow) AND "drivers for changes"	58
Scopus	ALL (("business process" OR workflow) AND "driver* for change*")	40
BASE	("business process" OR workflow) AND ("driver for change" OR "driver for changes" OR "drivers for change" OR "drivers for changes")	34

Database	Adapted Search Queries for Search Term "driver"	#Hits
GS	("business process" OR workflow) AND ("driver of change" OR "drivers of change" OR "driver of changes" OR "drivers of changes")	~2820
	("business process" OR workflow) AND "driver of change"	893
	("business process" OR workflow) AND "driver of changes"	51
	("business process" OR workflow) AND "drivers of change"	~1980
	("business process" OR workflow) AND "drivers of changes"	78
Scopus	("business process" OR workflow) AND "driver* of change*"	38
BASE	("business process" OR workflow) AND ("driver of change" OR "drivers of change" OR "driver of changes" OR "drivers of changes")	34

Table A.4.: Overview of search queries including the search term "driver" [Kap17, p. 71]

Database	Adapted Search Queries for Search Term "cause"	#Hits
GS	("business process" OR workflow) AND ("change cause" OR "change causes")	990
WoS	TOPIC: (("business process" OR workflow) AND change* cause*) Timespan: All years. Indexes: SCI-EXPANDED, SSCI.	147
Scopus	ALL (("business process" OR workflow) AND "change* cause*")	105
BASE	("business process" OR workflow) AND ("change cause" OR "change causes")	23
GS	("business process" OR workflow) AND ("cause for change" OR "cause for changes" OR "causes for change" OR "causes for changes")	329
Scopus	ALL (("business process" OR workflow) AND "cause* for change*"	4
BASE	("business process" OR workflow) AND ("cause for change" OR "causes for change" OR "cause for changes" OR "causes for changes")	46
GS	("business process" OR workflow) AND ("cause of change" OR "cause of changes" OR "causes of change" OR "causes of changes")	797
Scopus	ALL (("business process" OR workflow) AND "cause* of change*")	5
BASE	("business process" OR workflow) AND ("cause of change" OR "cause of changes" OR "causes of change" OR "causes of changes")	46

Table A.5.: Overview of search queries including the search term "cause" [Kap17, p. 72]

Database	Adapted Search Queries for Search Term "need"	#Hits
GS	("business process" OR workflow) AND "need for change"	~8510
WoS	TOPIC: (("business process" OR workflow) AND "need for change") Timespan: All years. Search language=Auto.	7
Scopus	ALL (("business process" OR workflow) AND "need for change")	4
BASE	("business process" OR workflow) AND "need for change"	61
GS	("business process" OR workflow) AND "need to change"	~17800
Scopus	ALL (("business process" OR workflow) AND "need to change")	14
BASE	("business process" OR workflow) AND "need to change"	61

Table A.6.: Overview of search queries including the search term "need" [Kap17, p. 73]

Database	Adapted Search Queries for Search Term "origin"	#Hits
GS	("business process" OR workflow) AND ("origin for change" OR "origin for changes" OR "origins for change" OR "origins for changes")	5
WoS	TOPIC: (("business process" OR workflow) AND origin* AND change*) Timespan: All years. Indexes: SCI-EXPANDED, SSCI.	124
Scopus	ALL (("business process" OR workflow) AND "origin* for change*")	–
BASE	("business process" OR workflow) AND ("origin for change" OR "origin for changes" OR "origins for change" OR "origins for changes")	2
GS	("business process" OR workflow) AND ("origin of change" OR "origin of changes" OR "origins of change" OR "origins of changes")	121
Scopus	ALL (("business process" OR workflow) AND "origin* of change*")	2
BASE	("business process" OR workflow) AND ("origin of change" OR "origin of changes" OR "origins of change" OR "origins of changes")	2

Table A.7.: Overview of search queries including the search term "origin" [Kap17, p. 74]

Database	Adapted Search Queries for Search Term "lever"	#Hits
GS	("business process" OR workflow) AND ("change lever" OR "change levers")	311
WoS	TOPIC: (("business process" OR workflow) AND change* AND lever*) Timespan: All years. Search language=Auto.	102
Scopus	ALL (("business process" OR workflow) AND ("change* lever*"))	7
BASE	("business process" OR workflow) AND ("change lever" OR "change levers")	2
GS	("business process" OR workflow) AND ("lever for change" OR "lever for changes" OR "levers for change" OR "levers for changes")	303
Scopus	ALL (("business process" OR workflow) AND "lever* for change*")	11
BASE	("business process" OR workflow) AND ("lever for change" OR "lever for changes" OR "levers for change" OR "levers for changes")	2
GS	("business process" OR workflow) AND ("lever of change" OR "lever of changes" OR "levers of change" OR "levers of changes")	252
Scopus	ALL (("business process" OR workflow) AND "lever* of change*")	4
BASE	("business process" OR workflow) AND ("lever of change" OR "lever of changes" OR "levers of change" OR "levers of changes")	2

Table A.8.: Overview of search queries including the search term "lever" [Kap17, p. 76]

Database	Adapted Search Queries for Search Term "source"	#Hits
GS	("business process" OR workflow) AND ("source for change" OR "source for changes" OR "sources for change" OR "source for changes")	122
WoS	TOPIC: (("business process" OR workflow) AND source* AND change*) Timespan: All years. Indexes: SCI-EXPANDED, SSCI.	162
Scopus	ALL (("business process" OR workflow) AND "source* for change*")	–
BASE	("business process" OR workflow) AND ("source for change" OR "source for changes" OR "sources for change" OR "sources for changes")	19
GS	("business process" OR workflow) AND ("source of change" OR "source of changes" OR "sources of change" OR "sources of changes")	~1,460
	("business process" OR workflow) AND "source of change"	649
	("business process" OR workflow) AND "source of changes"	133
	("business process" OR workflow) AND "sources of change"	722
	("business process" OR workflow) AND "sources of changes"	140
Scopus	ALL (("business process" OR workflow) AND "source* of change*")	69
BASE	("business process" OR workflow) AND ("source of change" OR "source of changes" OR "sources of change" OR "sources of changes")	19

Table A.9.: Overview of search queries including the search term "source" [Kap17, p. 75]

Bibliography

[17] *Enterprise Architecture at Work: Modelling, Communication and Analysis.* Springer, 2017.

[Aal16] Wil van der Aalst. *Process Mining: Data Science in Action.* 2nd ed. Springer, 2016. ISBN: 978-3-662-49850-7. DOI: 10.1007/978-3-662-49851-4.

[AB93] Robert Arnold and Shawn Bohner. "Impact Analysis - Towards a Framework for Comparison". In: *Proceedings of the Conference on Software Maintenance, ICSM 1993, Montréal, Quebec, Canada, September 1993.* 1993, pp. 292–301. DOI: 10.1109/ICSM.1993.366933.

[Aer+04] Ad Aerts, Jan Goossenaerts, Dieter Hammer, and Hans Wortmann. "Architectures in context: on the evolution of business, application software, and ICT platform architectures". In: *Information and Management* 41.6 (2004), pp. 781–794.

[AG] Janz Tec AG. *CODESYS - Entwicklungssoftware für Industriesteuerungen.* URL: https://www.janztec.com/embedded-pc/codesys (visited on 10/31/2017).

[AG14] Oscar Avila and Kelly Garcés. "Change Management Contributions for Business-IT Alignment". In: *Business Information Systems Workshops.* Springer, 2014, pp. 156–167.

[Aie+07] Giovanni Aiello, Marco Alessi, Manfredi Bruccoleri, Carlo D'Onofrio, and Giuseppe Vella. "An Agile methodology for Manufacturing Control Systems development". In: *2007 5th IEEE International Conference on Industrial Informatics.* Vol. 2. 2007, pp. 817–822.

[AJ00] Wil van der Aalst and Stefan Jablonski. "Dealing with workflow change: identification of issues and solutions". In: *Computer Systems Science and Engineering* 15.5 (2000), pp. 267–276.

[Ala+08] Ruth Alas et al. "Implementation of organizational changes in Estonian companies". In: *Journal of Business Economics and Management* 4 (2008), pp. 289–297.

[Ala07] Ruth Alas. "The triangular model for dealing with organizational change". In: *Journal of Change Management* 7.3-4 (2007), pp. 255–271.

[All10] Lindsay Allen. "Verification and Anomaly Detection for Event-Based Control of Manufacturing Systems". PhD thesis. University of Michigan, 2010.

[AM] System Analysis and Germany Modeling Group at the HPI/University of Potsdam. *Modular Rice University Bidding System (mRUBiS)*. URL: https://www.hpi.uni-potsdam.de/giese/public/mdelab/mdelab-projects/case-studies/mrubis/ (visited on 01/28/2019).

[Bas92] Victor Basili. *Software Modeling and Measurement: The Goal/Question/Metric Paradigm*. Tech. rep. University of Maryland, 1992.

[BB99] PerOlof Bengtsson and Jan Bosch. "Architecture Level Prediction of Software Maintenance". In: *Proc. of 3rd CSMR*. 1999, pp. 139–147.

[BCR94] Victor Basili, Gianluigi Caldiera, and H. Dieter Rombach. "The Goal Question Metric Approach". In: *Encyclopedia of Software Engineering*. Wiley, 1994.

[Bel18] Inna Belyantseva. "Eine domänenspezifische Sprache für Änderungsausbreitungsregeln". Masterarbeit. Karlsruhe Institute of Technology, 2018.

[Ben+04] PerOlof Bengtsson, Nico Lassing, Jan Bosch, and Hans van Vliet. "Architecture-level Modifiability Analysis (ALMA)". In: *Journal of Systems and Software* 69.1-2 (2004), pp. 129–147. ISSN: 0164-1212. DOI: 10.1016/S0164-1212(03)00080-3.

[Ber+11] Gábor Bergmann, Zoltán Ujhelyi, István Ráth, and Dániel Varró. "A Graph Query Language for EMF Models". In: *Theory and Practice of Model Transformations*. Ed. by Jordi Cabot and Eelco Visser. Springer Berlin Heidelberg, 2011, pp. 167–182.

[Ber68] Ludwig von Bertalanffy. *General system theory: foundations, development, applications*. International library of systems theory and philosophy. G. Braziller, 1968.

[Bif+15] Stefan Biffl, Emanuel Mätzler, Manuel Wimmer, Arndt Lüder, and Nicole Schmidt. "Linking and versioning support for AutomationML: A model-driven engineering perspective". In: *INDIN*. IEEE, 2015, pp. 499–506. ISBN: 978-1-4799-6649-3.

[BKR09] Steffen Becker, Heiko Koziolek, and Ralf Reussner. "The Palladio Component Model for Model-driven Performance Prediction". In: *Journal of Systems and Software* 82.1 (2009), pp. 3–22. ISSN: 0164-1212.

[BLO03] Lionel Briand, Yvan Labiche, and L. O'Sullivan. "Impact Analysis and Change Management of UML Models". In: *ICSM*. 2003.

[Bod+04] Thierry Bodhuin, Raffaele Esposito, Cristina Pacelli, and Maria Tortorella. "Impact Analysis for Supporting the Co-Evolution of Business Processes and Supporting Software Systems". In: *CAiSE Workshops (2)*. FCSIT, Riga TU, 2004, pp. 146–150.

[Boe+00] Barry Boehm et al. *Software Cost Estimation with COCOMO II*. Prentice Hall, 2000. ISBN: 0130266922.

[Boe+05] Frank de Boer et al. "Change impact analysis of enterprise architectures". In: *IRI -2005 IEEE International Conference on Information Reuse and Integration* (2005), pp. 177–181.

[Boh02] Shawn Bohner. "Software change impacts-an evolving perspective". In: *International Conference on Software Maintenance.* 2002, pp. 263–272. DOI: 10.1109/ICSM.2002.1167777.

[Bou+17] Safa Bougouffa, Kilian Meßzmer, Suhyun Cha, Emanuel Trunzer, and Birgit Vogel-Heuser. "Industry 4.0 interface for dynamic reconfiguration of an open lab size automated production system to allow remote community experiments". In: *2017 IEEE International Conference on Industrial Engineering and Engineering Management (IEEM)* (2017), pp. 2058–2062.

[BP95] Monica Bellgran and Öhrström Pernilla. "Design and Evaluation of Assembly Systems - A Study of Ten Swedish Manufacturing Companies". In: *Proceedings of the 13th International Conference on Production Research.* ICPR '95. 1995.

[Bra09] Jörg-Peter Brauer. *DIN EN ISO 9000: 2000 ff. umsetzen: Gestaltungshilfen zum Aufbau Ihres Qualitätsmanagementsystems.* Vol. 4. Hanser Verlag, 2009.

[Bra10] Jana Brauweiler. "Umweltmanagementsysteme nach ISO 14001 und EMAS". In: *Integratives Umweltmanagement: Systemorientierte Zusammenhänge zwischen Politik, Recht, Management und Technik* (2010), pp. 279–299.

[BRG01] BRG. *Business Rules Group.* http://www.businessrulesgroup.org. 2001.

[Bro+12] Franz Brosch, Heiko Koziolek, Barbora Buhnova, and Ralf Reussner. "Architecture-Based Reliability Prediction with the Palladio Component Model". In: *IEEE Transactions on Software Engineering* 38.6 (2012), pp. 1319–1339. DOI: 10.1109/TSE.2011.94.

[BRT93] Henri Barki, Suzanne Rivard, and Jean Talbot. "A keyword classification scheme for IS research literature: an update". In: *Mis Quarterly* (1993), pp. 209–226.

[BS09] Monica Bellgran and Kristina Säfsten. *Production Development: Design and Operation of Production Systems.* Springer, Jan. 2009. ISBN: 1848824955, 9781848824959. DOI: 10.1007/978-1-84882-495-9.

[Bus+18a] Kiana Busch, Robert Heinrich, Axel Busch, and Ralf Reussner. "Automated Analysis of the Co-evolution of Software Systems and Business Processes". In: *Software Engineering 2018, Fachtagung des GI-Fachbereichs Softwaretechnik, 06.-09. March 2018, Ulm, Deutschland.* 2018.

[Bus+18b] Kiana Busch et al. "A Cross-Disciplinary Language for Change Propagation Rules". In: *14th IEEE International Conference on Automation Science and Engineering (CASE).* IEEE, 2018, pp. 1099–1104. DOI: 10.1109/COASE.2018.8560364.

[Bus+18c] Kiana Busch et al. "A Model-Based Approach to Calculate Maintainability Task Lists of PLC Programs for Factory Automation". In: *IECON 2018 - 44th Annual Conference of the IEEE Industrial Electronics Society.* IEEE, 2018, pp. 2949–2954. DOI: 10.1109/IECON.2018.8591302.

[Cha+01] Ned Chapin, Joanne Hale, Khaled Kham, Juan Ramil, and Wui-Gee Tan. "Types of Software Evolution and Software Maintenance". In: *Journal of Software Maintenance* 13.1 (2001), pp. 3–30.

[Con68] Melvin Conway. "How do Committees Invent?" In: *Datamation* 14 (1968), pp. 28–31.

[DP05] Åsa Dahlstedt and Anne Persson. "Requirements Interdependencies: State of the Art and Future Challenges". In: *Engineering and Managing Software Requirements.* Ed. by Aybüke Aurum and Claes Wohlin. Berlin, Heidelberg: Springer Berlin Heidelberg, 2005, pp. 95–116. ISBN: 978-3-540-28244-0. DOI: 10.1007/3-540-28244-0_5.

[DR13] Zoya Durdik and Ralf Reussner. "On the Appropriate Rationale for Using Design Patterns and Pattern Documentation". In: *Proceedings of the 9th ACM SIGSOFT International Conference on the Quality of Software Architectures (QoSA 2013).* 2013.

[DT11] George Doukas and Kleanthis Thramboulidis. "A Real-Time-Linux-Based Framework for Model-Driven Engineering in Control and Automation". In: *IEEE Transactions on Industrial Electronics* 58 (2011), pp. 914–924. DOI: 10.1109/TIE.2009.2029584.

[Dur14] Zoya Durdik. "Architectural Design Decision Documentation through Reuse of Design Patterns". PhD thesis. Karlsruhe Institute od Technology, 2014.

[Dus+15] Kerstin Duschl, Denise Gramß, Martin Obermeier, and Birgit Vogel-Heuser. "Towards a taxonomy of errors in PLC programming". In: *Cognition, Technology & Work* 17.3 (2015), pp. 417–430. DOI: 10.1007/s10111-014-0307-x.

[DW10] Hoa Dam and Michael Winikoff. "Supporting change propagation in UML models". In: *2010 IEEE International Conference on Software Maintenance.* 2010, pp. 1–10.

[DW11] Hoa Dam and Michael Winikoff. "An agent-oriented approach to change propagation in software maintenance". In: *Autonomous Agents and Multi-Agent Systems* 23.3 (2011), pp. 384–452. ISSN: 1573-7454. DOI: 10.1007/s10458-010-9163-0.

[EKS08] Stefan Eicker, Jessica Kochbeck, and Peter Schuler. "Employee competencies for business process management". In: *International Conference on Business Information Systems.* Springer. 2008, pp. 251–262.

[EM12] Elisabet Estévez and Marga Marcos. "Model-Based Validation of Industrial Control Systems". In: *IEEE Transactions on Industrial Informatics* 8.2 (2012), pp. 302–310. DOI: 10.1109/TII.2011.2174248.

[EMO07] Elisabet Estévez, Marga Marcos, and Darío Orive. "Automatic generation of PLC automation projects from component-based models". In: *The International Journal of Advanced Manufacturing Technology* 35.5 (2007), pp. 527–540. DOI: 10.1007/s00170-007-1127-4.

[ES05] Anne Etien and Camille Salinesi. “Managing Requirements in a Co-evolution Context”. In: *13th IEEE International Conference on Requirements Engineering (RE 2005), 29 August - 2 September 2005, Paris, France.* 2005, pp. 125–134. DOI: 10.1109/RE.2005.37.

[EV06] Sven Efftinge and Markus Völter. “oAW xText: a framework for textual DSLs”. In: *Workshop on Modeling Symposium at Eclipse Summit* 32 (Jan. 2006), p. 4.

[Fay+15] Alexander Fay et al. “Enhancing a Model-based Engineering Approach for Distributed Manufacturing Automation Systems with Characteristics and Design Patterns”. In: *Journal of Systems and Software* 101.C (2015), pp. 221–235. ISSN: 0164-1212. DOI: 10.1016/j.jss.2014.12.028.

[Fdh+15] Walid Fdhila, Conrad Indiono, Stefanie Rinderle-Ma, and Manfred Reichert. “Dealing with change in process choreographies: Design and implementation of propagation algorithms”. In: *Information Systems* 49 (2015). DOI: 10.1016/j.is.2014.10.004.

[Fel+16] Stefan Feldmann, Florian Hauer, Sebastian Ulewicz, and Birgit Vogel-Heuser. “Analysis framework for evaluating PLC software: An application of Semantic Web technologies”. In: *ISIE*. IEEE, 2016, pp. 1048–1054.

[FL00] Georg Frey and Lothar Litz. “Formal methods in PLC programming”. In: *Proceedings of IEEE international conference on systems, man and cybernetics (SMC).* Vol. 4. 2000, pp. 2431–2436. DOI: 10.1109/ICSMC.2000.884356.

[Fow10] Martin Fowler. *Domain Specific Languages.* 1st. Addison-Wesley Professional, 2010.

[FRR12] Walid Fdhila, Stefanie Rinderle-Ma, and Manfred Reichert. “Change propagation in collaborative processes scenarios”. In: *CollaborateCom'12.* 2012, pp. 452–461.

[Gas08] Susan Gasson. “A Framework for the Co-design of Business and IT Systems”. In: *HICSS.* IEEE Computer Society, 2008, p. 348.

[GGS96] Michael Goldapp, Ulrich Grottker, and Gregor Snelting. "Validierung softwaregesteuerter Meßsysteme durch Program Slicing und Constraint Solving". In: *Statusseminar des BMBF Softwaretechnologie* (1996), pp. 405–425.

[GKB16] Arda Goknil, Ivan Kurtev, and Klaas van den Berg. "A Rule-Based Change Impact Analysis Approach in Software Architecture for Requirements Changes". In: *CoRR* abs/1608.02757 (2016).

[Gli07] Martin Glinz. "On Non-Functional Requirements". In: *15th IEEE International Requirements Engineering Conference (RE 2007)* (2007), pp. 21–26.

[Gok+11] Arda Goknil, Ivan Kurtev, Klaas van den Berg, and Jan-Willem Veldhuis. "Semantics of trace relations in requirements models for consistency checking and inferencing". In: *Software and Systems Modeling* 10.1 (2011), pp. 31–54. ISSN: 1619-1374. DOI: 10.1007/s10270-009-0142-3.

[Gok+14] Arda Goknil, Ivan Kurtev, Klaas Berg, and Wietze Spijkerman. "Change Impact Analysis for Requirements: a Metamodeling Approach". In: *Information and Software Technology* 56 (Aug. 2014). DOI: 10.1016/j.infsof.2014.03.002.

[Gol+15] Ursula Goltz et al. "Design for future: managed software evolution". In: *Computer Science - Research and Development* 30.3 (2015), pp. 321–331. ISSN: 1865-2042. DOI: 10.1007/s00450-014-0273-9.

[GV06] Stijn Goedertier and Jan Vanthienen. "Compliant and flexible business processes with business rules". In: *7th Workshop on BPMDS'06 at CAiSE'06*. CEUR-WS.org, 2006, pp. 94–104.

[HBK18] Robert Heinrich, Kiana Busch, and Sandro Koch. "A Methodology for Domain-spanning Change Impact Analysis". In: *2018 44th Euromicro Conference on Software Engineering and Advanced Applications (SEAA)*. IEEE, 2018, pp. 326–330. DOI: 10.1109/SEAA.2018.00060.

[HC93] Michael Hammer and James Champy. *Reengineering the Corporation: A Manifesto for Business Revolution.* HarperBusiness, 1993.

[Hei+15] Robert Heinrich et al. "A Platform for Empirical Research on Information System Evolution". In: *27th International Conference on Software Engineering and Knowledge Engineering.* 2015, pp. 415–420.

[Hei+17] Robert Heinrich, Philipp Merkle, Jörg Henss, and Barbara Paech. "Integrating business process simulation and information system simulation for performance prediction". In: *International Journal on Software & Systems Modeling* 16.1 (2017), pp. 257–277. ISSN: 1619-1366. DOI: 10.1007/s10270-015-0457-1.

[Hei+18] Robert Heinrich et al. "Architecture-based change impact analysis in cross-disciplinary automated production systems". In: *Journal of Systems and Software* 146 (2018), pp. 167–185. ISSN: 0164-1212. DOI: https://doi.org/10.1016/j.jss.2018.08.058.

[Hei14] Robert Heinrich. *Aligning Business Processes and Information Systems: New Approaches to Continuous Quality Engineering.* Springer, 2014.

[Her+08] Sebastian Herold et al. "CoCoME - The Common Component Modeling Example". In: *The Common Component Modeling Example: Comparing Software Component Models.* Ed. by Andreas Rausch, Ralf Reussner, Raffaela Mirandola, and František Plášil. Springer Berlin Heidelberg, 2008, pp. 16–53. DOI: 10.1007/978-3-540-85289-6_3.

[HKR11] Jens Happe, Heiko Koziolek, and Ralf Reussner. "Facilitating Performance Predictions Using Software Components". In: *IEEE Software* 28.3 (2011), pp. 27–33.

[HRR16] Robert Heinrich, Kiana Rostami, and Ralf Reussner. *The CoCoME Platform for Collaborative Empirical Research on Information System Evolution.* Tech. rep. KIT, 2016.

[HS15] René Hahn and Peter Schuller. *Architecture as Connection between Requirements and Quality Prediction to Support Design Decisions.* Praxis der Forschung: Modellbasierte semiautomatische Unterstützung des Architekturentwurfs nach Anforderungsänderungen. 2015.

[HZ04] Heinrich Hussmann and Steffen Zschaler. "The Object Constraint Language for UML 2.0 - Overview and Assessment". In: *Upgrade* 5.2 (2004), pp. 25–28.

[IEC13] IEC. *IEC 61131-3 Standard - Programmable controllers - Part 3: Programming languages.* International Electrical Commission, 2013.

[IEE11] IEEE. "Systems and software engineering – Life cycle processes –Requirements engineering". In: *ISO/IEC/IEEE 29148:2011(E)* (2011).

[IEE90] IEEE. "IEEE Standard Glossary of Software Engineering Terminology". In: *IEEE Std 610.12-1990* (1990).

[IEE98] IEEE. *IEEE Recommended Practice for Software Requirements Specifications.* 1998.

[ISO11] ISO/IEC 25010:2011. *Systems and software engineering – Systems and software Quality Requirements and Evaluation (SQuaRE) – System and software quality models.* 2011.

[ISO92] DIN ISO. "8402 Qualitätsmanagement und Qualitätssicherung". In: *Begriffe, Berlin* (1992).

[Jäg+11] Tobias Jäger, Alexander Fay, Thomas Wagner, and Ulrich Löwen. "Mining technical dependencies throughout engineering process knowledge". In: *ETFA2011.* 2011, pp. 1–7. DOI: 10.1109/ETFA.2011.6058985.

[Jam15a] Marcin Jamro. "POU-Oriented Unit Testing of IEC 61131-3 Control Software". In: *IEEE Transactions on Industrial Informatics* 11.5 (2015), pp. 1119–1129.

[Jam15b] Marcin Jamro. "SysML Modeling of Functional and Non-functional Requirements for IEC 61131-3 Control Systems". In: *Progress in Automation, Robotics and Measuring Techniques.* Springer International Publishing, 2015, pp. 91–100. ISBN: 978-3-319-15796-2.

[Jar+11] T. Jarratt, Claudia Eckert, Nicholas Calwell, and P. John Clarkson. "Engineering change: an overview and perspective on the literature". In: *Research in engineering design* 22.2 (2011), pp. 103–124.

[JM09] Dan Jurafsky and James Martin. *Speech and language processing : an introduction to natural language processing, computational linguistics, and speech recognition.* Pearson Prentice Hall, 2009. ISBN: 9780131873216 0131873210.

[JP12] Pooyan Jamshidi and Claus Pahl. "Business Process and Software Architecture Model Co-evolution Patterns". In: *MiSE'12.* IEEE, 2012, pp. 91–97.

[JT01] Karl-Heinz John and Michael Tiegelkamp. "Building Blocks of IEC 61131-3". In: *IEC 61131-3: Programming Industrial Automation Systems: Concepts and Programming Languages, Requirements for Programming Systems, Aids to Decision-Making Tools.* Springer Berlin Heidelberg, 2001, pp. 21–64.

[JT13] Marcin Jamro and Bartosz Trybus. "Testing Procedure for IEC 61131-3 Control Software". In: *IFAC Proceedings Volumes* 46.28 (2013), pp. 192–197.

[Kap+18a] Angelika Kaplan, Kiana Busch, Robert Heinrich, and Anne Koziolek. "Categories of Change Triggers in Business Processes". In: *2018 44th Euromicro Conference on Software Engineering and Advanced Applications (SEAA).* IEEE, 2018, pp. 252–259. DOI: 10.1109/SEAA.2018.00049.

[Kap+18b] Angelika Kaplan, Kiana Busch, Robert Heinrich, and Anne Koziolek. *Supplementary material for the study on categories of change triggers in business processes.* Tech. rep. 7. Karlsruhe: Karlsruhe Institute of Technology (KIT), 2018.

[Kap17] Angelika Kaplan. "Eine empirische Studie zu Änderungskategorien in Bezug auf Änderungsauslöser in Geschäftsprozessen". Diplomarbeit. Karlsruhe Institute of Technology, 2017.

[Kaz+94] Rick Kazman, Len Bass, Gregory Abowd, and Mike Webb. "SAAM: a method for analyzing the properties of software architectures". In: *Software Engineering, 1994. Proceedings. ICSE-16., 16th International Conference on.* 1994, pp. 81–90. DOI: 10.1109/ICSE.1994.296768.

[Kaz+98] Rick Kazman et al. "The Architecture Tradeoff Analysis Method". In: *Proceedings. Fourth IEEE International Conference on Engineering of Complex Computer Systems (Cat. No.98EX193).* Jan. 1998, pp. 68–78. DOI: 10.1109/ICECCS.1998.706657.

[Kee07] Staffs Keele. "Guidelines for performing systematic literature reviews in software engineering". In: *Technical report, Ver. 2.3 EBSE Technical Report. EBSE.* sn, 2007.

[KG99] Markus Kradolfer and Andreas Geppert. "Dynamic Workflow Schema Evolution Based on Workflow Type Versioning and Workflow Migration". In: *CoopIS'99.* 1999, pp. 104–114.

[Kil08] Malia Kilpinen. "The emergence of change at the systems engineering and software design interface". PhD thesis. University of Cambridge, 2008.

[KKF12] Sonja Kabicher-Fuchs, Simone Kriglstein, and Kathrin Figl. "Timeline Visualization for Documenting Process Model Change". In: *EMISA.* 2012, pp. 95–108.

[KMS05] Huzefa Kagdi, Jonathan Maletic, and Andrew Sutton. "Context-Free Slicing of UML Class Models". In: *ICSM.* IEEE Computer Society, 2005, pp. 635–638.

[Koc17] Sandro Koch. "Automatische Vorhersage von Änderungsausbreitungen am Beispiel von Automatisierungssystemen". Masterarbeit. Karlsruhe Institute of Technology, 2017.

[KR16] Karunanidhi Karthik and K. Janardhan Reddy. "Engineering Changes in Product Design-A Review". In: *IOP Conference Series: Materials Science and Engineering.* Vol. 149. 1. IOP Publishing. 2016, p. 012001.

[Kro12] Klaus Krogmann. *Reconstruction of Software Component Architectures and Behaviour Models using Static and Dynamic Analysis.* Vol. 4. The Karlsruhe Series on Software Design and Quality. KIT Scientific Publishing, 2012. DOI: 10.5445/KSP/1000025617.

[Kru04] Philippe Kruchten. *The Rational Unified Process: An Introduction.* The Addison-Wesley object technology series. Addison-Wesley, 2004. ISBN: 9780321197702.

[Kur+12] Tri Kurniawan, Aditya Ghose, Hoa Dam, and Lam-Son Lê. "Relationship-Preserving Change Propagation in Process Ecosystems". In: *Service-Oriented Computing.* Springer Berlin Heidelberg, 2012, pp. 63–78.

[Küs13] Martin Küster. "Architecture-Centric Modeling of Design Decisions for Validation and Traceability". In: *Proceedings of the 7th European Conference on Software Architecture (ECSA '13).* Vol. 7957. Lecture Notes in Computer Science. Springer Berlin Heidelberg, 2013, pp. 184–191.

[KV07] Uwe Katzke and Birgit Vogel-Heuser. "COMBINING UML WITH IEC 61131-3 LANGUAGES TO PRESERVE THE USABILITY OF GRAPHICAL NOTATIONS IN THE SOFTWARE DEVELOPMENT OF COMPLEX AUTOMATION SYSTEMS". In: *IFAC Proceedings Volumes* 40.16 (2007). 10th IFAC,IFIP,IFORS,IEA Symposium on Analysis, Design, and Evaluation of Human-Machine Systems, pp. 90–94. ISSN: 1474-6670. DOI: https://doi.org/10.3182/20070904-3-KR-2922.00016.

[KWN05] Udo Kelte, Jürgen Wehren, and Jörg Niere. "A Generic Difference Algorithm for UML Models". In: *Software Engineering.* Vol. 64. LNI. GI, 2005, pp. 105–116.

[Lad+13] Jan Ladiges et al. "Evolution of Production Facilities and its Impact on Non-Functional Requirements". In: *International Conference on Industrial Informatics (INDIN) 2013 - Proceedings of the 11th International Conference on Industrial Informatics.* IEEE, 2013.

[Lar04] Craig Larman. *Applying UML and Patterns: An Introduction to Object-Oriented Analysis and Design and Iterative Development (3rd Edition).* Prentice Hall PTR, 2004. ISBN: 0131489062.

[Leh11a] Steffen Lehnert. *A Review of Software Change Impact Analysis.* Tech. rep. Ilmenau University of Technology, Department of Software Systems / Process Informatics, 2011.

[Leh11b] Steffen Lehnert. "A Taxonomy for Software Change Impact Analysis". In: *Proceedings of the 12th International Workshop on Principles of Software Evolution and the 7th Annual ERCIM Workshop on Software Evolution.* IWPSE-EVOL '11. ACM, 2011, pp. 41–50. DOI: 10.1145/2024445.2024454.

[Leh79] Meir Lehman. "On understanding laws, evolution, and conservation in the large-program life cycle". In: *Journal of Systems and Software* 1 (1979), pp. 213–221.

[Lew47] Kurt Lewin. "Group decision and social change". In: *Readings in social psychology* 3 (1947), pp. 197–211.

[LFL16] Jan Ladiges, Alexander Fay, and Winfried Lamersdorf. "Automated Determining of Manufacturing Properties and Their Evolutionary Changes from Event Traces". In: *Intelligent Industrial Systems* 2.2 (2016), pp. 163–178. DOI: 10.1007/s40903-016-0048-7.

[LFR13] Steffen Lehnert, Qurat-ul-ann Farooq, and Matthias Riebisch. "Rule-Based Impact Analysis for Heterogeneous Software Artifacts". In: *17th European Conference on Software Maintenance and Reengineering, CSMR 2013, Genova, Italy, March 5-8, 2013.* 2013, pp. 209–218. DOI: 10.1109/CSMR.2013.30.

[LFV13] Christoph Legat, Jens Folmer, and Birgit Vogel-Heuser. "Evolution in industrial plant automation: A case study". In: *IECON Proceedings (Industrial Electronics Conference).* 2013, pp. 4386–4391. ISBN: 9781479902248. DOI: 10.1109/IECON.2013.6699841.

[LGJ07] Yuehua Lin, Jeff Gray, and Frédéric Jouault. "DSMDiff: a differentiation tool for domain-specific models". In: *European Journal of Information Systems* 16.4 (2007), pp. 349–361.

[Liu+11] Xumin Liu, Athman Bouguettaya, Qi Yu, and Zaki Malik. "Efficient change management in long-term composed services". In: *Service Oriented Computing and Applications* 5.2 (2011), pp. 87–103.

[LLE17] Lukas Linsbauer, Roberto Erick Lopez-Herrejon, and Alexander Egyed. "Variability extraction and modeling for product variants". In: *Software and System Modeling* 16.4 (2017), pp. 1179–1199.

[Llo94] JW Lloyd. "Practical advantages of declarative programming". English. In: Conference Proceedings/Title of Journal: Joint Conference on Declarative Programming. 1994, pp. 3–17.

[LMT08] Mario Lezoche, Michele Missikoff, and Leonardo Tininini. "Business Process Evolution: a Rule-based Approach". In: *the 9th Workshop on Business Process Modeling, Development, and Support (BPMDS'08)*. 2008.

[LOA00] M. Lee, A. J. Offutt, and R. T. Alexander. "Algorithmic analysis of the impacts of changes to object-oriented software". In: *Proc. 34th Intern. Conf. on TOOLS*. 2000, pp. 61–70.

[Löp18] Martin Löper. "Eine Sprache für die Spezifikation disziplinübergreifender Änderungsausbreitungsregeln". Bachelorarbeit. Karlsruhe Institute of Technology, 2018.

[LR11] Kevin Lano and Shekoufeh Kolahdouz Rahimi. "Slicing Techniques for UML Models". In: *Journal of Object Technology* 10 (2011), 11: 1–49. DOI: `10.5381/jot.2011.10.1.a11`.

[LS17] Arndt Lüder and Nicole Schmidt. "AutomationML in a Nutshell". In: *Handbuch Industrie 4.0 Bd.2: Automatisierung*. Ed. by Birgit Vogel-Heuser, Thomas Bauernhansl, and Michael ten Hompel. Springer Berlin Heidelberg, 2017, pp. 213–258. ISBN: 978-3-662-53248-5.

[LSB02] Kecheng Liu, Lily Sun, and Keith H. Bennett. "Co-Design of Business and IT Systems - Introduction by Guest Editors". In: *Information Systems Frontiers* 4.3 (2002), pp. 251–256. DOI: `10.1023/A:1019942501848`.

[Mai18] Timo Maier. "Automatic Derivation of Change Propagation Based on Requirement Changes in Automated Production Systems". Bachelorarbeit. Karlsruhe Institute of Technology, 2018.

[Mar+10] Marga Marcos, Elisabet Estévez, Nagore Iriondo, and Dario Orive. "Analysis and validation of IEC 61131-3 applications using a MDE approach". In: *ETFA*. IEEE, 2010, pp. 1–8.

[MB76] Robert M Metcalfe and David R Boggs. "Ethernet: Distributed packet switching for local computer networks". In: *Communications of the ACM* 19.7 (1976), pp. 395–404.

[MBR18] Timo Maier, Kiana Busch, and Ralf Reussner. "An Approach to Requirement Analysis in Automated Production Systems". In: *Workshop Software-Reengineering & Evolution and Workshop Design For Future*. Softwaretechnik-Trends, 2018.

[MG10] Sharon McGee and Des Greer. "Sources of Software Requirements Change from the Perspectives of Development and Maintenance". In: *International Journal on Advances in Software*. Vol. 3. 1 & 2. 2010.

[MGK96] John Mooney, Vijay Gurbaxani, and Kenneth Kraemer. "A Process Oriented Framework for Assessing the Business Value of Information Technology". In: *SIGMIS Database* 27.2 (1996), pp. 68–81. ISSN: 0095-0033.

[MHS05] Marjan Mernik, Jan Heering, and Anthony Sloane. "When and How to Develop Domain-specific Languages". In: *ACM Comput. Surv.* 37.4 (2005), pp. 316–344. DOI: 10.1145/1118890.1118892.

[Moo65] Gordon Moore. *Cramming More Components Onto Integrated Circuits, Electronics,(38) 8*. 1965.

[MR15] Klaus Müller and Bernhard Rumpe. "A Methodology for Impact Analysis Based on Model Differencing". In: *Softwaretechnik-Trends* 35.2 (2015).

[MT10] Nenad Medvidovic and Richard Taylor. "Software Architecture: Foundations, Theory, and Practice". In: *Proceedings - International Conference on Software Engineering*. 2010, pp. 471–472. ISBN: 978-1-60558-719-6. DOI: 10.1145/1810295.1810435.

[MW13] Simha Magal and Jeffrey Word. *Business Process Integration with SAP ERP*. 1st. Epistemy Press LLC, 2013. ISBN: 0985600861, 9780985600860.

[NCG08] Selmin Nurcan, Bruno Claudepierre, and Islem Gmati. "Conceptual Dependencies between two connected IT domains: Business/IS alignment and IT governance". In: *Research Challenges in Information Science, 2008. RCIS 2008. Second International Conference on*. IEEE. 2008, pp. 87–98.

[Nwo+18] Joshua Nwokeji, Faisal Aqlan, Tony Clark, Balbir Barn, and Vinay Kulkarni. "A Modelling Technique for Enterprise Agility". In: *HICSS*. AIS Electronic Library (AISeL), 2018.

[Obj11] Object Management Group. *Business Process Model and Notation (BPMN) Version 2.0*. Tech. rep. Object Management Group, 2011.

[OMG06] OMG. *Object Constraint Language Specification, version 2.0*. Ed. by OMG. OMG document formal/2006-05-01. Object Modeling Group. 2006.

[OMG12] OMG. *OMG Systems Modeling Language (OMG SysML), Version 1.3*. Object Management Group, 2012. URL: http://www.omg.org/spec/SysML/1.3/.

[OO84] Karl Ottenstein and Linda Ottenstein. "The Program Dependence Graph in a Software Development Environment". In: *SIGPLAN Not.* 19.5 (1984), pp. 177–184. ISSN: 0362-1340. DOI: 10.1145/390011.808263.

[OT07] John Oakland and Steve Tanner. "A new framework for managing change". In: *The TQM Magazine* 19.6 (2007), pp. 572–589.

[Pat] Richard Pattis. *EBNF: A Notation to Describe Syntax*. web site. https://www.ics.uci.edu/~pattis/misc/ebnf2.pdf.

[Pau01] Daniel Paulish. *Architecture-centric Software Project Management: A Practical Guide.* Addison-Wesley Educational Publishers Inc, 2001. ISBN: 0201734095.

[Pet18] Maximilian Peters. "Evaluation und Optimierung der Wartbarkeit von Software-Architekturen". Bachelorarbeit. Karlsruhe Institute of Technology, 2018.

[Pie+15] Christopher Pietsch, Timo Kehrer, Udo Kelter, Dennis Reuling, and Manuel Ohrndorf. "SiPL - A Delta-Based Modeling Framework for Software Product Line Engineering". In: *30th IEEE/ACM International Conference on Automated Software Engineering, ASE 2015, Lincoln, NE, USA, November 9-13, 2015.* 2015, pp. 852–857. DOI: 10.1109/ASE.2015.106.

[Poh95] Klaus Pohl. "A process centered requirements engineering environment". PhD thesis. RWTH Aachen University, Germany, 1995.

[Pow08] David Powers. "Evaluation: From Precision, Recall and F-Factor to ROC, Informedness, Markedness & Correlation". In: *Machine Learning Technologies* 2 (2008).

[Prä+16] Herbert Prähofer, Daniela Rabiser, Florian Angerer, Paul Grünbacher, and Peter Feichtinger. "Feature-Oriented Development in Industrial Automation Software Ecosystems: Development Scenarios and Tool Support". In: *Proceedings 14th IEEE International Conference on Industrial Informatics (INDIN 2016).* 2016, pp. 1218–1223. DOI: 10.1109/INDIN.2016.7819353.

[Rat13] Christoph Rathfelder. "Modelling Event-Based Interactions in Component-Based Architectures for Quantitative System Evaluation". PhD thesis. KIT, 2013. 358 pp. ISBN: 978-3-86644-969-5. DOI: 10.5445/KSP/1000032232.

[Rät17] Jannis Rätz. "Erweiterung eines Wartbarkeits-Frameworks für die Programmiersprache IEC 61131-3". Bachelorarbeit. Karlsruhe Institute of Technology, 2017.

[Rät18] Jannis Rätz. *Change Propagation Analysis in PLC-based Automated Production Systems.* Practical Course: Software Quality Engineering with Eclipse. 2018.

[RD98] Manfred Reichert and Peter Dadam. "Adeptflex—Supporting Dynamic Changes of Workflows Without Losing Control". In: *Journal of Intelligent Information Systems* 10.2 (1998), pp. 93–129. DOI: 10.1023/A:1008604709862.

[Rei+05] Manfred Reichert, Stefanie Rinderle, Ulrich Kreher, and Peter Dadam. "Adaptive Process Management with ADEPT2". In: *21st Intern. Conference on Data Engineering*. IEEE, 2005, pp. 1113–1114.

[Rep82] Thomas Reps. "Optimal-time Incremental Semantic Analysis for Syntax-directed Editors". In: *Proceedings of the 9th ACM SIGPLAN-SIGACT Symposium on Principles of Programming Languages*. POPL '82. ACM, 1982, pp. 169–176. ISBN: 0-89791-065-6. DOI: 10.1145/582153.582172.

[Res07] Respect-IT. *A KAOS Tutorial*. 2007.

[Reu16] Reussner, Ralf and Becker, Steffen and Happe, Jens and Heinrich, Robert and Koziolek, Anne and Koziolek, Heiko and Kramer, Max and Krogmann, Klaus, ed. *Modeling and Simulating Software Architectures – The Palladio Approach*. ISBN: 978-0-262-03476-0. MIT Press, 2016.

[RJ01] Balasubramaniam Ramesh and Matthias Jarke. "Toward Reference Models for Requirements Traceability". In: *IEEE Transaction on Software Engineering* 27.1 (2001), pp. 58–93. ISSN: 0098-5589. DOI: 10.1109/32.895989. URL: https://doi.org/10.1109/32.895989.

[RJB04] James Rumbaugh, Ivar Jacobson, and Grady Booch. *Unified Modeling Language Reference Manual, The (2Nd Edition)*. Pearson Higher Education, 2004. ISBN: 0321245628.

[Ros+15a] Kiana Rostami, Johannes Stammel, Robert Heinrich, and Ralf Reussner. "Architecture-based Assessment and Planning of Change Requests". In: *Proceedings of the 11th International ACM SIGSOFT Conference on Quality of Software Architectures*. ACM, 2015, pp. 21–30.

[Ros+15b] Kiana Rostami, Johannes Stammel, Robert Heinrich, and Ralf Reussner. "Architecture-based Assessment and Planning of Change Requests". In: *Proceedings of the 11th International ACM SIGSOFT Conference on Quality of Software Architectures*. QoSA '15. ACM, 2015, pp. 21–30. DOI: 10.1145/2737182.2737198.

[Ros+17a] Kiana Rostami, Robert Heinrich, Axel Busch, and Ralf H. Reussner. "Architecture-based Change Impact Analysis in Information Systems and Business Processes". In: *2017 IEEE International Conference on Software Architecture (ICSA)*. IEEE, 2017, pp. 179–188. DOI: 10.1109/ICSA.2017.17.

[Ros+17b] Kiana Rostami, Johannes Stammel, Robert Heinrich, and Ralf Reussner. "Change Impact Analysis by Architecture-based Assessment and Planning". In: *Software Engineering 2017, Fachtagung des GI-Fachbereichs Softwaretechnik, 21.-24. Februar 2017, Hannover, Deutschland.* 2017, pp. 69–70.

[Ros+17c] Kiana Rostami et al. "Reconstructing Development Artifacts for Change Impact Analysis". In: *19. Workshop Software-Reengineering und-Evolution*. 2017.

[Ros15] Kiana Rostami. "Domain-spanning Maintainability Analysis for Software-intensive Systems". In: *Gemeinsamer Tagungsband der Workshops der Tagung Software Engineering 2015, Dresden, Germany, 17.-18. März 2015.* 2015, pp. 106–108.

[RSS06] Gil Regev, Pnina Soffer, and Rainer Schmidt. "Taxonomy of Flexibility in Business Processes". In: *Business Process Modeling, Design and Support* 236 (2006).

[RT01] Barbara Ryder and Frank Tip. "Change impact analysis for object-oriented programs". In: *PASTE*. ACM, 2001, pp. 46–53.

[RT87] Thomas W. Reps and Tim Teitelbaum. "Language Processing in Program Editors". In: *IEEE Computer* 20.11 (1987), pp. 29–40. DOI: 10.1109/MC.1987.1663414.

[Run+12] Per Runeson, Martin Host, Austen Rainer, and Bjorn Regnell. *Case Study Research in Software Engineering: Guidelines and Examples.* 1st. Wiley, 2012. ISBN: 1118104358, 9781118104354.

[RWR06a] Stefanie Rinderle-Ma, Andreas Wombacher, and Manfred Reichert. "Evolution of process choreographies in DYCHOR". In: *On the Move to Meaningful Internet Systems 2006: CoopIS, DOA, GADA, and ODBASE*. Vol. 4275. Springer Berlin Heidelberg, 2006, pp. 273–290. DOI: 10.1007/11914853_17.

[RWR06b] Stefanie Rinderle-Ma, Andreas Wombacher, and Manfred Reichert. "On the Controlled Evolution of Process Choreographies". In: *Proc. 22nd Int'l Conf. on Data Engineering (ICDE'06)*. 2006, p. 124.

[SK16] Misha Strittmatter and Amine Kechaou. *The Media Store 3 Case Study System*. Tech. rep. 2016,1. Faculty of Informatics, Karlsruhe Institute of Technology, 2016.

[SKL12] Navid Karimi Sani, Shokoofeh Ketabchi, and Kecheng Liu. "The Co-design of Business and IT Systems: A Case in Supply Chain Management". In: *Information Systems, Technology and Management - 6th International Conference, ICISTM 2012, Grenoble, France, March 28-30, 2012. Proceedings*. 2012, pp. 13–27. DOI: 10.1007/978-3-642-29166-1_2.

[SL00] Lawson Savery and J Alan Luks. "Organizational change: the Australian experience". In: *Journal of Management Development* 19.4 (2000), pp. 309–317.

[SMO00] Sadiq Sadiq, Olivera Marjanovic, and Maria Orlowska. "Managing Change and Time in Dynamic Workflow Processes". In: *International Journal of Computational Intelligence Systems* (2000), pp. 93–116.

[SNH95] Dilip Soni, Robert Nord, and Christine Hofmeister. "Software Architecture in Industrial Applications". In: *Proceedings of the 17th International Conference on Software Engineering*. ICSE '95. ACM, 1995, pp. 196–207. ISBN: 0-89791-708-1. DOI: 10.1145/225014.225033.

[SO99] Shazia Sadiq and Maria Orlowska. "Architectural Considerations in Systems Supporting Dynamic Workflow Modification". In: *SABPM'99*. 1999.

[Som06] Ian Sommerville. *Software Engineering: (Update) (8th Edition) (International Computer Science).* Boston, MA, USA: Addison-Wesley Longman Publishing Co., Inc., 2006. ISBN: 0321313798.

[Sot07] Martín Soto. "Delta-P: Model Comparison Using Semantic Web Standards". In: *Softwaretechnik-Trends* 27.2 (2007).

[SR09] Johannes Stammel and Ralf Reussner. "KAMP: Karlsruhe Architectural Maintainability Prediction". In: *Proc. of 1st. L2S2 Workshop.* 2009, pp. 87–98.

[Sta15] Johannes Stammel. "Architekturbasierte Bewertung und Planung von Änderungsanfragen". PhD thesis. KIT, 2015.

[Sta73] Herbert Stachowiak. *Allgemeine Modelltheorie.* Springer Verlag, 1973.

[Ste+09] David Steinberg, Frank Budinsky, Marcelo Paternostro, and Ed Merks. *EMF: Eclipse Modeling Framework 2.0.* 2nd. Addison-Wesley Professional, 2009.

[Sun+13] Sagar Sunkle et al. "Analyzing Enterprise Models Using Enterprise Architecture-Based Ontology". In: *Model-Driven Engineering Languages and Systems: 16th Intern. Conference.* Springer, 2013, pp. 622–638.

[SV06] Thomas Stahl and Markus Völter. *Model-Driven Software Development: Technology, Engineering, Management.* Wiley, 2006. ISBN: 978-0-470-02570-3.

[Swa76] E. Burton Swanson. "The Dimensions of Maintenance". In: *Proceedings of the 2Nd International Conference on Software Engineering.* ICSE '76. IEEE Computer Society Press, 1976, pp. 492–497.

[SZ11] Andreas Scharf and Albert Zündorf. "Difference Visualization for Models (DVM) - Visualizing model changes directly within diagrams". In: 2011.

[THF08] Uttam Kumar Tripathi, Knut Hinkelmann, and Daniela Feldkamp. "Life cycle for change management in business processes using semantic technologies". In: *JCP* 3.1 (2008), pp. 24–31.

[Thr04] Kleanthis Thramboulidis. “Using UML in control and automation: a model driven approach”. In: *2nd IEEE International Conference on Industrial Informatics, 2004. INDIN ’04. 2004* (2004), pp. 587–593.

[Thr05] Kleanthis Thramboulidis. “Model-integrated mechatronics - toward a new paradigm in the development of manufacturing systems”. In: *IEEE Transactions on Industrial Informatics* 1 (2005), pp. 54–61.

[Thr10] Kleanthis Thramboulidis. “The 3 + 1 SysML View-Model in Model Integrated Mechatronics”. In: *Journal of Software Engineering and Applications* 3.2 (2010), pp. 109–118. DOI: 10.4236/jsea.2010.32014.

[Tip95] Frank Tip. “A Survey of Program Slicing Techniques”. In: *Journal of Programming Languages* 3 (1995), pp. 121–189.

[TMD09] Richard Taylor, Nenand Medvidovic, and Erik Dashofy. *Software Architecture: Foundations, Theory, and Practice.* Wiley Publishing, 2009. ISBN: 0470167742, 9780470167748.

[Van+07] Irene Vanderfeesten, Jorge Cardoso, Jan Mendling, Hajo Reijers, and Wil van der Aalst. “Quality Metrics for Business Process Models”. In: *BPM and Workflow Handbook 2007.* 2007.

[Vog+14a] Birgit Vogel-Heuser, Christoph Legat, Jens Folmer, and Stefan Feldmann. *Researching Evolution in Industrial Plant Automation: Scenarios and Documentation of the Pick and Place Unit.* Tech. rep. Institute of Automation and Information Systems, Technische Universität München, 2014.

[Vog+14b] Andreas Vogelsang, Sebastian Eder, Georg Hackenberg, Maximilian Junker, and Sabine Teufl. “Supporting concurrent development of requirements and architecture: A model-based approach”. In: *2014 2nd International Conference on Model-Driven Engineering and Software Development (MODELSWARD).* 2014, pp. 587–595.

[Vog+15] Birgit Vogel-Heuser, Alexander Fay, Ina Schaefer, and Matthias Tichy. “Evolution of software in automated production systems: Challenges and research directions”. In: *Journal of Systems and Software* 110 (2015), pp. 54–84.

[Vog+17] Birgit Vogel-Heuser et al. “Maintenance effort estimation with KAMP4aPS for cross-disciplinary automated PLC-based Production Systems - a collaborative approach”. In: *IFAC-PapersOnLine* 50.1 (2017). 20th IFAC World Congress, pp. 4360–4367. ISSN: 2405-8963. DOI: https://doi.org/10.1016/j.ifacol.2017.08.877.

[Vog14] Birgit Vogel-Heuser. “Usability Experiments to Evaluate UML/SysML-Based Model Driven Software Engineering Notations for Logic Control in Manufacturing Automation”. In: *Journal of Software Engineering and Applications* 7.11 (2014), pp. 943–973.

[Vog18] Thomas Vogel. “mRUBiS: An Exemplar for Model-Based Architectural Self-Healing and Self-Optimization (Artifact)”. In: *Dagstuhl Artifacts Series* 4.1 (2018), 1:1–1:4.

[VVL03] Eileen Van Aken, Dirk Van Goubergen, and Geert Letens. “Integrated enterprise transformation: case application in engineering project work in the Belgian Armed Forces”. In: *Engineering Management Journal* 15.2 (2003), pp. 3–16.

[Vya13] V. Vyatkin. “Software Engineering in Industrial Automation: State-of-the-Art Review”. In: *IEEE Transactions on Industrial Informatics* 9.3 (2013), pp. 1234–1249. DOI: 10.1109/TII.2013.2258165.

[WB98] D. Wright and N. Burns. “New organisation structures for global business: an empirical study”. In: *International Journal of Operations & Production Management* 18.9/10 (1998), pp. 896–923.

[Wei+11] Monika Weidmann et al. “Business process change management based on process model synchronization of multiple abstraction levels”. In: *2011 IEEE International Conference on Service-Oriented Computing and Applications, SOCA 2011*. 2011, pp. 1–4.

[Wei81] Mark Weiser. “Program Slicing”. In: *Proceedings of the 5th International Conference on Software Engineering*. ICSE ’81. IEEE Press, 1981, pp. 439–449. ISBN: 0-89791-146-6.

[Wer09] Benedikt Werner. "Object-oriented extensions for iec 61131-3". In: *IEEE Industrial Electronics Magazine* 3.4 (2009), pp. 36–39.

[WGK00] Brian Warboys, R. Mark Greenwood, and Peter Kawalek. "Systems Engineering for Business Process Change". In: Springer, 2000. Chap. Modelling the Co-Evolution of Business Processes and IT Systems, pp. 10–23.

[Wit13] Daniel Witsch. "Modellgetriebene Entwicklung von Steuerungssoftware auf Basis der UML unter Berücksichtigung der domänenspezifischen Anforderungen des Maschinen- und Anlagenbaus". PhD thesis. Technische Universität München, Lehrstuhl für Automatisierung und Informationssysteme, 2013.

[WKH07] Katharina Wolter, Thorsten Krebs, and Lothar Hotz. "Ontology-based Model Comparison". In: *Softwaretechnik-Trends* 27.2 (2007).

[Woh+00] Claes Wohlin et al. *Experimentation in Software Engineering: An Introduction.* Kluwer Academic Publishers, 2000.

[Woh14] Claes Wohlin. "Guidelines for snowballing in systematic literature studies and a replication in software engineering". In: *18th EASE.* ACM. 2014, p. 38.

[Wor99] Workflow Management Coalition Specification. *Workflow Management Coalition - Terminology & Glossary (WFMC-TC-1011).* Feb. 1999.

[WRR08] Barbara Weber, Manfred Reichert, and Stefanie Rinderle-Ma. "Change Patterns and Change Support Features - Enhancing Flexibility in Process-aware Information Systems". In: *Data & Knowledge Engineering* 66.3 (2008), pp. 438–466. ISSN: 0169-023X.

[WWM09] Matthias Weidlich, Mathias Weske, and Jan Mendling. "Change Propagation in Process Models Using Behavioural Profiles". In: *IEEE SCC.* IEEE Computer Society, 2009, pp. 33–40.

[Yin08] Robert Yin. *Case Study Research: Design and Methods (Applied Social Research Methods)*. Fourth Edition. Sage Publications, 2008. ISBN: 1412960991.

[Yoo+08] Sanghyun Yoo et al. "Rule-based Dynamic Business Process Modification and Adaptation". In: *2008 International Conference on Information Networking, ICOIN 2008, Busan, Korea, January 23-25, 2008*. IEEE, 2008, pp. 1–5. ISBN: 978-89-960761-1-7.

[Zha+14] He Zhang et al. "Investigating dependencies in software requirements for change propagation analysis". In: *Information and Software Technology* 56.1 (2014), pp. 40–53. ISSN: 0950-5849. DOI: https://doi.org/10.1016/j.infsof.2013.07.001.

Acronyms

ADL	Architecture Description Language 23
AIS	Actual Impact Set 2
AISeL	Association for Information System research electronic Library 216
ALMA	Architecture-level Modifiability Analysis 42
AML	Automation Markup Language 31
API	Application Programming Interface 21
aPS	automated Production Systems 3
ArchiMate	Architecture-Animate 49
AST	Abstract Syntax Tree 54
ATAM	Architecture Tradeoff Analysis Method 41
BASE	Bielefeld Academic Search Engine 216
BP	Business Processes 3
BPC	Business Process Change 223
BPF	Business Process Flexibility 213
BPM	Business Process Modeling 223
BPMN	Business Process Model and Notation 25
BPR	Business Process Reengineering 226
CAEX	Computer Aided Engineering eXchange 53
CAPTCHA	Completely Automated Public Turing test to tell Computers and Humans Apart 281
CBSE	Component-based Software Engineering 61
CIS	Candidate Impact Set 2
CM	Change Management 223
CMS	Change Management System 228
Co-BITS	Co-Design of Business and IT Systems 48
CoCoME	Common Component Modelling Example 252
COLLADA	COLLAborative Design Activity 53
CPRL	Change Propagation Rule Language 194
DSL	Domain Specific Language 20

DYCHOR	DYnamic CHOReographies	47
EA	Enterprise Architecture	49
EBNF	Extended Backus-Naur Form	22
EBSE	Evidence-Based Software Engineering	241
ECAD	Electronic Computer-Aided Design	54
EMAS	Eco-Management and Audit Scheme	237
EMF	Eclipse Modeling Framework	21
GoalBPM	Goal Business Process Management	56
GPL	General-purpose Programming Language	14
GQM	Goal Question Metric	246
GS	Google Scholar	215
HMI	Human Machine Interface	58
IDE	Integrated Development Environment	21
IEC	International Electrotechnical Commission	30
IS	Information Systems	3
IT	Information Technology	237
IT/BA	IT/Business Alignment	227
Java EE	Java Platform, Enterprise Edition	65
KAMP	Karlsruhe Architectural Maintainability Prediction	35
KAMP4aPS	Karlsruhe Architectural Maintainability Prediction for automated Production Systems	132
KAMP4BP	Karlsruhe Architectural Maintainability Prediction for Business Processes	97
KAMP4IEC	Karlsruhe Architectural Maintainability Prediction for International Electrotechnical Commission	132
KAMP4IS	Karlsruhe Architectural Maintainability Prediction for Information Systems	97
LCS	Longest Common Subsequence	51
MDSD	Model-Driven Software Development	19
MIM	Model Integrated Mechatronics	62
mRUBiS	modular Rice University Bidding System	256
OC	Organizational Change	226
OCL	Object Constraint Language	23
OOP	Object-Oriented Programming	313
PCM	Palladio Component Model	19
PDG	Program Dependence Graph	40
PLC	Programmable Logic Controllers	30
POU	Program Organization Units	31

PPU	Pick and Place Unit	68
RDF	Resource Description Framework	51
RFID	Radio-Frequency IDentification	266
RUBiS	Rice University Bidding System	256
SAAM	Software Architecture Analysis Method	41
SEFF	Service EFFect specification	36
SIS	Starting Impact Set	2
SOC	Service-Oriented Computing	228
SoMoX	Source Code Model eXtractor	36
SoMoX4KAMP	Source Code Model eXtractor for Karlsruhe Architectural Maintainability Prediction	36
SysML	Systems Modeling Language	57
TDD	Test-Driven Development	168
TUM	Technische Universität München	31
UML-PA	UML for Process Automation	61
UML	Unified Modeling Language	4
VQL	VIATRA Query Language	60
WfMS	Workflow Management Systems	226
WOS	Web Of Science	216
XMI	XML Metadata Interchange	51
XML	eXtensible Markup Language	46
xPPU	Extended Pick and Place Unit	32
XSD	XML Schema Definition	53

The Karlsruhe Series on Software Design and Quality

Edited by Prof. Dr. Ralf Reussner // ISSN 1867-0067

Band 1 **Steffen Becker**
Coupled Model Transformations for QoS Enabled Component-Based Software Design.
ISBN 978-3-86644-271-9

Band 2 **Heiko Koziolek**
Parameter Dependencies for Reusable Performance Specifications of Software Components.
ISBN 978-3-86644-272-6

Band 3 **Jens Happe**
Predicting Software Performance in Symmetric Multi-core and Multiprocessor Environments.
ISBN 978-3-86644-381-5

Band 4 **Klaus Krogmann**
Reconstruction of Software Component Architectures and Behaviour Models using Static and Dynamic Analysis.
ISBN 978-3-86644-804-9

Band 5 **Michael Kuperberg**
Quantifying and Predicting the Influence of Execution Platform on Software Component Performance.
ISBN 978-3-86644-741-7

Band 6 **Thomas Goldschmidt**
View-Based Textual Modelling.
ISBN 978-3-86644-642-7

Band 7 **Anne Koziolek**
Automated Improvement of Software Architecture Models for Performance and Other Quality Attributes.
ISBN 978-3-86644-973 2

Band 8 **Lucia Happe**
Configurable Software Performance Completions through Higher-Order Model Transformations.
ISBN 978-3-86644-990-9

Band 9 **Franz Brosch**
Integrated Software Architecture-Based Reliability Prediction for IT Systems.
ISBN 978-3-86644-859-9

Band 10 **Christoph Rathfelder**
Modelling Event-Based Interactions in Component-Based Architectures for Quantitative System Evaluation.
ISBN 978-3-86644-969-5

Band 11 **Henning Groenda**
Certifying Software Component Performance Specifications.
ISBN 978-3-7315-0080-3

Band 12 **Dennis Westermann**
Deriving Goal-oriented Performance Models by Systematic Experimentation.
ISBN 978-3-7315-0165-7

Band 13 **Michael Hauck**
Automated Experiments for Deriving Performance-relevant Properties of Software Execution Environments.
ISBN 978-3-7315-0138-1

Band 14 **Zoya Durdik**
Architectural Design Decision Documentation through Reuse of Design Patterns.
ISBN 978-3-7315-0292-0

Band 15 **Erik Burger**
Flexible Views for View-based Model-driven Development.
ISBN 978-3-7315-0276-0

Band 16 **Benjamin Klatt**
Consolidation of Customized Product Copies into Software Product Lines.
ISBN 978-3-7315-0368-2

Band 17 **Andreas Rentschler**
Model Transformation Languages with Modular Information Hiding.
ISBN 978-3-7315-0346-0

Band 18 **Omar-Qais Noorshams**
Modeling and Prediction of I/O Performance in Virtualized Environments.
ISBN 978-3-7315-0359-0

Band 19 **Johannes Josef Stammel**
Architekturbasierte Bewertung und Planung von Änderungsanfragen.
ISBN 978-3-7315-0524-2

Band 20 **Alexander Wert**
Performance Problem Diagnostics by Systematic Experimentation.
ISBN 978-3-7315-0677-5

Band 21 **Christoph Heger**
An Approach for Guiding Developers to Performance and Scalability Solutions.
ISBN 978-3-7315-0698-0

Band 22 **Fouad ben Nasr Omri**
Weighted Statistical Testing based on Active Learning and Formal Verification Techniques for Software Reliability Assessment.
ISBN 978-3-7315-0472-6

Band 23 **Michael Langhammer**
Automated Coevolution of Source Code and Software Architecture Models.
ISBN 978-3-7315-0783-3

Band 24 **Max Emanuel Kramer**
Specification Languages for Preserving Consistency between Models of Different Languages.
ISBN 978-3-7315-0784-0

Band 25 **Sebastian Michael Lehrig**
Efficiently Conducting Quality-of-Service Analyses by Templating Architectural Knowledge.
ISBN 978-3-7315-0756-7

Band 26 **Georg Hinkel**
Implicit Incremental Model Analyses and Transformations.
ISBN 978-3-7315-0763-5

Band 27 **Christian Stier**
Adaptation-Aware Architecture Modeling and Analysis of Energy Efficiency for Software Systems.
ISBN 978-3-7315-0851-9

Band 28 **Lukas Märtin**
Entwurfsoptimierung von selbst-adaptiven Wartungsmechanismen für software-intensive technische Systeme.
ISBN 978-3-7315-0852-6

Band 29 **Axel Busch**
Quality-driven Reuse of Model-based Software Architecture Elements.
ISBN 978-3-7315-0951-6

Band 30 **Kiana Busch**
An Architecture-based Approach for Change Impact Analysis of Software-intensive Systems.
ISBN 978-3-7315-0974-5